THE CAMBRIDGE
COMPANION TO
EUGENE O'NEILL

This is a volume of specially commissioned essays containing studies of
Eugene O'Neill's life, his intellectual and creative forebears, and his relation
to the theatrical world of his creative period, 1916–42. Also included are
descriptions of the O'Neill canon and its production history on stage and
screen, and a series of essays on "special topics" related to the playwright,
such as his treatment of women in the plays, his portrayals of Irish and
African–Americans, and his attempts to deal in dramatic terms with his
parental family culminating in his greatest play, *Long Day's Journey Into
Night*. One of the essays speaks for those who are critical of O'Neill's work,
and the volume concludes with an essay on O'Neill criticism containing a
select bibliography of full-length studies of the playwright's work.

CAMBRIDGE COMPANIONS TO LITERATURE

*The Cambridge Companion to Old English
Literature*
edited by Malcolm Godden and
Michael Lapidge

The Cambridge Companion to Dante
edited by Rachel Jacoff

The Cambridge Chaucer Companion
edited by Piero Boitani and Jill Mann

*The Cambridge Companion to Medieval
English Theatre*
edited by Richard Beadle

*The Cambridge Companion to Shakespeare
Studies*
edited by Stanley Wells

*The Cambridge Companion to English
Renaissance Drama*
edited by A. R. Braunmuller and
Michael Hattaway

*The Cambridge Companion to English Poetry,
Donne to Marvell*
edited by Thomas N. Corns

The Cambridge Companion to Milton
edited by Dennis Danielson

*The Cambridge Companion to British
Romanticism*
edited by Stuart Curran

The Cambridge Companion to James Joyce
edited by Derek Attridge

The Cambridge Companion to Ibsen
edited by James McFarlane

The Cambridge Companion to Brecht
edited by Peter Thomason and Glendyr Sacks

The Cambridge Companion to Beckett
edited by John Pilling

The Cambridge Companion to T. S. Eliot
edited by A. David Moody

*The Cambridge Companion to Renaissance
Humanism*
edited by Jill Kraye

The Cambridge Companion to Joseph Conrad
edited by J. H. Stape

The Cambridge Companion to Faulkner
edited by Philip M. Weinstein

The Cambridge Companion to Thoreau
edited by Joel Myerson

The Cambridge Companion to Edith Wharton
edited by Millicent Bell

*The Cambridge Companion to Realism and
Naturalism*
edited by Donald Pizer

The Cambridge Companion to Twain
edited by Forrest G. Robinson

The Cambridge Companion to Whitman
edited by Ezra Greenspan

The Cambridge Companion to Hemingway
edited by Scott Donaldson

*The Cambridge Companion to the
Eighteenth-Century Novel*
edited by John Richetti

The Cambridge Companion to Jane Austen
edited by Edward Copeland and Juliet
McMaster

The Cambridge Companion to Samuel Johnson
edited by Gregory Clingham

The Cambridge Companion to Oscar Wilde
edited by Peter Raby

*The Cambridge Companion to Tennessee
Williams*
edited by Matthew C. Roudané

The Cambridge Companion to Arthur Miller
edited by Christopher Bigsby

The Cambridge Companion to Virgil
edited by Charles Martindale

*The Cambridge Companion to Greek
Tragedy*
edited by P. E. Easterling

*The Cambridge Companion to the Modern
French Novel*
edited by Timothy Unwin

*The Cambridge Companion to the Classic
Russian Novel*
edited by Malcolm V. Jones and
Robin Feuer Miller

*The Cambridge Companion to English
Literature, 1650–1740*
edited by Steven N. Zwicker

Eugene O'Neill at his player piano "Rosie" in the early 1940s

THE CAMBRIDGE
COMPANION TO
EUGENE O'NEILL

EDITED BY
MICHAEL MANHEIM
Professor Emeritus of English,
University of Toledo, Ohio

CAMBRIDGE
UNIVERSITY PRESS

PUBLISHED BY THE PRESS SYNDICATE OF THE UNIVERSITY OF CAMBRIDGE
The Pitt Building, Trumpington Street, Cambridge CB2 1RP, United Kingdom

CAMBRIDGE UNIVERSITY PRESS
The Edinburgh Building, Cambridge CB2 2RU, United Kingdom
40 West 20th Street, New York, NY 10011–4211, USA
10 Stamford Road, Oakleigh, Melbourne 3166, Australia

© Cambridge University Press 1998

First published 1998

Printed in the United Kingdom at the University Press, Cambridge

Typeset in Sabon 10/13 pt. [CE]

A catalogue record for this book is available from the British Library

Library of Congress cataloguing in publication data

The Cambridge companion to Eugene O'Neill / edited by Michael Manheim.
p.   cm. – (Cambridge companions to literature)
Includes bibliographical references and index.
ISBN 0 521 55389 X (hardback). – ISBN 0 521 55645 7 (paperback)
1. O'Neill, Eugene, 1888–1953 – Criticism and interpretation.
1. Manheim, Michael.   11. Cambridge University Press.   111. Series.
PS3529.N5Z575   1998
812'.52 – dc21   97-42228 CIP

ISBN 0 521 55389 X hardback
ISBN 0 521 55645 7 paperback

CONTENTS

ILLUSTRATIONS

NOTES ON CONTRIBUTORS

JUDITH E. BARLOW is Professor of English and Women's Studies at the University at Albany, State University of New York. She is the author of *Final Acts: The Creation of Three Late O'Neill Plays* (1985), as well as articles on O'Neill, Lillian Hellman, Tina Howe, and the Provincetown Players. Professor Barlow is also the editor of *Plays By American Women, 1900–1930*, and *Plays By American Women, 1930–1960*.

NORMAND BERLIN is Professor Emeritus of English at the University of Massachusetts. He is the author of *O'Neill's Shakespeare* (1993), *Eugene O'Neill* (1982), *The Secret Cause: A Discussion of Tragedy* (1981), *Thomas Sackville* (1974), *The Base String: The Underworld in Elizabethan Drama* (1968), and numerous articles on subjects ranging from medieval poetry to modern drama and film.

STEPHEN A. BLACK, Professor of English at Simon Fraser University, is the author of books on Walt Whitman and James Thurber, and has published more than twenty articles on O'Neill. He studied psychoanalysis for nine years at the Seattle Psychoanalytic Institute.

JEAN CHOTHIA is a lecturer in the Faculty of English at Cambridge University and is a Fellow of Selwyn College. She is the author of *Forging a Language: A Study of the Plays of Eugene O'Neill* (1979), *André Antoine* [Cambridge Directors in Perspective Series] (1991), and *English Drama 1890–1940* (1996).

KURT EISEN is Associate Professor of English at Tennessee Technological University. He is the author of *The Inner Strength of Opposites: O'Neill's Novelistic Drama and the Melodramatic Imagination* (1995), as well as a variety of articles on modern drama.

DONALD GALLUP was curator of the Yale Collection of American Literature (including the principal O'Neill archive) for thirty-three years. He has edited O'Neill's *Inscriptions* (1960), *More Stately Mansions* (1964), *Poems* (1979), *Work Diary* (1981), and *The Calms of Capricorn* (1981), as well as works by Ezra Pound, Gertrude Stein, and Thornton Wilder. He is the author of bibliographies of both T. S. Eliot and Ezra Pound, and a book of memoirs, *Pigeons in the Granite* (1988).

MICHAEL MANHEIM, Professor Emeritus of English at the University of Toledo, is the author of *Eugene O'Neill's New Language of Kinship* (1982) and *The Weak King Dilemma in the Shakespearean History Play* (1973), as well as a good many related articles.

BRENDA MURPHY is Professor of English at the University of Connecticut. She is the author of *Miller: Death of a Salesman* (1995), *Tennessee Williams and Elia Kazan: A Collaboration in the Theatre* (1992), *A Realist in the American Theatre: Selected Dramatic Criticism of William Dean Howells* (1992), *American Realism and American Drama, 1880–1940* (1987), and, with George Monteiro, *John Hay-Howells Letters* (1980).

MARGARET LOFTUS RANALD is Professor Emerita of English, the City University of New York (Queens College). Her publications include *The Eugene O'Neill Companion* (1984), *Shakespeare and his Social Context: Studies in Osmotic Knowledge and Literary Interpretation* (1987), *John Webster* (1989). She is an Associate Editor of *The International Bibliography of Theatre* (1982–).

JAMES A. ROBINSON, Professor of English at the University of Maryland, is the author of *Eugene O'Neill and Oriental Thought: A Divided Vision* (1982), as well as numerous articles on O'Neill, Miller, Shepard and others.

EDWARD L. SHAUGHNESSY is Professor Emeritus of English at Butler University (Indianapolis). He is the author of *Eugene O'Neill in Ireland: The Critical Reception* (1988), *Down the Nights and Down the Days: Eugene O'Neill's Catholic Sensibility* (1996), and numerous essays on O'Neill's family and cultural background.

EGIL TÖRNQVIST is Professor of Scandinavian Studies at the University of Amsterdam. His publications include *A Drama of Souls: Studies in O'Neill's Super-naturalistic Technique* (1968), *Strindbergian Drama: Themes and Structure* (1982), *Transposing Drama: Studies in Representation* (1991), *Ibsen: "A Doll's House"* (1995), and *Between Stage and Screen: Ingmar Bergman Directs* (1995).

RONALD WAINSCOTT is Associate Professor of Theatre History, Dramatic Literature at Indiana University. He is the author of *The Emergence of Modern American Theater, 1914–1929* (1988), and *Staging O'Neill: The Experimental Years, 1920–1934* (1988), and has written numerous articles and entries in professional journals and books.

DANIEL J. WATERMEIER is Professor of Theatre at the University of Toledo. He is author/co-author of *Between Actor and Critic: Letters of Edwin Booth and William Winter* (1971), *Shakespeare Around the Globe: A Guide to Notable Post-War Revivals* (1986), *Edwin Booth's Performances* (1990), *Shakespeare*

Companies and Festivals: An International Guide (1995), and numerous articles on American theatre and drama, as well as on contemporary Shakespearean production.

MATTHEW H. WIKANDER is Professor of English at the University of Toledo. He is author of *Princes to Act: Royal Audience and Royal Performance, 1578–1792* (1993), and *The Play of Truth and State: Historical Drama from Shakespeare to Brecht* (1986), as well as numerous articles on drama and theatre from the Elizabethans to the present.

CHRONOLOGY

1877   James, Sr. (father) marries Ella Quinlan O'Neill (mother).

1878   James, Jr. (brother) born.

1883   Edmund (brother) born.

1885   Edmund dies.

1888   Eugene Gladstone O'Neill born on 16 October in New York City.

1895   To Mount Saint Vincent Academy boarding school (NYC).

1900   To Betts Academy (Stamford, Connecticut).

1906   To Princeton University (leaves 1907).

1909   Marries Kathleen Jenkins, followed by gold prospecting trip to Honduras.

1910   Eugene Gladstone O'Neill, Jr. (son) born. O'Neill sails to Buenos Aires as member of ship's crew.

1911   Returns to United States. Takes up residence at Jimmy-the-Priest's (tavern and room house in lower Manhattan, where he attempts suicide in 1912).

1912   Divorced from Kathleen Jenkins, returns to parental home (Monte Cristo Cottage in New London, Connecticut). Reporter for the New London *Telegraph*. Enters Gaylord Farm Sanatorium for tuberculosis on 24 December (where he stays for six months and writes his first one-act plays).

1914   To George Pierce Baker's class in playwriting at Harvard. Publishes *Thirst, and Other One-Act Plays*.

1916   To Provincetown, Massachusetts, where *Bound East for Cardiff* and *Thirst* are produced. *Bound East* also produced in New York later this year. *Before Breakfast* produced.

1917   *Fog, The Sniper, In the Zone, The Long Voyage Home*, and *Ile* produced.

1918   Marries Agnes Boulton. *The Rope, Where the Cross is Made*, and *The Moon of the Caribbees* produced.

1919   Son, Shane O'Neill, born. *The Dreamy Kid* produced.

1920   *Beyond the Horizon* produced (wins Pulitzer Prize). Father, James O'Neill, Sr., dies. *The Emperor Jones* and *Diff'rent* produced.

1921   *Anna Christie* produced (wins second Pulitzer Prize). *Gold* and *The Straw* produced.

1922   Mother, Ella Quinlan O'Neill, dies. *The Hairy Ape* and *The First Man* produced.

1923   Brother, James O'Neill, Jr., dies.

1924   *All God's Chillun Got Wings, Welded*, and *Desire Under the Elms* produced.

1925   *The Fountain* produced.

1926   Daughter, Oona O'Neill, born. *The Great God Brown* produced.

1928   *Lazarus Laughed* produced (in Pasadena, California). *Marco Millions* and *Strange Interlude* produced. (*Strange Interlude* wins third Pulitzer Prize.)

1929   *Dynamo* produced. Divorces Agnes Boulton, marries Carlotta
        Monterey (in France).

1931   *Mourning Becomes Electra* produced.

1933   *Ah, Wilderness!* produced.

1934   *Days Without End* produced.

1936   Awarded Nobel Prize. (During the late 1930s and into the 1940s,
        O'Neill is at work on his eleven-play Cycle, "A Tale of Possessors
        Self-Dispossessed," which includes the later-to-be-produced *A
        Touch of the Poet* and *More Stately Mansions*. See the essay by
        Donald Gallup in this collection.)

1937   Builds "Tao House" in Danville, California (where he writes his
        last plays).

1939   Writes *The Iceman Cometh*.

1940   Writes *Long Day's Journey Into Night*.

1943   Completes *A Moon for the Misbegotten*.

1946   *The Iceman Cometh* produced.

1947   *A Moon for the Misbegotten* produced (in Columbus, Ohio).

1950   Son, Eugene O'Neill, Jr., dies.

1953   O'Neill dies (27 November, in Boston).

1955   *The Iceman Cometh* revived by José Quintero in New York
        (starring Jason Robards, Jr.).

1956   *Long Day's Journey Into Night* produced in Stockholm, then
        New York. (Wins fourth Pulitzer Prize.)

1957   *A Touch of the Poet* produced.

1958   *Hughie* produced (in Stockholm).

1959   *Hughie* produced in New York.

1962   A version of *More Stately Mansions* produced (in Stockholm).

1962   Another version of *More Stately Mansions* produced in New York.

1972   *Long Day's Journey Into Night* revived in London (starring Laurence Olivier).

1973   *A Moon for the Misbegotten* revived by José Quintero in New York (starring Jason Robards, Jr. and Colleen Dewhurst).

From the 1960s on, there have been numerous successful revivals of O'Neill plays on stage and screen. See the essays by Ronald Wainscott and Kurt Eisen in this collection.

PLAYS AND POEMS
(listed by year of publication)

Thirst, and Other One-Act Plays (*Thirst, Fog, Warnings, The Web, Recklessness*). Privately Printed, 1914.

The Moon of the Caribbees, and Six Other Plays of the Sea (*Bound East for Cardiff, In the Zone, The Long Voyage Home, Ile, Where the Cross is Made, The Rope*). NY: Boni and Liveright, 1919.

Beyond the Horizon. NY: Boni and Liveright, 1920.

Gold. NY: Boni and Liveright, 1921.

The Emperor Jones, Diff'rent, The Straw. NY: Boni and Liveright, 1921.

The Hairy Ape, Anna Christie, The First Man. NY: Boni and Liveright, 1922.

All God's Chillun Got Wings, and *Welded.* NY: Boni and Liveright, 1924.

The Complete Works of Eugene O'Neill (including *The Dreamy Kid*). 2 vols. NY: Boni and Liveright, 1924.

Desire Under the Elms. NY: Boni and Liveright, 1925.

Plays. 4 vols. NY: Boni and Liveright, 1925.

The Great God Brown, The Fountain, The Moon of the Caribbees, and Other Plays (the "other plays" being those included among the (Other) *Six Plays of the Sea*). NY: Boni and Liveright, 1926.

Lazarus Laughed. NY: Boni and Liveright, 1927.

Marco Millions. NY: Boni and Liveright, 1928.

Strange Interlude. NY: Liveright, 1928.

Dynamo. NY: Liveright, 1929.

Mourning Becomes Electra. NY: Liveright, 1931.

Nine Plays. NY: Liveright, 1932.

Ah, Wilderness!. NY: Random House, 1933.

Days Without End. NY: Random House, 1934.

The Plays of Eugene O'Neill. 12 vols. NY: Random House, 1934–5.

The Iceman Cometh. NY: Random House, 1946.

Lost Plays of Eugene O'Neill (*Abortion, The Movie Man, The Sniper, Servitude,* and *A Wife for A Life*). NY: The Citadel Press, 1950.

The Plays of Eugene O'Neill. 3 vols. NY: Random House, 1951.

A Moon for the Misbegotten. NY: Random House, 1952.

Long Day's Journey Into Night. New Haven: Yale University Press, 1956.

A Touch of the Poet. New Haven: Yale University Press, 1957.

Hughie. New Haven: Yale University Press, 1959.

More Stately Mansions. Edited by Donald Gallup. New Haven: Yale University Press, 1964.

Ten "Lost" Plays (including the plays from *The Lost Plays of Eugene O'Neill* plus *Thirst, The Web*, and *Warnings*). NY: Random House, 1964.

Poems: 1912–1914. Edited by Donald Gallup. New Haven and NY: Ticknor and Fields, 1980.

Chris Christofersen. NY: Random House, 1982.

O'Neill: Complete Plays. 3 vols. NY: The Library of America, 1988. (Includes the following previously unpublished plays: *Bread and Butter, Now I Ask You, The Personal Equation, The Reckoning*.)

MICHAEL MANHEIM

Introduction

Not many today question the pre-eminence of Eugene O'Neill as America's leading playwright. The playwrights who followed him – Williams, Miller, and Albee, and, more recently, dramatists like Sam Shepard, David Mamet, and Tony Kushner – all have acknowledged their profound debt to him, as have younger playwrights in countries as remote from one another as Sweden and China. He is internationally recognized as the quintessential American dramatist of the twentieth-century world stage. Some are uncomfortable with what occasionally seems the melodramatic excess of even his most successful plays. There have been and continue to be vociferous nay-sayers about the playwright's work. But they are a relatively small minority, and many of those who express reservations about the excesses of earlier plays acknowledge that he "forged" those excesses (to use Jean Chothia's word) into a uniquely powerful medium that culminated in America's greatest tragedy, *Long Day's Journey Into Night*.

O'Neill has long been a fixture of the American educational curriculum. Before the Second World War, plays such as *Beyond the Horizon*, *The Emperor Jones*, *The Hairy Ape*, *Desire Under the Elms*, *Mourning Becomes Electra*, and *Ah, Wilderness!* were regularly assigned in high school and college literature courses; and if the emphasis on such plays faded in the post-war era, O'Neill's reputation was explosively revived with *The Iceman Cometh*, *Long Day's Journey*, and *A Moon for the Misbegotten* – in the context of which many of those earlier plays are now studied. Not insignificant in that revival have been productions of those late plays by director José Quintero working with actors Jason Robards and Colleen Dewhurst, and on-screen treatments by Sidney Lumet and Laurence Olivier.

What the future holds for that reputation no one can tell, but it may be significant that, as reported in the *New York Times* for 10 February 1997 (Section C, p. 11), "a series on performances of the entire O'Neill canon, 50 plays in all," is currently being contemplated at New York University,

Yale University, the Provincetown Playhouse, and Monte Cristo Cottage (O'Neill's boyhood home in New London, Connecticut and the setting of *Long Day's Journey*).

The Cambridge Companion to Eugene O'Neill, like the others in the Companion series, attempts to be comprehensive without ignoring more specialized approaches to the playwright. Three background discussions constitute the opening section. Stephen A. Black deals first with the subject which has probably been the most important in O'Neill study over the past thirty years, O'Neill's biography as it relates to his childhood home life – the subject first brought into prominence, of course, with the appearance of *Long Day's Journey*. This is followed by Egil Törnqvist's discussion of the several European philosophers and playwrights – notably Nietzsche, Ibsen, and Strindberg – who had the greatest influence on O'Neill's intellectual and artistic development. And third in this group is Daniel J. Watermeier's discussion of the theatrical world in which O'Neill and his father before him were such important figures.

The second section deals with the canon itself. The early and early-middle periods plays – plays such as the *S.S. Glencairn* series, *The Emperor Jones*, *The Hairy Ape*, and *Desire Under the Elms* that brought him his initial fame – are looked at in some detail by Margaret Loftus Ranald (who organizes her essay more around themes than strict chronology). Her essay is followed by James A. Robinson's probing discussion of the plays of O'Neill's middle period – plays such as *The Great God Brown*, *Strange Interlude*, and *Mourning Becomes Electra* – that solidified the playwright's reputation. The last-named won him the Nobel Prize for Literature in 1936. Finally, Normand Berlin discusses O'Neill's all-important late plays, including the two extant plays of his unfinished "Cycle" (which is discussed at length by Donald Gallup later in the volume). Berlin, one of the best-known assessors of O'Neill's later career, focuses chiefly, of course, on *The Iceman Cometh*, *Long Day's Journey*, *Moon for the Misbegotten*, and the one-act *Hughie*.

The third section of this Companion will be for some its most interesting in that it focuses on O'Neill's plays in performance. While space limitations prohibit a detailed history of the great number of productions of O'Neill's plays world-wide, Ronald Wainscott focuses on the best-known professional productions in America. Wainscott's discussion is particularly useful in juxtaposing discussions of initial productions of individual plays with important revivals of those plays. And Kurt Eisen follows up with an insightful look at the rapidly expanding production history of O'Neill plays in cinema and television – suggesting, among other things, which plays have worked best in which medium.

The last section is the longest and most varied – encompassing subjects as far-ranging as O'Neill's fascination with America's racial and religious minorities in his plays to a forthright questioning of the playwright's claim to greatness. Brenda Murphy leads off with a discussion of how the cultural mores of the period between the two world wars worked to shape O'Neill's plays of that period – notably *Strange Interlude*. She is followed by Edward L. Shaughnessy's look at O'Neill's treatment of African–Americans and Irish–Americans, the two most frequently included minority groups in his plays. And following this is Judith E. Barlow's feminist consideration of O'Neill's women characters.

Donald Gallup's essay on O'Neill's vast unfinished Cycle "A Tale of Possessors Self-Dispossessed," which comes next, is unique to this collection in its consideration of material from O'Neill's unpublished *Work Diary* at the Beinecke Library at Yale University. Gallup here summarizes plots and scenarios of unfinished and, in some cases, unwritten plays to give us a sense of the overall dimensions of the projected work.

The next two essays look from different perspectives at O'Neill's brilliance as a dramatist. Jean Chothia looks first at how O'Neill forged theatrical techniques suited to the writing of autobiographical drama throughout the latter part of the twentieth century. Following this, the editor of this collection examines aspects of *Long Day's Journey Into Night* which further certify its greatness.

The essay on *Long Day's Journey* just referred to is intentionally juxtaposed with the final essay in this section. My comments on that play seek unequivocally to place O'Neill in the pantheon of great world dramatists, while Matthew Wikander seeks equally unequivocally to undermine the playwright's pre-eminence. Wikander's essay will infuriate some O'Neill enthusiasts, but he effectively articulates attitudes of a vocal minority that need to be patiently considered in any final assessment of O'Neill's work.

The Companion concludes with a discussion and selected bibliography of O'Neill criticism.

I

STEPHEN A. BLACK

"Celebrant of loss"
Eugene O'Neill 1888–1953

On 2 February 1920 Eugene O'Neill saw his first major play, *Beyond the Horizon*, open at the Morosco. It was his first opening and first performance in a mainstream theatre. *Beyond* was about the thirtieth play he had finished since he began writing plays in 1913; he wrote it early in 1918 when he was twenty-nine. When it opened two years later, New York was in the throes of a lethal influenza epidemic, and the opening was an unpublicized "special matinee." Late in rehearsals, O'Neill took over direction from the lead actor, but despite all efforts, despaired of the production. Nevertheless, an audience came and accepted the play as a serious and absorbing work, and reviewers admired it. Though it is no great compliment, *Beyond* was clearly the best play yet written by an American and would win O'Neill the first of four Pulitzer Prizes. The production ran 144 performances and brought O'Neill over $6,000 which made him, at thirty-one, finally independent of his father's purse-strings. James O'Neill, the author's father, a celebrated heroic actor whose career went back more than fifty years, attended the performance and was seen to leave the theatre wiping tears of pride from his cheeks.

As with several events in the author's life, there was heavy irony in the occasion. Within a month, James O'Neill suffered a stroke and while he was recovering, intestinal cancer was diagnosed. Until adolescence, Eugene had worshipped his father as a hero – such are his words in a private autobiographical document. Then for many years Eugene seemed nearly as often to hate his father as to love him, although his father supported him in and out of trouble, and tolerated the youth's contempt. In 1912 a detente developed and in the last years of the aging actor's life, father and son became close in an increasingly collegial way. From March to August 1920 Eugene grieved deeply while watching his father die slowly and painfully, spending many hours and days at his father's bedside when James was unconscious or barely lucid.

As with many artists, bereavement set off in Eugene a spate of creative effort. For two years he had struggled with a promising, unwieldy play he called "Chris Christophersen." Almost immediately after James O'Neill's death on 10 August, Eugene began sweeping revisions, conceiving new characters for Chris's daughter and her lover, and a new setting and plot for Acts 2 and 3. He finished "*Anna Christie*" in less than six weeks. A day or so later he began another new play, *The Emperor Jones*, which he finished in about two weeks. When he was done, almost without pausing, he began and finished still another play, the undervalued *Diff'rent*.

In ordinary circumstances, O'Neill's mourning for his father would surely have been intense, but it would have run a normal course, such as is described by the psychoanalyst John Bowlby and others, and would have resolved itself in three or four years. (See, e.g. Bowlby, *Attachment and Loss* [New York: Basic Books, 1969.]) But O'Neill's life had never been ordinary, and his grief was to be greatly compounded. A year and a half after James died, Ella O'Neill, thirteen years younger than her husband and seemingly in good health, died suddenly from a brain tumor. Twenty months later, her first son, James Jr., ten years older than Eugene and idolized by him since childhood, succeeded in an oft-declared intent to drink himself to death. Within thirty-nine months, O'Neill lost all the members of his parental family.

The cluster of losses overwhelmed the playwright and put him in a state of mourning that lasted two decades and determined the qualities, themes and characters of everything he wrote from then on. After 1920, nearly every O'Neill play is either directly or indirectly about death, loss and mourning, and most have bereaved characters (such as Eben Cabot in *Desire Under the Elms* or Nina Leeds in *Strange Interlude*) who struggle unsuccessfully to let their dead be dead and to live their own lives without feeling haunted. Over the next two decades writing was the vehicle for O'Neill's mourning.

Finally he reached the point where, in privately dedicating the manuscript of the late autobiographical masterpiece, *Long Day's Journey Into Night* (1941), he could tell himself and his wife that he had faced his dead "at last" and written of them "with deep pity and understanding and forgiveness." O'Neill felt that he had finally come to terms with his dead by understanding the spirits that haunted them, and how they haunted him. How he reached that point of insight is as remarkable a story as how he came to be so haunted in the first place.

The most important event in O'Neill's early life, a youth marked by large events, was the discovery when he was not quite fourteen that his mother had become a morphine addict at his birth, he himself being the unwitting cause of her addiction. It was a discovery not unlike the discovery by one Oedipus that is celebrated in two plays by Sophocles; in one play Sophocles imagined the process of discovery, and in the other, the consequences of the discovery.

The young Eugene did not discover that he had killed his father and wed and begot children with his mother, but he learned that the birth of his eleven-pound natal self had caused his mother prolonged pain and depression for which morphine was prescribed. Ella O'Neill rapidly became addicted. The addiction plagued her and her family for the next quarter-century. Eugene grew up sharing the family assumption that they would all have been better off had he not been born. Guilt and responsibility preceding the possibility of deliberate choice, an old-fashioned idea even in Periclean Athens, became a topic of reflection and self-scrutiny for the future playwright. Given his birth into a theatrical family and his remarkable creative drive, Eugene had little more choice in the matter of becoming a tragic playwright than he had in causing his mother's affliction.

Before the discovery, life had been less difficult, though far from ordinary. Eugene was born on 17 October 1888 in a Manhattan hotel. He was nursed in the wings of theatres as his father travelled North America in an adaptation of *The Count of Monte Cristo*, a play he performed thousands of times during thirty years of almost constant touring. James O'Neill (1844–1920) and his wife Ella (Mary Ellen Quinlan 1857–1922) were deeply dependent on one another and although she hated the uncomfortable travelling, she almost always accompanied him. The first son, Jamie (1878–1923), travelled with his parents until he was seven when he was sent to school in South Bend, Indiana, where his mother had also been educated. A second son, Edmund Burke O'Neill, born in 1884, died a year and a half later of measles, caught from Jamie. Jamie was blamed for deliberately infecting his brother and carried the guilt all his life.

Despite a first-rate education and top marks at prep school and at St. John's College (later, Fordham University), Jamie could never settle into a career, and in fact, got himself expelled from St. John's for a prank a few months before he would have graduated. A sport and an athlete, a bon vivant, a heavy drinker from adolescence, Jamie seldom worked and was dependent on his father throughout his life. He acted sometimes in his father's company, but never fulfilled the talent his father thought he had. Eugene grew up idolizing his brother; later, when he rebelled against his father Eugene took his father's exasperation with Jamie as evidence of his brother's perfection. Eugene's idealization of his brother continued almost unchanged until shortly before Jamie died.

Like Jamie, Eugene travelled with his parents until he was seven; but unlike Jamie he was cared for by a nanny, hired to help his mother who was not recovering from her addition to morphine. Insatiably curious herself, the nanny took young Eugene to see the sights wherever they travelled. At seven he had a wider acquaintance with the natural wonders and oddities of America than most Americans ever acquire. All the while Eugene absorbed the grammar of theatrical artifice, a native language.

At seven everything changed. He was sent to a Catholic boarding school which he loathed in suburban New York. There, and at a Catholic prep school in Manhattan, he drew into himself and counted the weeks and days until he would rejoin his parents and brother for summers in New London, Connecticut, where the family had a seaside cottage. He earned good marks, but virtually ignored school life; he read voraciously, and wrote a stream of letters and poems. Until sent to school, he had known almost no children; he had been the only child, the boss's son, in a world of actors. Throughout his life he remembered hating school for immersing him in the dogma of Sin, pervasive and original – this before he knew of his own primal crime. Although his father was deeply devout, family Catholicism was relaxed. At school, nuns and priests ruled their boys with severe hands. Eugene, an obedient, cooperative child, had probably never been punished before going to school, and he never forgot or forgave injuries and injustices. He remained in Catholic schools until he was thirteen.

In late summer, 1902, Ella O'Neill ran out of morphine and tried to drown herself. James and Jamie decided Eugene had to be told about her addiction, and they could not conceal that they held his birth to be its cause. The shameful secret and blame gave Eugene leverage in an old argument with his father, to let him escape Catholic school. Eugene transferred to the secular Betts Academy in Stamford, Connecticut. At Betts he made a good academic record and acquired a solid education, which he amplified by constant wide reading, by writing poems, by writing daily letters to parents, brother, nanny, and others. He had learned as early as primary school that through letter writing he could escape the immediate and create a world more pleasant than the world of nuns surrounding him. Fellow students remembered him at Betts, as at his previous schools, a loner, even tempered, very determined, somewhat more decadent in rebellion than was typical for the time.

The discovery of his mother's addiction caused his adolescence to abort and set off a decade-long binge of self-destructive behavior. He started drinking heavily and was probably a full-blown alcoholic before he was fifteen. His father's fame made it easy for Eugene, guided by Jamie, to wander casually through New York theatre dressing rooms. Tall and lean, exceptionally handsome, the son of a prominent father, Eugene fell easily into carousing with show girls, prostitutes, married women, women of affairs. He enrolled at Princeton in the fall of 1906 to take a science program, but attended so few classes that he was dropped for excessive cuts before the end of the spring term.

For the next two years Eugene drank and carried on with his brother and other wild friends, having numerous casual affairs. In 1909 he became involved with Kathleen Jenkins, daughter of a prominent, troubled family, who soon became pregnant. Fearing he would be sued by Kathleen's family, James arranged for Eugene to leave the country on a gold-prospecting expedition to Honduras. Before he left, however, Eugene secretly married Kathleen, apparently out of a sense of guilt or honor, a sense which did not extend to attempting to be husband or father. He saw Kathleen and his son only once more before the boy was eleven. The trip to Honduras gave Eugene a taste for adventure and over the next two years he made at least three more voyages as a sailor, attaining on his last the rating "able-bodied." His "A-B" certificate, which he cherished all his life, was the first sign that he might ever become self-supporting.

Although Eugene never lived with Kathleen, the marriage had an important consequence beside the birth of Eugene Jr. Late in 1911 Kathleen filed for divorce asking for neither support nor alimony. The petition seemed to bring home to Eugene the reality of the marriage and touched the enormous guilt he carried for his mother's addiction. His guilt led him to procure from several druggists enough of the opiate veronal to kill himself. In a Fulton Street flophouse where he was staying, he went to his room, hooked the door and ingested the lot. By chance a friend found him several hours later and, unable to rouse him, got help. The proprietor, afraid of having a death on the premises, called for a cab. Eugene was taken to Bellevue Hospital where his stomach was pumped and he was held several days for observation.

The psychoanalyst Erik Erikson once wrote that certain wayward young people need to "touch rock-bottom" before they can begin to find themselves. The nearly successful suicide attempt had such an effect on Eugene. He made a partial detente with his father (who had thanklessly supported Eugene since he left Princeton), and got a job writing features and occasional reportage for a New London newspaper. (His father secretly underwrote his salary.) He also fell romantically in love with a local girl whom he tried to educate by foisting on her his favorite authors: Nietzsche, Schopenhauer, Wilde, Whitman, Swinburne, Baudelaire, Fitzgerald's Omar Khayyam, Dowson and the like. His adolescence having in effect aborted in 1902, he now returned to it for another try. He would have other such romantic affairs over the next five years, each time begging his beloved to marry him, addressing letters to "own little wife" whether or not she would entertain his proposals.

Just as the resumed adolescence was getting under way, Eugene developed tuberculosis. The case was diagnosed in November 1912 and he entered a sanatorium where he cooperated fully with his treatment and was discharged the following June. While in the "san" he began thinking about writing plays. Within a year he had finished at least ten, one of them "Bound East for Cardiff," a play still frequently revived. He persuaded his father to send him to Harvard where he attended George Pierce Baker's play-writing course. From Baker he learned to write detailed scenarios before beginning composition and to work methodically. He intended to take a second year with Baker, but some dispute led his father to cancel the plan. Eugene returned to New York where he lived on a dollar a day from his father and whatever he could beg from drinking friends or earn for a few days' work on the docks. When he was sober he wrote. Once again he was living rough, hanging out with artists, philosophers, journalists and radicals. In six years at least five close friends died, three by suicide.

In 1916 a friend introduced him to people who had begun an anti-commercial theatre group the previous summer, The Provincetown Players. O'Neill became intimate with the journalists John Reed and Louise Bryant, members of the group who were living together and would soon marry. O'Neill had met them the previous winter, and during the summer he and Bryant became lovers. The affair continued off and on for over a year, before and after Bryant married Reed.

On 28 July 1916 the first performance of an O'Neill play took place. "Bound East for Cardiff" was produced by the Players in a makeshift theatre on the end of a pier in Provincetown. For the next ten years O'Neill worked with the Players in their several forms; they would produce several of his best-known early plays including *The Emperor Jones* and *The Hairy Ape*. In fall, when the Players and O'Neill returned to New York, "Cardiff" opened the group's first New York bill in Greenwich Village. Over the next two seasons the players produced several more O'Neill plays, including "Before Breakfast," "In the Zone" and "The Long Voyage Home." Reed and Bryant went to Russia to witness the Revolution, which ended her affair with O'Neill.

Late in 1917 Eugene met Agnes Boulton and two months later, the two eloped to Provincetown where they married on 12 April. As a wedding gift, James O'Neill bought for Eugene and Agnes a former life-saving station near the outer tip of Cape Cod, elegantly remodelled by Mabel Dodge. The couple used it as a summer home for the next several years. On 30 October

1919, their son Shane was born. Shortly after came the premiere of *Beyond the Horizon*. Then his father died.

James's death changed everything among the O'Neills. After his father stopped touring about 1914, Jamie always lived near his parents in a different hotel, drinking and carrying on with women at night but spending an hour or two with his mother most mornings. If James was present, Jamie would irritate and provoke his father, drink James's whiskey, and win his mother's sly approval for small victories over the family tyrant. After he married, Eugene grew particularly close to his father, tended to side with him in quarrels, and was uncomfortable with his mother. Ella, for her part, never got over feeling guilty toward Eugene, partly for being unable to care for him in his childhood, partly for blaming him for her affliction, and partly because simply seeing him reminded her of the addiction which she had escaped in 1914 and hated to remember.

With James dead, Ella and Jamie began spending much of every day with each other. For the first time since adolescence, simply because Ella asked him to, Jamie stopped drinking. He developed a successful system for betting on horses, and he and his mother often went to watch them run. In her memoir, Agnes recounted an anecdote Jamie had told her and Eugene. Ella would take her bath in the late morning after she and Jamie had breakfasted in her hotel room, then would retire to dress. While her bath water drained, Jamie would go to the tub, dabble his fingers in the water; immersing himself in her odor gave him a kind of bliss. He seemed happy and contented for the first time in his life, having his mother to himself. He became her secretary as she tried to straighten out James's complicated real estate and other holdings, writing lawyers, brokers and agents, evicting delinquent tenants, and the like.

Jamie and Ella went to Los Angeles where a property in Glendale had become valuable. While they arranged to sell it, Ella had a stroke caused by a brain tumor. All Jamie's reformation was instantly undone. Urged by a woman he knew, and again drinking heavily, Jamie tried to persuade his mother to give him the most valuable property in the estate rather than sharing it with Eugene. After wavering, Ella resisted the pressure. An old friend who was present during Ella's last days and who witnessed her will, described all the sordid events in a letter which was passed on to Eugene. When his mother died, Eugene lost both her and his idealization of his brother. With both he had much unfinished business.

Under any circumstances Eugene's mourning for his mother would have been difficult. On both sides their relations had always been overburdened with irrational guilt. Bowlby and others have shown that the more complex one's relations with the dead, the more difficult and slow the work of mourning. Although in part Eugene adored his mother, he also feared and mistrusted her, and on the whole, negative feelings outweighed the positive. The extremes of his feelings about her are evident in portraits in many plays of women who are mad, incapable of growing to adulthood, destructive to their husbands or seductive with their children.

Eugene's attraction to his mother and his fear of her are also evident in the extremes of romantic passion he attached to his many love affairs and to his ideals for marriage. Troubles in his marriage to Agnes that emerged after his father died led him to consult a psychoanalyst in the fall of 1921. When word came that Ella was dying in California, he returned to the analyst. For the next several years he would consult several psychiatrists to try to resolve the depression that engulfed him in his bereavement.

As Eugene gradually realized that Jamie had tried to cheat him out of his share of the estate, he increasingly avoided his brother. Jamie now told everyone he wanted to drink himself to death, and often provoked his friends to rage. Sixteen months after his mother died, he fell into an alcoholic psychosis and was taken to a sanatorium. His once athletic body was bloated, his hair was white, and he told people he was impotent. In the sanatorium he found ways to have liquor brought in and continued to drink. He suffered a stroke in September 1923 and lingered until 8 November when he died, aged forty-five. In the last year Jamie lived, Eugene saw him only once; he refused to visit him in the sanatorium, and later refused to go to the funeral or have anything to do with burial arrangements.

After Jamie died Eugene reverted to drinking so heavily that it affected his writing, something he had seldom done since he married Agnes. When sober, he tried to be writing constantly, since he could isolate himself from the world while writing, but his work in these circumstances was erratic. *Desire Under the Elms*, written just after Jamie died, was probably his most successful play from the mid-1920s. Drinking heavily through 1924–25 O'Neill began to feel he must stop drinking or give up writing and die and made several attempts to stop. Nevertheless, he was drinking heavily in May 1925 when his daughter Oona was born. He spoke several times to psychiatrists and other doctors about his drinking. His melancholia deepened and in early 1926 he saw an analyst frequently over about six weeks and called the experience "my analysis." From this point on, except for several isolated episodes, O'Neill drank little or nothing.

The psychotherapy was probably too brief to have much effect in itself, but it gave form to O'Neill's own efforts at self-analysis. Stuck in his mourning, mostly denying his losses, and when accepting them, so overwhelmed that he soon reverted to denial, O'Neill creates characters like Eben Cabot in *Desire Under the Elms* and Nina Leeds of *Strange Interlude* who are overwhelmed by their losses but have so little insight that they can neither go back nor move ahead. Although progress was slow and a long time coming, writing of his own past and his own psychic processes eventually brought the playwright insight. Little by little, with help from doctors he sometimes consulted, he assimilated what he learned.

Together with other changes he was making in his life, sobriety decisively affected his troubled marriage. Always taciturn except sometimes when drinking, he withdrew further from Agnes, who continued to drink and complained that he had become boring. In the summer of 1926 O'Neill met the actress Carlotta Monterey and sometime later began an affair with her. He and Agnes were living in Bermuda at the time, and had recently begun to remodel an early eighteenth-century house. In the winter of 1927, with the greatest ambivalence and guilt, he left Agnes, and in March 1928, eloped with Carlotta to the south of France where he remained until 1931. Bitter divorce negotiations estranged him from his children Shane and Oona, although he remained on good terms with his first son, Eugene Jr., who would become a classics scholar. While his father and Carlotta lived in France, Eugene Jr. studied classics at Yale where he would later teach. The new marriage and Eugene Jr.'s early success were important satisfactions to O'Neill in a very troubled time.

While at Princeton O'Neill was greatly affected by Nietzsche, and over the years an impulse toward what might be called scientific mysticism had become increasingly prominent. As he stopped drinking and tried to accept his dead, his plays show him turning increasingly toward a view of the world influenced by Nietzsche, psychoanalysis and the ancient Greeks. He read about pre-Pythagorean philosophies and ancient cultures and mythologies. Plays of the late twenties like *Strange Interlude*, *Lazarus Laughed*, and *Dynamo* reflected these interests, and simultaneously, O'Neill struggled with his mourning. The Lazarus he imagines has survived death but lost his humanity, which the play seems to see defined by the dread of death. *Interlude* is about the unresolvable mourning of Nina Leeds and Charlie Marsden for parents who died while Charlie and Nina were children. The unresolvable mourning for lost parents inhibits all their relations with the living, and makes every subsequent loss the more unbearable.

The title *Strange Interlude* arises from a reflection by Nina Leeds that life is merely an interlude in the grand electrical display of God the Father. Her meditations lead her to contrast God the Father with God the Mother who evokes (in the audience if not in Nina) the ancient earth god Geia. The male "modern science God" of *Interlude* is superseded in the next play, *Dynamo*, by a modern female god of the hydro-electric dynamo, worshipped by

Reuben Light as his dead mother, in the course of which rites he electrocutes himself.

Having arrived in such a state of mind in 1929, O'Neill began another play about bereavement, *Mourning Becomes Electra* which he finished in 1931. In writing the very end of *Mourning Becomes Electra*, O'Neill was able for the first time since his father died to imagine a character, Lavinia Mannon, who could accept the permanence of her losses and could imagine surviving. At the end she closed herself in the old house to remain there with her dead until she could forgive them and herself.

Writing *Electra* effected a change in O'Neill's state of mind and his writing. Shortly after he finished it, he wrote the nostalgic comedy *Ah, Wilderness!* In an experiment few would have predicted, he next attempted a "return toward Cath[olicism]. [*sic*] away from the tragic sense of life." The experiment lasted two years and led O'Neill not only to a failed play, *Days Without End* (1934), but to the verge of a breakdown. On doctor's orders he stopped writing for six months, and turned "back to the tragic sense of life" which was apparently healthier for him. (The quotations are from a private document, "Cycles," published by Virginia Floyd, *Eugene O'Neill at Work* [New York: Ungar, 1981, appendix, p. 387].)

When he resumed writing, he began a vast epic of immigrant Irish life in America that he called "A Tale of Possessors, Self-Dispossessed," often called the "Cycle." He projected as many as eleven plays in the epic, which would begin in the mid-eighteenth century and carry on to 1931. Struggling with depression and various illnesses, including nearly fatal complications of appendicitis in 1937, O'Neill worked on the Cycle between 1935 and 1939. In November 1936, not long after he began this work, he was awarded the Nobel Prize. The medal had to be brought to his hospital bed. Later O'Neill referred to the episode as a "crack-up." For six months or so he could work very little. Of the Cycle material, he finished only one play to the point of being performable, *A Touch of the Poet*, which he drafted in 1935–36 and revised in 1942. Most other material from the Cycle was destroyed, but a draft of *More Stately Mansions* survived and has been published.

In what survives of the Cycle, especially *Mansions*, it seems that O'Neill delved as deeply as he could into his relations with and fantasies of his mother whom he represents as Deborah Harford; he represents himself as her son, Simon. The exploration of the relationship seems to go so deep into a world of explicit Oedipal fantasies, which must have been his own, that O'Neill surely would never have allowed it to become public. (He wrote on the typescript that it was to be destroyed at his death; later he thought he destroyed it with other material; apparently by accident it survived and was found among papers given to the Yale Libraries in 1951.) It appears to be the material of the self-analysis, necessary to the working through of his old relationships with his parents and brother, and accessible as drama in the age of Freud. Such is the work that occupied O'Neill until June 1939, a labor that seemed to end in nothing.

Struggling with the Cycle yielded little in itself, but its real consequence was that it enabled O'Neill to write the four important plays that marked the end of his writing life. On 5 June 1939, O'Neill laid the Cycle aside and wrote out detailed scenarios for two plays that had recently come to him, *The Iceman Cometh* and *Long Day's Journey Into Night*. In these plays all the work of self-analysis and mourning would finally be realized.

Set in 1912 *Iceman* takes place in a waterfront saloon that brings together various people and places of the playwright's youth. Jimmy Tomorrow is a representation of the friend who saved O'Neill's life when he tried to kill himself, and who himself died a suicide the next year. The boy Parritt is a version of O'Neill's youthful self, full of guilt, driven by a compulsion to find truth. Parritt's alter ego in the play, the salesman, Hickey, represents aspects of Jamie. Between them they enact versions of O'Neill family crimes, guilt and atonement. Through his identifications with these and other characters, O'Neill consolidates and develops the fragments of insight he has accumulated and goes much further than before in understanding his youthful self. Through private and public means O'Neill creates tragedy far greater than anything he has written thus far. He arranges *Iceman* around the insight of Parritt who acknowledges his hatred of his mother and sentences himself to die, and the guilt of Hickey who goes mad to disavow the knowledge that hatred of his wife has led him to kill her.

In a certain sense, allowing for the condensations and distortions of the unconscious and the poetic mind, the fates of Parritt and Hickey reflect O'Neill's understanding of the reactions of himself and Jamie to their mother's life and death. The most important biographical meaning of *Iceman* is this: understanding allows O'Neill to go beyond the distorted and unconscious to write his next play in a style and manner that, compared to *Iceman*, seems in its private meanings clear and undisguised.

Writing *Iceman* brought O'Neill to see more clearly than he could have seen before how deeply rooted were the self-destructive impulses that had driven him since 1902. Expressing them now dramatically in the torment of Parritt and Hickey somehow made it possible for O'Neill to go even farther, to write with seeming simplicity and directness about his dead and his relations with them. The result was a work so private and personal that for the remaining thirteen years of his life, he reiterated legal safeguards which he intended to prevent the play from ever being performed and from being published until twenty-five years after his death.

Whatever O'Neill's feelings in the matter, once he died control passed from his hands. He had made Carlotta executrix of his estate and she had the power to override O'Neill's blocks on publication. She arranged for the play to be performed in Stockholm, where it opened in Swedish on 2 February 1956. The first performance in English was in Boston the following 15 October. In the light of O'Neill's lifelong protection of his privacy it is yet another irony that *Long Day's Journey Into Night* has become one of the most celebrated and often performed of twentieth-century tragedies.

Long Day's Journey represents the O'Neill family, called Tyrone in the play, on an imagined day in August 1912 when the younger son (called Edmund) discovers that he has tuberculosis and when his mother, Mary, resumes taking morphine after being free of her addiction for some time. O'Neill seeks a neutral point of view from which to tell the story, but it is not a detached neutrality; like an analyst, and like many a playwright, he seeks to be empathically neutral. He requires neutrality if he is to escape the habits of the past during his re-immersion in his family. From his neutral standpoint he presents a family in which there is no possibility of neutrality but only of guilt or innocence. Nearly every word spoken in the play accuses or defends in the question of who caused Mama's addiction. The form and substance of the question preclude the Tyrones from neutrality. Most audiences find themselves compelled to participate silently in the accusations and defenses, and find it as hard as the Tyrones to be neutral.

With a play so harrowing for an audience, it is common to question whether O'Neill reaches the "deep pity and understanding and forgiveness for *all* the four haunted Tyrones" that he says he did in the dedication to Carlotta. Apart from his own testimony, there is indirect evidence of the forgiveness in the plays O'Neill wrote after *Long Day's Journey*: *A Moon for the Misbegotten* and *Hughie*. These are plays of reconciliation, written from a sense of life as tragic as ever. Writing about death and bereavement finally teaches O'Neill how to return to life.

As before in the past two decades, O'Neill's subject is mourning, but in both plays, there is hope that one may recover from grief and return to life somehow enlarged and more coherent as a result of the experience. In *Hughie*, in the space of an hour, O'Neill shows the gambler Erie Smith mourning his friend Hughie and passing beyond mourning and tragedy to that strange sort of drama written after a lifetime immersion in tragedy by Sophocles in *Oedipus at Colonus* and by Shakespeare in *The Winter's Tale* and *The Tempest*. Few people who have seen a good performance of *Hughie* can doubt that Erie has known his friend and mourned him, and has earned his return to life and his new friend.

In *A Moon for the Misbegotten* (1943) Josie Hogan lets herself fall in love with Jim Tyrone, who has inherited her father's farm and whose mother has just died. Here O'Neill recapitulates from Jamie's point of view the whole sordid story of his behavior at the time his mother died and afterwards. By doing so he, like Josie, can learn something about who Jamie really was. After two decades he lets himself understand at last why Jamie had to betray his brother and drink himself to death. Knowing Jamie at last, at last he can mourn him, both in life, and in the play in the guise of Josie, as well. He and Josie find that Jim could neither love nor tolerate being loved and so, hating himself, he could stand to live no longer. Josie's act of knowing and loving Jim, and of being able to mourn her lost image of him, effects a noteworthy change. At the end she is more comfortable with herself than before and has abandoned much of her former dependency on her father. This was to be the last play O'Neill would finish.

After the breakdown of 1937 the playwright's health gradually declined. A rare, nameless hereditary condition gradually destroyed Purkinje cells in his cerebral cortex, large neurons which control fine motor coordination, causing a tremor he had always had to worsen, so that much of the time he could not feed himself or light a cigarette or write, or walk well, or even speak clearly enough to be understood. The condition, however, did not in the least affect his thinking. It is yet another of his life's ironies that he spent his last decade an alert witness to his own disintegration. The marriage with Carlotta, happy much of the time and organized almost entirely around maintaining the conditions he needed to write, began to disintegrate when he could write no longer. Carlotta was herself ill much of the time. There were dreadful quarrels and separations. O'Neill died in a Boston hotel room on 27 November 1953. Shortly before he died he said to Carlotta, "God damn it, I knew it! Born in a hotel room and dying in a hotel room."

BIBLIOGRAPHICAL NOTE

O'Neill has been the subject of numerous biographies, many by journalists beginning in the early 1920s; three dozen of these are collected by Mark W. Estrin in *Conversations with Eugene O'Neill* (Jackson and London: University of Mississippi Press, 1990). It does not contain one of the most important such essays, "O'Neill, the Man with a Mask" by Elizabeth Shepley Sergeant which appears in her collection *Fire Under the Andes* (New York: Knopf, 1927). The first book-length biography is by Barrett Clark, *Eugene O'Neill* (New York: Robert McBride,

1926). (Four revised editions were published as *Eugene O'Neill: The Man and his Plays*: in 1929, 1933, 1936 by McBride; and in 1947 by Dover.) Other book-length biographies include *The Curse of the Misbegotten* by Croswell Bowen, with assistance from Shane O'Neill (New York: McGraw Hill, 1959); *The Tempering of Eugene O'Neill* (on O'Neill's life to 1920) by Doris Alexander (New York: Harcourt, Brace and World, 1962); *O'Neill* by Arthur and Barbara Gelb (New York: Harper, 1962; 1973); *O'Neill: Son and Playwright* (Boston: Little, Brown, 1968), and *O'Neill: Son and Artist* (Boston: Little, Brown, 1973) by Louis Sheaffer. Of these works, those by the Gelbs and Sheaffer are considered standard. In addition, several works emphasize autobiographical qualities in O'Neill's plays, including: Doris Falk, *Eugene O'Neill and the Tragic Tension* (New Brunswick: Rutgers University Press, 1958); Travis Bogard, *Contours in Time: The Plays of Eugene O'Neill* (New York: Oxford University Press, 1972); Michael Manheim, *Eugene O'Neill's New Language of Kinship* (Syracuse University Press, 1982); Judith E. Barlow, *Final Acts: The Creation of Three Late O'Neill Plays* (Athens: University of Georgia Press, 1985); and Doris Alexander, *Eugene O'Neill's Creative Struggle: The Decisive Decade, 1924–1933* (University Park: Pennsylvania State University Press, 1992).

2

EGIL TÖRNQVIST

O'Neill's philosophical and literary paragons

Against the wall between the doorways is a small bookcase, with a picture of Shakespeare above it, containing novels by Balzac, Zola, Stendahl, philosophical and sociological works by Schopenhauer, Nietzsche, Marx, Engels, Kropotkin, Max Stirner, plays by Ibsen, Shaw, Strindberg, poetry by Swinburne, Rossetti, Wilde, Ernest Dowson, Kipling, etc.

Rarely has a writer been so explicit about his literary preferences in a fictive work. Edmund Tyrone's bookcase in *Long Day's Journey Into Night* tells us what his alter ego, the young Eugene O'Neill, was reading round 1912. Significantly, Shakespeare is present only in the form of a picture. His collected works are found in the living room's other *"large, glassed-in bookcase,"* representing the contrasting taste of James Tyrone, Edmund's father. Naturally, O'Neill has arranged the two book collections to fit the generation conflict in the play: old versus new values. A more authentic version of Edmund's, alias the young O'Neill's, bookcase would have included London and Conrad rather than Marx, Engels and Kropotkin.[1] But by and large, the authors in the small bookcase accurately indicate O'Neill's favorite reading at the time.

In the next couple of years, he told his first biographer,

I read about everything I could lay hands on: the Greeks, the Elizabethans – practically all the classics – and of course all the moderns. Ibsen and Strindberg, especially Strindberg.[2]

Later many other writers were to have an impact on him: Thoreau, Melville, Dostoevski, Gorki, Joyce – to mention but a few.[3] Whether or not as a reaction against the taste of his father-cum-actor, Shakespeare seems to have meant surprisingly little to him.[4] And whether or not his early acquaintance with the Catholic confessional made him specially attuned to them,[5] "those works O'Neill particularly valued are confessional."[6]

It was in 1907, five years after he had given up Catholicism, that O'Neill became acquainted with Nietzsche's writings,[7] and it is likely that it was above all as a meaningful substitute for his shattered faith that Nietzsche's philosophy appealed to him. Nietzsche's *Thus Spake Zarathustra*, he later declared, has influenced me more than any book I've ever read. I ran into it [...] when I was eighteen and I've always possessed a copy since then and every year or so I reread it and am never disappointed, which is more than I can say of almost any other book.[8]

A testimony to O'Neill's concern with *Zarathustra* are the copious excerpts, now in Yale University Library, that he made from this work.

When Barrett Clark met him in 1926 he carried a worn copy of another work by Nietzsche in his coat pocket – *The Birth of Tragedy*[9] – and in the playbill of *The Great God Brown* produced the same year there were two considerable quotations from this book.

Like Nietzsche, O'Neill considered Greek tragedy the unsurpassed example of art *and* religion. Enacted in theatres that were also temples, it had a religious spirit that O'Neill found "completely lacking in modern life." To recreate the Greek spirit was the goal he set for himself. The mystical, Dionysian experience of being part of the Life Force that Nietzsche found communicated in the plays of Aeschylus and Sophocles, O'Neill hoped to impart, through his plays, to a modern audience. "What has influenced my plays the most," he stated in 1929, "is my knowledge of the drama of all time – particularly Greek tragedy."[10]

The "pessimism of strength" inherent in Greek tragedy, Nietzsche found, has nothing to do with pessimism in the everyday sense. O'Neill agreed wholeheartedly. Tragedy, he declared, "is the meaning of life – and the hope. The noblest is eternally the most tragic. The people who succeed and do not push on to a greater failure are the spiritual middle classers."[11]

The struggle of Nietzsche's ideal man to turn himself into a superman (*Übermensch*) is the struggle also of the O'Neill protagonist. As the playwright put it in an early interview: "A man wills his own defeat when he pursues the unattainable. But his *struggle* is his success!"[12]

Martha Jayson in *The First Man* is one of O'Neill's Nietzschean creators. She voices the superman's willingness not only to endure the inevitable but to love it, his *amor fati*.

Nietzsche's view of tragedy as a metaphysical solace and of the theatrical experience as effecting a sense of Dionysian oneness with one's fellows and with the universe led him to believe that the pre-Socratic Greeks "*could* not endure individuals on the tragic stage,"[13] and that the protagonists in the plays of Aeschylus and Sophocles are, in fact, only masks of the original hero: Dionysus.

This assumption had a definite impact on O'Neill in his attempts to recapture what he considered the Greek tragic spirit. What was essential to Nietzsche in life as in tragedy – the two should be interchangeable! – was the rapturous feeling of being, not an individual but part of the Life Force. O'Neill shared this mystical feeling: "I'm always, always trying to interpret Life in terms of lives, never just lives in terms of character. I'm always acutely conscious of the Force behind."[14]

For Nietzsche the tragic spirit equalled a religious faith. In an age when it was becoming increasingly difficult to conceive of man or his actions as noble, he called for a revival of the tragic hero not only in tragedy but in life. Out of the need to justify existence after the death of the old God was born the concept of the superman, the man who welcomes pain as a necessity for inner growth and who, like the protagonists in Greek tragedy, achieves spiritual attainment through suffering.

More esoteric is Nietzsche's doctrine about eternal recurrence, the gist of which is found in the following words by Zarathustra, excerpted by O'Neill:

> Now I die and vanish and in a moment I shall be nothing. Souls are as mortal as bodies.
>
> But the knot of causes recurreth in which I am twined. It will create me again. I myself belong unto the cause of eternal recurrence.
>
> I come back not for a new life, or a better life, or an eternal life, but back eternally unto this one and the same life, in the greatest and the smallest things.[15]

We find an echo of this in *The Fountain*, where Juan Ponce de Léon's dying revelation discloses to him that his individual soul will be absorbed like a drop by "the Fountain of Eternity" – Life – and that, as part of the Fountain, it will eternally recur. His final words are: "Oh, Luis, I begin to know eternal youth! I have found my Fountain! O Fountain of Eternity, take back this drop, my soul!" Zarathustra uses the same imagery for his identical longing; in the version excerpted by O'Neill: "When, well of eternity? Thou gay, shuddering abyss of noon! When drinkest thou my soul back into thyne."[16]

The full title of Nietzsche's first book is *The Birth of Tragedy from the Spirit of Music*. To Nietzsche tragedy is essentially the "manifestation and illustration of Dionysian states, as the visible symbolisation of music, as the dream-world of Dionysian ecstacy."[17] The musical element in Greek tragedy was embodied in the choral songs. When these were reduced in favor of the dialogue, the very foundation of tragedy was threatened.

Folk song, Nietzsche claims, should be regarded as "the original melody," a musical mirroring of the cosmos, and "every period which is highly productive in popular songs has been most violently stirred by Dionysian currents."[18] O'Neill's plays are full of music, mostly popular

songs or folk songs. In *The Great God Brown*, Cybel, the prostitute and
Earth Mother, has a player-piano on which she is banging out "'*Mother-
Mammy' tunes.*" Her music is Dionysian in the Nietzschean sense. As Dion
(!) puts it: "Every song is a hymn. They keep trying to find the word in the
beginning." In the operatic *Lazarus Laughed*, the Dionysian spirit of music
is brought out not only in the dance music played by Lazarus' followers but
also in the pervasive laughter, which O'Neill borrowed straight from
Zarathustra.

The premise of Nietzsche's entire philosophy is the postulate that "God is
dead," that we have destroyed our faith in Him. Nietzsche saw it as his task
to fill the terrifying void that had arisen by providing modern man with a
faith in which he could believe. O'Neill accepted Nietzsche's postulate.
What teaching could be more attractive to a man who shunned the creed of
the Church, yet who claimed that he was primarily concerned with
ultimates! In an often quoted statement O'Neill declared that

> The playwright today must dig at the roots of the sickness of today as he feels
> it – the death of the old God and the failure of science and materialism to give
> any satisfying new one for the surviving primitive religious instinct to find a
> meaning for life in, and to comfort its fears of death with.[19]

Some ten years earlier he had indicated that the only cure for the
"sickness of today" was to be found in Zarathustra's gospel. "The only way
we can get religion back," he said, "is through an exultant acceptance of
life."[20]

Zarathustra admonishes the higher men to flee from the market place
and from the city of shopkeepers out into the wilderness, up into the
mountains; in O'Neill's quotation:

> Thy neighbors will always be poisonous flies. That which is great in thee –
> that itself must make them still more poisonous and ever more like flies. Fly,
> my friend, into thy lonliness [*sic*] and where the rough, strong wind bloweth.
> It is not thy lot to be a fly-brush.[21]

"Out into the woods! Upon the hills!" exclaims O'Neill's Lazarus.
"Cities are prisons wherein man locks himself from life." "You're like a
swarm of poisonous flies," Curtis Jayson in *The First Man* shouts to the
"small minds" that surround him before he leaves to climb the Himalayas
in search for "the first man" – clearly not so much an archeological
expedition as a moral and religious one, a search for the antithesis of
Nietzsche's last man, for the superman to come.

O'Neill even tried to incorporate Nietzsche's exultant, aphoristic style into some of the experimental plays of the middle period, notably *Lazarus Laughed*. The result was hardly satisfactory.[22]

Enlarging upon Agnes Boulton's observation that O'Neill more or less identified himself with the German philosopher, the Gelbs point out that

> Many aspects of O'Neill's later life strikingly parallelled those of Nietzsche's. The drooping black mustache O'Neill grew in his late twenties, the solitude in which he spent his last years, the tremendous strain he put on his creative spirit, the somber satisfaction he took in being misunderstood, and the final collapse – all are a mirroring of Nietzsche.[23]

However, rather than identification or mirroring we may speak of a fundamental spiritual affinity leading to similar manifestations, an affinity which explains the scope and depth of Nietzsche's impact on O'Neill's writings.

While O'Neill readily acknowledged his indebtedness to Nietzsche, he always protested against the frequently heard claims that his plays were too closely patterned on the findings of psychoanalysis.[24]

> There is no conscious use of psychoanalytical material in any of my plays. All of them could easily have been written by a dramatist who had never heard of the Freudian theory and was simply guided by an intuitive psychological insight into human beings and their life-impulsions that is as old as Greek drama. [...] I have only read two books of Freud's, "Totem and Taboo" and "Beyond the Pleasure Principle." The book that interested me the most of all those of the Freudian school is Jung's "Psychology of the Unconscious" which I read many years ago. If I have been influenced unconsciously it must have been by this book more than any other psychological work.[25]

Yet O'Neill had personal contacts with at least three psychoanalysts. And the "Working Notes" for *Mourning Becomes Electra* indicate a certain familiarity with psychoanalysis. Thus Christine's hatred of her husband is said to be determined by "sexual frustration by his puritan sense of guilt turning love to lust"; and the characters' desire to leave for their South Sea island is said to express a "yearning for prenatal non-competitive freedom from fear."[26] After the play is completed O'Neill speaks of "the life and death impulses that drive the characters on to their fates."[27] In the notes for *Days Without End* he refers to "mother worship, repressed and turned morbid," changing into "Death-love and longing," and he calls the wife of the protagonist a "mother substitute."[28]

Possibly inspired by Jung's concept of persona, O'Neill believed the mask to be the most satisfying solution for the

> new form of drama projected from a fresh insight into the inner forces motivating the actions and reactions of men and women ...

> For what, at bottom, is the new psychological insight into human cause and effect but a study in masks, an exercise in unmasking?[29]

O'Neill applied the idea of the unconscious not only to his characters but also to his audience. Our emotions, he once declared with a reasoning that calls to mind the Jungian collective unconscious,

> are a better guide than our thoughts. Our emotions are instinctive. They are the result not only of our individual experiences but of the experiences of the whole human race, back through all the ages.[30]

Of central importance to him as a playwright was how to find a modern equivalent of the Greek sense of fate. His first working note for *Mourning Becomes Electra* reads: "Is it possible to get modern psychological approximation of Greek sense of fate [...], which an intelligent audience of today, possessed of no belief in gods or supernatural retribution, could accept and be moved by?"[31] In 1925, a year before this question was posed, O'Neill implied an answer to it. In the posthumously published "Author's foreword" to *The Great God Brown* he says: "if we have no gods, or heroes to portray we have the subconscious the mother of all Gods and heroes."[32] Yet these and other similar statements hardly prove more than that O'Neill was attuned to what was very much in the air in the twenties and thirties, when psychoanalysis had become *commune bonum*.

If the critics, on the whole, have failed to show any marked influence from psychoanalysis on O'Neill, the reason is not merely a lack of thorough investigation. It is also a consequence of the difficulty of comparing theoretical writings with fiction and of classifying ideas too fundamental to be strictly limited to any one writer or school of thought as psychoanalytic.

Of the dramatists who were profound psychologists before psychoanalysis was invented,[33] Ibsen and Strindberg take a special place within O'Neill's literary canon.[34]

It was Bernard Shaw's *The Quintessence of Ibsenism*, around 1905 O'Neill's "favorite reading,"[35] that first familiarized him with the Norwegian playwright. A few years later William Archer's translation of Ibsen's collected works was published. In the season of 1906–07 Broadway paid homage to the recently dead playwright by staging *A Doll's House*, *Hedda Gabler* and *The Master Builder*. O'Neill went to see them all and "he talked Ibsen all that year."[36] Especially *Hedda Gabler* impressed him:

> I do remember well the impact upon me when I saw an Ibsen play for the first time, a production of "Hedda Gabler" at the old Bijou Theatre in New York – and then went again and again for ten successive nights [...]. That experience

discovered an entire new world of the drama for me. It gave me my first conception of a modern theatre where truth might live.[37]

Much later O'Neill would recognize his indebtedness to this play when writing *Ah, Wilderness!*, where he contrasts the events and characters of Ibsen's play with those of his own.[38] The play's protagonist, O'Neill's sixteen-year-old alter ego Richard Miller, keeps quoting from *Hedda Gabler* and likes to think of himself as another Eilert Løvborg.

At Harvard, one of O'Neill's classmates, William Laurence, some six years later further stimulated his interest in Ibsen by seeing *Brand* and *Peer Gynt* as Nietzschean characters.[39]

When O'Neill first discovered Ibsen, he linked him, via Shaw, with the modern, realistic European drama. But in the twenties the Ibsen formula was no longer a vital issue. O'Neill now, his second wife reports, "considered the author of *A Dream Play* and *The Dance of Death* a greater and much more profound playwright than Ibsen, whom he liked to belittle as being conventional and idealistic."[40] However, as his last plays indicate, O'Neill was to change his mind once more. In the public letter appearing in *Nordisk Tidende* he states:

> Not long ago I read all of Ibsen's plays again. The same living truth is there. Only to fools with a superficial eye cocked to detect the incidental can they have anything dated or outworn about them. As dramas revealing the souls of men and women they are as great to-day as they will be a hundred years from now.[41]

Of all Ibsen's plays, *A Doll's House* has left particularly obvious traces in such early plays as *Recklessness*, *Fog*, and *Servitude*. Somewhat later the impact of *Peer Gynt* can be sensed. Incarnating the biblical archetype of him who loses his soul while gaining the world, Ibsen's roaming self-made man has a counterpart in the title figures of *The Emperor Jones* and *Marco Millions*. Starting out as the son of a poor crofter, Peer, ironically crowned "Emperor of Himself," has turned into

> a prosperous man of business in America, highly respectable and ready for any profitable speculation: slave trade, Bible trade, whisky trade, missionary trade, anything! His commercial success in this phase persuades him that he is under the special care of God.[42]

Jones and Marco are explorers and exploiters akin to Peer. "The American 'success story' in black-face,"[43] Jones, too, believes that he is under special protection: only a silver bullet can kill him. And in Marco we witness the same development as in Peer from youthful innocence to an ever-increasing materialism and loss of self.

Ibsen's impact on O'Neill ironically reaches an apogee in the play that was hailed in Europe as a sign that America was at last living up to its New World reputation in the field of drama. The play is *Anna Christie*. Engel notes in passing that like Ibsen's Ellida, in *The Lady from the Sea*, Anna Christie longs for the open sea.[44] As a matter of fact there is a close affinity not only between the two heroines but also between the plots of the two plays. This appears not least from Shaw's synopsis of Ibsen's drama in *Quintessence*. But whereas Ellida abstains from her seaman, Anna decides to marry hers.

House-building as a symbolic occupation is the noteworthy resemblance between Ibsen's *The Masterbuilder* and *The Great God Brown*. Having designed villas for years, Solness decides once more to erect a tower, not on a church, however, but on the house he is building for himself. Like Dion's cathedral design in O'Neill's play, it may be regarded as a Nietzschean mock-church. For both men it is to be their last construction.

Already when *The Iceman Cometh* was first performed, American critics pointed out its similarity not only to Gorki's *Night Asylum* (also called *The Lower Depths*) – especially with regard to environment and the protagonist-cum-savior – but also its thematic resemblance to Ibsen's *The Wild Duck*.[45] Both plays stress the necessity of the life-lie, that is, the idea that man cannot live without illusions – about himself. Although a common theme in modern drama, it is arguably more pronounced in *The Wild Duck* and *The Iceman Cometh* than in any other plays to date. Drinking sustains the pipe dreamers in either drama and just as Ibsen's characters figuratively dwell on "the bottom of the sea," so O'Neill's human wrecks drink themselves to oblivion in "The Bottom of the Sea Rathskeller."

The transparently autobiographical nature of *Long Day's Journey Into Night* tends to disguise its relationship to other plays in the same realistic vein. Ibsen's *Ghosts* is a case in point. Adhering faithfully to the three unities, both *Ghosts* and *Long Day's Journey* cover a time of about sixteen hours. In each play there are five characters. Both dramas are highly retrospective, gradually revealing past guilt which has resulted in present misery in what appears to be a fated chain of events. The guilt is in both cases distributed on several hands, and in the last instance life itself seems to be "responsible" for the course of events. The intimate mother–son relationship plays a central part in both plays. Alcohol and morphine appear in both. The secret, shameful illness – syphilis in *Ghosts*, morphine addiction in *Long Day's Journey* – is not revealed until late in the plays and in both cases the revelation is followed by insanity on the part of the victims (Osvald, Mary). Last but not least: in both dramas we witness a struggle against blinding forces, symbolized by the fog. When the fog is dispelled in *Ghosts*, the struggle is over: Osvald's insanity is made manifest. In *Long Day's Journey* the fog, far from being dispelled, is denser than ever when the play closes. Ibsen ends his tragedy with an ironical sunrise, whereas in O'Neill's tragedy of survival the characters are plunged into fog-bound darkness.

Ibsen's *Wild Duck* again flaps its broken wings in *A Touch of the Poet*, where Cornelius Melody, another pipe dreamer, recalls Old Ekdal in Ibsen's play. Melody's killing of the mare – O'Neill's "wild duck" – means a violation both to his pipe dream and to his innermost self.

Paradoxically, O'Neill is never closer to Ibsen than at the peak of his artistry and integrity, when he is able to use the old master's tools, notably his retrospective technique, with perfection and insight, free in his indebtedness to the father of modern drama and, through his own work, pointing to the Ibsen tradition as a viable alternative in the search for a tragedy of our time.

Even more important for O'Neill than Ibsen was the Swede August Strindberg. Significantly, half of O'Neill's Nobel Prize acceptance speech in 1936 was devoted to Strindberg:

> It was reading his plays when I first started to write back in the winter of 1913–14 that, above all else, first gave me a vision of what modern drama could be, and first inspired me with the urge to write for the theater myself. If there is anything of lasting worth in my work, it is due to that original impulse from him, which has continued as my inspiration down all the years since then – to the ambition I received then to follow in the footsteps of his genius as worthily as my talent might permit, and with the same integrity of purpose.
>
> Of course, it will be no news to you in Sweden that my work owes much to the influence of Strindberg. That influence runs clearly through more than a few of my plays and is plain for everyone to see. Neither will it be news for anyone who has ever known me, for I have always stressed it myself. [...]
>
> For me, he remains, as Nietzsche remains in his sphere, the Master, still to this day more modern than any of us, still our leader.[46]

Already in the early Twenties O'Neill had lauded the Swedish playwright in a program note for the Provincetown Players' production of *The Spook Sonata*:

> Strindberg still remains among the most modern of moderns, the greatest interpreter in the theater of the characteristic spiritual conflicts which constitute the drama – the blood – of our lives today. He carried Naturalism to a logical attainment of such poignant intensity that, if the work of any other playwright is to be called "naturalism," we must classify a play like *The Dance of Death* as "super-naturalism," and place it in a class by itself,

exclusively Strindberg's since no one before or after him has had the genius to qualify.

[...]

Strindberg knew and suffered with our struggle years before many of us were born. He expressed it by intensifying the method of his time and by foreshadowing both in content and form the methods to come. All that is enduring in what we loosely call "Expressionism" – all that is artistically valid and sound theater – can be clearly traced back through Wedekind to Strindberg's *The Dream Play, There Are Crimes and Crimes, The Spook Sonata*, etc.[47]

At about the same time he told a newspaper reporter that he considered Strindberg "the last undeniably great playwright."[48]

O'Neill undoubtedly read all the twenty-four Strindberg plays appearing in the original Scribner edition, 1912–16, in Edwin Björkman's translation. Agnes Boulton has reported how strong Strindberg's impact was on her husband around 1920: "Nietzsche, Strindberg – he kept these always with him, discussed them and quoted from them."[49] Similarly, O'Neill's third wife, Carlotta Monterey, has said that before Strindberg he would kneel.[50]

O'Neill's veneration is reflected in one of his earliest – and worst – pieces, *Recklessness*, which is little more than a rewriting of Strindberg's *Miss Julie*. Julie's concluding suicide has also left traces both in *Diff'rent* and in *Before Breakfast*, a monodrama which, as O'Neill himself surmised, is patterned on Strindberg's *The Stronger*.

When Strindberg, in the famous preface to *Miss Julie*, describes his characters as "conglomerates, made up of past and present stages of civilization," he is touching on an idea that O'Neill has taken to heart in *The Emperor Jones*, where he lets Jones experience past stages of civilization, both those that belong to his own past and those that belong to the past of his race.

Miss Julie, daughter of a Count, lowers herself socially when she descends from the noble environment where she belongs to the servants' kitchen in the basement. A metaphysical counterpart of her descent appears in *A Dream Play*, where Indra's Daughter descends to Earth to share the lot of mankind. O'Neill obviously had both plays in mind when he had Mildred Douglas in *The Hairy Ape*, daughter of the President of the Steel Trust, descend from her first-class cabin of an ocean liner to the dark, hot and murky stokehole. As Clara Blackburn has demonstrated, there are striking similarities between Strindberg's coalheavers and O'Neill's stokers.[51]

In quite another way *A Dream Play* figures again in the uncompleted *More Stately Mansions*, this time in the form of an enigmatic door. Both doors are visible on the stage, one as part of a theatre corridor, the other of a summer house. Both are related to childhood memories. And both function as suspense-evoking elements. But whereas Strindberg refrains from commenting explicitly on the significance of the door and what is behind it – since the riddle of life is insoluble – O'Neill, whose concern is here psychological rather than metaphysical, provides a complicated, explicit interpretation.

In *Miss Julie* Strindberg touches on the idea of a psychological family fate when he has Julie say that "now it is my mother's turn to revenge herself again, through me." This idea is expressed visually in *Mourning Becomes Electra*, where Lavinia in the third part has become a kind of reincarnation of the dead mother – a circumstance that Orin draws attention to when he tells her: "you're Mother."

There are, in fact, several resemblances between Julie (and her kins-woman Hedda Gabler) and Lavinia. Of about the same age, they both come from venerable old families on their father's side, who inhabit stately manor houses. Julie has been brought up like a boy by her father, and Lavinia is also, when we first meet her, very boyish in appearance as a token of her repressed femininity. In the third part she is completely changed; she now resembles her mother. At the end of the trilogy she returns to her puritan, Mannon self. Even more than Strindberg, O'Neill in this way illustrates his heroine's vacillation between her parents. Julie's self-characterization – "half woman and half man" – fits Lavinia.

In his "Working Notes" for the trilogy O'Neill declares that, unlike the Attic tragedians, he wants to give his Electra (Lavinia) a tragic end "worthy of her character."[52] Both in Hedda and Julie he could find figures who fulfilled this demand. In his preface to *Miss Julie* Strindberg points out that Julie, being of noble birth, is inclined to "take vengeance upon herself" and "would be moved to it by that innate or acquired sense of honor which the upper classes inherit – whence?" The fact that she is the last member of her family makes the ending seem very definite. It is not only an individual who dies, it is a whole social class and the values that go with it that is extinguished. The same could be said about Lavinia. She is, in an even more literal sense than Julie, the last member of her family. After all, Julie's father survives her, but no one survives Lavinia.

The spatially circular composition of *The Emperor Jones* may owe something to *To Damascus I*, often considered the first expressionist drama. In a sense, Strindberg's play is essentially one long monologue, the protagonist's talking to himself. This is literally true about the major part of *The Emperor Jones*, where the fleeing protagonist is the only speaker. The characters who function as reminders of the Stranger's past guilt in

To Damascus correspond to the phantoms that Jones has to face in the jungle.[53]

Alternatively, the characters in Strindberg's play can be seen as conflicting selves within the protagonist. As such, they resemble the two selves constituting the man John Loving in *Days Without End*. Thus Falk regards the Stranger, the Beggar and the Doctor in *To Damascus* as a conglomerate character comparable to John, "while the Tempter is the voice of rationality and experience – Loving. There is even an all-knowing 'Confessor,' comparable to Father Baird in *Days Without End*."[54]

Also with regard to more limited stage effects, Strindberg may have inspired O'Neill. At the beginning of *The Pelican* Elise tells her son Fredrik to turn on "only a couple" of lights, because they must save on electricity, while later, when feeling forsaken, she herself *"turns on all the electric lights."* When Elise's daughter Gerda enters and *"turns off all the electric lights but one,"* the former situation is reversed:

MOTHER [...] Don't put out the lights!

GERDA Yes, we have to economize!

In the final act of *Long Day's Journey*, similarly, Tyrone first asks his son to put out the light in the hall because "there is no reason [...] burning up money!" A little later he himself turns on the bulbs in the living room. But after a while he clicks them out again.

In both plays the electric lights are used to demonstrate the discrepancy between a seemingly objective and acceptable motivation – the need to economize – and the underlying true reason, the subtext. It is likely that the light symbolism in Strindberg's chamber play has inspired O'Neill to his more extensive and psychologically more penetrating handling of this symbolism in *Long Day's Journey*.

"Strindberg," the Gelbs declare, "was more than a literary kindred spirit to O'Neill; [...] he became in some ways a pattern for O'Neill's life."[55] The reason for this is indicated by Sheaffer when he states:

Perhaps the most important thing he [O'Neill] took from Strindberg was the courage to explore in his writings the darkest corners of his own character.[56]

In Strindberg's depiction of family relations O'Neill could recognize his own situation. Thus Strindberg's feeling that he was an unwanted child is frequently expressed in O'Neill's work, most explicitly in *Long Day's Journey*. After his mother's death O'Neill told a friend that as a semirecluse she had reminded him of the Mummy in *The Spook Sonata*, the old lady who lives in a cupboard.[57] *The Dance of Death* "struck an overwhelmingly responsive chord," because it "put into words [...] what O'Neill had for a long time recognized as one of the motivating forces of his parents' relationship with each other and the resultant effects upon him."[58]

But the biographical explanation is not exhaustive. O'Neill's profound concern with Strindberg must also be sought in the Swedish playwright's power to deal with psychological and metaphysical problems in a dramatically convincing and arresting way. The Strindbergian method, George Jean Nathan once remarked, is "the intensification of the dramatic action, of which O'Neill was so fond. If he stems from anyone, he stems from Strindberg."[59]

In the manner in which he depicts people fighting themselves, torn between contrasting loyalties, vacillating between love, hatred and self-hatred, driven by impulses and desires that they cannot restrain or of which they are not aware, searching for a meaning of life, a justification for the suffering of mankind – in all this Strindberg is, as O'Neill put it in 1924, "the most modern of moderns." And in all this, O'Neill is his inheritor.

Early in his career O'Neill declared that he would never let himself be influenced by any consideration but one: "Is it the truth as I know it – or, better still, feel it? If so, shoot, and let the splinters fly wherever they may."[60] Some forty years later he wrote a dedication to his wife on the script of *Long Day's Journey* that begins: "I give you the original script of this play of old sorrow, written in tears and blood." The two statements form a fitting epitaph for a life which, like Nietzsche's, Ibsen's and Strindberg's, was inextricably intertwined with his creative writing – and reading.[61] Like theirs, his work, characterized by unusual integrity and sincerity, is in the confessional mode. O'Neill rarely forgot Zarathustra's admonishment to the creator: "Write in blood, and thou shalt learn that blood is spirit."

NOTES

1 For Conrad's influence on O'Neill, see Travis Bogard, *Contour in Time: The Plays of Eugene O'Neill* (New York: Oxford University Press, 1972), pp. 39–42.

2 Barrett H. Clark, *Eugene O'Neill: The Man and his Plays* (New York: Dover Publications, 1947), p. 25.

3 For a good discussion of "O'Neill's literary biography," see Jean Chothia, *Forging a Language: A Study of the Plays of Eugene O'Neill* (Cambridge: Cambridge University Press, 1979), pp. 43–52, 198–206, 230–32.

4 The comparisons made by Normand Berlin in his *O'Neill's Shakespeare* (Ann Arbor: University of Michigan Press, 1993) are usually too general to indicate a direct influence.

5 Cf. John Henry Raleigh, "The Last Confession: O'Neill and the Catholic Confession," in Virginia Floyd, ed., *O'Neill: A World View* (New York: Frederick Ungar, 1979), pp. 212–28.

6 Chothia, *Forging a Language*, p. 44.

7 For an extended discussion, see Egil Törnqvist, "Nietzsche and O'Neill: A Study in Affinity," *Orbis Litterarum*, 23 (1968): 97–126.

8 Letter to Benjamin De Casseres (22 June 1927), quoted from Louis Sheaffer, *O'Neill: Son and Playwright* (Boston: Little Brown, 1968), p. 123.

9 Clark, *Eugene O'Neill*, p. 5.

10 Arthur Nethercot, "The Psychoanalyzing of Eugene O'Neill," *Modern Drama*, 3 (December 1960): 248.

11 *The New York Tribune*, 13 February 1921.

12 Mary B. Mullett, "The Extraordinary Story of Eugene O'Neill," *American Magazine* (November 1922), quoted from Ulrich Halfmann, ed., *Eugene O'Neill: Comments on the Drama and the Theater* (Tübingen: Gunter Narr Verlag, 1987), p. 26.

13 *The Birth of Tragedy*, tr. William A. Haussmann (Edinburgh and London: T. N. Foulis, 1909), Section 10.

14 Arthur Hobson Quinn, *A History of the American Drama from the Civil War to the Present Day*, vol. II (New York: Harper, 1937), p. 199.

15 *Thus Spake Zarathustra*, tr. A. Tille (New York: Macmillan, 1896), part III, chapter 13.

16 *Zarathustra*, part IV, chapter 10.

17 *The Birth of Tragedy*, section 14.

18 *The Birth of Tragedy*, section 6.

19 Letter to George Jean Nathan published in *American Mercury* (January 1929): 119.

20 Arthur and Barbara Gelb, *O'Neill* (New York: Harper, 1962), p. 520.

21 *Zarathustra*, part I, chapter 12.

22 See Chothia, *Eugene O'Neill*, pp. 96–98.

23 Gelbs, *O'Neill*, p. 121.

24 For an extended discussion of O'Neill's relationship to psychoanalysis, see Nethercot's article, mentioned in note 10, and its sequel in *Modern Drama*, 4 (February 1961): 357–72.

25 Letter to Martha Carolyn Sparrow (13 October 1929), quoted from Nethercot (1960): 248.

26 Horst Frenz, ed., *American Playwrights on Drama* (New York: Hill and Wang, 1965), pp. 5, 8–9.

27 Oscar Cargill et al., eds., *O'Neill and His Plays: Four Decades of Criticism* (New York: New York University Press, 1961), p. 120.

28 Doris Falk, *Eugene O'Neill and the Tragic Tension* (New Brunswick, NJ: Rutgers University Press, 1965), p. 150.

29 O'Neill, "Memoranda on Masks" (1932), quoted from Cargill et al., p. 116.

30 Mullett, "The Extraordinary Story," in Halfmann, *Eugene O'Neill*, p. 22.

31 Frenz, *American Playwrights*, p. 3.

32 Virginia Floyd, ed., *Eugene O'Neill at Work: Newly Released Ideas for Plays* (New York: Frederick Ungar, 1981), p. 52.

33 O'Neill's statement to Clark, in his *Eugene O'Neill*, p. 136.

34 For an extended discussion of their impact on O'Neill, see Egil Törnqvist, "Ibsen and O'Neill: A Study in Influence," *Scandinavian Studies*, 37 (Aug. 1965): 211–35, and Egil Törnqvist, "Strindberg and O'Neill," in Marilyn Johns

Blackwell, ed., *Structures of Influence: A Comparative Approach to August Strindberg* (Chapel Hill: University of North Carolina Press, 1981), pp. 277–91.

35 Lawrence Langner, *The Magic Curtain* (New York: Dutton, 1951), p. 288.

36 Doris Alexander, *The Tempering of Eugene O'Neill* (New York: Harcourt, Brace, and World, 1961), p. 128.

37 *Nordisk Tidende* [Brooklyn, NY], 2 June 1938, quoted from Halfmann, Eugene O'Neill p. 135.

38 The observation is Chothia's in *Forging a Language*, p. 50.

39 Gelbs, *O'Neill*, p. 277.

40 Agnes Boulton, *Part of a Long Story* (Garden City, NY: Doubleday, 1958), p. 76.

41 Halfmann, *Eugene O'Neill*, p. 135.

42 George Bernard Shaw, *The Quintessence of Ibsenism* (1891), quoted from his *Major Critical Essays* (London: Constable, 1955), p. 135.

43 Edwin Engel, *The Haunted Heroes of Eugene O'Neill* (Cambridge, Mass.: Harvard University Press, 1953), p. 49.

44 *Ibid.*, p. 23.

45 Cf. Sverre Arestad, "*The Iceman Cometh* and *The Wild Duck*," *Scandinavian Studies*, 20 (February 1948): 1–12.

46 *New York Times* (11 December 1936), quoted from Frenz, *American Playwrights*, pp. 41–42.

47 "Strindberg and Our Theatre," *Provincetown Playbill* (Season 1923–24), quoted from Cargill *et al.*, *O'Neill and his Plays*, pp. 108–09.

48 Gelbs, *O'Neill*, p. 585.

49 Boulton, *Part of a Long Story*, p. 76.

50 Karl Ragnar Gierow, "Ett teaterprogram," *Svenska Dagbladet*, 15 September 1958.

51 Clara Blackburn, "Continental Influences on Eugene O'Neill's Expressionistic Drama," *American Literature*, 13 (May 1941): 119–21.

52 Frenz, *American Playwrights*, p. 3.

53 Blackburn, "Continental Influences," pp. 115–16.

54 Falk, *Eugene O'Neill*, p. 153.

55 Gelbs, *O'Neill*, p. 234.

56 Sheaffer, *O'Neill: Son and Playwright*, p. 254.

57 *Ibid.*, p. 317.

58 Gelbs, *O'Neill*, p. 233.

59 *Ibid.*, p. 731.

60 Clark, *Eugene O'Neill*, p. 163.

61 Chothia, *Forging a Language*, p. 45.

3

DANIEL J. WATERMEIER

O'Neill and the theatre of his time

From the end of World War I to the onset of the Great Depression marked the most dynamic period in the history of the American stage. Over the course of this era, the theatre experienced unprecedented growth. Expansion, stimulated by mounting economic prosperity and a burgeoning urban, middle-class population, resulted in an increased demand for theatrical entertainment. Demand sparked competition and an openness to invention and change, forcing the theatrical establishment to vie with new emerging talents and innovative approaches for audiences and critical attention. O'Neill's career, which began on the cusp of this theatrical Renaissance, was impacted by theatre's expansionist tendencies and the prevailing tensions between the forces of tradition and those of change. A survey of the existing conditions and innovative trends manifest in this milieu illuminates O'Neill's artistic and commercial success in the theatre of his time.

Art versus commercialism

By the late Teens, professional theatre in America was centralized in New York. Indeed, "Broadway" and "American theatre" had become virtually synonymous terms. Broadway, in turn, was largely controlled by producers driven primarily by commercial, rather than artistic interests. These were relatively recent developments in the annals of our national stage and there were many who criticized, in particular, the trend towards commercialism which did little to elevate theatrical tastes and standards. To understand the rise of Broadway and commercialism, one must go back a generation to the immediate post-Civil War era.

When O'Neill's celebrated actor–father made his theatrical debut in 1867, the American theatre was organized around the so-called stock and star system. Most cities had at least one resident stock company; major metropolitan areas had several. For the most part, these companies presented standard, traditional dramatic fare, mixed with an occasional new play, on a repertory basis – productions were changed or rotated weekly, bi-weekly, or more often. Visiting stars, bravura actors travelling alone from city to city, were regularly engaged to supplement the resident company. At the head of the company was an actor–manager, usually an experienced and respected performer. This system had been in place since the 1820s. It had its shortcomings and critics, but it offered artistic familiarity, a certain stability and financial security for common players, handsome incomes for many stars, and a respectable profit for managers.

Beginning in the mid-1870s, the organization of theatrical performance changed significantly. Stars would remain a permanent fixture in the theatrical cosmos, but the stock system was steadily eroded, initially by the long-run. In a highly competitive arena, new plays increasingly replaced traditional fare to attract audiences. Since new plays were usually more expensive to mount than revivals of old plays, to recoup their investment – and when box office demand warranted it – managers would run a production continuously night after night, rather than rotating it with other productions. A run of one hundred continuous performances soon became the benchmark for a commercially successful production. Stock was also affected by the rise of the "combination," a theatrical company organized to tour a single popular play, or a small repertoire of plays, featuring a prominent star, or, occasionally, stars. Combination companies travelled with their own stock of scenery, properties, and costumes, and a cadre of at least essential support personnel. They were basically travelling long-runs. A number of factors contributed to the rise of the combination, but the most significant was the growth of railroads. In 1860, there were about 30,000 miles of track. With the laying of transcontinental lines in the late 1860s, railways expanded rapidly. By the mid-1880s, there were over 130,000 miles of track. Railroads gave combinations access to cities and towns across America. Local stock companies could not compete with the popularity and glamor of touring combinations. Managers abandoned stock, turning their theatres into "road" houses in which they booked a steady stream of combinations. Although local autonomy was lost, touring was highly profitable for tour organizers and, especially, for stars, many of whom earned fortunes at the head of their own combinations. By the turn of the century, several hundred combinations were on the road each season.

Since time immemorial, theatre had balanced artistic objectives with business interests, but the long-run and the combination tipped the scales away from art and towards commercialism. In an age of industrial monopolies, entrepreneurial producers, booking agents, and theatre owners soon began to organize monopolistic partnerships that controlled both production and the lucrative touring circuit. These monopolies brought stability and efficiency to the complex touring circuit; they renovated old theatres and built new ones; most importantly they made money for the partnership and its clients. But monopolies could act ruthlessly. Actors, managers, and theatre owners who did not come into the fold were squeezed out of the business. Plays that appealed to conventional tastes and were likely to be profitable took precedence over innovation, experimentation, or genuine literary merit. A few stars, long accustomed to selecting their own repertoire and arranging their own engagements without middle-men, some independent producers and theatre owners, and several prominent critics railed against the leading monopolies. The venerable dean of American theatre critics, William Winter, for example, called them, with some justification, organizations of "sordid, money-grubbing tradesmen," and decried the movement of theatre away from "the hands either of Actors who love and honor their art or of men endowed with the temperament of the Actor and acquainted with his art and its needs" (*Other Days*, 30–37). The monopolies, however, ignored their critics and stymied efforts to break their stranglehold on theatrical organization and production.

Ironically, touring, which in large measure was responsible for the rise of theatrical monopolies, declined precipitously in the second decade of the new century. The causes for the decline are multiple and include growing production costs which reduced profitability, the rise of a cheaper priced vaudeville touring circuit, even cheaper movies, and free radio. By 1920, the number of productions on the road had shrunk to about forty a year, although a popular Broadway hit could still be successful on the road. The goal for most producers, actors, and playwrights alike was a successful – meaning profitable – long-run of several hundred performances on Broadway, followed, if possible, by a tour of major cities. Theatrical monopolies were weakened, but not destroyed. Indeed, the commercial model they had fostered was widely emulated by their managerial successors and competitors. The number of productions on Broadway steadily increased from about one hundred annually in the period 1902–03, to 192 in 1920–21, to 297 in 1926–27. Nearly 2,500 productions were mounted during the Twenties, an average of 250 a season. The risks of producing a Broadway show were great – more productions failed than succeeded – but the potential profits were greater. General prosperity and "war profits" provided capital for almost any enterprise. Commercial producers multiplied. However, discontent with Broadway's commercialism steadily mounted on several fronts.

Even at the height of the monopolists' power, a few independent producers struggled to preserve and promote dramatic art over standard commercial fare. Minnie Maddern Fiske, for example, a prominent star and manager, and her husband Harrison Grey Fiske, a producer and director and the publisher of the influential *New York Dramatic Mirror*, both arch-opponents of the theatrical monopolies, were early champions of realistic drama. In the early 1900s, Mrs. Fiske achieved *succès d'estime* in Ibsen's *A Doll's House, Hedda Gabler, Rosmersholm*, and *The Pillars of Society*. She also starred in several American realistic social comedies and dramas, including Langdon Mitchell's *The New York Idea* (1906), a satire of marriage and divorce among New York's affluent elite, and at the other end of the social scale, Edward Sheldon's *Salvation Nell* (1908), a somber portrayal of the squalor and conflicts of lower-class life. Both productions had excellent, if limited, runs on Broadway. The Fiskes were not alone.

In 1909, a consortium of wealthy businessmen established what they hoped would be an American equivalent of Europe's great national theatres – like the Théâtre Français or the Vienna Burgtheater. Not only did they build the architecturally splendid New Theatre, but they endowed or subsidized its operation, presumably freeing its management and repertoire from commercial interests. Winthrop Ames, a young director from Boston, with a Harvard education, a private income, and first-hand knowledge of contemporary European theatre, was installed as the New Theatre's artistic director. For two seasons, Ames mounted an ambitious repertoire, alternating revivals of classics with productions of new, modern European and American plays, including, for example, Shakespeare's *Antony and Cleopatra*, John Galsworthy's *Strife*, Maeterlinck's *The Blue Bird*, and Edward Sheldon's provocative *The Nigger*. The productions were generally distinguished, but insufficiently popular to break even in the cavernous, 2,500-seat New Theatre. The debt grew larger than the consortium was willing to sustain; they sold the New Theatre to the monopolistic Shubert brothers who used it as a house for popular musicals and operettas. Ames, however, had learned an important lesson. He built two intimate theatres – the 500-seat Little Theatre (1912) and the 800-seat Booth Theatre (1913) – where he successfully mounted productions of plays by Galsworthy, Shaw, Schnitzler, Maeterlinck and other modern dramatists.

Some mainly commercial producers also occasionally aimed beyond mere financial success. In 1911, veteran producer William A. Brady built the small, 1,000-seat Playhouse, where he starred his actress-wife Grace George in a number of modern plays, including Shaw's *Major Barbara* (1915) and *Captain Brassbound's Conversion* (1916). (Their daughter Alice Brady would later star as Lavinia in *Mourning Becomes Electra*.) Producer–director John D. Williams propelled John Barrymore into stardom with a production of Galsworthy's *Justice* (1916) and then two seasons later did the same for Lionel Barrymore in Augustus Thomas's Civil War drama *The Copperhead*. (Williams would subsequently produce *Beyond the Horizon*.) In 1918, producer–director Arthur Hopkins scored successes featuring John Barrymore in Tolstoy's *The Living Corpse* (re-titled *Redemption*) and the Russian emigré actress Alla Nazimova in revivals of Ibsen's *The Wild Duck*, *Hedda Gabler*, and *A Doll's House*. (Hopkins would produce *Anna Christie*, while Nazimova would be the original Christine in *Mourning Becomes Electra*.)

Certain external forces also impacted the commercial theatrical establishment and theatrical tastes. In the second decade of the new century, a number of non-profit, mostly amateur theatrical groups, collectively called "Little Theatres," began springing up across America. The founders of Little Theatres were usually dissatisfied with commercial theatrical fare. They modeled their organizations after late nineteenth-century European art theatres such as André Antoine's Théâtre-Libre, Otto Brahms's Freie Bühne, J. T. Grein's Independent Theatre, the Moscow Art Theatre, and Dublin's Abbey Theatre, all of which had been founded by talented, dedicated amateurs. Like their models, Little Theatre organizers were interested in modern European drama; new, serious American drama; and dramatic classics – all plays which were not ordinarily mounted by the typical commercial producer. By 1920, there were hundreds of such Little Theatres scattered across America. Some would retain an amateur community theatre status, while others became semi or fully professional. The Provincetown Players, in particular, and the Washington Square Players, to a lesser degree, were two Little Theatres that would figure importantly in O'Neill's development.

The Provincetown Players began informally in the summer of 1915 when a score of aspiring performers and playwrights, including O'Neill, staged a series of one-act plays in a makeshift theatre on an old wharf in Provincetown, Massachusetts. They repeated the experiment the following summer; and then flush with enthusiasm, they relocated to a small theatre in New York's bohemian Greenwich Village, becoming one of the first of what would later be called an Off-Broadway theatre. Organized formally as the Provincetown Players: The Playwrights' Theatre, they continued to mount their own plays and encouraged plays that aspired to high dramatic standards. Over the course of its first six seasons, the Provincetown Players mounted over ninety new plays, mostly one-acts, by American playwrights. For these playwrights, the Provincetown Players offered a first opportunity to see and hear their plays performed, and as such the company contributed significantly to nurturing their talent and honing their skills.

Although after a few seasons, some of its members were paid, the Provincetown Players remained mainly amateur and resolutely experimental. But it established a growing reputation for inventive stagings of compelling dramas. All of O'Neill's early plays were staged by the Provincetown Players, including *Bound East for Cardiff* (1916), *The Long Voyage Home* (1918), and *The Moon of the Caribbees* (1919). After O'Neill was established as a young playwright to be reckoned with, the Provincetown continued to provide a venue for the daring experimentation of *The Emperor Jones* (1920), *The Hairy Ape* (1922), *All God's Chillun Got Wings* (1923), and *Desire Under the Elms* (1924). Without the Provincetown Players, plays of this sort probably would not have been produced. (After their initial downtown successes, furthermore, *The Hairy Ape* and *Desire Under the Elms* transferred to commercial Broadway theatres.)

The Washington Square Players was founded in 1914 to present realist and symbolist plays, preferably new plays in these styles by American authors. During four seasons, they presented over sixty productions, predominantly one-act plays, most by American writers, but including plays by Chekhov, Maeterlinck, Shaw, and Wilde. In the fall of 1917, the Washington Square Players presented O'Neill's *In the Zone*. They remained an amateur, volunteer organization – although some actors and business and technical personnel did receive token salaries. The Washington Square Players steadily built a critical and popular following, but when key members were conscripted for service in World War I, the organization disbanded in May 1918. A year later, however, the Washington Square Players reformed as the Theatre Guild.

Like its parent organization, the Guild was mainly interested in modernist plays, especially pieces that were anti-realist in style, although some of their notable successes were essentially realist plays. The Guild intended to be self-supporting. It never sought subsidies or endowments, but it privileged artistic merit over commercial interests. To capitalize their enterprise and to organize interested playgoers, the Guild offered tickets by season subscription. Subscription tickets were discounted from a per-production, single-ticket rate, even though Guild prices were comparatively cheaper than tickets to commercial productions. Subscriptions were common for concert and operatic series, but they were unusual for theatre companies. The Guild's subscription system got off to a slow start with only 150 subscribers in 1919, but the numbers grew significantly with each season. By the mid-1920s, the Guild had over 20,000 subscribers and was an established, mainstream Broadway institution with its own permanent company and theatre. Not all of its productions were financially successful, but a commercial failure was invariably offset by one or more successes. With innovative business savvy, the Guild maintained high artistic standards and commercial viability. Beginning with *Marco Millions* (1927), the Guild would produce O'Neill's next six plays. Indeed, it is unlikely that any other organization of the time had the capital, artistic resources, and managerial acumen to take on O'Neill's increasingly challenging, lengthy dramas.

Interest in modern drama was also stimulated by new theatrical publications. The Drama League of America, for example, was founded in 1909 to stimulate interest in modern drama and the role of theatre as a cultural force. It sponsored playreading circles and circulated playscripts and information about meritorious productions. In 1911, the Drama League began publishing a quarterly journal, *The Drama*, with articles by important critics and new playscripts. By 1920 the Drama League had tens of thousands of members and 100 centers nation wide. *Theatre Arts*, a quarterly journal founded in 1916, introduced readers to modernist ideas and practices in European and American theatre. In the mid-1920s, *Theatre Arts* expanded to monthly publication. How directly organizations like the Drama League and publications like *Theatre Arts* influenced Broadway standards is difficult to determine, but they suggest that there was a growing audience for modern drama and an intense interest among some theatre professionals in elevating the overall artistic quality of American theatre and drama.

Popular entertainment versus modern drama

Popular entertainment, however, not modern drama ruled on Broadway in the Teens and Twenties. Before World War I, the longest running Broadway play was *Peg o' My Heart*, a light-hearted sentimental comedy. Opening in 1912, it had 604 performances in New York, played in London for a season, then was toured for several seasons more. *Lightnin'* (1918), a rural comedy-melodrama, surpassed *Peg o' My Heart* with 1,291 performances; it subsequently toured season after season until 1925. The greatest hit of the era was *Abie's Irish Rose* (1922), a romantic ethnic comedy, pitting young lovers – a Jewish boy and an Irish Catholic girl – against their hidebound parents. It ran five years for over 2,500 performances, a record that held until the sensational, rural melodrama, *Tobacco Road* (1933), chalked up over 3,000 continuous performances. Running not far behind these hits were such plays as *The Gold Diggers* (1919; 720 performances), a farce about chorus girls searching for wealthy husbands, and *The Bat* (1920; 867 performances), a mystery "whodunit."

Typically a Broadway season offered a range of melodramas, farces, light romantic comedies, and lavishly staged musical comedies, revues, and operettas. The 1919–20 season, in which *Beyond the Horizon* premiered, was, in most respects, representative of the era. About 150 productions were mounted. They included a number of claptrap melodramas with titles like *The Challenge*, *The Storm*, and *The Purple Mask*; a range of light romantic comedies and farces, some vapid like the bedroom farce *Nighty-Night*, others more skillfully wrought, like Booth Tarkington's *Clarence*; historical dramas, such as *Abraham Lincoln* and *George Washington*; and exotic "Oriental" plays, such as John Masefield's *The Faithful*, set in ancient Japan, and David Belasco's Chinese melodrama, *The Son–Daughter*.

Popular entertainment held sway, but a few plays of dramatic merit always managed to find an audience. O'Neill's *Beyond the Horizon*, which ran for a respectable 111 performances, is a case in point. Zoë Akins's society drama *Déclassé*, although marred by melodramatic plotting, was also a serious attempt to address sexual double standards and class snobbery. Helped by Ethel Barrymore's compelling performance in the leading role, *Déclassé* enjoyed a very long run of 257 performances. Rachel Crothers's *He and She* was more deftly structured than *Déclassé* and a more probing examination of American gender issues, but its troubling realism and lack of a star undoubtedly prevented it from attracting the audience it deserved. It ran for a mere twenty-eight performances. But Crothers had succeeded on Broadway as early as 1906 with *The Three of Us*, which ran for an entire season, and again, though to a lesser extent, with *A Man's World* (1910; 71 performances). Writing a play a year over the next two decades, and usually directing them as well, Crothers would add to her reputation as a skillful and thoughtful playwright.

Indeed, in the early decades of the new century, a handful of older playwrights had sown the seeds for the harvest that O'Neill and his generation would reap. It is certainly untrue, as some writers have suggested, that O'Neill was the first American playwright to bring dramatic literature to Broadway (Gelbs, *O'Neill*, 409; Sheaffer, *O'Neill: Son and Playwright*, 481). Histories of American drama regularly cite such meritorious dramatic antecedents as William Vaughan Moody's *The Great Divide* (1906), Mitchell's *The New York Idea* (1906), Clyde Fitch's *The City* (1909), Sheldon's *Salvation Nell* (1908), *The Nigger* (1909), and *The Boss* (1911), and Eugene Walter's *The Easiest Way* (1909). Although tending towards melodrama in structure and with visions less penetrating and encompassing than O'Neill's masterpieces, these plays were in their time critically well-regarded and commercially successful.

O'Neill may also have benefited from the fact that there was a dearth of dramatic talent in the years immediately preceding the premiere of *Beyond the Horizon*. Fitch died prematurely in 1909 at age forty-four; Moody in 1910 at age forty-one; Sheldon, incapacitated by rheumatoid arthritis, became less active and productive; neither Eugene Walter nor Langdon Mitchell, although they continued to write, fulfilled their early promise. Percy MacKaye had shown promise with *The Scarecrow* (1909), but after the war, he had turned his attention to historical pageantry. The prolific Augustus Thomas, active on Broadway since the 1890s, with over sixty plays to his credit, had his last critically acclaimed success with *The Copperhead*. But past his prime and written-out, Thomas's output dwindled. Furthermore, before O'Neill, few outstanding young talents emerged to replace the older generation of notable playwrights. A survey of the five Broadway seasons from 1914–15 to 1919–20 reveals only two new American playwrights who, like O'Neill, would have lasting reputations. Elmer Rice (still, however, writing under his given name, Elmer L. Reizenstein) was represented by three plays, including *On Trial* (1914), a powerful court-room drama which used a then novel flash-back technique to recreate the crime being tried. *On Trial* ran for 365 performances. Rachel Crothers had at least one play on Broadway in almost every one of the five seasons, including two commercial successes, *Old Lady 31* (1916; 160 performances) and *A Little Journey* (1918; 252 performances). The most popular playwrights of the time – Edward Knoblock, Frederic and Fanny Hatton, and Roi Cooper Megrue, to name a few, authors of light sentimental comedies, situation farces, and melodramas of contemporary life – have largely been forgotten.

European masters of modern drama were also consistently neglected. There were undistinguished mountings of Ibsen's *Ghosts* and *John Gabriel Borkman*. In 1919, Arthur Hopkins followed his productions of Tolstoy and Ibsen with a revival of Gorki's *The Lower Depths* (as *Night Lodging*), but it was not successful. The most popular modernist dramatist was Shaw, a number of whose plays were successfully premiered or revived between 1914 and 1920, including *Pygmalion, Misalliance, Captain Brassbound's Conversion*, and *Mrs. Warren's Profession*. John Galsworthy, Somerset Maugham, and, especially, James M. Barrie were also popular; and the Theatre Guild in its first season had an unexpected success with St. John Ervine's Irish tragedy *John Ferguson* (1919). There was a smattering of adaptations of contemporary European dramas and boulevard comedies. Broadway producers were probably not consciously nativistic, but, with a few notable exceptions, most of the plays they presented were by American authors.

The new stagecraft and natural acting

A tendency towards representational, illusionistic *mise-en scène* marked the nineteenth-century American stage. In the early years of the new century, David Belasco's productions epitomized this tradition. Since his apprentice years in San Francisco in the 1870s, Belasco had championed scenic realism. "Everything must be real" was his aesthetic dictum. He was not a designer himself, but he was the guiding force behind this visual ideal. When he built his own theatre in 1906, he took realism to new heights with solid three-dimensional scenic units, actual objects, and costumes that, depending on the play, were historically or contemporaneously accurate. He was a pioneer in the use of electrical lighting to create moods and naturalistic effects. He eliminated the traditional and distracting footlights and developed a system of overhead, diffused lighting that simulated natural-looking sunsets and sunrises or strikingly lit interiors. The plays Belasco chose to produce, usually his own, were invariably romantic, sentimental, and melodramatic, but their dramaturgical shortcomings were often masked by the extraordinary realism of their *mise-en-scènes*. Indeed, so famous were Belasco's lighting effects that they sometimes became the subject of sardonic commentary. In *A Moon for the Misbegotten*, for example, Jim Tyrone, according to the stage direction, is "profoundly moved ... [by] an exceptionally beautiful sunrise," but he caustically observes, "God seems to be putting on quite a display. I like Belasco better. Rise of curtain. Act-Four stuff" (*Complete Plays*, III, 942). By the late Teens, Belasco-style realism was increasingly challenged by modernist, European scenic practices. Inspired principally by the visionary designs and theoretical writings of Edward Gordon Craig and Adolphe Appia and by the inventive, eclectic directorial approach of Austrian *régisseur* Max Reinhardt, the New Stagecraft, as it was called, rejected detailed, photographic realism in favor of abstraction, suggestion, selective and simplified realism, and visual symbolism and metaphor.

New Stagecraft design was introduced to the American stage as early as 1911–12 by Austrian émigré designer Joseph Urban at the Boston Opera and by American designer Livingston Platt at Boston's Toy Theatre, an early "Little Theatre." Reinhardt himself brought the New Stagecraft to Broadway when he toured his exotic Arabian Nights-style pantomime *Sumurun* to New York in 1912. Three years later, English director–playwright Harley Granville-Barker, demonstrated his own variation on

New Stagecraft with his New York presentations of *A Midsummer Night's Dream*, Shaw's *Androcles and the Lion* and Anatole France's *The Man Who Married a Dumb Wife*, a farcical curtain-raiser set in the Middle Ages. American designer Robert Edmond Jones's scenery and costumes for the latter, which wittily suggested Medievalism without resorting to heavy-handed historical accuracy, signaled his allegiance to the New Stagecraft. In the next few years, Jones would enhance his own reputation and the cause of the New Stagecraft with imaginative, strikingly minimalistic settings for a number of Broadway productions. Jones was soon joined by other young advocates of New Stagecraft design, including Rollo Peters, Lee Simonson, and Cleon Throckmorton. By the early 1920s, although realistic stage design remained dominant, the New Stagecraft was an established, accepted, and admired alternative.

At the turn of the century, stage direction was not generally held to be a separate, distinct theatrical craft. Plays were usually staged by an actor-manager, by its producer, or sometimes by the playwright him/herself. As long as plays and their production adhered to established nineteenth-century conventions, this approach sufficed. Unconventional modern plays, however, and the scenic approaches of the New Stagecraft required specialized directors to unify the sometimes competing demands of script, *mise-en-scène*, and acting ensemble. Jones, Simonson, and Throckmorton would design the scenery for most of O'Neill's plays in the 1920s.

O'Neill was particularly fortunate to have several first-class directors to stage his often theatrically challenging plays. George Cram Cook (1873–1924), the inspirational founder of the Provincetown Players, imaginatively staged *The Emperor Jones*. James Light, who began his career as an actor and designer with the Provincetown Players, but gradually moved almost exclusively towards directing, staged *Diff'rent* (1920), *The Hairy Ape*, *All God's Chillun Got Wings*, and *S.S. Glencairn* (1924). Arthur Hopkins, a skillful director as well as a daring producer, staged *Anna Christie* (1921). Robert Edmond Jones both designed and directed *Desire Under the Elms*, the historical epic *The Fountain* (1925), and *The Great God Brown* (1926). Rouben Mamoulian, Russian-born and trained at Moscow's famous Vakhtangov Studio Theatre, staged O'Neill's sprawling *Marco Millions*. Subsequently, Mamoulian would become one of the American stage's leading directors, highly regarded for his ability to integrate music, drama, and dance into an artistically unified production. Philip Moeller, a founder of the Theatre Guild and an especially gifted and experienced director, staged five O'Neill plays, including the extraordinarily successful *Strange Interlude* (1928) and *Mourning Becomes Electra* (1931).

Ironically, as modern stage practice sought alternatives to illusionistic realism, the growing tendency in acting was towards an increasingly realistic or "natural" style. This trend had, in fact, been developing since the latter part of the nineteenth century. In the mid-1870s, for example, the acting of the great Shakespearean tragedian Edwin Booth (1833–93) was variously described as "quiet," "colloquial," "conversational," emotionally "restrained," and "natural." Indeed, "quietude" in particular was regarded as the chief quality distinguishing Booth's acting from the often violent excesses of the earlier Romantic school. But Booth's widely admired techniques were at the service of heroic, poetic characters, drawn from Shakespeare and historical romances; it was a realism tinged with romantic idealism and grandiloquence, suitable to the mainstream aesthetic values of the high-Victorian era, but not to an emerging modernism. Booth, however, pointed the direction for further developments; other interlocking forces contributed to the trend. Turn-of-the-century performers, like Minnie Maddern Fiske and William Gillette, practiced and promoted an acting style characterized by skillful, economical underplaying, emotional reserve or restraint, and a convincing, psychological truthfulness. The Italian actress Eleanora Duse during her four tours of America (1892, 1896, 1903, and 1923–24) impressed critics and playgoers with her subtle, naturalistic playing. The founding of schools to teach acting and influential acting teachers also made a contribution. Belasco, for example, as both a director and gifted acting teacher championed a natural, spontaneous, emotionally truthful acting style. Modern psychology, pioneered in America by William James, with its interest in the complexities of consciousness was a significant influence. Perhaps the foremost factor was the development of a contemporary realistic drama, both native and foreign, that focused not on extraordinary, heroic figures, but on ordinary people, and, in particular, on their inner psychological lives. Indeed, realism of this sort was increasingly pervasive in *fin-de-siècle* American literature and art. Playgoers were not immune to these cultural and theatrical tendencies. By the second decade of the new century, popular stars like James O'Neill, William Faversham, even the great Sarah Bernhardt, might still impress and thrill many playgoers, but their performance style was widely regarded as old-fashioned, melodramatic (increasingly used as a pejorative term), or "hammy." The American tours of Stanislavski and the Moscow Art Theatre (MAT) between 1923 and 1925 reinforced the trend towards realistic acting and promoting a systematic approach to learning its techniques. Realistic acting, however, was the norm on the American stage even before the MAT's first visit.

In the Twenties, O'Neill and his producers and directors could draw on an unusually large pool of experienced, talented performers who had successfully melded magnetic stage personalities with a realistic stage technique. Richard Bennett, for example, who created the role of Robert Mayo in *Beyond the Horizon*, had been a leading man for a decade, playing in dozens of contemporary social comedies and dramas. Handsome and dynamic, he had a reputation as a matinee idol, but he was a serious actor, and, in fact, was instrumental in bringing *Beyond the Horizon* to the stage. He would subsequently create such memorable characters as Tony in Sidney Howard's *They Knew What They Wanted* (1924) and Judge Gaunt in Maxwell Anderson's *Winterset* (1935). In the 1940s, he appeared in a number of films, most notably Orson Welles's *The Magnificent Ambersons* (1942). Charles Gilpin, the original Emperor Jones, had moved from black minstrelsy and vaudeville to a range of roles in leading black stock companies and finally to Broadway where he was one of the first black legitimate actors to be integrated into a "white" production. Louis Wolheim was a mechanical engineer and adventurer who drifted into acting after World War I. His riveting performance as Yank in *The Hairy Ape* was his first leading role and it brought him stardom. As Captain Flagg in Maxwell Anderson's and Laurence Stallings's anti-war drama *What Price Glory?* (1924), Wolheim solidified his reputation as a compelling character actor, particularly in rugged, tough-guy roles. Pauline Lord, who had been on stage since the age of thirteen, created the role of Anna Christie and then later was Nina for the tour of *Strange Interlude*. She also played Amy opposite Bennett in *They Knew What They Wanted*. Often compared to Duse for her subtle variety and quiet power, Lord was a leading performer for over thirty years. Mary Morris, Abbie in *Desire Under the Elms*, made her debut in 1916 with the Washington Square Players. She subsequently toured with the noted British actor George Arliss, then played leads in productions of Ibsen, Shaw, and Barrie, and in Greek tragedies mounted in Berkeley's famous amphitheatre, before joining the Provincetown Players. Later she was a member of both Eva LeGallienne's Civic Repertory Theatre and the Group Theatre and then a distinguished acting teacher at Carnegie Mellon University. Walter Huston was on stage for twenty years before the role of Ephraim Cabot in *Desire Under the Elms* made him a star. For another twenty years, he was frequently acclaimed for his realistic, magnetic performances on stage and screen. Other notable performers who brought O'Neill's characters vividly to life on stage include Alfred Lunt and Morris Carnovsky, Marco Polo and Ghazan, the Khan of Persia, respectively, in *Marco Millions*; Lynn Fontanne, who created Nina; Judith Anderson, who succeeded Fontanne as Nina and later played Lavinia; and Paul Robeson (1898–1976), who created Jim Harris in *All God's Chillun Got Wings* and the title role in revivals of *The Emperor Jones*. They and numerous lesser known but no less talented actors contributed significantly to the popular success of O'Neill's plays.

New critical voices

At the turn of the century, theatrical criticism in New York was dominated by an older generation of critics who generally represented a traditional and conservative point-of-view. They were not always particularly sympathetic to modern drama. Chief among these critics were William Winter, critic of the *New York Tribune* from 1865 to 1909, English-born John Ranken Towse, who came to America in 1869 and served as critic of the *New York Evening Post* from 1874 to 1927, and Edward Dithmar, critic of the *New York Times* from 1884 to 1901. James G. Huneker was an older, but generally more liberal and enlightened critic, who wrote for several different papers in the late 1890s and early 1900s, including the *New York Sun* from 1905 to 1917. Huneker opposed conservative critics like Winter and promoted the cause of the new European drama. His *Iconoclasts: A Book of Dramatists* (1905) was a seminal study of Ibsen, Strindberg, Shaw and other major European dramatists. Huneker's critical style and views encouraged a new generation of critics emerging in the early 1900s.

George Jean Nathan was among the leaders of this new generation. In 1909, he became the drama critic of *Smart Set*, a rising, intellectually oriented periodical, and quickly found his *métier* ridiculing outmoded theatrical traditions and conventions. He would become one of O'Neill's staunchest critical supporters. In 1906, Adolph Klauber (1879–1933) became the critic of the *New York Times*, replacing the aging Dithmar. Before joining the *Times*, Klauber had worked as a theatrical producer. In the late Teens and Twenties, he resumed this occupation, co-producing several notable hits featuring his actress-wife Jane Cowl. Klauber would also co-produce O'Neill's *The Emperor Jones* and *Diff'rent*. Alexander Woollcott replaced Klauber at the *Times*. A founder of the famous "Algonquin Round Table," Woollcott was a witty and enthusiastic champion of modernism. In the 1920s, Woollcott left the *Times*, but he continued to write theatrical criticism for several leading New York dailies, including the *Sun*, the *Herald*, and the *World*. Burns Mantle became critic for the *New York Evening Mail* in 1911, moving to the *Daily News* in 1922. An erstwhile advocate of new American drama, Mantle initiated the annual *Best Plays of the Year* series in 1919. At the end of each season, he selected ten plays which he considered the "best," then he published what he called "descriptive synopses" of them. His anthologies also included a comprehensive record of every play produced during the New York season. Mantle compiled and edited this respected series until 1947. (In the 1930s, he published two supplementary volumes, covering 1899–1909 and 1909–19. Under various editors, the *Best Plays* series has continued to be published until the present day.) Stark Young, who reviewed for the influential journal *New Republic* from 1922 to 1947, and was also a contributing editor for *Theatre Arts*, was one of the more intellectual critics of the era. A proponent of the New Stagecraft and a friend of both O'Neill and Robert Edmond Jones, Young directed *Welded* in 1924, although the production was not a success. In 1926, Brooks Atkinson (1894–1984) became the chief critic of the powerful *New York Times*. He held the post until 1960 and gained a reputation as one of the theatre's most literate and humane critics. Joseph Wood Krutch, critic for *The Nation* from 1924 to 1952, was, like Young and Atkinson, also respected for his thoughtfulness and erudition.

By the early 1920s, theatrical criticism in New York's dozen or so dailies, as well as in a half dozen important weekly and monthly magazines, was in the hands of critics who were contemporaries of O'Neill and were, like him, generally receptive to theatrical experimentation and modernist thought. This is not to say that every critic was impressed with O'Neill. Percy Hammond, critic of the *Tribune* from 1921 to 1936, was not generally an O'Neill fan. Even O'Neill's supporters among the critics found some of his plays lacking in one respect or another. O'Neill himself was often irritated with the critical response to his plays and their productions. Yet he also regularly consulted Nathan, Atkinson, and Krutch about drafts of his plays and plans for plays. One must at least consider that New York's new wave of critics fostered a critical milieu where O'Neill's plays would be seriously reviewed, analyzed, and discussed; and in so doing, they promoted playgoer receptivity to O'Neill's inventive, different dramaturgy.

By 1920 then, the New York stage was set, even primed, for O'Neill's theatrical ascent. Institutional art theatres and commercially successful producers were available to mount his plays; imaginative scenic designers could provide them with a new look; actors armed with solid stage technique could compellingly and plausibly embody their psychologically conflicted characters; skillful directors could shape them into exciting stage productions; and a new breed of critics could explain and champion the work. Lastly, there was a playgoing population whose sensibilities had been nurtured by an earlier generation of American and foreign playwrights and by organizations and institutions like the Drama League, the Theatre Guild, and the Little Theatres, and who were, thus, prepared for O'Neill's plays. In this context, his success is easily understood.

Between 1920 and 1931, O'Neill had sixteen new plays produced in New York. In addition, his *The Ancient Mariner*, adapted from Coleridge's poem, was also produced; *Beyond the Horizon* was revived in 1926; his early sea plays were collectively revived as *The S.S. Glencairn* in 1924 and again in 1929; *Before Breakfast* was also revived in 1929; and *The Emperor Jones* was reprised in 1924, in 1925, and finally in 1926 on a double bill with *The Dreamy Kid*. Eleven of these productions were commercial successes, most running for more than one hundred performances. Including its various revivals, *The Emperor Jones* had a total of 387 performances; *Desire Under the Elms* had 208 performances; *The Great God Brown* had 271 performances; and *Strange Interlude* had 426 performances. Seven plays were selected by Burns Mantle as a Best Play of their respective seasons: *Beyond the Horizon* (1919–20), *The Emperor Jones* (1920–21), *Anna Christie* (1921–22), *Desire Under the Elms* (1924–25), *The Great God Brown* (1925–26), *Strange Interlude* (1927–28), and *Mourning Becomes Electra* (1931–32). O'Neill would also win Pulitzer Prizes for *Beyond the Horizon*, *Anna Christie*, and *Strange Interlude*. It was a singular record unmatched by any other modernist American dramatist of the Twenties.

Playwrights often thought to be as talented as O'Neill were, unlike him, unable to sustain a body of work that was both artistically and commercially successful. Sidney Howard, for example, succeeded only with *They Knew What They Wanted* (1924; 192 performances) and *The Silver Cord* (1926; 130 performances); Elmer Rice's daring, expressionistic *The Adding Machine* (1923) had only seventy-two performances, although the naturalistic *Street Scene* (1929) ran for 601 performances; Robert Sherwood (1896–1955) succeeded with *The Road to Rome* (1927; 392 performances); S. N. Behrman with *The Second Man* (1926; 178 performances). Philip Barry had several hits, including *Paris Bound* (1927; 234 performances) and *Holiday* (1928; 230 performances). George Kelly had two major hits, including *The Show-Off* (1923; 571 performances). Rachel Crothers scored with *Nice People* (1920; 247 performances.) Most of these plays, however, were essentially realistic, contemporary social comedies, a genre invariably more popular with audiences than serious, experimentally structured dramas. Maxwell Anderson, whose reputation as a dramatist of distinction ranks second only to O'Neill, co-authored with Laurence Stallings the popular anti-war play *What Price Glory?* (1924; 299 performances), which also has decided comedic overtones. Although he continued to produce – usually with a co-author – through the Twenties, Anderson did not come into his own until the Thirties.

O'Neill's output slowed significantly in the 1930s. The charming comedy *Ah, Wilderness!* was produced by the Theatre Guild in 1932. Featuring the popular Broadway producer, playwright, and musical star George M. Cohan, *Ah, Wilderness!* ran for 289 performances. The Guild's production of *Days Without End* in 1934, however, was a critical and commercial failure, running for a mere fifty-seven performances. O'Neill, professionally disappointed and buffeted by illness and family crises, retreated from the hurly-burly of Broadway. In 1937, the Federal Theatre Project mounted revivals of *Diff'rent*, which ran, however, for only two performances, and the *S.S. Glencairn*, which, with the novelty of an entirely African–American cast, ran for a respectable sixty-eight performances. Not until the 1946 production of *The Iceman Cometh* would a new O'Neill play be mounted in New York. In the interim, Broadway underwent a radical sea-change. Feeling the economic pinch of the great Depression, weakened by Hollywood's increasing inroads on its talent and audiences and by its own organizational tensions, Broadway's stock plummeted. The number of productions fell to about one hundred in the 1939–40 season, one-third of what it had been a decade earlier. Theatres stood empty or were converted into movie palaces. A few leading producers and theatrical organizations survived. The Theatre Guild, for example, despite financial set-backs and internal fissures, remained afloat, but mainly by presenting popular social comedies and musicals, often featuring well-known stars like Alfred Lunt and Lynn Fontanne. The social and political turmoil of the times would give rise to new theatrical organizations and new dramatic voices and subject matter. With the onset of World War II, theatrical production rebounded slightly, but the American theatre would never recapture its glory days of the Teens and Twenties. Artistically, O'Neill was detached from these currents and largely forgotten by the theatrical world. Only after his death would there once again develop an American theatre both able and eager to embrace his plays.

WORKS CITED AND CONSULTED

Bordman, Gerald, *American Theatre: A Chronicle of Comedy and Drama, 1869–1914* (New York: Oxford University Press, 1994).
    American Theatre: A Chronicle of Comedy and Drama, 1914–1930 (New York: Oxford University Press, 1995).
    American Musical Theatre: A Chronicle (second edition, New York: Oxford University Press, 1992).

Gelb, Arthur and Barbara, *O'Neill* (Second, enlarged edition, New York: Harper and Row, 1973).

Leiter, Samuel L., *The Encyclopedia of the New York Stage, 1920–1930* (New York: Greenwood Press, 1985).

The Encyclopedia of the New York Stage, 1930–1940 (New York: Greenwood Press, 1989).

Londré, Felicia and Daniel J. Watermeier, *The History of North American Theater: The United States, Canada, and Mexico, From Pre-Columbian Times to the Present* (New York: Continuum Publishing Group, forthcoming).

Mantle, Burns and Garrison, P. Sherwood, *The Best Plays of 1909–1919* (New York: Dodd, Mead and Company, 1934).

The Best Plays of 1919–1920 (Boston: Small, Maynard and Company, 1920).

O'Neill, Eugene, *Complete Plays, 1932–1943*. Edited by Travis Bogard (The Library of America, 1988).

Poggi, Jack, *Theatre in America: The Impact of Economic Forces, 1870–1967* (Ithaca, NY: Cornell University Press, 1968).

Robinson, Alice M., Vera Mowry Roberts, and Milly S. Barranger, *Notable Women in the American Theatre: A Biographical Dictionary* (New York: Greenwood Press, 1989).

Sheaffer, Louis, *O'Neill: Son and Playwright* (Boston: Little, Brown and Company, 1968).

O'Neill: Son and Artist (Boston: Little, Brown and Company, 1973).

Watermeier, Daniel J., "*The Iceman Cometh* Twice: A Comparison of the 1946 and 1956 New York Productions" in *Eugene O'Neill in China: An International Centenary Celebration*. Haiping Liu and Lowell Swortzell, eds. (New York: Greenwood Press, 1992, 211–22).

Wilmeth, Don B. and Tice L. Miller, eds. *Cambridge Guide to American Theatre* (New York: Cambridge University Press, 1993).

Winter, William, *Other Days: Being Chronicles and Memories of the Stage* (New York: Moffat, Yard and Company, 1908).

4

MARGARET LOFTUS RANALD

From trial to triumph (1913–1924): the early plays

In 1912–13, while a tuberculosis patient in the Gaylord Sanitarium, Eugene O'Neill decided to become a dramatist. As a result American drama during the first half of the twentieth century was totally changed, and a new high seriousness came into the theatrical market place. Dissatisfied with the old histrionic romantic theatre of his father (James O'Neill, the perennial Count of Monte Cristo), Eugene O'Neill made profitable use of his three-month hospital stay by reading philosophy, drama, and absorbing the influence of new theatrical movements in Ireland, France, Sweden, and Germany, led by J. M. Synge, Eugène Brieux, August Strindberg and Gerhart Hauptmann.

On his release from Gaylord he started to write, using his own life experiences as creative matrix. Thus he set the autobiographical pattern that was to culminate in the great family plays of his last years: *Long Day's Journey Into Night* and *A Moon for the Misbegotten*, with a return to the dissipation of his youth in *The Iceman Cometh*.

His devotion to his own personal "drama of souls" never ceased, and hence writing exacted a tremendous physical and psychological toll. He was also self-taught in dramatic technique, educating himself by reading and closely observing stage performances. From the theatrical touring world of his childhood he had repeatedly observed *The Count of Monte Cristo*, and James O'Neill's sometimes distinguished attempts at classics like *Hamlet*. Also, after his suicide attempt (1910),[1] Eugene toured with the entire family in *The White Sister*, in the "made" position of assistant manager. Consequently, he became aware of dramatic structure, the possibilities of stage effects and the intellectual limitations of the theatrical audiences of his day.

Like his father, O'Neill was an autodidact. His Princeton year (1906–07) was essentially one of self-directed study, because he despised his course assignments, being suspended for "poor scholarship." He learned from wide, undisciplined reading, rather than academic instruction, claiming

51

that the only result of his year in George Pierce Baker's English 47 Workshop (1914–15) at Harvard was his practice of first writing a scenario and then the dialogue, which he did throughout his productive life.[2]

One cannot explain the workings of genius, and Eugene O'Neill must be so considered. He saw the theatre as an enlightening, quasi-religious experience, a place where serious matters were to be dramatized, and audiences would empathize with the intensely human problems put before them. His was also a nationalistic view. He took the United States as his major theme documenting its collision of old with new in its attempt to make a dynamic world out of the curse of the old. As a result, he created a new theatre with a sense of a shared past and present, even projecting the future in *Strange Interlude*. More importantly, he created a family mythology which ascends to universality, dramatizing experiences which tease the alert beholder into empathy.

His early experimental plays (1913–24) demonstrate the structural influence of his father's theatre of melodrama, in his instinctive ability to build a scene or action toward a sometimes explosive conclusion, skillfully varying the pace of a play. Just as his audience's emotion or body flags, he revivifies attention by means of a gunshot, a sudden revelation, or a death. Like Chekhov and Ibsen he also knew that a weapon or important object once displayed on stage must eventually be used, something surely learned from *Monte Cristo*.

The influence of the vaudeville skit is also obvious in his very first play, *A Wife for a Life* (1913) written during his post-sanitarium residence in New London. In this piece, based on O'Neill's miserable mining experiences in Honduras, The Older Man (unnamed) renounces his claim on Yvette, the wife he has abused and abandoned (yet still loves) in favor of Jack, his young mining-assistant and friend in a final, banal vaudeville-style line: "Greater love hath no man but this, that he giveth his wife for his friend." This playlet also marks the beginning of O'Neill's use of monologue, a device he later used with singular skill.

It also initiates another theme: Woman as the intruder who destroys masculine ambition, or disturbs an enclosed, companionable male universe.[3] This theme recurs throughout his career, finding its final statement in two of his last plays, *The Iceman Cometh* and *Hughie*.

"Thirst" and Other One-Act Plays (1914), the first published collection of O'Neill's plays, is important as indicating his future development. Published by Gorham Press, Boston, and underwritten by a $450 subvention from his father, O'Neill was to receive 25 percent of the profits, which did not materialize.[4] These five plays are important both for what they are and what they prefigure. *Thirst* (1913), portrays a raft as a microcosm,

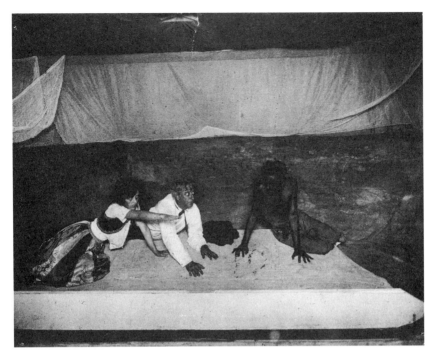

1   Louise Bryant, George Cram Cook, and O'Neill in the 1916 Provincetown Players
    production of *Thirst* at the Wharf Theatre in Provincetown

with its three unnamed shipwreck survivors of Dancer, Gentleman, and
West Indian Mulatto Sailor. While introducing the theme of woman as
whore, along with interracial and class conflict, it also portrays the
behavior of individuals pushed to their emotional and physical limits, even
to proposed cannibalism, after the Dancer dances herself to death. The
stage directions demonstrate O'Neill's visual and aural sense as he instructs
both stage designer and actors to evoke suitable audience reactions.

In *Fog* (1914) a lifeboat serves as a microcosm, this time with a Poet, a
Man of Business, a Polish Peasant Woman and her dead child. Now
O'Neill makes a notable advance in the use of sound and scenic effects:
steamer whistles, dripping water, and the fog, still endemic to New
London, which will recur as late as *Long Day's Journey*. Fog is used to
evoke mood, and also a sense of supernatural mystery, when a passing
steamer turns aside from its course after the sailors hear the cry of the dead
child over the noise of their engines. This is O'Neill's first foray into the
eerie world of supernatural fantasy.

Also in this collection are three plays dealing with the relationship of
man and woman, which will later become a major topic of the O'Neill

canon. In *The Web* (1913), a one-act melodrama, he presents a sympathetic portrait of a tubercular prostitute exploited by her pimp. A neighbor, who attempts to save her, is shot by the pimp, and the prostitute is accused of murder. In *Recklessness* (1913), reminiscent of Strindberg's *Miss Julie*, O'Neill moves into another important theme – marriage. Here Baldwin, a wealthy man whose wife, Mildred, has been forced by her family into a loveless, money-based marriage, causes the death of the chauffeur with whom she has found consolation. This clumsy piece, ending with the sound of an automobile crash, is highly contrived, while the chauffeur, Fred Burgess, is too ineffectual to be a believable suitor.

With *Warnings* (1914), O'Neill embarks on his first play in which a woman is responsible for the death of her husband. This simplistic piece, loosely modeled after Joseph Conrad's *The End of the Tether*, portrays a radio operator who, despite his growing deafness, is forced back to sea because of financial worries, a nagging wife, and too many children. When he realizes that his deafness has caused the loss of his ship he shoots himself in despair.

With the exception of *A Wife for a Life* (1912), all O'Neill's plays up to and including the *"Thirst"* volume conclude with sometimes savage and shocking violence. In the title play the two survivors drown after a struggle. *Recklessness* ends with a constructive murder by automobile, *Warnings* with suicide, *The Web* with murder and wrongful accusation. *Fog*, though ending with rescue, includes proposed suicide and near cannibalism.

Perhaps as the result of his almost total early immersion in melodrama, suicide and death offer a frequent solution for O'Neill at this time. In *Abortion* (1914), a play outside the *"Thirst"* collection, the college–athlete hero shoots himself after being threatened by the brother of his girl friend, dead after a botched abortion financed by his own father. The final scene, with its noisy victory parade outside the room of the suicide victim, remains a clever piece of ironic theatre, arousing sympathy for the young man's blighted promise, rather than for the "townie" girl.

Also ending with a death, *Bound East for Cardiff* (1914), originally called "Children of the Sea," is an astonishing dramatic advance from the melodramatic clumsiness of *Abortion*. The first written of the *S.S. Glencairn* series, it repeats the supernatural theme of *Fog*, concentrating on the central figure of the dying sailor, with his dream deferred, a theme to which O'Neill will often return. "Yank" greets death as "a pretty lady in Black," and with his death the fog lifts. Notable here are O'Neill's ability to create a sustained mood and a sense of community in this forecastle populated by an international (though all-white) crew. Repetitive sound in the snoring of the sleeping men and the blast of the steamship's whistle maintain atmosphere.[5]

This play also has continuing fame as the first O'Neill work to be publicly staged, 28 July 1916, in Provincetown, Massachusetts. It figures prominently in the history of the Provincetown Players, who nurtured the author's talents until his successes on Broadway eventually undermined the "faith" with which they began. Susan Glaspell, wife of George Cram Cook, founder of the group, tells of hearing from Terry Carlin, a well-known Provincetown and Greenwich Village anarchist, that O'Neill had "a trunk full of plays," and when in mid-July 1916 he read *Bound East for Cardiff* to the assembled members, "Then we knew what we were for."[6] Despite its frequent repetition this account should be reconsidered, and Gary Jay Williams has persuasively argued that O'Neill had unsuccessfully offered *The Movie Man*, along with the *Thirst* volume, a month before the celebrated reading took place.[7] He agrees with Sheaffer that O'Neill had probably submitted *Cardiff* to George Pierce Baker's English 47 course at Harvard, revising it there.[8] The play was again presented in New York in November 1916 as part of the successful opening bill at the Playwrights' Theatre, attended by both O'Neill's parents.

The three other plays of this group were written in 1917–18. *In the Zone* is a conventional submarine-warfare potboiler, spiced with some violence, with Smitty as the alcoholic lover, a failure driven to sea by a woman's rejection, while *The Long Voyage Home* is a predictable Shanghai-ing drama, including the reappearance of the dream-forever-deferred theme in Olson's wish to retire to a farm.

The greatest advance, however, comes with *Moon of the Caribbees* (1918) where O'Neill, in addition to developing mood, also experiments with the impact of black culture upon whites, and this, his first truly multicultural play, foreshadows also his interest in "total theatre." Character, theme, and mood become interdependent, with the old donkey-man as wise observer, a *persona* who reappears in *The Iceman Cometh* as Larry Slade, "the old foolosopher." The clash of cultures leads to a bacchanal and consequent violence, reinforced by music and dance as the bumboat women bring liquor to the ship. Then the mood changes, and the play comes full circle to the moonlit mystery of the opening, the final stage direction identifying the "brooding music ... like the mood of the moon-light made audible." Here is a prophecy of future experimentation, and when the entire "*Glencairn*" series opens with *Moon of the Caribbees*, as is customary, that atmosphere gives spiritual form to the entire group. At the same time, it also prefigures O'Neill's later practice of frequently putting important details into stage directions to bring his readers also into emotional communion with text and staging – both aural and visual. John Ford's film of this series, entitled *The Long Voyage Home* (the only film of his plays O'Neill liked) offers a conflation of the individual plays and emphasizes the human conflicts.

O'Neill's evocation of mood to draw the audience into the action goes even further in *Where the Cross Is Made* (1918), where in a single act he attempts to seduce his audience into a collective hallucination as the ghosts of dead sailors return to the Captain's home with their chest of bogus treasure. Its reworking into the four-act drama *Gold* (1920) is less successful. Here the action is opened up to cover a number of years, from the discovery of the "treasure" through the captain's destruction of his familial relationships. The focus of this version is thus splintered and over-explication detracts from the mysterious supernaturalism when the drowned men reappear before the lunatic father and son.

Directly after *Gold*, O'Neill revised his previously unsuccessful sea play *Chris Christophersen* (1919), which offers insights into his revisionary techniques. Originally the emphasis is almost entirely on Chris the coal bargeman, while his daughter, Anna, is an unbelievable construct. Brought up by her mother's English family in Leeds, she descends upon Chris as a typist with a distinctly refined accent and a desire to gain a college degree. Nevertheless, there is a germ of what Anna will become as a character in the two later revisions, "*The Ole Davil*" and finally "*Anna Christie*." In *Chris* she is something of a salvific angel, the cause that Paul Andersen, second mate of the steamer that rescues them from Chris's drifting coal barge, discovers ambition (in order to become worthy of Anna), while Chris accepts the position of boatswain on the same vessel. His two tags of "the ole davil" (the sea) and the song "My Yosephine" appear in all three versions.

The intermediate draft, '*The Ole Davil*" (1920) is very close to the final version, "*Anna Christie*" (1921), which won O'Neill his second Pulitzer Prize. Anna is now from a Minnesota farm driven by familial sexual abuse to a life of prostitution, while Mat Burke, a sentimental and sexually radiant Irishman, sweeps her off her feet. He is a virile shipwrecked sailor, a savior who has risen from the sea to demonstrate the truth of love. But what really changes Anna is her discovery that the sea is in her spirit and in her veins, while the fog which leaves her in suspension from reality purifies her. Over-emphasis on the baleful influence of "the Ole Davil sea" comes entirely from Chris, but the happiness of the young couple indicates his error, and the second version ends in laughter.

It remains doubtful which conclusion was used at the first performance of "*Anna Christie*." Reviewers generally thought it comic,[9] the published version looks like an ambivalent compromise and O'Neill steadfastly insisted that the play was incipiently tragic. There is a minor comedic flurry over the religious difference between Mat and Anna, then all three drink to their future, with Mat and Chris as shipmates, leaving Anna waiting at home for her men. Her defiant toast is "Here's to the sea, no matter what." But Chris with his complaints about losing one's way in the fog has the last word: "Only that ole davil sea – she knows."

O'Neill also disclaimed the drama, omitting it from his self-chosen selection *Nine Plays* (1932). Certainly it is creakily designed with somewhat predictable, even sentimental, stock characters. And if one looks closely at Mat's dialogue, one can see little beyond the stage Irishman. However, in performance, when the lines are rephrased by a strong Irish actor, sexual chemistry can make powerful drama.

Another dominant theme in O'Neill's work at this time is the masculine idealist, or artist destroyed by the predatory philistinism of woman or wife. *Bread and Butter* (1914) is the first of these, and its action culminates in the offstage suicide of the husband forced by his wife into the family hardware business, rather than developing his talent as a painter.

Before Breakfast (1916) is a bitter little monologue in which the wife, having tricked her honorable husband (the son of a millionaire) into marriage with an alleged pregnancy, finally drives him to offstage suicide, by refusing to divorce him so that he can marry the woman he loves.

In *Ile* (1917), Captain Keeney's gently stubborn, delicate wife, who has insisted on going to sea with him, has brought bad luck to his whaling expedition. When the vessel finally sights a school of whales, he breaks free, asserts his masculinity, follows his calling and will make the voyage a success. She, the intruder into his masculine world, pays with her sanity – frantically playing hymns on her harmonium as the curtain falls.

However, the most important treatment of this theme of woman as hindrance to man's self-expression, whether artistic or otherwise, came with O'Neill's first Broadway success and the first of his four Pulitzer Prize dramas. In *Beyond the Horizon* (written 1918, produced 1920) Ruth Mayo is a Strindbergian character who ruins the lives of two brothers as well as her own by her selfish romanticism. She wants to possess both Robert and Andrew Mayo, the romantic and the stolid farmer. Finally she is left alone, in total inanition, incapable of saving herself. With this play O'Neill first tasted prestige and satisfaction, even earning the reluctant approval of his father, who was to die within a few months. He, of all people, understood the extraordinary feat his son had achieved – though he still clung to his experientially validated and market-driven opinion that people came to the theatre to be entertained. "What are you trying to do – send them home to commit suicide?" he asked.[10]

For O'Neill, the life of the farmer was confining, while freedom would be found elsewhere. When at the conclusion the sun rises over the delimiting hills, and Robert Mayo follows into eternity that road not taken, one recalls the conclusion of Ibsen's *Ghosts* and looks ahead to the end of *Desire Under the Elms*. Those who live on in the light of full day have been beaten down, or have not followed their dreams.

With this play O'Neill singlehandedly started an intellectual and emotional revolution in Broadway theatre, to which he continued to contribute throughout his writing career. Yet there is still something simplistic in this undeniably moving play. Quite legitimately one can argue that Robert Mayo would either have been destroyed by the physical hardships of the sea, or have developed the same emotional carapace as the less sensitive Andrew, but the sincerity of O'Neill's realism and the colloquialism of his dialogue give strength to this groundbreaking play. The action also reaches mythic proportions and transcends specific locality.

But what did O'Neill expect from marriage both in life and in drama? *Servitude* (1914), often considered a satire, may well provide an answer. "Love means servitude; and my love is my happiness" (Act 2), says Alice Roylston, who is editor, housekeeper, mother, and lover to her writer–husband. When she finds Ethel Frazer in her house she immediately offers to step aside so that her husband's happiness will be completed, but fortunately the "other woman," amazed both by her self-abnegation and Roylston's selfishness, returns to her own husband.

Further, when one looks at *Now I Ask You* (1916), *The Straw* (1919), and *The First Man* (1921), the last two written during his second marriage, to Agnes Boulton, the "requirement" of servitude is again important. In all of these plays the necessity of the husband's self-fulfillment is paramount and the woman is expected to sacrifice herself for the career of her beloved. Even the appreciative dedication written by O'Neill in the printed copy of *Mourning Becomes Electra* (1933) which he presented to Carlotta Monterey O'Neill, his third wife, can be read as a statement of his continuing expectations: "... mother, and wife and mistress and friend, ... and collaborator, I love you."[11]

Now I Ask You (1916) is an unsuccessful attempt at comedy, a triple satire of Ibsen's *Hedda Gabler*, melodrama, and feminine self-expression, with roots in O'Neill's Greenwich Village period. The circular three-act structure, with Prologue and Epilogue, inverts Ibsen by opening with a young woman's onstage suicide by pistol shot to the temple. But then O'Neill dramatizes the foolish events which have led to this action. This still unperformed play offers a happy ending when the Epilogue reveals that the initial "gunshot" was the sound of a blownout tire.

With *The Straw* (1919), an autobiographical drama set in a tuberculosis sanatorium, O'Neill again celebrates feminine sacrifice. Stephen Murray, the author *manqué*, finds his courage and inspiration in Eileen Carmody, a young woman fellow patient who has spent her life serving her ungrateful family. She risks her health to bid him farewell and finally accepts the fact that he cannot love her. But then, as she lies dying, Stephen, now a successful, yet dissipated author, marries her in an ambiguous conclusion, admitting that without her self-sacrifice he would have been a failure. Through her he finds a kind of salvation – a theme that appears much later in *Days Without End* (1933), which celebrates his third wife, Carlotta Monterey. There, Elsa Loving, who survives near fatal pneumonia, is instrumental in the religious conversion of her husband, and lives to serve again.

Similarly, *The First Man* (1921) insists upon the necessity of a wife's duty as helpmeet, supporter of her husband's career, even at the expense of her biological imperative. A child will discommode Curtis Jayson's archeological expedition to China, by depriving him of his wife's assistance. He considers himself betrayed, but not as much as does his wife in the hostile and suspicious middle-class environment of his family. She dies in graphic childbirth agony and he sets out on his scientific expedition, planning that his work will be continued by his son. He has learned very little from the devotion of his wife, Martha.

Another theme here, recalling the earlier *Bread and Butter*, is the relentless hostility of middle-class values to anything creative, with the added suspicion of a woman who is more than a housewife. Jayson's family even doubts the paternity of the child. Money is usually the god of the families to which O'Neill's major characters of this period belong, or into which they marry. Artistic or intellectual creativity is despised as impractical. Overall, O'Neill reacted against this convention-ridden class – except in *Ah, Wilderness!* (1933), which depicts a happy, well-adjusted, bourgeois family with empathy, tolerance, and understanding.

Another, and earlier, destructive woman is the domineering character of *Diff'rent* (1920), where Emma Crosby, a sexually repressed and hyperidealistic woman, given to the reading of romantic novels, falls so much under their influence that she cannot forgive her fiancé's single South Seas sexual peccadillo. The distraught whaling captain, Caleb Williams, waits thirty years to gain her forgiveness only to discover that she believes herself in love with his ne'er-do-well nephew. In despair he hangs himself in the offstage barn, and she follows him there as the curtain falls.

The psychology of both characters is rather clumsy, yet the play achieved considerable Broadway success at its opening. As is frequent in O'Neill's developing career, the play looks backward and forward. The hanging in the barn recalls the earlier one-acter, *The Rope* (1918), and the theme of sexual freedom in "The Blessed Isles," the typical subject of sailor yarns (found also in *Gold* and *Moon of the Caribees*), is repeated as a tale told of Lavinia in the final play of the trilogy *Mourning Becomes Electra* (1929–31). Here, in Emma's expectations of chaste masculine behavior there may be an autobiographical reference to Ella Quinlan O'Neill's early disillusionment when her husband was the successful defendant in a marriage and paternity suit.[12]

Politics and political awareness also intrude upon O'Neill's consciousness in his early plays, as his treatment of the Pancho Villa expedition in *The Movie Man* (1914) indicates. However, this pedestrian, melodramatic piece is a major regression after "Children of the Sea" (in its later version *Bound East for Cardiff*). The central idea that the battles of the Mexican uprising be orchestrated at the behest of a film company is politically explosive and based on the frequent and thorough coverage appearing in North American papers. However, the treatment lacks verisimilitude while both dialogue and characterization are stereotypical and unconvincing. O'Neill had probably read the Mexican news dispatches of John Reed, though he may not have yet met him.[13] Certainly the play proves that O'Neill was not very successful when he was writing propagandistically. He soared highest when working out of, and transforming, his own personal experience.

His Harvard war play, *The Sniper* (1915, but begun earlier), is insightful in its pacifist questioning of the values epitomized by World War I. On a human level it indicates O'Neill's understanding of war's cost, as the French peasant tries to shoot Germans in revenge for their destruction of his family and farm. Predictably, he dies before an ad hoc firing squad, with a sympathetic priest having the last word, "Alas, the laws of men!" This play was submitted to George Pierce Baker's English 47 workshop at Harvard where it did not receive the first prize, much to O'Neill's chagrin. As he wrote to his then girl friend, Beatrice Ashe (Maher), Baker indicated that the reason was the unpopularity of the war topic, though he recognized the drama's emotional power.[14]

Again O'Neill returned to war with *In the Zone* (1917) and the unperformed one-acter *Shell Shock* (1918). Showing little psychological insight, the later play skims across the surface of the action, with affinities to a simplistic vaudeville skit. The central character's addiction to cigarettes, and the final revelation that his friend still lives are awkwardly contrived. In view of what O'Neill had already written in *Moon of the Caribbees* and *Beyond the Horizon*, *Shell Shock* disappoints.

Another forgettable unperformed play, *The Personal Equation* (1915) has a political topic drawn from O'Neill's Greenwich Village period. Even here, he is autobiographical. Notable is the absent mother (dead for a number of years, as in effect his drug addicted mother had been to him) and an obsessive father, a second engineer, more attached to his ship and its engines than anything else. When his anarchist son, Tom, is deputed to destroy these engines to further a labor dispute, the father shoots him, leaving him a vegetable. Then he and Olga, the young man's fiancée, dedicate themselves to Tom's care, renouncing politics for familial duty. Once again, the sea scenes have validity while the political ones smack of mere propaganda, and the conclusion is contrived.

In 1919 O'Neill moves into the politics of race relations with his one-act play *The Dreamy Kid* (1918) in which Gary Jay Williams detects an autobiographical resonance with Jamie as the prodigal son and O'Neill's "Darker Brother."[15] This interpretation gains probability when one recalls that James O'Neill, Sr. had recently played the role of Jesse, the father of that biblical wastrel, in *The Wanderer*. Dreamy, a black gangster, though warned by Irene, a black prostitute, that the white police are coming, stands his final watch over his grandmother's deathbed. For once there is no concluding shot as he crouches down, revolver cocked, while the police wait outside, and Mammy prays.

Though this small suspense drama engages in stereotypes, particularly in the figure of Dreamy and the matriarchal Mammy, it treats black people sympathetically as human beings, victims of society, with emotions and family ties. O'Neill was playing with fire here, and perhaps that is why he did not make the character of Irene a white prostitute, as he had once considered.[16] But even more important he broke new ground by seeing that the Provincetown Players engaged black actors for the roles, rather than having whites perform in blackface.

His much more significant African–American play, *The Emperor Jones*, came the following year (1921). This time the cast was integrated, with the white colonialist, Smithers, a distinctly unlikable character and Brutus Jones the first modern black hero to be played on Broadway by an African–American actor, Charles Gilpin. Essentially an expressionistic psychodrama, it goes beyond language into total theatrical experience. Not only does it give a reverse historical account of African–American history, but also draws the audience into sensory and emotional participation, aurally by the continually responsive sound of the tom-tom, and visually by the repeated action of disrobing, as Jones confronts the Little Formless Fears and his later adversaries.

Emperor Brutus Jones, the ex-Pullman porter, either throws off, or loses the trappings of white civilization as he moves through eight scenes back to his African origins, making a personal journey of internal discovery, reliving in reverse his own life and the Black Experience. He kills Jeff a former friend, then sequentially a prison guard, an auctioneer and a planter bidding at a slave auction, and re-imagines the slave ship. Finally, wearing only a breech-cloth, he confronts the crocodile god and his witch doctor, calling on Jesus in his terror. Gradually mime takes the place of words, while lighting, projections, the evocative setting, and the ever-quickening beat of the drums combine to strip away the appurtenances of so-called civilization and evoke collective hallucination in the audience. Everything leads inexorably to the inevitable final pistol shot when Brutus Jones lies dead from a silver bullet cast by the hands of his own people. But since Jones has refused the ultimate return to his past by invoking Christianity before putting the witch doctor and crocodile god to flight with his own silver bullet, he has signed his death warrant. Perhaps O'Neill drew back at this last step, or perhaps he was condescending towards black culture by "redeeming" Jones through a return to the white man's religion.

Racism was covertly charged against this play by Charles Gilpin in his frequent changes in the text to avoid racist language. Consequently, O'Neill was happy to replace him in the London production with Paul Robeson, a graduate of Rutgers University and Columbia Law School, rather than a "mere" actor. The play was an astounding success and after a month in Greenwich Village it moved uptown and thereby helped hasten the demise of the idealistic Provincetown Players.

In *The Hairy Ape* (1921), another foray into expressionism, O'Neill combines a number of themes from his earlier sea plays, and also the symbiotic relationship of the second engineer with his engines in *The Personal Equation*. He develops further his interest in labor politics, and even more importantly, his commitment to expressionistic total theatre. This time he documents the downward spiral of a white man. The fellowship of the forecastle in the S.S. *"Glencairn"* series now becomes a dance of the damned, imprisoned in an inferno, sleeping in a crowded steel-barred space like a prison cage for Neanderthal man, dehumanized by the shipowners and big business. Much the same forecastle cast from the *Glencairn* is to be found here – the white human race in microcosm – but the unifying force is engines, steel, and coal. The filth of the stokehole has supplanted the sea's cleansing, uplifting power while the Irishman's romantic remembrance of sailing ships is ridiculed by these slaves to machines. The aptly named Yank is the leader of those who feed the engines in a repetitive, grotesque, infernal parody of brutal sexual intercourse.

Yank represents the unthinking, voiceless working class, unquestioning of their lot, perceiving themselves as the first moving principle, while Long, the typical labor agitator, spouts anarchistic clichés, but does nothing. It is

Yank's demoralizing confrontation with the bored, bred-out young society woman, Mildred, that destroys him psychologically, leading him to question both himself and society.

O'Neill faced a difficult problem here: how to make an inarticulate character communicate ideas. As before with *The Emperor Jones*, he resorts to expressionistic techniques, especially in the Fifth Avenue scene, where the effetely oblivious members of the upper class are unaffected by Yank's superior strength. O'Neill here used masks for the first time – though they were an afterthought, suggested by Blanche Hays, the costume designer. The repeated image of the cage with Yank as the "beast," which the whiteclad Mildred had called him, dominates the rest of the play, as the "hairy ape," who has lost his sense of "belonging," tries to find his place in a hostile universe which rejects him to the last. Like Emperor Brutus Jones he moves downward, rejected by Fifth Avenue and labor agitators, imprisoned briefly, and even rejected there, until he finds his death in a cage, whose gorilla occupant, like capitalist society, casually destroys him in an instant. Finally Yank considers himself no more than a grotesque beast in a sideshow where "perhaps, the Hairy Ape at last belongs." Once again, O'Neill had a major success, particularly in the performance of Louis Wolheim, with the production moving from Greenwich Village to Broadway.[17]

Returning to the theme of race relations in 1923 with *All God's Chillun Got Wings*, O'Neill met trouble. The only reason *The Emperor Jones* had been acceptable was that there was no question of miscegenation, but an interracial marriage was still anathema to the theatrical establishment. Howls of rage came from press and public alike when it was known that Paul Robeson would actually kiss a white woman onstage as his wife.[18] So, in a futile attempt to defuse audience hostility, and fill a hiatus caused by the illness of Mary Blair, the star of the new play, the Provincetown Playhouse presented Robeson in a limited run of *The Emperor Jones* to introduce this handsome, well-educated actor/singer to the New York audience.

O'Neill's choice of music is important in *Chillun* because he always tailors musical selections to fit the situation. The black music is warm and joyous, e.g. "I Guess I'll Have to Telegraph my Baby," while the white folk sing constrainedly of sentimental social limitation, "She's Only a Bird in a Gilded Cage." Expressionistic techniques are also used in the careful division of black and white in the scene of the doomed wedding underlined by contrasting lamentations of slavery – a spiritual, "Sometimes I feel Like a Mourning Dove," and Stephen Foster's banal "Old Black Joe." Then the disapproving church bell "clangs one more stroke, instantly dismissing."

Expressionism is repeatedly invoked in the growing dominance of the African mask, given to Jim by his Afrocentric sister, and through the physically contracting size of the room in which Jim and Ella live. As Brutus Jones strips off all his clothes, so Jim's attempts to succeed in a hostile white world diminish. Ella wishes him to fail, because she feels her own selfhood and power threatened by his intellect and potential upward mobility. Her attempt to kill Jim and her stabbing of the African mask signify both her assertion of white superiority, and her own insanity. With his last failure to complete his law examinations Jim regresses to his happy ignorant childhood, when the world seemed friendly and racism had neither tainted his ambition nor destroyed his love. Thus, they again become as little children in order to enter the kingdom of heaven, where "All God's Chillun Got Wings," as the spiritual says. Jim gives up his hopes and dreams to serve his now insane wife. And as with *Jones*, the conclusion can appear racist.

However, *Chillun* has more to it than simple race relations. Its real theme is the destruction of a good man by a selfish or inappropriate wife. Almost alone among reviewers, Heywood Broun understood that fact: "this tiresome play ... gives to a first rate Negro a third rate white woman," documenting her slide into insanity (*New York World*, 16 May 1924). There are also autobiographical overtones in the names James and Ella – like O'Neill's own parents. Indeed this play may point ahead to *Long Day's Journey into Night*, demonstrating O'Neill's continuing anger at his once drug-addicted mother.

Even more autobiographical is *Welded* (1923), O'Neill's tribute to his marriage with Agnes Boulton, the mother of his children Shane and Oona. Its subject is one evening of misunderstanding in the union of two artists, a playwright and his actress-muse – with a double attempted revenge. The wife tries to rekindle a relationship with an old flame, who brings her to understand her dependence on her husband, while he seeks out a prostitute, who cannot comprehend him. By the end of the third act, the pair, whose separateness has been defined by the use of individual spotlights, merge into one single illumination as they climb the stairs to their bedroom, pausing in an embrace that forms a cross, to signify an interdependence both sacrificial and redemptive. Unsuccessful at its first production and not revived in New York until 1981, the play does have some good moments, despite its depressing title. Yet O'Neill's attitude toward woman is unchanged. While ostensibly celebrating his own marriage, O'Neill has his playwright character dominate his wife, who as the interpreter of his roles is his puppet. Again he celebrates masculine creativity and feminine servitude to it.

A more affirmative attitude is found in *The Fountain* (1922, produced 1926) written just before *Welded*. This long experimental play embraces the total theatre espoused also by his designer/director, Robert Edmond Jones. Produced by the "Triumvirate" of O'Neill, Jones, and Kenneth McGowan ("The Experimental Theatre, Inc."), this successor to the earlier Provincetown Players was heavily influenced by the innovative dramatists and stage designers of Europe.

The Fountain deals with Juan Ponce de Léon and his search for emotional fulfillment. However much one may think that he seeks "the finer perfection of Love," the Fountain of Youth, or the eternal return, he initially looks for wealth, joining Columbus to pillage the New World. There, he exhibits the shabbiest qualities of Christianity, inflicting genocide, torture, and mayhem. Then in his old age he discovers the love he had denied in his youth, after the aptly named Beatriz, daughter of his once-beloved Maria, comes as his ward to Puerto Rico. She represents what he has lost by following an avaricious goal, and in her marriage to the young Luis, she becomes Juan's symbol of life. Her dream-appearance as the fountain spirit leads him to understand the conflict between emotions and cold intellect, demonstrating the inclusiveness of the world soul of Neo-platonic thinkers, and the oneness of all religions. Then, like her Dantean equivalent, Beatriz leads the dying hidalgo out of life into a new paradisal world. In marriage to her beloved she trusts love, where Juan did not.

Though this play tries to include too much, and suffers from O'Neill's lack of true poetic instinct, its importance lies in its experimentation, its circularity, and its attempt to go beyond the conventions of act division. The two-generation action is developed by symbolic scenes to evoke the cyclical quality of human existence, the power of love and the central mystery of human life.

O'Neill's next play, *Desire Under the Elms* (1924), established him as a dramatist of true genius and is the culmination of his first period of composition. The modern world is often thought hostile to tragedy, but in this play O'Neill discomfits the naysayers. He manipulates into an astonishingly successful tragic whole such different elements as the conflict between duty and joy, the Apollonian and the Dionysian (even more notable in *The Great God Brown*), the dysfunctional family, and a combination of Greek myth with the then current philosophical–psychological ideas of Friedrich Nietzsche and Sigmund Freud. These disparate ideas are melded together in a thoroughly American New England setting which carries with it the mythico-religious tradition of Puritanism, along with the dream of monetary success, the pioneering spirit of breaking new land, and the world of gold in the far West. In effect, within this single play O'Neill prefigures

Mourning Becomes Electra and the totality of his uncompleted saga "A Tale of Possessors, Self-Dispossessed," demonstrating the dour and acquisitive quality of the Great American Myth, which he was to examine not only in the Mannon family, but also in the Harford and Melody families of *A Touch of the Poet* and the unfinished *More Stately Mansions*.

Desire also recalls the hardscrabble misery of *Beyond the Horizon* (1920), and *The Rope* (1918). Particularly important in *The Rope* is the second marriage of the old farmer Abraham Bentley, to a much younger woman (now dead), by whom he had a son, Luke. Bentley also has a secret hoard of gold pieces, keeping it for the son of his passionate old age. Also, like the later Ephraim Cabot of *Desire*, Bentley speaks in a biblical manner, especially when his prodigal son returns.

In *Desire*, everything falls into place. The gloomy farmhouse was presented in a much-praised set, superbly executed by Robert Edmond Jones from O'Neill's descriptions and drawings, its brooding trees reinforcing the sense of doom that pervades the play. In addition, O'Neill also solves the problem of the inarticulate central figure, which had been problematic in *The Hairy Ape*, by giving Ephraim Cabot the incantatory cadences of the Bible, particularly the *Song of Solomon*. But equally effective is Ephraim's long dialect-based monologue where he insists that "God's hard, not easy" (II.ii), in telling his new young wife of his earlier decision to return to his rocky farm rather than remain in the fertile Midwest.

The cycle of the seasons is also important for all these characters who are creatures of the soil. All members of this family are subject to it, none more than Ephraim, who rode out in an earlier spring to test himself in the Midwest, only to discover that his Puritan heritage was too strong, and happiness is not to be found in this world. Now in this later spring season the older brothers follow their father's example in seeking their freedom, departing for California after an act of betrayal that combines aspects of Jacob, Esau, and Judas Iscariot – selling their patrimony to their half-brother Eben for the thirty pieces of gold that Ephraim had hoarded.

But the newly aroused Ephraim has returned from his latest spring-wandering with a young bride through whom he hopes to restore his own fertility and that of the farm, bypassing all his sons. In so doing he unleashes on the family the mythic horrors of Oedipus, Phaedra, and Medea, in Greek tragedy. In the background are the sternly religious conflict between joy and duty, the familial psychology of Freud, and the racial unconscious of Jung. Thus Abbie seduces Eben in the front parlor that signifies his dead mother's personal space, claiming her son and the farm as her own. And here Eben also follows his father; just as all three sons had succeeded their father in their patronage of Min, the village prostitute, so Eben impregnates Abbie, in an Oedipal union, with Phaedrian overtones.

In the celebrations for the birth of "his" son, Ephraim becomes a capering satyr figure, ignorant of what all the world knows – the child is Eben's, and the instrument of his own disinheritance. So, in a rewriting of *Medea*, Abbie suffocates their child to keep Eben's love, driving the griefstricken young father to report her to the sheriff. But the power of his passion calls him back to share her fate, and in a repetition of the ending of *Beyond the Horizon*, the two lovers walk forth into the sunrise to face their all too certain future. This conclusion seems more affirmative than in the earlier play, and O'Neill leaves the audience with a sense of love's eternity.

With this play, initially banned in Boston on moral grounds and refused a public performance in England until 1940, O'Neill reached true international status. This was not merely because of the steamy plot, but the extraordinary transmutation of mythology into modern garb. It also demonstrated one of O'Neill's greatest strengths – as myth user rather than myth maker. Here and in *Mourning Becomes Electra* he combined ancient myths with modern psychology to examine American emotional and cultural equivalents.

NOTES

1 He dramatized this attempt in "Exorcism," which he withdrew and destroyed after a single performance from the Provincetown Players (1920).
2 For discussion of O'Neill's intellectual background, see Egil Törnqvist's essay "O'Neill's Philosophical and Literary Paragons" in this collection.
3 See Ann C. Hall, *"A Kind of Alaska": Women in the Plays of O'Neill, Pinter, and Shepard* (Carbondale and Edwardsville: Southern Illinois University Press, 1993).
4 Louis Sheaffer, *O'Neill: Son and Playwright* (Boston: Little, Brown, 1968), p. 273.
5 Timo Tiusanen, *O'Neill's Scenic Images* (Princeton, NJ: Princeton University Press, 1968), p. 45, notes this idea of the "sound coulisse," described by Otto Kioischwitz, *O'Neill* (Berlin: Junker und Dünnhaupt, 1938), p. 73.
6 Susan Glaspell, *The Road to the Temple* (New York: Frederick Stokes, 1927), see pp. 253–54.
7 Gary Jay Williams, "Turned Down by Provincetown: O'Neill's Debut Reexamined," *Theatre Journal* 37 (1985): 155–66. Reprinted in *The Eugene O'Neill Newsletter*, 12, i (1988): 17–27. See also Williams's entry "The Provincetown Players" in Margaret Loftus Ranald, *The Eugene O'Neill Companion* (Westport, Connecticut: Greenwood Press, 1982).
8 Sheaffer, *O'Neill: Son and Playwright*, p. 242.
9 Travis Bogard, *Contour in Time: The Plays of Eugene O'Neill* (New York: Oxford University Press, 1972), p. 162n.

10 Sheaffer, *O'Neill: Son and Playwright*, p. 477.

11 See Eugene O'Neill, *Inscriptions: Eugene O'Neill to Carlotta Monterey*. Privately printed: New Haven: Yale University Press, 1960, n.p.

12 Though the accusations were not upheld in court, James O'Neill made at least two financial settlements on the young man, who later tried to claim against his estate.

13 John Reed, *Insurgent Mexico* (New York: D. Appleton, 1914), most of which comes from articles originally appearing in the *Metropolitan* magazine.

14 See undated letter in the Beatrice Ashe Maher correspondence, Berg Collection, New York Public Library, and a corroborative news item of 4 March 1915 in the *New London Morning Telegraph*.

15 Gary Jay Williams, "*The Dreamy Kid*: O'Neill's Darker Brother," *Theatre Annual* 43 (1988): 3–14.

16 Sheaffer, *O'Neill: Son and Playwright*, p. 430.

17 When the play moved uptown the role of Mildred was played by Carlotta Monterey, later O'Neill's third wife.

18 Attempts were made to abort the play, and child labor laws were invoked to prevent the first performance, forcing James Light, the stage director, to read the children's lines. Children appeared only in summer performances when school was not in session.

5

JAMES A. ROBINSON

The middle plays

By the time *Desire Under the Elms* closed in the fall of 1925, Eugene O'Neill was firmly established as the leading artistic playwright of the American theatre. The "Triumvirate" of O'Neill, Kenneth Macgowan and Robert Edmond Jones had successfully reorganized the Provincetown Players into The Experimental Theatre, an off-Broadway company ready to stage virtually anything which O'Neill could conceive. Guided by the tenets of the Art Theatre movement which Macgowan promoted, O'Neill indulged his imagination, composing the historical extravaganzas "*Marco Millions*" and *Lazarus Laughed* and the allegorical *The Great God Brown*, and sketching out two studies of modern bourgeois America, *Strange Interlude* and *Dynamo*, as well. But *Marco*, *Interlude* and *Dynamo* were not produced by the Triumvirate but the Theatre Guild, a prestigious Broadway company whose embrace of O'Neill signalled his arrival as a popular dramatist. The Guild also premiered O'Neill's Civil War trilogy *Mourning Becomes Electra*, and the autobiographical dramas *Ah, Wilderness!* (a domestic comedy) and *Days Without End* (a dogmatic miracle play). The artistic and commercial failure of the latter in early 1934 combined with the Great Depression to motivate O'Neill to compose an epic Cycle of historical plays exploring his country's greedy self-dispossession. No Cycle plays were to be staged until the series was complete. But he never finished it; so no new O'Neill play appeared until *The Iceman Cometh* in 1946, ten years after his receipt of the Nobel Prize for Literature made official the worldwide recognition of his genius.

The international award seemed particularly appropriate for a playwright openly indebted to major European dramatists and thinkers, including Aeschylus, Sophocles, Henrik Ibsen, August Strindberg, Friedrich Nietzsche, Sigmund Freud and Carl Jung. During this middle period these foreign currents ebbed and flowed through his work, their influence sometimes challenged and sometimes fortified by mystical philosophy from Asia, and by techniques from medieval and Elizabethan theatre and the modern

European novel. O'Neill thus continued to expose his audiences, critics and fellow playwrights to unfamiliar ideas and forms from abroad. But his emphasis on strong narratives and powerful feelings carried on an older American tradition of melodrama, as amended by more recent conventions of naturalism and realism that O'Neill himself had helped plant and nurture.

This combining of ancient and modern, foreign and native, pervades *Desire Under the Elms*, the 1924 play that foreshadows the works of O'Neill's middle decade. Its plot (like that of *Electra*) enacts ancient Greek myths in nineteenth-century New England; its characters, native folk-drama rustics, are viewed (like those of *Interlude*) through the filter of modern depth psychology; its vision betrays debts to Eastern mysticism (*Marco*), American Gothicism (*Electra*), and Dionysus via Nietzsche (*Lazarus* and *Brown*). Like *Interlude*, *Dynamo*, *Electra* and *Wilderness*, *Desire* pictures overt intrafamilial conflict; the more covert struggle within Eben Cabot between Jungian male and female principles assumes transcultural form in *Marco*, becomes theological in *Interlude* and *Dynamo*, and is exorcized in the Freudian family romance of *Electra*. Finally, the 1924 play's identification of transcendent forces in the land and in love reveals O'Neill's religious sensibility, his desire (expressed in a program note that year) to penetrate like his master, Strindberg, to a realm "behind life" where "our souls, maddened by loneliness and the ignoble inarticulateness of flesh, are slowly evolving their new language of kinship."[1] In the exalted speeches of *Brown* and *Lazarus*, the mysterious larger force controlling human destiny in *Interlude* and *Electra*, and the design for *Dynamo* and *Days* to compose two parts of a trilogy exploring the death of God, we witness O'Neill's consistent ambition during this phase for the restoration of theatre to its formerly sacred place in Western culture.

Indeed, the phase's three initial plays form an unintended trilogy on a theological theme: the spiritual emptiness of material desires. The first of the three to be composed (though not produced until 1928), *Marco* offers a protagonist who is part explorer, part tourist, part inventor, part local mayor, but mainly eager merchant: a variation on Sinclair Lewis's George Babbitt, without his redeeming moral sense. Blending history with romance, satire and tragedy, O'Neill creates from the famous Venetian's exploits a pageant worthy of David Belasco (the Broadway producer of dazzling theatre spectacles who in fact took out the first option on the play). The first act places Polo's entourage in a series of gorgeous, exotic Asian settings on their way to the Chinese emperor Kublai Khan's sumptuous court – the site of several subsequent scenes during Polo's fifteen-year residence in China and subsequent return to Venice, where he is nicknamed "Marco Millions" for the fabulous wealth he conspicuously displays. The nickname points up Marco's identity (in Kublai Khan's words) as "a shrewd and crafty greed" who "has not even a mortal soul," but only "an acquisitive instinct."[2] This vulgar materialism is underscored by a romantic story line involving the beautiful princess Kukachin, the Khan's grand-daughter, who dies of her unrequited love for a man who fails to recognize a passion he is incapable of sharing or returning. As an emblem of the female, the intuitive and the spiritual (qualities O'Neill associated with the East), Kukachin offers the *yin* to the *yang* symbolized by Polo, whose male, rational and acquisitive attributes identify him as quintessentially Western (that is, modern American) – rich without, impoverished within.

The dualistic opposition between Kukachin and Marco Polo epitomizes a play that features vivid contrasts in its costumes, settings, characters and themes: West vs. East, matter vs. spirit, death vs. life, division vs. unity. A similar polar vision, prominent in the moral absolutism of American melodrama and reinforced by O'Neill's reading of Emerson, Jung, and Taoist texts, characterizes most of O'Neill's plays. It certainly informs *The Great God Brown*, a masked drama about the struggles between and within two architects. Externally, creative spirit battles obtuse matter in the conflict between the sensitive, artistic Dion Anthony and his rival Billy Brown, who employs and exploits Dion. Like Marco Millions, Brown is "inwardly empty and resourceless," O'Neill explained in a letter to New York newspapers shortly after the play opened in January 1926. He also outlined Dion's inner battle between "Dionysus and St. Anthony – the creative pagan acceptance of life, fighting eternal war with the masochistic, life-denying spirit of Christianity as represented by St. Anthony"; and he identified a "mystical pattern" of "conflicting tides in the soul of Man" as the play's central rhythm.[3]

A testimony to O'Neill's theatrical instinct, the play proved popular despite its mystical ambitions, despite the visual masks worn by Dion, Brown, Dion's wife Margaret, and Cybel (a prostitute who is mistress to both agonists), despite a bizarre plot spanning fourteen years that features two climaxes. At the first climax, the wealthy bachelor Brown – who envies Dion his wife, his mistress, and his talent – assumes Dion's cynical mask upon his rival's premature death, convincing even Dion's family that he is Dion. A more elaborate (often comic) masquerade follows in scenes drenched in dramatic irony, as Brown manically alternates between the mask of Dion, a new mask of his former complacent self, and a face increasingly *"ravaged and haggard"* (11, 516) that is revealed only to Cybel upon Brown's death (the second climax) a few weeks after Dion's.

The play suffers from its implausible story, excessive rhetoric and stereotypical characterization – especially that of the gold-hearted, earth-mother prostitute Cybel. But it is among O'Neill's most intriguing plays, especially for biographical critics. Dion's Dionysian mask, "distorted by morality" (O'Neill's letter observes) "from Pan into Satan, into a Mephisto-pheles mocking himself in order to feel alive," strongly resembles O'Neill's self-contemptuous, cynical brother Jamie, prematurely dead from alcoholism in 1923.[4] Dion's hostility toward Brown, moreover, suggests O'Neill's intuition of the threat to his talent posed by his recent fame and success; he did not want to follow his father, whose fabulous popularity as *The Count of Monte Cristo* had led him to sacrifice his talent for wealth. Finally, Dion's inner battle between Dionysus and St. Anthony projects the playwright's own struggle between the Nietzschean doctrines of affirmation and tragic joy he repeatedly espoused in the mid-1920s, and Roman Catholic values that he could only half-repudiate. No doubt he regarded the Christian asceticism which tortures Dion as "masochistic"; but Dion's spiritual growth implies nonetheless the redemptive value of suffering, the central tenet of Christian faith. The same holds true for Brown, out of whose brief anguish (claims O'Neill's letter) "a soul is born, a tortured Christian soul such as the dying Dion's."[5]

If Dion is tormented by his deeper faith, Brown is murdered by Dion's superficial mask. The masking constitutes the play's most provocative feature. Presumably inspired by ancient Greek theatre, its implications are modern. It reveals the playwright's interest in contemporary depth psychology, which posited a private, authentic self beneath the personality presented to others. Only Cybel witnesses this sensitive, poetic, and vulnerable self; and this suppression of his genuine nature hastens Dion's self-destruction.[6] O'Neill himself, however, privately lamented that the play's production "suggested only the bromidic, hypocritical and defensive double-personality of people in their personal relationships" rather than the mystical "drama of the forces behind the people" that his public letter had stressed.[7] And from a third perspective, *Brown*'s masks enunciate what W. B. Worthen terms O'Neill's deepest project, the "exfoliation of an unconscious, intensely private, and interior self in the public action of the theatre." The masking thus questions the identification of character and actor that modern realistic acting style asserts; moreover, the masked characters' painful awareness of audience implies that "'character' in this drama never escapes its subjection to and falsification by the coercion of the spectator, by the spectators in the audience, those on the stage, and those haunting the theatre of the self."[8] But on the deepest level, the suffering of the souls beneath the masks simply dramatizes the central theme of O'Neill's work, indeed of his life: the anguish of human lone-liness.

The inability of Billy Brown to incorporate into himself the "Satan" which Dion's mask has become also reveals the influence of Jung, who argued that personal development required integration of one's hidden evil side, or shadow, into oneself. Jung's presence expands in *Lazarus Laughed*, the final drama of O'Neill's informal anti-materialist trilogy. The intricate masking schemes for its series of crowds follow the seven personality categories proposed by Jung's *Psychological Types* (1921), with each type divided into seven periods of life, then multiplied even further by race, gender, class, nationality and religious sect so that the play's production requires literally hundreds of masks. Not surprisingly, this most audacious of O'Neill's plays has never been produced on Broadway, and rarely elsewhere.[9] It follows the progress of the biblical Lazarus – the only unmasked character – from the days after his miraculous restoration to life by Jesus through a fictional journey with legions of followers to imperial Rome, where he is eventually executed by the old, decadent emperor Tiberius. But his true antagonist is the young, perverse Caligula, the self-proclaimed "Lord of fear, Caesar of death" (II, 627), who symbolizes corrupt and fallen mankind. Like all others, however, the Roman general responds to Lazarus' irresistibly contagious laughter, the consequence of the Jew's realization – proclaimed repeatedly – that "there is no death."

Lazarus' words echo Christ's, as do his charisma, radiance, loving nature and ultimate fate. But Lazarus' gospel of the ego's unreality draws more upon Hinduism, Buddhism and Gnostic faiths of the early Christian era; and his youthful personality and intoxicating effect resemble Nietzsche's Zarathustra and Dionysus. Most important, the God he worships offers not salvation but the enlightened insight that humans, like all material beings, participate in a process of "eternal change and everlasting growth, and a high note of laughter soaring through chaos from the deep heart of God!" (572). Jesus wept; Lazarus laughed. And the laughter, chanting and dancing of his mobs of followers (many of whom literally die laughing) is elaborately choreographed by a playwright who characteristically attends to rhythm, both in the texture and structure of this unique divine comedy. Perhaps only in *Lazarus* did O'Neill realize his middle period ambition (proclaimed in 1933) for a theatre that served as "a Temple where the religion of a poetical interpretation and symbolic celebration of life is communicated to human beings, starved in spirit by their soul-stifling daily struggle to exist as masks among the masks of living."[10] But the spectacle offered by this play (like religious theatre generally) has attracted few modern spectators.

The same cannot be said of *Strange Interlude*, which ran on Broadway from January 1928 to June 1929, sold 100,000 copies, and established O'Neill as a bankable playwright. It presents variations on another Nietzschean theme, the will to power, in the form of emotional possessiveness. "Forgive us our possessing as we forgive those who possessed before us" (II, 650), muses novelist Charles Marsden in one of this nine-act play's countless thought asides – a version of the Elizabethan soliloquy which exposes most of the spoken exchanges as verbal masks. Like Ibsen's Hedda Gabler, *Interlude*'s Nina Leeds seeks dominion over the men who love and surround her, including her family friend Marsden, husband Sam Evans, lover Ned Darrell, and son Gordon – named after her fiancé Gordon Shaw, who died in World War I before consummating their love. Gordon's ghost haunts Nina's mind, first prompting promiscuity, then marriage (promoted by Ned, her doctor) to Gordon's boyish admirer Sam, then intercourse with Ned to conceive Gordon II after her discovery of congenital insanity in Sam's family causes her to abort Sam's child. Their intermittent affair destroys Ned's promising scientific career over the following twenty years, while the blissfully unaware Sam prospers and young Gordon grows and marries in spite of his jealous mother's fierce covert resistance. Shortly after Sam's death in his late forties, Nina and Marsden plan a passionless marriage that signals her retreat from possessiveness.

A compelling character, Nina combines features of the Romantic eternal feminine (as in her *"unchangeably mysterious eyes"* [II, 675]), the Victorian *femme fatale*, Strindberg's castrating women, and Anne Whitefield of G. B. Shaw's *Man and Superman*. Embodying the instinctual Life Force (a version of Arthur Schopenhauer's Will), she deviously manipulates her male admirers, especially the scientist Ned who considers himself *"immune to love"* (661). Nina's cunning also aligns her with the predatory villains of melodrama, whose conventions *Interlude* both follows and critiques. As Kurt Eisen has observed, the play's two levels of dialogue (of speech and thoughts) strive to achieve the total emotional expressivity of melodrama. But that dialogue, modelled upon the conflicting discourses of the modern novel (as described by Mikhail Bakhtin), also ironically contrasts melodrama's sentimental values – celebrating home and motherhood – with the ideologies of business (Sam), psychoanalysis (Darrell), and fictional art (Marsden).[11]

Sam's discourse is the least complicated of the three, for this dense, complacent advertising executive has little inner life, hence rarely soliloquizes after little Gordon's birth confers (apparent) fatherhood upon him. His subtle power over others lies in the bourgeois honor code, associated with Gordon Shaw, that he carries on: a code honored by Nina and Ned, who protect Sam from knowledge of their adultery at heavy cost to the anguished Ned. The conflict between morality and sexuality, superego and id, points up the influence of Freud, whose popular psychoanalytical discourse shapes the words and thoughts of Dr. Darrell. Having himself briefly undergone psychoanalysis in 1926, O'Neill treats Ned with ambivalence. On the one hand, the neurologist offers acute insight into Marsden's Oedipal fixation and Nina's promiscuity; on the other, his Freudian ideas and language are often parodied. Thus, his promotion of Sam as a surrogate for Gordon Shaw and cure for Nina's neurosis backfires disastrously, with himself the primary victim. And his *"cold, emotionless, professional"* words as Nina seduces him at Act 4's conclusion satirically highlight the arrogant blindness of a theorist who succumbs to the sexual force to which he has claimed immunity (II, 709).

Not just Ned's language, but language itself is questioned by a work whose protagonist sees "how we poor monkeys hide from ourselves behind the sounds called words" (II, 667), hinting at mysterious depths of existence lurking beneath its characters' speeches and thoughts. Appropriately, the play also satirizes its language specialist as one who hides from himself. Charles Marsden's deep fear not just of sex but "of life" (II, 670), and the timid conventionality of his fiction, suggest O'Neill's mild contempt. Yet Marsden's *"indefinable feminine quality"* allows him penetrating intuitions about Nina's behavior (II, 633), and his numerous thought asides (which open and close the play) often provide a central consciousness to this novelistic drama. After all, the asides constitute a simplified, conventionally syntactical version of the stream-of-consciousness technique of the modern novel: Marsden's domain. And Marsden resembles Nina in a crucial respect. In a play structured around Nina's alternating moods of adjustment and alienation, Marsden's emotional life vacillates between a mild detached contentment and deep grief over the loss of loved ones. He moves symbolically between life and death: the deepest rhythm not just of this play, but of all O'Neill's drama.

In *Interlude*'s final scene, Nina declares their lives to be "merely strange dark interludes in the electrical display of God the Father" (II, 817), concluding a series of allusions to a distant, punishing father god who competes with an immanent, mystical mother god for her allegiance. In O'Neill's next play another neurotic protagonist, Reuben Light, repudiates the Puritanical father God of his parents and seeks forgiveness for his mother's subsequent death from the maternal god he discovers in electricity. *Dynamo* ends in a hydro-electric plant with Reuben's murder of his girl friend Ada, then sacrificial suicide to a generator, *"huge and black, with something of a massive female idol about it"* (II, 871). The play's titular symbol clearly alludes to "The Dynamo and the Virgin" chapter from *The Education of Henry Adams*, the famous American autobiography which introduced this powerful symbol for our modern technological god. But credibility of character falls victim to the play's schematic presentation of the "big subject" (as O'Neill described it after finishing *Dynamo* in August, 1928): the "sickness of today" and the "death of the old God and the failure of Science and Materialism to give any satisfying new One for the surviving primitive religious instinct to find a meaning for life in."[12] Another letter written while he wrote the play betrays the tired imagination of a playwright who consciously borrowed *Dynamo*'s interior/exterior domestic settings from *Desire Under the Elms*, its industrial sounds from *The Hairy Ape*, and its thought asides from *Interlude*.[13] The characters also seem borrowed from earlier O'Neill plays (especially *Desire*), resulting in unintended self-parody. The Oedipal Reuben is a modern Eben Cabot without the dignity, his minister father a cowardly, watered-down Ephraim; Ada's mother, subject to spells of moody dreaminess around the dynamo she worships, recalls *Brown*'s Earth Mother, Cybel; Ada's father mocks like Dion Anthony, is a scientist like Ned Darrell.

Dynamo failed on Broadway in 1929, as did O'Neill's final religious play, *Days Without End*, in 1934. Again, he reworks old material. Resembling Dion Anthony, protagonist John Loving is split between two selves, one attracted tentatively to his abandoned Christian faith (John, an unmasked character), the other toward Mephistophelean nihilism (Loving, who wears *"the death mask of a John who has died with a sneer of scornful mockery on his lips"*).[14] Their word duel forms the central conflict of a play about John's progress on an autobiographical novel, whose plot reveals his recent adultery and current desire (fueled by Loving) for his ailing wife Elsa to die. But with the aid of a Catholic priest, John finally slays his masked alterego by recovering his lost faith in church at the foot of a crucifix, and Elsa miraculously recovers. The play does not. While *Days* offers in John's past a mildly intriguing résumé of O'Neill's own spiritual journey, its underdeveloped characters, overloaded exposition, and blunt (and highly atypical) Christian conclusion render it O'Neill's dullest mature drama.[15] Perhaps sensing this, O'Neill cancelled plans for the third of the "Myth Plays for the God-Forsaken" trilogy begun by *Dynamo* and *Days*, and never ventured onto religious terrain again.

In fact, a previous trilogy of myth plays had already given O'Neill's spiritual sensibility its most powerful expression. T. S. Eliot once observed that good poets borrow, while great poets steal; the plot for *Mourning Becomes Electra*, produced in 1932, was stolen from Euripides, Sophocles and (especially) the *Oresteia* of Aeschylus. But Electra's title indicates

O'Neill's interest in the daughter, Lavinia Mannon, who avenges the murder of her father Ezra (Agamemnon) by his wife Christine (Clytemnestra) and her lover, Ezra's cousin Adam Brant (Aegisthus). Part 1 of the trilogy, *Homecoming*, describes Ezra's poisoning upon his return to New England in 1865 from serving as a Union general in the American Civil War; part 2, *The Hunted*, depicts the outraged Lavinia manipulating her neurotic, Oedipal brother Orin (Orestes) into killing Brant and goading Christine into taking her life. The final play, *The Haunted*, finds Lavinia worried that Orin, driven half-insane by guilt and incestuous desire, will confess and tarnish the Mannon name. She drives her brother to suicide, then entombs herself within the family Greek revival mansion for the remainder of her life. She is helped by Seth, the family's old gardener, who also hosts the various choruses of townspeople whose gossip about the aristocratic Mannons opens each part of the trilogy.

Doris Alexander notes that *Electra* places O'Neill "in direct rivalry" with the ancient Greek playwrights.[16] Indeed, that competition of modern playwright with revered forefathers enacts the rebellion of child against parent at the heart of the play. O'Neill also challenged another father figure, Kenneth Macgowan, in his abdication of the theatrical expressionism his colleague had encouraged. "Hereafter I write plays primarily as literature to be read," he wrote Macgowan in June 1929; "my trend will be to regard anything depending on director or scenic designer for collaboration to bring out its full values as suspect."[17] *Electra* nonetheless betrays a lingering trace of the Art Theatre in the "*strange life-like mask*" expression of all the Mannons in repose (II, 897), a visual sign of their shared destiny as members of a cursed family. Moreover, the play's major relationships pattern themselves according to the Freudian family romance that Macgowan had helped popularize in a 1929 book he co-authored, *What is Wrong with Marriage*. Each Mannon child is enamored of the opposite-sex parent in a drama which features frequent fleeting glimpses of unconscious suppressed desires (as in Vinny's attraction to Brant, who resembles her father), and which exposes the repetition compulsion of characters whose later words and gestures re-enact moments from earlier scenes, from the recent past.

The stranglehold of past on present is the play's central theme. *Electra* itself takes place in the past, participating in the broad alternation between historical and modern settings that marks O'Neill's middle period. Starting in 1934, however, the playwright set all his plays in prior periods, concurring with Mary Tyrone of *Long Day's Journey* that "the past is the present. It's the future, too" (III, 765). The line could summarize *Electra*. The past is governed by one's ancestors, the ancestral Mannon family portraits whose *"intense, bitter life, with their frozen stare"* (II, 1034) so dominates the sitting room that Lavinia addresses them like characters. Scenes occur there that underscore Lavinia's growing resemblance to Christine, Orin's to Ezra, and Ezra's to the zealots, generals and judges who preceded him. O'Neill's determinism was in large part itself determined by the Greek tragedians, Freud, and early twentieth-century American culture, all of which figured the family as a form of fate.[18] Hence, "fate springing out of the family" became O'Neill's conscious intention as he revised the first draft;[19] and as Travis Bogard concludes, fate deliberately shapes the plot, the character descriptions, and even the Mannon speech rhythms.[20] The grim protagonist Lavinia, who ceaselessly prods others into action but herself moves *"like some tragic mechanical doll"* (II, 974), is fate's fool until her resignation to the Mannon destiny – and possible ironic triumph over it – in her final gesture of self-imprisonment.

The male family portraits also suggest another prominent theme: the sins of the fathers. The earliest colonial Mannon burned witches, but the family is not doomed until Ezra's father (recalling Cain) expels his brother, Brant's father, from the family when both lust after the same woman. If the theme of primal sin recalls Nathaniel Hawthorne's fiction, other Gothic features point toward Poe. *Electra* describes the fall of the house of Mannon, a powerful and respectable New England family; ghosts haunt the house; incestuous love and death commingle in the plot. Ultimately, death conquers all. At the play's heart, thematically and structurally, lies the corpse of Ezra Mannon, who himself killed Christine's love by his Puritanical Mannon belief (perceived and forsworn too late) that "life was a dying. Being born was starting to die. Death was being born" (II, 937–38). Though the carefree pagan life of the Blessed Isles in the South Pacific entices Adam and Christine, and briefly seduces Orin and Lavinia, "death becomes the Mannons," as Orin tells Ezra's corpse (II, 975). Mourning becomes Electra.

The play is quintessential O'Neill in its length (over five hours in performance), its repetitions, its power, its enactment of ancient tragic actions on native grounds. Also typically, tragedy shares the stage with melodrama in the play's strong narrative elements (blackmail, murder and revenge), the emotional intensity of its stage directions, and the manipulativeness of Lavinia and Christine – misogynistic nightmares who descend directly from Nina Leeds. But the family focus on this heaviest of the middle plays also points toward the lightest, *Ah, Wilderness!*, produced in 1933 on Broadway where it ran for a year. Several factors account for its popularity. It is set in a small Connecticut seaport – the New London of O'Neill's childhood – on 4 July 1906, in an era that offers not tragic entrapment but fond memories of simpler times. (The play thus aligns itself with numerous later nostalgic narratives of the 1930s, particularly Wilder's *Our Town*.) It also displays the familiar stereotypes of comedy (a clumsy servant, a funny drunk, an old maid, a Puritanical elder, even a traveling salesman) in familiar, hence reassuring patterns. Boy (the teenaged Richard Miller) briefly loses girl (the chaste, pretty Muriel Macomber), then fails to lose his virginity to a "tart" before he reunites with girl. The equilibrium of a social unit, the Miller family, is briefly upset by Richard's mild rebellion and his uncle Sid's alcoholic episode (upsetting the maiden Aunt Lily, whom he courts), then is restored upon their repentance. Finally, the play sentimentally affirms the respectable bourgeois family – headed by Richard's mother Essie and father Nat – as a source of love, support and wisdom. Recognizing that Richard is "just as innocent and as big a kid as Muriel" (III, 20), Nat tempers discipline with understanding when he lectures his son the day after Richard's drunken return from a bar. In the previous scene, a sober Richard and Muriel had reunited in innocent love on a moonlit beach; but the last moments extol the seasoned love of Essie and Nat, the latter wooing his wife with lines from a romantic text admired by both father and son, "The Rubaiyat of Omar Khayyam."

The source of the play's title, "The Rubaiyat" also provides several of the play's numerous allusions to *fin de siècle* texts. For Richard's adolescent rebellion is mediated by Swinburne's poetry, Wilde's fiction, and Ibsen's *Hedda Gabler*. Though never quoted, O'Neill's true Penelope is the Shaw of *Arms and the Man*: another initiation story about the partial disillusion of an appealing young protagonist whose temperamental romantic idealism expresses itself in a theatrical manner learned from art. The most literary of O'Neill's middle plays, *Wilderness* (anticipating the late work) foregrounds, questions, and sometimes parodies its sources. Richard's melodramatic poses and language are similarly recognized and more thoroughly mocked. "He ought to be on stage," his mother chuckles after one histrionic exit (III, 33), suggesting O'Neill's acknowledgment of the theatrical form (parodied again in *A Touch of the Poet*, the first Cycle play) that had both enriched and weakened his own work. Intriguingly, Richard's alternation between a *"plain simple boy and a posey actor solemnly playing a role"* (III, 12) finds O'Neill employing the favorite device of the middle period – the mask – in a strictly behavioral manner that deepens in the psychologically realistic portraiture of *Poet*, *Long Day's Journey* and *A Moon for the Misbegotten*.

Those final masterworks, rich in allusions, continue the project initiated in *Electra* to write for a literary audience. But O'Neill's earlier, expressionistic plays from 1925 to 1930 also advanced his own literary development, for they expanded his dramatic actions and deepened his characterizations while they indulged – and finally tempered – the obsession with "big subjects" that often threatened to turn his dialogue into rhetoric. Along with *Electra* and *Wilderness*, those middle plays contributed crucially to the artistic growth of the modern American theatre as well. O'Neill's earnestness during this phase about theatre's religious mission, for instance, has immeasurably influenced countless more secular successors, elevating their aims for their dramatic medium (with Arthur Miller's concern about tragedy and the common man only the most obvious example). Moreover, O'Neill's bold and restless imagination, whether playing with masks or incorporating novelistic techniques into commercially successful drama, has inspired subsequent generations of American playwrights to experiment without foregoing the hope of earning a living through their art. Perhaps most important, these plays exposed the large audiences of mainstream American theatre to the concerns and techniques of European dramatists. O'Neill thus paved the way for the Ibsenesque moral realism of Miller, the Strindbergian sexual battles of Tennessee Williams, the expressionistic allegories of early Edward Albee, even the Absurdist – and mythic – families of later Sam Shepard. Whatever their flaws, then, the plays of this phase by themselves merit our attention, for they represent what most playwrights would consider a lifetime's worth of achievement; but the full flowering of O'Neill's genius lay in the future, when he was borne back ceaselessly into the past.

NOTES

1 *Provincetown Playbill* for Strindberg's *The Spook Sonata*, January 3, 1924; rpt. in Ulrich Halfmann, ed., *Eugene O'Neill: Comments on the Drama and the Theater* (Tübingen: Gunter Narr Verlag, 1987), p. 32.

2 Travis Bogard, ed., *Eugene O'Neill: Complete Plays* (New York: The Library of America, 1988), II, p. 420. Hereafter documented in the text.

3 Rpt. in Halfmann, *Eugene O'Neill*, pp. 66–67.

4 Halfmann, *Eugene O'Neill*, p. 66.

5 Halfmann, *Eugene O'Neill*, p. 67.

6 For a New Historicist deconstruction of O'Neill's drama as both expression and critique of depth psychology, see Joel Pfister's *Staging Depth: Eugene O'Neill and the Politics of Psychological Discourse* (Chapel Hill: University of North Carolina Press, 1995), which claims that Brown's quick destruction by Dion's mask implies a parody of the "anxious quest for pseudo-spiritual depth" in which O'Neill's bourgeois audience was itself engaged (p. 83).

7 June 1927 Letter to Benjamin de Casseres, *Selected Letters of Eugene O'Neill*, eds. Travis Bogard and Jackson R. Bryer (New Haven: Yale University Press, 1988), p. 246.

8 *Modern Drama and the Rhetoric of Theatre* (Berkeley: University of California Press, 1992), pp. 64–67.

9 The play was staged in April 1928 at the Pasadena Playhouse by an amateur company directed by Gilmore Brown. For a scholarly analysis of the productions of this and other O'Neill plays from this period, see Ronald H. Wainscott, *Staging O'Neill: The Experimental Years, 1920–1934* (New Haven: Yale University Press, 1988).

10 "A Dramatist's Notebook," *The American Spectator*, 1, 3 (1933): 2. The last segment of a piece O'Neill wrote for George Jean Nathan's new journal also presents his final opinion on the theatrical potential of masks in general and for his work in particular. Rpt. in Halfmann, *Eugene O'Neill*, pp. 107–12.

11 *The Inner Strength of Opposites: O'Neill's Novelistic Drama and the Melodramatic Imagination* (Athens: University of Georgia Press, 1994), pp. 28, 106ff.

12 *Letters*, p. 311.

13 June 1928 letter to Theresa Helburn, *Letters*, pp. 300–01.

14 Bogard, ed., *Eugene O'Neill: Complete Plays* (New York: Random House, 1988), III, p. 113. Hereafter documented in the text.

15 See Bogard, *Contour in Time: The Plays of Eugene O'Neill*, rev. edn. (New York: Oxford University Press, 1988), p. 327.

16 *Eugene O'Neill's Creative Struggle: The Decisive Decade, 1924–1933* (University Park: Pennsylvania State University Press, 1992), p. 149. Though it persistently overinterprets the play as evidence of psychobiography, this is a valuable source study.

17 Quoted in Bogard, *Contour*, p. 340.

18 See Pfister, pp. 20–30, on the cultural construction of family as determinant.

19 Work Diary, 27 March 1930; rpt. in Halfmann, *Eugene O'Neill*, p. 90.

20 Bogard, *Contour*, 336–39.

Other sources relevant to this chapter include:

Floyd, Virginia, ed., *Eugene O'Neill at Work: Newly Released Ideas for Plays* (New York: Frederick Ungar, 1981).

Robinson, James A., *Eugene O'Neill and Oriental Thought: A Divided Vision* (Carbondale: Southern Illinois University Press, 1982).

Manheim, Michael, *Eugene O'Neill's New Language of Kinship* (Syracuse, New York: Syracuse University Press, 1982).

6

NORMAND BERLIN

The late plays

After the fifty-seven performances of *Days Without End* in 1934, just enough to cover the Theatre Guild subscribers, Broadway would not see another O'Neill play until *The Iceman Cometh* was produced in 1946. The twelve years between the play that affirmed a sunny faith in God and the play that revealed O'Neill's dark existentialism are referred to as O'Neill's "silence." Many believed that O'Neill's supposed return to Catholicism, as revealed in *Days Without End,* marked the end of his artistic powers. Of course, O'Neill did not return to Catholicism, nor did he feel spiritual peace. Quite the contrary, during his absence from Broadway he was engaged in his most intense exploration of his country and himself. Beset by continual physical illness, troubled by his relations with his children and wife Carlotta, deeply disturbed by the miserable state of the world – with Hitler, the world's "iceman," on the march – O'Neill, exhausted physically and perhaps spiritually, was at the end of his tortuous journey. He was ready to write the plays of his history Cycle, "A Tale of Possessors Self-Dispossessed," a task not completed, and to write the four last plays which crown his formidable career, plays of the highest accomplishment – *The Iceman Cometh* (1939), *Hughie* (1940), *Long Day's Journey Into Night* (1940), and *A Moon for the Misbegotten* (1943).

The rare public interview given by O'Neill after his "silence," in anticipation of the opening of *Iceman,* clearly reveals his attitude toward America. His oft-quoted words provide the context to any evaluation of his history Cycle. America, he said, "instead of being the most successful country in the world, is the greatest failure. It's the greatest failure because it was given everything, more than any other country ... Its main idea is that everlasting game of trying to possess your own soul by the possession of something outside of it."[1] Possession and greed, he believed, had destroyed the soul of America, and this was the theme of his projected history Cycle. The plan and composition of the eleven-play Cycle, stretching from the Revolutionary War to the Great Depression, are discussed by Donald

Gallup in this volume. That O'Neill was unable to complete so ambitious a project represents a major loss for American drama. The one play he did complete, *A Touch of the Poet*, although part of the cycle – in fact, the most important part of the cycle because here O'Neill treats the union of Irish Sara melody and Yankee Simon Harford – has wholeness and depth; it can stand by itself, as O'Neill must have realized when he decided to complete the play after he wrote the other plays of his last period. *A Touch of the Poet* is closer to those last autobiographical plays than to the unfinished *More Stately Mansions* which was to come immediately after *Poet* in the Cycle. In *Mansions* Simon Harford epitomizes America's lost dream, a dream connected with freedom and equality and charity, and also represents America's spiritual death, a cynicism connected with ruthless power and greed. On the personal level, Simon is torn between wife and mother, a struggle that eventually destroys him and changes them, a family struggle that seems typical O'Neill. But O'Neill's method of presentation – the spoken asides and the use of extended time – is closer to his earlier plays, although we should be very tentative in evaluating the unfinished work of a meticulous artist.

A Touch of the Poet belongs with the late plays in method as well as theme, if not in tone. The play is a crucial link in the family-nation drama of the projected cycle but O'Neill seems to have forgotten his large theme of possessors self-dispossessed in his portrayal of Major Cornelius Melody, surely the play's emotional center. It is Con Melody's relation with his daughter Sara and his wife Nora that charges the play. It is Con Melody's attitude toward himself that gives the play is complexity and depth. A self-styled Byronic hero, Major Melody falls from his high deluded self-esteem – "I have not loved the World, nor the World me; . . . I stood / Among them, but not of them." – to a peasant innkeeper drinking with his lowly Irish buddies in the tavern. The fall is the dissolution of his pride, a recognition that he was living a lie. Con's facing reality instead of the mirror that reflected his glorious past is really the death of the man as his daughter Sara knew him.[2] When Con kills the beautiful mare that represented his past conquests he kills the romantic illusion of his self, but now Sara, who wanted her father to face reality, wants him to return to illusion because she realizes his pride was her pride too. This clearly reflects O'Neill's relationship with his father, who casts his shadow on this play, pushing *Poet* away from "history" and closer to the last autobiographical plays. In *Poet* the autobiographical pressure comes from the father; in *Mansions* it comes from the mother, Deborah Harford, an earlier portrait of Mary Tyrone.[3] It seems that O'Neill had to suffer through the history Cycle in order to confront more directly his personal life. This he does in his four last plays, his crowning achievements, his most autobiographical and most modern plays.

The step from Con Melody's 1828 tavern in Boston to Harry Hope's 1912 saloon in New York City is a short one – with Con Melody, like Hope's drinking buddies, living a life-lie; with Con, like Hickey and Larry Slade, both a comic and tragic character; with Sara, like Hickey, wishing to destroy illusion. We know that O'Neill was thinking about *Iceman* and *Long Day's Journey* while he was writing the history Cycle. These plays were always inside him; now they came out. Simon Harford's words in *Mansions* clearly anticipate *Iceman* when Simon, probably speaking for O'Neill, asserts that men's lives "are without any meaning whatever – that human life is a silly disappointment, a liar's promise … a daily appointment with peace and happiness in which we wait day after day, hoping against hope, listening to each footstep, and when finally the bride or the bridegroom cometh, we discover we are kissing Death."[4] His words describe the situation of *Iceman* and point to the play's unusual title. His phrase, "the bridegroom cometh," comes directly from the Bible: "While the bridegroom tarried, they all slumbered and slept. And at midnight there was a cry made, Behold, the bridegroom cometh" (Matthew 25: 5–6). O'Neill, always paying special attention to his titles, combines the archaic word "cometh" with the "iceman" of a bawdy joke told by Hickey whenever he comes to Harry Hope's saloon. According to O'Neill's friend, the writer Dudley Nichols, when Evelyn married Hickey she took Death to her breast, and "her insistence on her great love for Hickey and his undying love for her and her deathlike grip on his conscience … is making Death breathe hard on her breast as he approaches ever nearer – as he is about to 'come' in the vernacular sense."[5] This combination of the biblical and the vulgar reflects the realistic–symbolic nature of the play, revealed by Larry Slade's words when he describes Hope's saloon:

> It's the No Chance saloon. It's Bedrock Bar, The End of the Line Cafe, the Bottom of the Sea Rathskeller! Don't you notice the beautiful calm in the atmosphere? That's because it's the last harbor. No one here has to worry about where they're going next, because there is no farther they can go.
>
> (III, 577–78)

This saloon is a dying place containing sleepy men filled with booze and pipe dreams, men who are waiting for death to come. Death comes in the person of Hickey, the son of a preacher who, Jesus-like, wishes to be their savior but becomes the "death" of them, just as he was the death of his wife. Simon Harford's words point not only to the play's title but to the *waiting*, exactly what Harry Hope's lodgers are doing in anticipation of

Hickey who, they believe, will bring them a little "peace and happiness," again Simon's phrase. (The first three acts in this four-act play end with the word "happy," always uttered by Hickey.) The play could have been given the less interesting, but more clearly descriptive, title, "Waiting for Hickey," a title that would prod us to think about *Iceman* in relation to the great modern play of our time, *Waiting for Godot*. Although Harold Bloom rejects such a comparison because he believes O'Neill and Beckett have only Schopenhauer in common,[6] I find that *Iceman* and *Godot* share characteristics that help us to appreciate O'Neill's modernity and to understand the great success of the revival of *Iceman* in 1956 after the tepid reception of the 1946 production. Hickey's arrival is so long in coming, so eagerly anticipated, takes on such significance when it comes, that he is certainly more than a mere salesman; he is, as Willie Oban, the youngest of Hope's roomers, labels him, the "Great Salesman," more than a mere mortal. Those waiting for Hickey, like Didi and Gogo waiting for Godot, are in a frozen condition, a boundary situation, the "last harbor," to use Larry Slade's phrase. Sustained by their pipe dreams and alcohol, the waiters in Hope's saloon belong together and feed off each other; they are family. They fill their time with sleep and repetitive talk. They wait for a tomorrow that will never come. They also wait for Hickey who, unlike Godot, comes, and when he does, death enters the play. His illusion-destroying, salvationist activity converts Harry's place to a morgue. He puts all the derelicts on ice, so to speak, and Hickey becomes the iceman of death for them *and* the iceman of his own bawdy joke when he reveals, at play's end, that he murdered his sleeping wife, with the word *come* taking on sexual overtones.

O'Neill and Beckett share the same metaphysical ground. Their dramatic art, so different in particular traits, makes waiting and the atmosphere of death reflections of the bedrock reality of human existence. Their dramatic representations of illusion and despair strike deep responsive chords in a modern audience, and it seems that O'Neill's audience was more "modern" in 1956 than in 1946 when, despite the fanfare connected with O'Neill's return to Broadway after his twelve-year absence, *Iceman* closed after only 136 performances. In 1956, three years after O'Neill's death, *Iceman* began O'Neill's revival, and it had the longest run of any O'Neill play ever (565 performances). Much credit must go to José Quintero's brilliant direction and Jason Robards' memorable portrayal of Hickey, and perhaps the intimacy of the Circle-in-the-Square Theater allowed the hooks to go in, as Beckett would say, but also the ten-year gap between 1946 and 1956 made an enormous difference, with America catching up to an O'Neill whose attitude toward life, whose confrontation with the terrifying prospect that there are no firm values, no ultimate meanings, made him contemporary with such modern existential thinkers as Camus and Sartre – and Beckett. 1956 is the year *Waiting for Godot* came to Broadway, opening on 19 April, two weeks before *The Iceman Cometh*. America was ready for both dramatists, both children of their century, with Beckett writing his early plays, O'Neill having written his last plays.

In the same 1946 press conference in which he lamented the spiritual emptiness of America, O'Neill makes this revealing comment:

> It's struck me as time goes on, how something funny, even farcical, can suddenly without any apparent reason, break up into something gloomy and tragic ... A sort of unfair non sequitur, as though events, as though life, were being manipulated just to confuse us. I think I'm aware of comedy more than I ever was before; a big kind of comedy that doesn't stay funny very long. I've made some use of it in *The Iceman*. The first act is hilarious comedy, *I think*, but then some people may not even laugh. At any rate, the comedy breaks up and the tragedy comes on.[7]

O'Neill directly confronting his own play's genre, seems to be describing the kind of tragicomedy Beckett gives us in *Godot*. Comedy veering toward tragedy, a difficult linkage which prods critical debate. There's no doubt that O'Neill considers *Iceman* finally to be a tragedy. A letter to Lawrence Langner (11 August 1940) makes this crystal clear: "There are moments in it that suddenly strip the soul of a man stark naked, not in cruelty or moral superiority, but with an understanding compassion which sees him as a victim of the ironies of life and of himself. Those moments are for me the depth of tragedy, with nothing more than can possibly be said." But he also knows – despite his tentative "*I think*" – that his dark play contains comedy, and it does, almost every kind of comedy: jokes of all kinds, especially sexual jokes; comic wordplay, including semantic differences (tart vs. whore); comic types (parasite, drunkard, trickster, braggart soldier); comic physical activity; clichéd comic participants in the battle of the sexes (shrewish wife, henpecked husband, cuckold). And, of course, his presentation of characters who are both comic and tragic help to complicate our response to the play. For example, how should we take Hickey – tragic protagonist or comic catalyst? O'Neill's description of him – a bald "*stout roly-poly figure*" with a "*salesman's winning smile of self-confident affability and hearty good fellowship*" – together with his glad hand, his singing, his verbal retorts, all suggest a comic character. Those waiting for him expect to laugh and drink; he will be the life of the party. The Hickey they knew belongs to a comic holiday world. The affable salesman who arrives does want to make them "happy," but he is selling death without realizing it. When he forces his buddies to face themselves, when he attempts to destroy their pipe dreams, they figuratively die. Even their whiskey has no kick. He shatters their contentment, their family feeling, by forcing them to face the truth of their lives. Larry Slade, on the other hand, understands that "the lie of a pipe dream is what gives life to the whole misbegotten lot of us." Larry's own pipe dream is that he is not involved with the others, that he's merely an observer of mankind, and that he wants to die. By play's end Larry, very much connected to Don Parritt, whom he sends to his death, loses his pipe dream and faces the truth about himself. In *Iceman* the truth means death. As Larry realizes, he is "the only real convert to death Hickey made here." Hickey, the truth-teller, has his own pipe dream, that he loved his wife, but this becomes shattered momentarily when he, during his long confessional speech taking fifteen minutes of stage time, reveals that he laughed when he killed his wife and said to her: "Well, you know what you can do with your pipe dream now, you damned bitch!" But this unconscious slip, revealing his deeply buried hatred and his desperate need to rid himself of his wife's forgiveness and his own guilt, does not lead him to face the truth about himself. "Good God, I couldn't have said that! If I did, I'd gone insane! Why, I loved Evelyn better than anything in life!" (III, 700). He leaves the stage with pipe dream intact. The derelicts, latching on to Hickey's insanity as the reason for his strange behavior, can sink back into their illusions about yesterday and tomorrow. At play's end they, again filled with pipe dream and alcohol, continue to survive in their self-contained "comic" world, whereas Hickey, also holding on to his pipe dream, is going to his death, and Parritt, having no pipe dream to sustain him, has committed suicide, and Larry is staring at death. Larry Slade, who throughout the play was the critical commentator, the old "Foolosopher" who functioned much like the Fool in Shakespearean comedy, who saw things with clear eyes and sardonic humor, emerges as the play's tragic character. When O'Neill says, "the comedy breaks up and the tragedy comes on," he is tracing both the mood of the play *and* the development of Larry Slade as a character. Before the final curtain drops on *Iceman* we hear the bums carousing and we see Larry, oblivious to the noise, facing the truth of things. We witness the life of illusion and the death of illusion, and we recognize that O'Neill's vision of life, tragic though it unquestionably is, contains the important dimension of comedy, thereby offering us, as do Beckett and Shakespeare, the deepest sense of reality.

After writing *Iceman* and while writing *Long Day's Journey* – these plays O'Neill's finest, both highly autobiographical, both blending the comic and tragic, both marathon plays, both observing the classical unities – O'Neill is working on a one-act play called *Hughie*. Set in the summer of 1928 between 3 am and 4 am in a dingy lobby of a third-rate hotel in midtown New York City, it can be considered a kind of epilogue to *Iceman* because here too contact between men must be made, illusions must be shared, in order for life to continue. The men on stage are Erie Smith, a Broadway sport, "a teller of tales," probably modelled in part on Jamie O'Neill, and a usually silent night clerk called Charles Hughes. The man that Erie talks about is the former night clerk, Hughie, now dead. We get to know all three men – Erie Smith through his talk, almost an extended monologue; Charles Hughes by way of O'Neill's stage directions which give us his inner thoughts; Hughie because of what is said about him by Erie and because of what Charles Hughes is. Perhaps we get to know most about Hughie "by way of obit," the collective title of a projected cycle of six one-act plays, with *Hughie* the only one completed. O'Neill effectively captures the depressing loneliness of men in a hostile city. The vigorous prose of his stage directions describes the chaotic sounds – garbage cans, fire engines, ambulance sirens, etc. – which shatter the city's forbidding early morning silence. Silence is the enemy to Charles Hughes because it means death to him, so he listens for, and internally responds to, the harsh sounds. Silence is the enemy to Erie Smith for the same reason, so he must talk and talk, even to an unwilling listener, just as he used to talk to Hughie, a willing listener and a man he grew to like and to need. For Erie the alternative to talk is to enter his hotel room, alone, to face the forbidding silence. Only at play's end is contact made between Erie and Hughes. They begin to play a crap game. The two men will get through the night, at least, with Charles Hughes becoming Hughie. Like the lost men in Harry Hope's saloon, they have traveled from isolation to union, from death to life. The final effect of the play depends on a delicate blending of the tragic and comic, a balancing act brilliantly performed by O'Neill in a one-act play that can stand proudly next to the one-act plays of Chekhov and Synge.

In the same year, 1940, that he wrote *Hughie*, not performed until 1958 in Sweden, 1964 in America, O'Neill wrote the play he had to write, *Long Day's Journey Into Night*, his most autobiographical play, in which he faces himself and his brother and father and mother most directly but still by way of his dramatic art. The task was painful, as the words of Carlotta O'Neill reveal: "When he started *Long Day's Journey* it was a most strange experience to watch that man being tortured every day by his own writing. He would come out of his study at the end of a day gaunt and sometimes weeping. His eyes would be all red and he looked ten years older than when he went in in the morning."[8] O'Neill's own words in his dedication of the play to Carlotta testify to the agony of his converting memory to theatre. The play was "written in tears and blood ... with deep pity and understanding and forgiveness for all the four haunted Tyrones." So personal was the play to O'Neill that he expressed the wish that it never be performed and that it not be published until twenty-five years after his death. Carlotta disregarded his request when she decided to give the play to the world in 1956, much to the chagrin of the dramatist's friends and the Random House publishers to whom the request was made. Justifiable or not, Carlotta's decision to have Quintero direct *Long Day's Journey* six months after he had directed his highly acclaimed *Iceman* absolutely ensured continuing admiration for the reborn O'Neill. Quintero's production, which opened on Broadway on 7 November 1956, received praise from almost all the reviewers and brought O'Neill a posthumous Pulitzer Prize, his fourth, thirty-six years after his first for *Beyond the Horizon*.

In *Long Day's Journey*, as in *Iceman*, O'Neill makes large demands on his audience, forcing it to listen to the talk of members of a family for four hours, stuck in a room, as we were stuck in Harry Hope's saloon for four hours, physically entrapped as the characters are entrapped. O'Neill observes the classical unities here, as in all of his last plays, incrementally offering us secrets of the past, progressively bringing us deeper into his characters. The play contains no exciting outward action, but two family events seem climactic: Mary Tyrone has returned to her dope addiction, and Edmund Tyrone (O'Neill's portrait of himself as a young man) learns that he has tuberculosis. O'Neill rivets our attention to what the characters are saying (as each Tyrone uncovers a little more of the past or modifies someone else's view of the past) and what the characters are feeling (as the rhythm of accusation-regret, harshness-pity, hate-love, beats throughout the play). The repetition of the rhythmic pattern and the familial picking on the same sore of who is to blame – as well as the repetition of sounds and gestures and movements and words – perfectly reflect the play's main theme that "the past is the present," to use Mary's phrase.

The play's passing time can be measured by the extent of each character's withdrawal into self and need to reveal that self. In more commonplace terms, the time can be measured by the family's gathering for breakfast (Act 1), lunch (Act 2), dinner (Act 3), bedtime (Act 4). The flow of time can also be felt by the increasing darkness of the day and the thickening of the atmosphere. The increasing darkness and the developing fog outside – punctuated by the sound of the foghorn – will make the Tyrone house seem more and more isolated, with the family alone inside to face each other. Each member of the family will be alone as well. Isolation within isolation, but, at the same time, isolation within a togetherness because the family remains a family, listening to each other's accusations and complaints and regrets. As the play journeys into night, time will be moving toward revelations and confessions, but the circles of repetition will also be felt, resulting in a strange kind of stalemate, similar to the sense of frozen time an audience experiences in *Iceman* and *Godot*.

Throughout *Long Day's Journey* the present and the past have come together in the search for the cause of the present misery. Each Tyrone gives a heart-rending account of the past. James Tyrone tells about the poverty that made him a miser and caused him to latch on to the money-making play, *The Count of Monte Cristo*, which destroyed his considerable talent; he "could have been a great Shakespearean actor." Edmund reflects on his days at sea, a mystical experience, where "for a second you see – and seeing the secret, are the secret." He claims that "it was a great mistake, my being born a man, I would have been much more successful as a sea gull or a fish. As it is, I will always be a stranger who never feels at home, who does not really want and is not really wanted, who can never belong, who must always be a little in love with death!" (III, 812). The cynical and most lost of the Tyrones, Jamie, tells of his great dependence on his mother, how his drinking is connected to his mother's drug addiction – "I'd begun to hope, if she'd beaten the game, I could, too." He recalls the moment he first saw her "in the act with a hypo. Christ, I'd never dreamed before that any women but whores took dope!" (III, 818). And he reveals that he hates his brother, a hatred also connected with his feelings about Mama: "And it was your being born that started Mama on dope. I know that's not your fault, but all the same, God damn you, I can't help hating your guts!" (III, 820). This immediately followed by, "I love you more than I hate you." And Mary Tyrone tells of her early days when she thought she'd be a nun or a concert pianist, but then she met the dashing actor James Tyrone and her life was changed forever. Each Tyrone informs us about a past for which each is and is not responsible. The hellish life each lives now has been made by the past they all helped and did not help to make. Mary Tyrone's words on life's strange determinism ring true: "None of us can help the things life has done to us. They're done before you realize it, and once they're done they make you do other things until at last everything comes between you and what you'd like to be, and you've lost your true self forever" (III, 749). She sensitively touches this important idea again when she tells her husband, "James! We've loved each other! We always will! Let's remember only that, and not try to understand what we cannot understand, or help things that cannot be helped – the things life has done to us we cannot excuse or explain" (III, 764).

That the Tyrones try to understand the past, that they listen to one another, that they endure together, is the measure of their heroism. We share in their experience because it is a significantly lived experience, complex and deep and passionate, mirroring the experience of all of us. We all are to blame and not to blame for the "now" of our lives; we all await helplessly the approach of our nights. The plight of the Tyrones is presented with such directness and truth that they, isolated in their fog-bound New London home on an August day in 1912, come to represent every loving-hating family, close and far apart, together and alone, vulnerable and heroic, enmeshed in a tragic net.

The universal quality of the play must be stressed because too often *Long Day's Journey* is approached almost exclusively by way of autobiography. Yes, we get to know O'Neill the man because he was courageous enough to face his dead and because the very writing of the play served his personal need for atonement and forgiveness. Yes, the raw material of his life is placed before us in the text and on the boards, and he has gone more deeply into himself and his family than ever before. But *Long Day's Journey* is the product of a shaping creative imagination; it is great art. If it were anonymous, we would still feel the presence of the dramatist in his work because the play itself contains such personal intensity, such tragic feeling. It is interesting, even heart-rending, to learn about the personal agony of O'Neill and his family, but it is not of the highest importance. The Tyrones are Everyfamily; their experience is universal. The love-hate within a family, the closeness-distance, the loneliness within a togetherness, the guilt and need for forgiveness, the knowing and not knowing a loved one, the bewilderment in the face of a mysterious determinism – this is the human condition, so remarkably dramatized by O'Neill in America's finest play. Has any other American dramatist created so haunting a scene as we experience in the last minutes of *Long Day's Journey*? The three men are sitting in that ever-darkening living room, sharing the death of hope, the agony of loss, as they helplessly watch the center of their lives, Mary, enter the room. In her dope dream she is completely separated from the men, as she recalls her past, and ends the play with the by-now famous words: "That was in the winter of senior year. Then in the spring something happened to me. Yes, I remember. I fell in love with James Tyrone and was so happy for a time." At that moment, just before the final curtain, O'Neill's stage directions tells us that *"Tyrone stirs in his chair"* while *"Edmund and Jamie remain motionless."* Tyrone stirs, of course, because he was directly involved in that past. The sons remain completely frozen because they were not part of that particular past when "something happened" to Mary. But all are involved *now*, as they helplessly watch this precious woman who is taking leave of them. They watch; they endure. They do not leave the room that has imprisoned them, and we the audience

– the extended family – also remain frozen in that larger room, the theatre, as we helplessly watch the three Tyrone men watch the lost Mary. The dramatic moment, the stage action, takes in actors and audience. The human bond seems to transcend the stage, and this feeling, this personal feeling, that we are participating in the agony of the Tyrones, responding in pity and fear, but unable to do anything, touches the very heart of tragedy.

In *A Moon for the Misbegotten*, his last play, O'Neill continues the story of Jamie Tyrone, thereby satisfying a personal need to give his brother more "deep pity and forgiveness and understanding" than he received in *Long Day's Journey*, *Misbegotten* (written in 1943, produced on Broadway in 1957) can be considered an epilogue to *Long Day's Journey*, just as *Hughie* was an "epilogue" to *Iceman*. (It seems that O'Neill could not easily break away from his two most autobiographical plays, attaching to each another play.) He sets *Misbegotten* in the autumn of 1923, the year of Jamie O'Neill's death, eleven years after the summer of 1912, when we heard Jamie's confession to Edmund, a confession which revealed the agony of a son closely attached to a mother. In *Misbegotten* Jamie – now James Tyrone Jr., called Jim – again reveals his deep love for his mother, his feeling of guilt because he betrayed that love, and his need for a mother-substitute. O'Neill, allowing his play to fulfill a wish that had no relation to autobiographical reality, gives Jamie Tyrone a peaceful death. Jamie O'Neill died in a sanatorium of cerebral apoplexy, nearly blind and mad from too much alcohol. In *Misbegotten* he goes gentle into that good night.

Like the other plays of O'Neill's last period, *Misbegotten*, besides being autobiographical, observes the unities of place, time, and action, it treats family relations, and it is both comic and tragic. However, here the setting is not an enclosed room or dark saloon or hotel lobby but out-of-doors, in front of the dilapidated Hogan farmhouse in Connecticut. The play's time moves from noon (Act 1) to night (Acts 2 and 3) to dawn (Act 4). In both outdoor setting and time O'Neill is touching comedy. Beginning in laughter on a clear hot day, the play moves to a moonlit night filled with dark tragic lyricism, and ends in the dawn of a new day. Death is a strong focus of the play, as always with O'Neill, but the dark is balanced against the light, O'Neill himself referring to the play as "a fine unusual tragic comedy."[9] The laughter of the play's beginning stems from the Irishness of the three main characters – Jim (a drinker, still possessing some of his youthful "*Irish charm*," very much the son of a father who thought that Shakespeare was Irish Catholic); Phil Hogan (who likes his whiskey and speaks "*with a pronounced brogue*"); Josie Hogan ("*the map of Ireland is stamped on her face*"). They confront and baffle the Yankee, T. Stedman Harder, in a scene filled with Irish earthiness and linguistic playfulness, with O'Neill's comic writing so effective it brings to mind Synge. Still, even the comedy of Act I cannot erase that first image of Jim, described by Josie, as he's walking up the road: "Look at him when he thinks no one is watching, with his eyes on the ground. Like a dead man walking slow behind his own coffin" (III, 874). The description is apt. Jim Tyrone is spiritually dead and physically drinking himself to death because of a great burden of mind, which he eventually reveals to Josie in Act 3, the play's tender and lyrical climax. Under the moon, sitting on the steps of the farmhouse, with his head on Josie's ample bosom, Jim Tyrone makes his agonizing confession to Josie, telling a story that holds autobiographical truth. Jim reveals his deep affection for his mother and his dependence on her. When she gave up her dope, he gave up his drink, but when she was dying he began drinking again, and this filled him with guilt because his mother saw that he had returned to drink. When she died, he brought her body back to New York from California, where they were living together, and on the train carrying his mother's coffin he slept every night with a blonde hooker. This act – prodded by dark Oedipal urges and by "revenge" against his mother for leaving him – causes his deepest guilt. He needs his mother's forgiveness, but she is dead. Josie, recognizing Jim's desperation and realizing that he is really a dead man who needs a mother more than he needs a lover, becomes Jim's mother: "... I do forgive! ... As *she* forgives, do you hear me! As *she* loves and understands and forgives!" She then speaks of a dawn that "will wake in the sky like a promise of God's peace in the soul's dark sadness" (III, 933). That is the dawn of the next day, of the last act, but now in moonlight, Jim asleep, his face *"calm with the drained, exhausted peace of death,"* Josie holds him tightly – a memorable stage image. Comedy and tragedy have led us to this point, and here O'Neill has created his Pietà. Josie Hogan – grounded in reality, an earth woman, strong and sensitive, the virgin playing the whore, lover and mother, feisty Irish daughter and Virgin Mary – here acquires mythic proportions; surely, she is O'Neill's most powerful and sympathetic creation of a woman.

At play's end, after Jim leaves the stage, walking back down the road, still following his own coffin, but now prepared to die, now the reborn child having been forgiven, at peace with himself, Josie offers these words of benediction: "May you have your wish and die in your sleep soon, Jim, darling. May you rest forever in forgiveness and peace." She then goes to the door of her house, ready to continue her life with father, returning us to comedy in the large sense, an affirmation of life. The door of the Hogan farmhouse bears no resemblance to the door Lavinia Mannon closed behind her to face, as O'Neill faced, the ghosts of the dead, nor is it like the doors of O'Neill's last plays – the door Con Melody closes behind him when he enters the tavern in a world of ordinary men, or the door to the fearful outside world in *The Iceman Cometh*, or the door to the silent room that Erie Smith is afraid to open in *Hughie*, or the door to Mary Tyrone's upstairs room where she escapes the world with her drugs. The ending of *Misbegotten* is sad but positive, with O'Neill offering a final blessing to his brother and perhaps to himself as life goes on. The life that went on for O'Neill the dramatist was not a "happy" one, to use a charged O'Neill word. Of course, he did not know that *A Moon for the Misbegotten* would be his last play. His fertile imagination was always at work, with new plays conceived in his mind, but his hands couldn't stop shaking, his body couldn't accommodate his mind. He officially died ten years after writing *Misbegotten* but he was no longer really alive when he couldn't write. Still, O'Neill's last plays seem so right as last plays, seem so perfect "by way of obit," that perhaps the body was responding to impulses of the soul that were deeper than even O'Neill, that gazer into abysses, could realize.

In these last plays O'Neill fully displays his instinctive knowledge of what works in the theatre. Stripped of the theatrical devices of his experimental plays, the late plays are products of a realistic imagination working with sound and silence and light and gesture and movement and setting to produce highly emotive situations. These are essentially naked plays offering us "a drama of souls,"[10] appealing to our emotions, with O'Neill's dramatic art uncannily turning his compassion and understanding to our compassion and understanding. So intense in his personal commitment to what he is dramatizing, so sincere is his attempt to express the frustrations of our lives, the mystery of the force behind, the absurdity and sadness of our condition, that his own feelings seem palpable. Always aware that the darkly inexpressible cannot be expressed, giving voice to the inadequacy of language and to his own inadequacy through the words of Edmund Tyrone: "I couldn't touch what I tried to tell you just now. I just stammered. That's the best I'll ever do, I mean if I live. Well, it will be faithful realism, at least. Stammering is the native eloquence of us fog people." He nevertheless managed in his best work, and certainly in his last plays, to produce works of art that can stand with the very best in modern drama.

NOTES

1 O'Neill, quoted in Louis Sheaffer, *O'Neill: Son and Artist* (Boston: Little, Brown, 1973), p. 577.

2 Travis Bogard makes perceptive use of the "mirror" idea throughout *Contour in Time: The Plays of Eugene O'Neill* (New York: Oxford University Press, 1972). I discuss Con Melody's mirror in relation to the mirrors in Shakespeare in *O'Neill's Shakespeare* (Ann Arbor: University of Michigan Press, 1993), pp. 145–48.

3 Michael Manheim offers insightful discussion of the autobiographical dimension of *More Stately Mansions* in *Eugene O'Neill's New Language of Kinship* (Syracuse, New York: Syracuse University Press, 1982), pp. 18–19.

4 *More Stately Mansions*, vol. III, page 528. All quotations from O'Neill's last plays will come from volume III of *O'Neill: Complete Plays*, edited by Travis Bogard, published by the Library of America, New York, 1988. Hereafter all citations will appear in the essay, specifying volume number and page number.

5 Nichols, quoted in Arthur and Barbara Gelb, *O'Neill* (New York: Harper and Row, 1962), p. 831.

6 Harold Bloom, *Eugene O'Neill's 'The Iceman Cometh'* (New York: Chelsea House, 1987), p. 4. Juxtaposing Bloom's view of *Iceman*, as presented in his Introduction to this collection of essays, and my view, as found in the last chapter of by *Eugene O'Neill* (New York: St. Martin's Press, 1982), excerpted in Bloom, helps to illuminate the problematic nature of O'Neill's great play.

7 O'Neill, quoted in Sheaffer, *Artist*, p. 577.

8 Carlotta O'Neill, quoted in Sheaffer, *Artist*, p. 505.

9 O'Neill, quoted in Virginia Floyd, *The Plays of Eugene O'Neill* (New York: Frederick Ungar, 1985), p. 580.

10 O'Neill, phrase found in "Memoranda on Masks," in Oscar Cargill, N. Bryllion Fagin, and William Fisher (eds.), *O'Neill and his Plays* (New York: New York University Press, 1961), p. 116.

7

RONALD WAINSCOTT

Notable American stage productions

When attempting to select the important American productions of the plays of Eugene O'Neill, I was struck by the unavoidable conflicting views of what should make a production of a play significant in presenting a capsule stage history of the work of one of our most enduring playwrights. How important are the first productions of a play compared to revivals since the production personnel were the first to attempt to solve the problems of the plays? Yet some later efforts were clearly more finished or exciting. Furthermore, if a first production occurred while O'Neill was still living he often participated in production. And what of plays which are revived professionally nearly every year, like *Long Day's Journey Into Night* or *Ah, Wilderness!* versus important but only occasionally revived plays like *Anna Christie* or *The Great God Brown*? What of popularity versus critical approval? And what of the literary value of the play? Is a clear but uninspiring production of *Mourning Becomes Electra* more important than a fascinating interpretation of *Welded*? What of early amateur stagings of plays before 1920, many of which contributed to the notoriety of O'Neill before Broadway productions? Most of them were poorly acted and directed. Nonetheless, some of these productions caught the imagination of reviewers and artists and opened the door to O'Neill's professional career.

Obviously, I have tried to include all great or near-great productions of the most exciting and influential plays, but I have also included important examples of the other types outlined above to present a sense of the sweep, variety and ongoing remarkable volume of O'Neill productions which have graced the American theatre since 1916. All productions discussed are professional productions except for important plays which were first produced by amateur organizations like the Provincetown Players, Washington Square Players or the Pasadena Playhouse. Because the sweep of productions extends from 1916 to the 1990s, it is not possible, though it is tempting, to linger long with any one production. I will discuss O'Neill's plays as they appeared in first production chronologically, but if I treat more than one production of a play, the subsequent productions will be discussed after the first, before I go on to the next play.

Bound East for Cardiff is important because it was first. In the second summer season at the ramshackle Wharf Theatre in Provincetown, Massachusetts, O'Neill had his first performance for a small audience watching the efforts of the inventive and intrepid Provincetown Players, a group of intelligent amateurs led by George Cram Cook, who played the dying character of Yank. Opening on 28 July 1916 on a bill with other one-acts, this sea play was stunning in its evocation of haunting mood and sustained emotionally. Apparently the production was directed by O'Neill and E. J. Ballantine, who also played Cocky. Direction or co-direction by the playwright was common in the early days of Provincetown since it was the company's philosophy to have the play interpreted precisely as the playwright desired. It was clear to O'Neill early on, however, that he was not inclined to direct his own work. He also had no gift for acting, but like so many of the early Provincetown productions, it was necessary for him to appear in small roles from time to time as he did in *Bound East* both in July and later in New York and also in his own *Thirst* (1916) and *Before Breakfast* (1916). The setting of *Bound East* was extremely simple, created by three tiers of stacked bunks with cloth hangings above to suggest the sleeping quarters in the forecastle of a tramp steamer, a location to which O'Neill would often return.

Bound East was repeated in New York on 3 November at the Provincetowners' new venue, the Playwrights' Theatre in Greenwich Village. It appears that the production had much of the same cast and direction, but this time O'Neill's work started reaching a larger audience and important members of the theatrical/critical community. This was also the first New York production for any O'Neill play, and although not an overnight sensation, was instrumental in calling attention to the efforts of the Provincetown Players.

Bound East also appeared periodically when four of the early sea plays were collected as *S.S. Glencairn*, first produced together professionally on 3 November 1924, the eighth anniversary of O'Neill's New York premiere, at the restructured Provincetown, now known as Experimental Theatre, Inc. Directed by James Light, who was the first to stage many O'Neill plays, *Bound East* was performed last in the series, and appropriately so, since Yank dies in his bunk while hallucinating at the climax. This production, which also included *The Moon of the Caribbees*, *The Long Voyage Home*, and *In the Zone*, inspired many subsequent revivals of the sea plays.

Some of O'Neill's plays received much better direction beginning in 1917 when Nina Moise joined the Provincetowners. Unfortunately her efforts at improving staging and ensemble work were in the service of plays which were not among O'Neill's best one-act efforts: *The Sniper*, *Ile*, and *The Rope* (1918). *The Long Voyage Home* (produced in 1917 after Moise's arrival) was performed in a set so horribly executed that it could stand as an exemplar of the worst aspects of some amateur theatre, but this uncredited production was not hers. Curiously, given the subject matter and period, five of the early O'Neill productions were directed by women, with Ida Rauh staging *Where the Cross Is Made* (1918) and *The Dreamy Kid* (1919). It would be many years before a woman directed O'Neill in the professional American theatre.

The first professional productions of an O'Neill play stemmed from the mountings on 31 October 1917 of *In the Zone* by the Washington Square Players. Although this was an amateur theatre, it got considerable attention from the press for its theatrical experiments. Throughout 1918 the play appeared in the professional vaudeville circuit (a staging scheme similar to the original *Bound East for Cardiff* was used), and was viewed as timely due to the war references in the play. *In the Zone* joined the *Glencairn* plays in 1924.

The Moon of the Caribbees, the longest of the *Glencairn* plays, and a perfect evocation of mood, opened under the aegis of the Provincetowners on 20 December 1918 and caught the attention of director Arthur Hopkins, critic George Jean Nathan, and John Williams, who would first produce *Beyond the Horizon*. The production featured Charles Ellis as Smitty, an actor who performed in many O'Neill productions, most notably *Desire Under the Elms*. The *Glencairn* plays have reappeared periodically in professional theatres, most significantly with the Federal Theatre Project in 1937 with an all-black cast led by Canada Lee as Yank. It also gained critical attention in 1977 at the Long Wharf Theatre in New Haven, Connecticut, but was last seen in major presentation in New York in 1948 in a José Ferrer production.

The first production of *Beyond the Horizon* (3 February 1920) was remarkably important for O'Neill's career as his first full-length play to get professional presentation, but was a sad example of theatrical methods of the period. Producer John D. Williams was unwilling to risk a regular opening and had director Homer Saint-Gaudens open the play in trial matinees in poorly executed stock scenery with a makeshift cast from two other productions running at night. It was fortunate for O'Neill that a very experienced actor, Richard Bennett, was playing Robert Mayo and coaching the other actors, and that critics and audiences could hear and sense what was startling and moving in this American tragedy of misalliance and shelved dreams. Because the critical and popular reception were so strong, the production was partially recast, spruced up scenically, though never effectively, and reopened for a regular run. One of the biggest problems of this production was a failure to solve the need to shift regularly and rhythmically from exterior to interior without awful delays which spoiled the development of the action.

A 1926 revival by Actors' Theatre directed by James Light fixed the scenic problems with quick-shifting, jack-knife scenery on wagons designed by Cleon Throckmorton. The role of Robert Mayo was this time taken by Robert Keith who was the first to create Dion Anthony earlier in the year in *The Great God Brown*. A 1974 revival of *Beyond the Horizon* directed by Michael Kahn at the McCarter Theatre in New Jersey further simplified the interior/exterior problem by utilizing a stylized, framework setting which could accommodate the shifting locales simultaneously, more like Lee Simonson's skeletal 1929 interpretation of *Dynamo*. Although *Beyond the Horizon* has long been considered important to the career and development of O'Neill, its professional revivals are rare and its realism less enduring than that of *Anna Christie* or the late realistic plays like *Moon for the Misbegotten*.

Few plays by O'Neill have garnered more attention than his experimental *The Emperor Jones*. The 1 November 1920 production directed by George Cram Cook and designed by Cleon Throckmorton was the first Provincetown production to make the journey to a Broadway run and helped to transform the original mission of that little theatre. Although Cook was not a particularly talented director, his intuitive, visionary, if undisciplined choices were very apt for this play. His insistence on equipping the Playwrights' Theatre with a permanent concrete skydome lent *The Emperor Jones* an apparent endless depth of field and enchanting lighting possibilities, which were no small part of the play's success. Most dynamic, however, was the brave casting of Charles Gilpin, an African–American actor, in the leading role of Brutus Jones (despite the absurd fact that white actors took the supporting and incidental black roles).

Clearly, this play taxed the production methods of the American theatre, and the choices made by Cook and Throckmorton not only provided imaginative visual interpretations, but simple ones which coaxed stage design in America toward three-dimensional evocations of the New Stagecraft's expanses of color and moody lighting which since 1915 had usually been defined in predominantly two-dimensional scenic presentations. Perhaps the production's most dynamic visual impact, however, was felt in its nearly perfect creation of nightmare aesthetics and mysterious tableaux which dramatically arose from the imagination, terror and dreams of the protagonist. The nightmare was enhanced by aural counterpoint of incessant offstage drumming that ultimately affected the audience's sensibilities as strongly as anything else, with the possible exception of Gilpin's extraordinary tour-de-force acting. His vocally scintillating depiction of out-of-control arrogance mixed with his powerful display of the agony and horror resulting from centuries of institutional racism, left many who witnessed his performances either emotionally drained or remarkably exhilarated. This production stands as one of a handful of productions which defined the best of American theatrical experiment between the world wars.

Although this play has had important and technically proficient revivals, none has generated the critical and popular excitement of the original. Paul Robeson recreated a physically powerful and vocally stunning Brutus Jones with Experimental Theatre, Inc. on 6 May 1924 for a limited run under the direction of James Light, before opening as the young African–American in *All God's Chillun Got Wings*. On 16 February 1926, this time under the direction of James Light, Gilpin returned to the Provincetown space to revisit the role which he periodically toured. *The Emperor Jones* has also found its way to traditional radio and film interpretations throughout the century with such performers as Robeson and James Earl Jones, but finally reached something of a deconstructed, de-textualized, post-modern apotheosis with the Wooster Group on 24 March 1994 at their New York Performance Garage under the direction of Elizabeth LeCompte and starring Kate Valk. In our own time the once startling, but subsequently antique (at least in racial terms), *The Emperor Jones* has re-entered the avant-garde.

In the months following the premiere of *The Emperor Jones* New Yorkers saw a serviceable Provincetown production of a mediocre effort, *Diff'rent* (27 December 1920), and a perfectly horrid production (again by John Williams) on 1 June 1921 of *Gold*, a full-length play unwisely elongated from an earlier one-act, *Where the Cross Is Made*. Five months later, however, one of O'Neill's most enduring plays, *Anna Christie*, opened under the direction of Arthur Hopkins. This production (2 November 1921) benefited from arguably the most efficient and sensitive directing any O'Neill play received in the 1920s, as well as superb performance from Pauline Lord in the title role and moody, almost mysterious settings from Robert Edmond Jones in his first of nine productions with O'Neill.

In a much inferior form, this play had first been presented by producer George C. Tyler as *Chris Christophersen* in 1920, but both play and production suffered from overproduced settings and an underdeveloped Anna horribly miscast with prim Lynn Fontanne. This production closed out of town, and uncharacteristically, O'Neill rewrote the play and was lucky to secure Hopkins as producer–director.

In the Hopkins production the waterfront saloon setting with its playing area split between male bar and "family" back room was lauded in the press for its perfectly authentic environment from pre-Prohibition days. Yet the decorative details were selective rather than complete, a practice typical of Jones whose lighting in the saloon created a sense of grayed-out light from filthy windows which lent the space an eerie, almost magical quality. Hopkins's penchant for orchestrating simultaneous action with the actors was easily achieved in such a space. Subsequent scenes in a confined barge cabin, and topside in the night fog, enhanced the intimacy and violence of the mid and late scenes of the play.

It was Lord's interpretation of Anna, however, which stamped this production with unusual power. The image of this actress in the role was difficult to replace; in fact was not equaled or surpassed until late in the century. Her presentation of the nervous, often barely articulate, desperate woman was virtually hypnotic on the audiences who witnessed her fervent and charismatic display. This highly emotional and intuitive actress is arguably the first to start capturing fully the frightened, half-revealing, lost soul of so many O'Neill characters, some of whom have been more fully developed in post-1950 performances. Before World War II O'Neill productions were usually most fully realized in direction and design. Since that time the focus has shifted to actors and the directors who encourage or enhance the power of the actor.

Despite the splendid production, O'Neill strongly objected to what he saw as Hopkins's interpretation of the final moments of the play as a happy ending. It was very difficult for an American audience at the time, however, to ferret out the subtlety, as is barely implied by the text, that the future of Matt and Anna may be doomed. Most of the serious plays which graced Broadway stages in the early 1920s were melodramas with obvious happy endings or unambiguous tragedy or dramas of destruction like *Beyond the Horizon* and *The Emperor Jones*. Near the end of the 1920s, ambiguity was making its way more successfully onto the American stage.

Lord's defining interpretation of Anna was not seriously challenged on the American stage until 1993 despite José Quintero's casting of a real Scandinavian, Liv Ullman, opposite a dirty and tattooed, young John Lithgow on 14 April 1977. This Broadway production featured an unusual unit set for the last three acts, combining the cabin interior with the deck of the barge, thus opening up both locations to expansive staging. Although practical for effecting variety in use of the space, Ben Edwards' settings violated the confining, almost claustrophobic nature of the last two acts.

More importantly, the performances of Ullman and Lithgow remained too decorous and polite to create the edge which the play demands. Audiences and critics were more intrigued with seeing a famous star than getting involved with the world of Anna.

It was the stunning sensuality and consistent toughness of Natasha Richardson as Anna on 14 January 1993, however, which has provided an *Anna Christie* that fully exploited for late-century audiences the sexual power and emotional yearning of O'Neill's most fully drawn fallen woman. With the Roundabout Theatre Company and orchestrated by director David Leveaux, this production focused less on Anna as victim and her sea-obsessed father Chris (here played by Rip Torn) and more on the unsentimental passion so mercurially displayed by Richardson, and on Liam Neeson's strong but boyish and very virile Mat. The erotic in this play was finally unleashed, and the "happy ending" was modified by opening the setting to a final vision of gloomy mist from the sea. Much of the production as designed by John Lee Beatty was underscored by considerable fog.

The first *Anna Christie* was followed eight days later (10 November 1921) by a disappointing production by George C. Tyler of the sad tuberculosis play *The Straw*. Then just five days before *The Hairy Ape*, another failure, *The First Man* (4 March 1922), premiered under the direction of Augustin Duncan at the Neighborhood Playhouse. Both poor productions were quickly forgotten, however, when on 9 March 1922 the Provincetown Players produced their final O'Neill premiere, *The Hairy Ape*. Under the direction of James Light (overseen by Arthur Hopkins who moved it to Broadway) this fully expressionistic nightmare journey seemed to explode from the tiny downtown stage, due largely to the violent performance of Louis Wolheim as Yank, the open brawls of the stokers, the mechanized choric action of the socialites on Fifth Avenue, and periodic cacophonous voices and sound effects. Wolheim's overwhelming brutish physical and vocal power, as well as his profound ability to reveal the loneliness and suffering in Yank, alternately repelled and fascinated the audience. The stunning production captured the violence, cynicism, and anguish of this early American expressionistic play.

Co-designed by Cleon Throckmorton and Robert Edmond Jones, the settings featured angularity, fragmentation, and distortion – but recognizable locations. Most of the late scenes, however, heightened stylization, which helped to accentuate the destruction of the protagonist. The play as produced enhanced the expressionistic device of distorted scenery as a reflection of the anxiety of the central character. Although not called for in the text, the production put masks designed by Blanche Hays on the chorus of socialites, introducing a device to which O'Neill would return in four subsequent plays.

Although *The Hairy Ape* has enjoyed many important European revivals and numerous university productions, the play has had a limited American professional record since the premiere. Nonetheless, the play has received occasional productions in regional theatres, such as the Pittsburgh Public Theatre in 1987, which had an African–American as Yank and a racially mixed cast directed by George Ferencz, with percussive jazz music by Max Roach. Most recently, the play has undergone another avant-garde transformation in an adaptation by the Wooster Group in 1995 – which was performed in New York with Willem Dafoe in 1997.

O'Neill shifted his allegiance to the new Experimental Theatre, Inc. in late 1923 where his next six plays premiered. The first of these, *Welded* (17 March 1924), was directed by critic Stark Young and designed by Robert Edmond Jones. Although some scenes were imaginatively staged with effective stage pictures, side-by-side crosstalk, and experimental pauses, the love/hate dialogue was so excessive and the casting of the leading roles so inappropriate, that the self-conscious play had little chance of success. Rarely revived after audiences made fun of the original, *Welded* was nonetheless attempted by José Quintero on 10 June 1981 in a bungled effort to straddle a workshop atmosphere with finished production, combining stylization (a staircase to nowhere) and a sense of reality. The cast, headed by Philip Anglim as Michael Cape, suffered anxieties similar to those of the original production, and audiences and critics were just as condemning as those of 1924.

On 15 May 1924 O'Neill taxed censorship laws and racial bigotry with *All God's Chillun Got Wings*, produced by Experimental Theatre, Inc. Once again James Light and Cleon Throckmorton collaborated to create in the opening scenes an angular city exterior at the cross-roads of black and white living quarters. Subsequent settings, however, did not live up to the spatial demands of the play. This mixed success with the scenery was typical of the direction as well, which was irritatingly uneven. The mixed-race married couple was played by statuesque, deep-voiced Paul Robeson and tiny, emotional Mary Blair. Robeson, the second African–American to create an O'Neill character, presented a powerful presence and moving anxiety which underscored the suffering of Jim Harris. Mary Blair, however, was only effective in her emotional outbursts after the character of Ella spirals into madness. The group scenes sometimes created startling effects, but at other times managed only pedestrian execution. What got more attention than the produced play was the opening scene written for and rehearsed with children in the leading roles. Local government would not allow this in a mixed cast show and refused to license the use of children (apparently hoping to stop the production). Instead the director read the first scene to the audience on opening night; for subsequent performances the stage manager read the scene before shifting to dramatized action. The bigoted outcry and sensationalism surrounding the miscegenation outstripped the company's efforts to interpret the play.

American revival has been rare with this play which is now seen as too dated in its racial presentation. George C. Scott attempted reviving it on 20 March 1975 at Circle in the Square. With Robert Christian and Trish Van Devere in the leading roles, the action which was once so disturbing, now fairly bored audiences due largely to unimaginative direction (except for unexpected levels of violence between Jim and Ella). Scott's first directional effort, it was found by many to be marred by casting his own wife (a neophyte to the professional stage) as Ella. Critics found Van Devere physically attractive but emotionally and vocally bland. Ming Cho Lee's setting of the interior of the last scenes of the play attempted to capture O'Neill's request for a shrinking room by having the ceiling periodically lowered. Although the performances were critically panned, critics nearly unanimously claimed that even had the production been effective, the play no longer spoke to the social problems it was intended to address.

One of the most sensational of O'Neill's plays, both in disturbing subject matter and ongoing popular successes has been *Desire Under the Elms*, which premiered 11 November 1924 with Experimental Theatre, Inc. Directed as well as designed by Robert Edmond Jones, this experiment in space and mood called for simultaneous interior/exterior locations within a unit set which in this first production utilized movable walls so that the exterior of the New England farmhouse could dominate the stage when interiors were not necessary. The advantage of having removable walls allowed the mysterious, ghostly parlor to remain hidden until it was needed for the seduction of Eben by Abbie. The downside of this choice was a delay in removing and restoring wall units throughout the performance.

The Cabot house in 1924 was placed as close to the audience as the proscenium would allow. Some critics complained that the action was uncomfortably close, which was probably the point. Tall elm trees (mostly seen as foliage) stood as sentinels beside the house, which in its ordinariness created earthy counterpoint for the volatile sexual repression, sexual outbursts, greed and excruciating anguish performed effectively and disturbingly by Mary Morris as Abbie and Charles Ellis as Eben. It was the Ephraim Cabot of Walter Huston, however, which most fascinated audiences with his rock-hard, angry personality and inflexible manner. The results resonated like the audience responses to Pauline Lord, Charles

Gilpin and Louis Wolheim before him. Although this play and production also aroused would-be censors, who attempted to close the production as a work of obscenity once it moved to a Broadway house, the 1924 *Desire Under the Elms*, along with Hopkins' *Anna Christie*, stands as the most complete interpretation of O'Neill before his Theatre Guild years.

Desire Under the Elms had a traditional revival opening 16 January 1952, directed by Harold Clurman and designed by Mordecai Gorelik with Karl Malden as Ephraim Cabot. Once again two levels with removable walls were utilized with minor variations from the original. When José Quintero revived the play (8 January 1963), however, the theatre itself necessitated reconceiving some of *Desire*'s central images. At Circle in the Square, the use of a thrust stage eliminated the farmhouse altogether. With set and lights designed by David Hays, Quintero opened all the action in a fluid movement with the house activity generally upstage and the outside scenes downstage, with the kitchen party and dancing changed to an exterior scene. Most definitions of space were achieved with lights. Except for leaf projections, no elm trees were in sight. Critics were split in their assessment of these choices. It is clear that the staging was intriguing to watch, but thematically and symbolically much was lost. The fiery performances of George C. Scott as Ephraim and Colleen Dewhurst as Abbie were especially riveting, although the intimacy of the space made many audience members feel uncomfortable, just as they had in 1924. This production, along with *Moon for the Misbegotten*, cemented Dewhurst as one of the two leading acting voices for O'Neill in the post-war theatre. Rip Torn's Eben also was the first of several forays for this intriguing actor with O'Neill revivals. Since 1963 *Desire Under the Elms* has been revived by most regional theatres across the country.

The casting of Walter Huston as the protagonist could not save *The Fountain* in 1925, but this was followed by one of O'Neill's most mysterious and difficult-to-interpret experiments, *The Great God Brown*. Opening on 23 January 1926, this experiment with masks was again directed and designed by Robert Edmond Jones for Experimental Theatre, Inc. Although the audience was often confused by O'Neill's inconsistent, even contradictory uses of masks, they remained fascinated with the playwright's most challenging flight into the theatrical ether. O'Neill was lucky to have such an intuitive director as Jones who also brought his artistic skills to bear in creating two-dimensional, emblematic drops for each setting surmounted by real but selective furniture, which allowed the action to be placed realistically, but in isolated pools of space. The entire production had a dream-like presentation which supported the stylized activity with mask removal and exchange so startling in each new phase of the Dionysian play. The masks, designed by James Light, were sometimes problematic since they were full face masks, which sometimes distorted sound. How to execute the masks has been a recurring problem in subsequent productions. It is significant that the only remaining mask play professionally produced in O'Neill's lifetime was *Days Without End*, which used a half-mask, leaving the mouth area completely free.

The play's complexity and confusing mask work have probably contributed to *The Great God Brown* having only occasional revivals. Stuart Vaughan directed it for the Phoenix Theatre Company, which opened it on 6 October 1959 with Fritz Weaver as Dion and Robert Lansing as Brown in what may have been the finest production of this play. Performed on mobile platforms in moody, ghostly lighting, this energetic and extremely emotional interpretation captured the torment of the action and solved the vocal difficulties experienced in the first production by utilizing half-masks which left the actors' mouths free. Although there was high praise for this production, critics and audiences continued to be frustrated by the play.

When Harold Prince revived it for the revitalized Phoenix on 10 December 1972, the period was updated in a busy design by Boris Aronson. The mask work was altered yet again, this time using oversize, clear plastic, hand-held masks with cartoon-like visages. Many found the choice silly or pretentious, and always awkward, especially since gesture was severely curtailed. John Glover's performance as Brown, however, was stunning.

In 1928 O'Neill moved to the Theatre Guild for his base of operations and the first outing was a marvelous display of sweeping staging and beautiful designs all in service of a minor play with grand aspirations. *Marco Millions* (9 January 1928) benefited from a remarkable stage orchestration by director Rouben Mamoulian as the anti-commercial themes of the play resonated ironically in an obviously commercial production. Brightly colored Asian costumes decorated a series of international locations, most being variations on an adaptable unit set cleverly designed by Lee Simonson. As an evocation of Asian sounds, music, chant, rhythmic movement, and spectacular processions, the effort was stunning, but the play and the acting did not engage the audience. Although Alfred Lunt, who played Marco Polo, was an accomplished and popular actor, he was unsuited for this boyish, empty-headed Babbitt. A moderate run was managed primarily due to the majestic spectacle and the reputations of the Guild and O'Neill.

When José Quintero revived *Marco Millions* with Hal Holbrook as Marco on 20 February 1964 with the new Lincoln Center Repertory Company, the action was moved into a modified thrust space. This not only reduced the possibilities for detailed spectacle, but demanded a radically different treatment of the material. The design by David Hays had to meld with the central design of Arthur Miller's *After the Fall* designed by Jo Mielziner as the heart of the rotating repertory. The resultant space for *Marco* was dominated by a central revolve. Consequently the pageantry was often radically simplified, made emblematic, or even cute, in its execution. With a much smaller cast the majestic nature of the first production was not approached. Although some critics and audiences were intrigued by the choices, the same attacks on the import of the play again arose and the life of the production was not long.

In the same month that the Theatre Guild opened *Marco Millions* it also premiered *Strange Interlude* (30 January 1928) under the direction of Philip Moeller, who was an intuitive director and proved to be the most successful interpreter of O'Neill's plays arguably until José Quintero. Both directors became famous for making few decisions about the shape of a production until they were already rehearsing with actors. One of the most successful O'Neill productions ever, *Strange Interlude* was everywhere lauded or satirized and had long touring seasons after an initial run of 426 performances. It was the first of his productions to be so long that a supper break intermission was required. The inordinate length of nine acts also led to Equity granting seven weeks of rehearsal time. The famous extensive asides (conscious interior monologues) of the play were performed by having all actors except the speaker cease activity in subtle freezes. Freedom of movement went to the speaker only, thus creating unusual patterns of movement as the asides moved from actor to actor. Although all four principal actors were praised for their complete characterizations, which had to age twenty-five years in the play, Lynn Fontanne especially made Nina Leeds her own and was long identified with this intense, calculating, intelligent and erotic character, much as Pauline Lord had been with Anna Christie.

Although the stage designs by Jo Mielziner appear to be realistic and pedestrian, the use of furniture proved to be very useful for interpretation. The representational rooms always had less furniture than such rooms would have in life and Moeller scattered the chairs across the room not allowing conversational groupings or intimacy. The isolation of the characters was enhanced by the placement of the chairs. Moeller went on to direct four more O'Neill plays.

On 11 March 1963 José Quintero revived *Strange Interlude* for the newly formed Actors Studio Theatre starring Geraldine Page as Nina. The design by David Hays attempted to simplify the multiple set changes by using a revolve, but most attention went to the performance style which approached the material much more naturalistically (using "Method" acting techniques as popularized by the Actors Studio). The result was a blurring of the asides with the dialogue utilizing no freezes. The asides were downplayed as if they were not interruptions to ongoing action. The major effect of this technique was the escalation of emotion during asides rather than during dialogue.

Another major reinterpretation of the play was not mounted here until 21 February 1985, when Glenda Jackson took on Nina under the direction of Keith Hack. Although a British production in conception and major roles, its New York run helped to redefine American conceptions of this play. This production was the first to discover the humor and fun in this play, especially in the performances of Jackson and Edward Petherbridge as Marsden, something which O'Neill had assiduously fought in 1928. It was received by many critics as an almost satirical comedy played in a stylized, large but confining, gray clapboard box designed by Voytek. The result came to many audiences and critics as something like relief after the nearly sixty-year reputation for elongated angst which followed this play.

Less than three months following the premiere of *Strange Interlude* O'Neill's largest cast play, *Lazarus Laughed*, opened in an amateur performance at the Pasadena Playhouse (9 April 1928). It never enjoyed a professional production, but the vast, dithyrambic production of masks and resurrection directed by Gilmor Brown received considerable attention in national periodicals of the theatre. The pageantry of the play called for more than four hundred roles filled by 174 performers, and all but Irving Pichel as Lazarus wore masks (some three hundred in all). The huge set of gray stairs, platforms and screens, designed by James Hyde, were reminiscent of Appia and Craig. The almost omnipresent musical score and extensive crowd and choric action and chant transformed much of the performance to recitative and pageantry.

While O'Neill was out of the country the Theatre Guild attempted to produce *Dynamo* (11 February 1929). Although a physically remarkable production designed by Lee Simonson, especially in his evocation of a Connecticut Power plant which ascended to four different playing levels, the scenery and forceful, imaginative staging by Philip Moeller could not save this "strange interlude" of the working class. This time the asides were found precious or laughable and *Dynamo* entered the ranks of fabulous failures.

O'Neill's next production, however, has been one of his most frequently revived plays despite its inordinate length. The Theatre Guild opened *Mourning Becomes Electra* on 26 October 1931 and like *Strange Interlude* included a dinner break and had no matinees. This remarkable production, directed by Philip Moeller, was surely the finest of any O'Neill play in the dramatist's lifetime. This seemed the perfect material to combine the intuitive style of Moeller and the sensitive, mysterious designing powers of Robert Edmond Jones. Images of the façade of the Mannon mansion, Alice Brady's lonely but proud Lavinia, and Alla Nazimova's brooding, serpentine Christine grace the pages of myriad theatre history books, and for good reason. This play links O'Neill forcefully to Greek tragedy and represents him at his best until the realism of three great plays at the end of his life. The production, both in New York and various national tours, left audiences spellbound by its emotional intensity, stunning beauty, and New England repression.

Four colors dominated Jones's sets and costumes: gray, white, green and black. Sometimes Jones even put black on black; for example, placing a black dress before an even deeper black open doorway. The entire staging area was surrounded by black velvet. Although the production's three domestic interiors were essentially realistic, their austerity lent them a quality akin to the funeral parlor. The façade of the mansion exterior was a majestic antebellum temple of doom, suggestive of both the palatial central door of Greek tragedy and of nineteenth-century American wealth. The clipper ship setting was fragmented and dominated by darkness. Moeller's production ultimately was masterful at evoking a sense of wonder in the audience despite more than five hours of playing time, the play's gloomy message of horror and torment, and acts of vengeance and self-destruction. The tempo was intentionally slow, much slower than would be possible now, but in 1931 this deliberation and power was equated with unequivocal grandeur.

Despite the trilogy's size, *Mourning Becomes Electra* has appeared in many regional theatres across America, especially since two important revivals in the early 1970s. In 1971 Michael Kahn directed Sada Thompson as Christine and Jane Alexander as Lavinia at the American Shakespeare Festival. The following year (15 November), Circle in the Square offered Colleen Dewhurst and Pamela Payton-Wright as mother/daughter under the direction of Theodore Mann in a thrust space, which severely altered the power of the mansion's exterior. This production also cut the play to four hours despite the otherwise reverent approach to revival. Since 1972 many productions have reduced the length of *Mourning Becomes Electra*.

While *Ah, Wilderness!* has proven to be the most frequently revived of all O'Neill plays, due in no small part to its comic action, penchant for nostalgia, and happy conclusion, the first production can almost stand for all successful productions of this play, which is fixed in its physical realism and cheerful energy. The premiere, which opened 2 October 1933 with the

Theatre Guild, was directed by Philip Moeller and designed by Robert Edmond Jones. The first production received much attention for its casting of George M. Cohan in the role of Nat Miller, who emerged as a genial but in-control father who helps his anxious, adolescent son Richard (Elisha Cook) to navigate the vicissitudes of growing up. The play demands and, despite the presence of a star, received a family ensemble which emblematizes a sentimental image of a gentler time before the horrors of world war.

Although nearly every season since the late 1950s has seen a professional revival either in New York or in the regional theatres, one of the most memorable was directed by Arvin Brown at the Long Wharf Theatre in 1974 and was remounted with minor cast changes the following season at Circle in the Square in New York (18 September 1975). Geraldine Fitzgerald as Essie drew special attention for this and other performances in O'Neill's work, and she ultimately became a director of several O'Neill revivals.

Like *Dynamo* in 1929, *Days Without End* received a splendid first production opening on 8 January 1934 directed by Philip Moeller for the Theatre Guild. The modern morality play was a mask experiment featuring a split character with the evil side wearing a half-mask and heard by all other characters, but seen by no one but the audience. Austere settings by Lee Simonson and imaginative staging and interpretation by Moeller almost turned this dramatic misfire into a success.

After a twelve-year hiatus with no new plays appearing from O'Neill, the Theatre Guild attempted to launch another phase of the playwright's career with the premiere of *The Iceman Cometh* on 9 October 1946. For the last time O'Neill benefited from a set design both dreamy and gritty by Robert Edmond Jones. The direction by Eddie Dowling, however, did not reflect the care and sensitivity of Moeller, who was no longer with the Guild. Dowling failed to produce the ensemble work the dark play demanded; to be fair, however, Dowling was forbidden by O'Neill and unwisely by the Guild to go beyond O'Neill's written stage directions regarding blocking. James Barton as Hickey was certainly efficient in the leading role, but it was the Harry Hope of Dudley Digges which was most frequently praised for his acting performance (a skewing of the dynamics of the play). Although by no means a failure, this production did not kick off a revival of interest in O'Neill. That came a decade later. The Guild *Iceman* was O'Neill's last New York premier during his lifetime.

The revival of *The Iceman Cometh*, directed by José Quintero, which opened on 8 May 1956 at Circle in the Square, quickly became associated with salvaged masterpieces (like Quintero's famous revival of Tennessee Williams' *Summer and Smoke* with Geraldine Page in 1952). Two features

2   Eugene O'Neill, *The Iceman Cometh*, Martin Beck Theatre, New York, 1946. Directed by
Eddie Dowling, with James Barton as Hickey

of Quintero's *Iceman* were significant to the future of O'Neill production:
intimacy and the performance of Jason Robards as Hickey. Quintero and
designer David Hays exploited the thrust stage and created a close and
dingy environment for the play. Like Moeller before him, Quintero proved
to be an organic and intuitive director who often served O'Neill's plays
splendidly. Despite the nature of the worn-out characters, this was a
youthful production, especially with the casting of Robards, which signaled
a gravelly, hard-edged, anxiety-ridden approach to O'Neill's characters
echoed in later performances by Colleen Dewhurst as well.

Another important revival of *Iceman* also appeared at Circle in the

3   Josie (Colleen Dewhurst) and Tyrone (Jason Robards) in the José Quintero production of
A Moon for the Misbegotten, New York, 1974

Square on 13 December 1973. This time directed by Theodore Mann in
perhaps his best outing with O'Neill, the director cast James Earl Jones,
who brought a charismatic and inspired presentation to Hickey. In fact the
production became very much about Jones's interpretation rather than the
director's.

When Quintero revived *Iceman* with Robards again on 29 September
1985 (this time for proscenium), the results were reverent but somewhat
dull. Intimacy was lost and the vigor of the 1956 production, especially in
the comparatively subdued performance of Robards, was missing. The
setting by Ben Edwards as lit by Thomas Skelton, however, although
lacking in decorative detail, recalled the grayed-out scenic wonders of
Robert Edmond Jones in *Anna Christie* and the first *Iceman*.

A Moon for the Misbegotten was first produced in 1947, but the Theatre
Guild production closed out of town and never officially opened. The play
opened in earnest ten years later in a highly praised production carefully
directed by Carmen Capalbo (2 May 1957). Despite the unlikely casting of
Wendy Hiller as Josie Hogan and Franchot Tone as James Tyrone, critics
lavished praise on the earthiness of Hiller's performance and the alcoholic

foppishness of Tone's. These interpretations were deemed appropriate for more than fifteen years.

The most famous production of this play was the José Quintero revival of 29 December 1973, which united Jason Robards and Colleen Dewhurst. Quintero had directed Dewhurst in the play twice before – in Buffalo, New York and Spoleto, Italy – but the performances of this production are usually seen as the defining interpretations of Tyrone and Josie. Designed by Ben Edwards, the house was defined by back-latticed, skeletal upstage walls and platforming which allowed free movement from interior to exterior. The simplicity of the setting matched the intuitive work of Quintero with two remarkable and transforming actors who revealed excruciating pain remembered and lives of anguish stripped bare on the nearly open stage.

Eleven years later (1 May 1984) another remarkable Josie appeared in British actress Kate Nelligan (who hid her own obvious beauty) directed by David Leveaux on a moody, abstracted set. This emotional, passionate production, which began in London before New York transfer, served as something of preamble to Leveaux's *Anna Christie*. Unfortunately the Tyrone of Ian Bannen did not match the achievement of Nelligan; otherwise Broadway might have had two "defining" *Moon*s in the late twentieth century.

O'Neill's most famous play, *Long Day's Journey Into Night*, was never produced in his lifetime, and had its American premiere on 7 November 1956, only six months after the Quintero *Iceman*. With the blessing of O'Neill's widow, José Quintero with Circle in the Square this time opened a play in a proscenium Broadway theatre and shifted Jason Robards from Hickey to Jamie Tyrone. Fredric March, Florence Eldridge and Bradford Dillman completed the family which startled audiences with this most agonizing of dramatic journeys. Visually, the design of David Hays stressed time passage through the uncomfortable house, but the stark, uncut text wore down the enthralled audience until emotionally spent.

Equally effective was Laurence Olivier's National Theatre production in 1972 directed by Michael Blakemore. Although this British production was never performed in the United States, it reached American audiences through television broadcast. Perhaps the most important aspect of this production was Olivier's presentation of a faded nineteenth-century ro-mantic–rhetorical acting star, an aspect of Tyrone which has eluded twentieth-century American actors in the role.

The American theatre has seen many professional revivals of *Long Day's Journey*, with nearly every season witnessing new incarnations. Opening on 21 April 1971, Arvin Brown directed it with Robert Ryan, Geraldine

Fitzgerald, and Stacy Keach. Fitzgerald would go on to direct it herself with an all African-American cast led by Earle Hyman off-Broadway on 3 March 1981. Jason Robards turned director at the Kennedy Center and Brooklyn Academy in 1976 casting himself as Tyrone, Sr. this time opposite Zoe Caldwell. Jack Lemmon attempted Tyrone beginning 28 April 1986 under the direction of Jonathan Miller, who escalated the speed of production by not only increasing tempo but introducing overlapping dialogue. At the same time, like Hack's *Strange Interlude*, this production captured many possibilities for humor in this play.

José Quintero returned to the play in one more Broadway production on 6 June 1988, after working the show at the Yale Repertory Theatre. Jason Robards and Colleen Dewhurst were reunited and alternated the play with *Ah, Wilderness!* directed by Arvin Brown first at the Long Wharf. In New York they used the same setting for the house interiors with adaptations by two designers, Ben Edwards for Quintero and Michael Yeargan for Brown. Although the two stars gave powerful performances, they were somewhat forced into these roles, which begged more fragility from Mary and more faded grandeur from Tyrone.

A Touch of the Poet did not premiere until 2 October 1958 in a production directed by Harold Clurman, who inspired very impressive performances of fully drawn characterizations from Helen Hayes and Kim Stanley as Nora and Sara Melody, and a powerful display in the wasted Cornelius Melody of Eric Portman. Although Denholm Elliott created an interesting Cornelius for the National Repertory Company in 1967 he was surrounded by ineptitude and unintelligible dialects. More dialect problems arose with Jason Robards's interpretation of Cornelius under the direction of José Quintero. Opening on 28 December 1977, with Geraldine Fitzgerald as Nora, this production nonetheless captured the edge and dissipation missing from earlier productions, but most critics found that Robards could only capture one side of this intriguing character.

The one-act virtual monologue of *Hughie* was not produced until 22 December 1964 under the direction of José Quintero with Jason Robards as Erie Smith. The action was performed in a vast (too large for such a small play), nearly bare, inhospitable space dominated by the night clerk's desk. Ben Gazzara also performed the role beginning 11 February 1975, but Martin Fried's direction opted for a comparatively crowded and completely enclosed hotel lobby and coupled the play with an unrelated one-act. Most recently Al Pacino has created a wonderfully seedy interpretation (August 1996), directing himself and Paul Benedict as the clerk at Circle in the Square after first mounting the production at the Long Wharf Theatre. This time the sparsely furnished setting of the lobby suggests a run-down, small hotel, and the critics seem satisfied at last that the play has been well-assayed.

The last play of O'Neill to reach the stage was *More Stately Mansions*, directed by José Quintero in Los Angeles (13 September) and New York (31 October 1967). The cast included Colleen Dewhurst, Ingrid Bergman and Arthur Hill, but Bergman's performance was an inappropriate star turn. The woefully unfinished play had to be adapted and failed to pass as completed work and was proclaimed by most as misconceived work. It is unfortunate that the final O'Neill premiere proved such a disappointment.

As this survey demonstrates, the plays of O'Neill have had a most uneven production history, but the work of three directors has repeatedly served the playwright well: Jones, Moeller and Quintero.

SOURCES

For photographs, reviews and detailed examination of the history of most of these productions the following sources are recommended:

Bogard, Travis, *Contour in Time: The Plays of Eugene O'Neill*, revised edn. (New York: Oxford University Press, 1988).

Bryer, Jackson, ed. *"The Theatre We Worked For": The Letters of Eugene O'Neill to Kenneth Macgowan* (New Haven: Yale University Press, 1982).

Gelb, Arthur and Barbara, *O'Neill* (New York: Harper and Row, 1973).

McDonough, Edwin J., *Quintero Directs O'Neill* (Chicago: A Capella, 1991).

Miller, Jordan Y., *Eugene O'Neill and the American Critic*, 2nd edn. (Hamden, Connecticut: Archon, 1973).

New York Theatre Critics' Reviews (New York: Critics Theatre Reviews, 1940–96).

Sarlos, Robert Karoly, *Jig Cook and the Provincetown Players* (Amherst: University of Massachusetts Press, 1982).

Sheaffer, Louis, *O'Neill: Son and Artist* (Boston: Little, Brown, 1973).

 O'Neill: Son and Playwright (Boston: Little, Brown, 1968).

Theatre World, ed. Daniel Blum, John Willis (New York: Crown, 1946–94).

Vena, Gary, *O'Neill's The Iceman Cometh: Reconstructing the Premiere* (Ann Arbor: UMI Press, 1988).

Wainscott, Ronald H., *Staging O'Neill: The Experimental Years, 1920–1934* (New Haven: Yale University Press, 1988).

8

KURT EISEN

O'Neill on screen

> Life then was simply a series of episodes flickering across my soul like the
> animated drawings one sees in the movies, and I could not then see how the
> continuity of my own seeking flight ran through them as a sustained pattern.
>
> O'Neill on his days as a sailor (letter to Carlotta Monterey, 1927)[1]

If Eugene O'Neill here employs a cinematic image to recall his experiences
as a young man at sea, directors and writers have sought for more than six
decades – with varying degrees of success – to illuminate his drama in
adaptations for the screen. Even when his reputation was at its lowest ebb
in the decade between the premiere of *The Iceman Cometh* in 1946 and its
triumphant 1956 revival, O'Neill's plays continued to appear with
regularity in versions for film and television. The legacy of O'Neill on the
screen has become essential to understanding the sustained patterns of his
art and how it corresponds to more general patterns within American
culture.

Producing O'Neill for the stage can be daunting enough, forcing compro-
mises of the kind O'Neill himself struggled to avoid in his writing. How
much more difficult, then, to get O'Neill "right" in a different medium
altogether. Though sometimes critical financial failures, screen versions of
his drama have been offered for the past seven decades on the premise that
the works of Eugene O'Neill merit production and preservation regardless
of their box-office appeal, Nielsen ratings, or the unavoidable trade-offs of
refitting a stage drama for cinema or television. Film and television have
offered performances of such works as *The Hairy Ape*, *Mourning Becomes
Electra* and *Strange Interlude* that are seldom revived outside New York or
London.

The work of American dramatists has not always translated well to the
big screen. For every *Streetcar Named Desire* or *Who's Afraid of Virginia
Woolf* there are many less distinguished renderings. Great plays no more
inevitably make great cinema than a beautiful face produces memorable
portraiture; in fact, as Burton Cooper has noted, Hollywood's approach to
O'Neill's plays has been hampered by "a vulgar prejudice that a play is
necessarily superior to a film."[2] O'Neill's drama, perhaps more than any
other American playwright's, carries an imposing prestige that draws

interest to adaptation, but can also get in the way of creating film versions that are genuinely moving or important in their own right.

Since its early decades, television has also looked to O'Neill for a measure of cultural legitimacy, with more generally favorable results. After truncated presentations in the 1950s of *Ah, Wilderness!* (three times), *The Emperor Jones* (twice), and *Anna Christie* (twice, once with Richard Burton playing the role of Mat Burke) on the three commercial networks,[3] O'Neill's major full-length plays began to appear on television in more or less complete form, including Sidney Lumet's 1960 PBS version of *The Iceman Cometh* with its masterful performance by Jason Robards, Jr., as Hickey; ABC's 1973 broadcast of *Long Day's Journey Into Night* featuring Laurence Olivier and London's National Theatre cast; and the 1975 Mobil Showcase presentation, again on ABC, of José Quintero's staging of *A Moon for the Misbegotten*, starring Robards and Colleen Dewhurst. More recently, public television has taken up the task of broadcasting O'Neill's work, including *A Touch of the Poet* (1974), *Beyond the Horizan* (1996), *Mourning Becomes Electra* (1978), *Long Day's Journey Into Night* (1987) and *Strange Interlude* (1988), as well as a feature-length documentary about O'Neill's life and work, *Eugene O'Neill: A Glory of Ghosts* (1986), and a one-hour docudrama, *Journey into Genius* (1987). In 1989, the Arts and Entertainment cable network included O'Neill's seldom performed one-act play of 1918, *The Rope*, in its American Playwrights series, with Elizabeth Ashley and José Ferrer.

The relatively consistent success of adaptations of O'Neill for television suggests a more compatible relationship between television and theatre than between theatre and film. In her influential 1966 essay Susan Sontag notes a "basic disapproval of films which betray their origins in plays."[4] Though a filmmaker is expected to reinvent the play as cinema, television adaptations often retain the cast of significant stage revivals. The more limited technical resources of television actually become its strengths, complementing and reinforcing stage techniques. Moreover, the spatial and temporal conventions of the proscenium stage seem more congruous with those of television than those of film. In Sontag's terms, the use of space on stage is "continuous," whereas film relies on the more "discontinuous" effect of edited camera shots.[5] Especially for interior scenes, the more continuous space of stage performance has strong affinities with such television genres as the soap opera and the situation comedy, and in general the effect of televisual "flow" (as described by Raymond Williams) seems a closer analogue to the shifting visual images within the spatial continuity of stage performance.[6]

O'Neill's own early enthusiasm for cinema was largely disappointed by the film adaptations of the 1920s and 1930s. He came to assume any movie would more than likely distort his work. Despite his sincere admiration for John Ford's 1940 treatment of the Glencairn plays in *The Long Voyage Home*, O'Neill dismissed as "a fantastically impossible notion" that "Hollywood ever could treat a subject of depth and integrity with depth and integrity."[7] Though O'Neill acknowledged that film and television could become useful outlets for dramatic writing, he believed that "neither films nor the waves will ever take the place of reality" – that is, the stage play.[8]

That one of his least favorite should be the first of his plays to reach the screen only underscores O'Neill's ambivalent relationship to film adaptation. O'Neill was generally pleased with the 1923 silent version of *Anna Christie* with Blanche Sweet, William Russell (Mat Burke) and George Marion (Chris Christopherson), despite regarding the play itself as "the very worst failure I have experienced" (notwithstanding its Pulitzer Prize) because "its success depends on the audience believing just what I did not want them to" – that is, the essentially comic finale with the imminent marriage of the heroine and the seeming reconciliation of her father and fiancé.[9] In its first version, as the title *Chris Christophersen* suggests, O'Neill had focused not on Anna but on the destiny of Chris, her mariner father. O'Neill regarded this early script as a failed "experiment by which I tried to compress the theme for a novel into play form without losing the flavor of the novel."[10]

In some respects producer Thomas Ince and his director John Griffith Wray were truer than O'Neill was himself to this original vision of the play, rendering its novelistic elements more fully by adding scenes that had been left implicit in the play. The extensive location shooting exploits cinematic resources to advantage, beginning with a sustained shot of waves breaking on a beach, a nice visual introduction to the play's predominant motif of life at sea in conflict with life on land. This is followed by images of Anna's early childhood in a Swedish coastal village. Playing alone on the beach, she hops playfully into a small boat and begins drifting out to sea. Her mother rescues her, but this scene establishes the sea's powerful claims on Anna, in spite of her father's misguided, ultimately self-serving conviction that farm life will shield her from the sea's ill effects. In the eloquent closing shot, a forlorn, worried Chris in the doorway of his barge cabin looks out at the fog and the sea as Mat and Anna embrace inside the cabin, successfully conveying the ominous mood of fatality that O'Neill felt was missing from early stage productions.

O'Neill reportedly thought the Ince–Wray *Anna Christie* a "fine and faithful work."[11] Its fidelity to O'Neill is exemplary for cinematic adaptation. Not only are visual elements deployed instead of verbal content (intertitles are used sparingly), but it also manages to convey its own vision

4   Greta Garbo brooding over her whiskey and ginger ale in the 1930 MGM film of
Anna Christie

of the story and characters without violating O'Neill's. One key to achieving this goal is to use O'Neill's play not as the film's point of departure but as its point of return – that is, to take liberties with the play right from the start so the process of converging with the playwright's vision may be realized ultimately in terms established as the filmmaker's own. In the best instances, a film version will reveal dimensions of the O'Neillian "truth" unavailable in stage productions.

The 1930 "talkie" version of *Anna Christie*, starring Greta Garbo and directed by Clarence Brown, likewise adds scenes and otherwise departs from O'Neill's play. But it also diverges more than the Ince–Wray silent version from the play's original mood and vision, offering more of "the kiss-marriage-happily-ever-after tradition" that O'Neill hated.[12] Not surprisingly, Francis Marion's adaptation clearly foregrounds the physical presence and especially the voice of Garbo, not O'Neill's fatalistic vision of the sea, and the scenic space is expanded to include views of New York's East River, the Brooklyn Bridge, and a long Coney Island episode that as much as any other change may be responsible for the film's inability to reconnect with the spirit of O'Neill's play. As John Orlandello observes, the characters are "generally softened," and in particular Anna "is more obviously and sentimentally romantic" (32), with the Coney Island sequence rendering her too "girlish" (35).[13] Garbo's performance is compelling, and her famous first words on screen, "Gimme a vhiskey – ginger ale on the side – and don't be stingy, baby," still have the ring of a major cultural event. Yet the shots of Mat and Anna enjoying the roller coaster at Coney Island establish a distinctly Hollywood image of future happiness that tames the ominously rolling waves of O'Neill's sea.

To capture the spirit of an O'Neill play in cinematic form requires not a literal fidelity to the original stage version but a comparably defiant attitude towards easy formulas – to film against the grain of Hollywood, just as O'Neill always tried to write against the prevailing norms of Broadway – including the very norms his own work helped to establish. In the case of the 1933 *The Emperor Jones*, even the prodigious talents of Paul Robeson could not overcome the awkward attempt to incorporate stage expressionism within the linear narrative conventions of mainstream cinema. The first half of the film is almost wholly invented from hints and details in the published play, and just as frequently contrived to showcase Robeson's celebrated singing voice or to provide exoticized images of black culture for white audiences. Paradoxically, the supposedly "realistic" linear exposition, dominated by images of the physically imposing, willful, brash, and savvy black hero, actually conveys a far stronger expressionistic effect – as it surely must have to white audiences in 1933 – than does the more stage-derived expressionism of the final scenes that show the self-haunted Jones fleeing through rather unconvincing jungle scenery. Instead of an odyssey into the depths of Jones's psyche, the jungle scenes reassuringly end the threat posed by an intelligent, ambitious, and ruthless black tyrant, and present the triumph of the conventions of cinema over the renegade power of the self-fashioning black artist. Moreover, by leaving this climax to its own (stage) devices the film seems determined to expose the limits of O'Neill's stage expressionism while also reminding viewers of the film's highbrow origins as a distinguished stage play.

The problem of creating a faithful yet fully cinematic vision continued to challenge adapters in such films as *Ah, Wilderness!* (1935), *Mourning Becomes Electra* (1947), and *Desire Under the Elms* (1958). Full, perceptive analyses of these and other films, including three that will be taken up later in this essay – *Strange Interlude* (1932), Sidney Lumet's *Long Day's Journey Into Night* (1962), and John Frankenheimer's *The Iceman Cometh* (1973) – may be found in John Orlandello's *O'Neill on Film*.[14] Two films of the early 1940s, John Ford's *The Long Voyage Home* (1940) and Alfred Santell's *The Hairy Ape* (1944) – both of them built on the quintessential O'Neillian predicament of life at sea – offer two very different approaches to reconciling O'Neill's vision of human destiny to the exigencies of Hollywood in a time of national crisis.

The Long Voyage Home remains a model of adaptation not only for the excellence of its cast, director, screenwriter, and cinematographer, but for its assertive approach both towards Hollywood conventions and the four very good O'Neill one-acters it is based on: *Bound East for Cardiff*, *The Moon of the Caribbees*, *In the Zone*, and *The Long Voyage Home*. O'Neill's own strong endorsement of the film also demonstrates that his objections to most film versions of his work stemmed less from changes in plot or characterization than from bowing to Hollywood industry standards. He admired director John Ford and producer Walter Wanger for making a "no plot, no sex, no slop, honest picture" out of the early sea plays that marked his own "first real break from theatrical traditions."[15] Matthew Bernstein explains that Ford signals his defiance of Hollywood right away by opening the film with five minutes (27 shots) with no dialogue – none of the narrative exposition usually deemed necessary to get the story moving. "The opening minutes," Bernstein writes, "establishing mood over character and stasis over narrative development, initiate a different relationship with its spectator from that of the typical Hollywood film."[16] With World War II underway in Europe and overseas markets therefore declining, United States studios were anxious to expand domestic markets and began to offer "prestige" or "arty" films that would appeal to better educated Americans.[17] *The Long Voyage Home* represents one attempt to do for American cinema what O'Neill himself had tried to for Broadway in the previous two decades: to bring the claims of art to a medium otherwise driven by standards of mass entertainment.

The shift to a World War II setting also changes what is at stake in the film's image of human history, especially against the O'Neillian backdrop of the timeless sea. Worried that Ford's wordless opening would leave some viewers disoriented, producer Wanger hedged somewhat by insisting that the following statement be added as prologue: "With their hate and desires men are changing the face of the earth – but they cannot change the Sea. Men who live on the Sea never change – for they live in a lonely world apart as they drift from one rusty tramp steamer to the next, forging the life-lines of Nations."[18] This world of lonely, separate, yet deeply connected lives is suggested in cinematographer Gregg Toland's persistently low-angle, deep-focus shots (perfecting the techniques he would use so prominently in *Citizen Kane* the following year) and by screenwriter Dudley Nichols's deft merging of O'Neill's four short plays into an ensemble of characters and episodes that reveal both the stark isolation and the intimately linked destinies of the S.S. Glencairn's sailors.

In 1940 these postures of isolation and engagement had special urgency as the United States contemplated its role in a war threatening to engulf the world. The film's most decisive departure from O'Neill's eponymous one-acter, shows the indomitable Irishman Driscoll (Thomas Mitchell) rescuing fellow sailor Olson (played valiantly with a Swedish accent by John Wayne) only to suffer Olson's fate himself – forced labor aboard the tyrannical ship Amindra, and then (in another added twist) death when that ship is torpedoed by a German U-boat. If this script change promotes the need to take action against tyrants who threaten liberty, it also sustained an O'Neillian tone by refusing to romanticize the destructive consequences of that necessity or to exaggerate the limits of human freedom.

The film version of *The Hairy Ape*, released in 1944 with the United States and its allies nearing victory, works mostly against the grain of O'Neill's expressionistic play. Directed by Alfred Santell, this film is not without its strengths, including lively performances by William Bendix in the lead role (here called Hank instead of O'Neill's more pointed nickname Yank) and Susan Hayward as his nemesis, the idly rich socialite Mildred Douglas. Their final, wordless showdown is an especially memorable twist on the original. But in the first half of the film, the scenic "opening up" of the action removes the cramped tension that gives poignancy to Hank's boast that it is he, the great stoker of furnaces, and not the ship's owners or officers, who "makes things go."[19] Unfortunately, what sounds like a troubled *cri de coeur* in the cramped stokehole of O'Neill's play comes across more as tiresome bluster in the film's more varied settings, such as the Lisbon waterfront where the film begins. As with *The Emperor Jones*, the play's expressionism has been largely naturalized, with only fitful attempts to use cinematic means to convey Hank's inward struggle.

The most important changes to the original play are two major new characters in a second plotline, and the updating of the action to a World War II setting. The historical shift means that the coal-burning freighter where Hank works – and with which he identifies so strongly – can no longer symbolize modern industrial technology. Coal-fueled engines are themselves presented as obsolete, superseded by the newer, faster "oil-burners"; Hank and his fellow stokers thus embody a modernist nostalgia for a time when men worked in harmony with their machines. Indeed, Mildred's selfish, manipulative treatment of others is most villainous in its obstruction of honest labor and the pursuit of noble careers. Mildred's devastating encounter with Hank in the stokehold destroys his will to work, the very quality that had distinguished him as a "boss stoker." Her corrupting idleness is contrasted to the benign sincerity of her friend Helen Parker (a character created for the film), who works to secure sea berths to

America for desperate European emigrants while Mildred enjoys Lisbon's posh night spots. To exploit his position of authority on the ship, Mildred seduces Tony Lazarre (another added character), the ship's bright, ambitious second engineer beloved by Helen, only to discard him when the ship reaches New York, thus shattering his promising career as a maritime officer.

The attempt to ennoble labor in *The Hairy Ape*, especially the worthy life of "following the sea" as the wise Captain MacDougall describes it to Helen Parker, marks a major contrast to the much more fatalistic – and O'Neillian – view prevalent in Ford's *The Long Voyage Home*. In the very intriguing climax that recalls *King Kong* (just as earlier scenes in the stokehold somewhat resemble the workers' inferno in Fritz Lang's *Metropolis*), Hank asserts his power over Mildred by reversing the terms of their earlier confrontation. Shot without dialogue, this sequence reinstates some of the expressionism lost in the play's translation to screen. As Hank climbs the stairs to Mildred's penthouse we see his shadow like a second, alienated self that becomes reintegrated when he triumphs over Mildred and her idle wealth. Finally, Hank carries the drunken Tony back on board the freighter as Captain MacDougall looks on from above with fatherly understanding. Ultimately, the wartime context – again in stark contrast to the end of *The Long Voyage Home* – has vanished. The upbeat finale transforms O'Neill's tragic-modernist angst to an almost cheerful look ahead to a postwar order driven by a revitalized industrial labor force, anchored by sagacious authority, and dedicated to propping up the wavering ambitions of corporate middle managers epitomized by Tony Lazarre.

If any development typifies this postwar American world it is the emergence of television and what Cecilia Tichi has called the "TV environments" that came increasingly to shape American private and public reality during the Cold War.[20] Though four more feature-length movies were made from plays by O'Neill, following the condensed hour-long adaptations that appeared on the home screen in such 1950s programs as Celanese Theater, Front Row Center, and Hallmark Hall of Fame, television began to show increasing fidelity to the play as written. More important, television offers an inherently home-centered medium generally more congruent with the naturalistic, domestic elements of O'Neill's work after 1927, of which only the expressionistic (and critically unesteemed) *Dynamo* (1929) and *Days Without End* (1934) have not been adapted for television. As John Fiske and John Hartley observe, television "is in a literally 'familiar' environment, and each viewer or family group is able to respond to the television message in terms that are intimately meaningful for themselves personally."[21] This mass-mediated intimacy creates a post-

Freudian psychodrama in which, as Roland Barthes argues, "Television condemns us to the Family, whose household utensil it has become."[22]

Conventions of such postwar television genres as soap opera and situation comedy have served in particular to shape our perception of family, especially in terms of gender. Whereas women in big screen adaptations such as *The Hairy Ape* are usually drawn according to one of two contrary archetypes – predatory (Mildred) or angelic (Helen) – the rhythm and sensibilities of television can often accommodate greater complexity, nuance, and even subversion in representing women and their roles within and beyond the home. Likewise, these television genres have specialized in portraying men in family roles while featuring their public careers as marginal or in conflict with these roles. Except for a new cinematic *Long Day's Journey* based on the acclaimed 1994 and 1995 stage productions of that play (directed by David Wellington), which appeared as this volume was being readied for publication, no O'Neill play has been made into a theatrical film since the 1973 *Iceman Cometh*. Television productions have, however, provided a new outlet for his drama. This is true in large part because television emphasizes the continuities of American domestic life; at the same time, in contrast to the film adaptations, O'Neill's plays on television tend to convey a subtler critique of those very elements of American individualism and community that television itself has so effectively propagated.

Comparing the 1932 movie version of *Strange Interlude* with the PBS American Playhouse production broadcast in 1988, one is struck by how media standards of frankness have changed since 1932 and by the slower, more elaborate pacing of the PBS production. The film, with Norma Shearer and Clark Gable badly miscast as Nina Leeds and Dr. Ned Darrell, is so truncated that virtually all the interesting themes in O'Neill's play have been erased, especially its critique of American materialism, its treatment of male sexual anxiety, and its focus on female desire. Though the "thought-aside" narrative device is retained by means of postsynchronized dubbing, the characters' thoughts have been so cleansed of anything provocative or subversive that the whole point of distinguishing their secret thoughts from their audible speech is mostly lost. Allusions to the Great War and its moral devastation – focalized in the lingering influence of Nina's dead fiancé Gordon Shaw – are also kept minimal. Perhaps most significant is the cutting of Nina's declarations concerning "God the Mother" and the "one complete beautiful male desire" supplied collectively by her three devoted men (*CP* II, 756): if O'Neill's play gestures toward the critique of a patriarchal order, the film seems determined to turn this critique back into an affirmation of conventional American motherhood and the business ethic.

The 1988 American Playhouse *Strange Interlude* focuses immediately on these more provocative themes with some prefatory footage of a World War I dogfight that implies the death of Gordon Shaw and the demise of an entire heroic mythology. Robert Enders's script retains most of O'Neill's script, including the thought-asides. Rather than dubbing them over close-up shots of the relevant character, the television production renders the thought-asides as spoken monologues slightly but decisively set off (usually with medium close-up shots) from speech understood to be audible to others; also, one thought-aside often overlaps with another character's audible lines, effectively conveying the sense that thinking and speaking can happen simultaneously. This contributes to the richer aural and physical density in the world of this adaptation compared to the 1932 film version.

With its almost languid tempo, the PBS *Strange Interlude* draws most effectively on the generic conventions of television soap opera, which, according to Ruth Rosen, is a modern counterpart of "the serialized morality novels of the eighteenth and nineteenth centuries which also exaggerated the ordinary, examined every problem from everyone's point of view, and extended plots for months, even years."[23] Rosen explains that despite its complications and intrigues, soap opera actually invokes a simpler American past in which "the traditional values of the community and family are reaffirmed."[24] Despite some clear deviations from this formula, O'Neill's themes in *Strange Interlude* translate well to the mode of soap opera. The Great War marks this very kind of discontinuity in traditional values, especially those concerning domestic values and gender roles. As Nina, Glenda Jackson commands the play's center with her resolute if often desperate pursuit of happiness following the death of Gordon Shaw. In retaining O'Neill's original, more ambivalent finale, this *Strange Interlude* reaffirms "the traditional values of the community and family" while reminding us that these values represent a form of escape or resignation more than a source of vitality or hope.

By the time O'Neill began work on *The Iceman Cometh* in 1939 an even more catastrophic world war was about to break out, and escape or resignation seemed to him the only way to salvage some kind of hope from the wreckage of modern history. Just as *Strange Interlude* anticipates soap opera, the genre most comparable to *Iceman* in its two adaptations for the screen, despite its gloomy overtones, may be the situation comedy. David Grote's account of the TV sitcom might almost be confused with a description of O'Neill's play: "The principal fundamental situation of the situation comedy is that things do not change. No new society occurs at the end. The only end is death, for characters as well as for the situation itself, the precise opposite of the rebirth and new life promised in the celebrations of the traditional comedy…"[25] If this formulation seems a bit weighty for *Gilligan's Island* or *Cheers*, it is also true that *The Iceman Cometh* contains a persistent comic dimension easily lost when a director stresses the play's status as a great American tragedy. In fact, the play's tragedy derives from the very denial of comic rebirth or change, a denial that the postwar TV sitcom represents as humorous and socially desirable.

Seen in this light, the 1960 television adaptation of *Iceman* directed by Sidney Lumet and starring Jason Robards, Jr., in a landmark performance as the salesman Hickey, aptly conveys the mixed spirit of the play. *Iceman* is unique among O'Neill's drama in that the television version preceded the version shown in movie houses, setting a standard against which the film version would inevitably be judged. Besides the presence of Robards (as well as a young Robert Redford as Don Parritt), Lumet's *Iceman* demonstrates television's capacity to deploy a wide range of camera techniques while retaining much of the spatial aesthetic of a stage performance, with the television screen as a kind of postmodern proscenium connecting the home and the stage. Already an accomplished film director by 1960, in the television *Iceman* Lumet utilizes the shifting movements of the camera and characters, along with an abundant use of close-up and deep-focus shots, to create a complex intimacy that very effectively brings out the play's central dynamic of personal illusion – the characters' various "pipe dreams" – as a performance that must be constantly legitimated by someone else, a listener who needs a credulous audience. Robards's increasingly manic Hickey threatens this arrangement with his insidious performance to end all performance, a vaudeville Mephistopheles badgering his audience to renounce their most cherished self-delusions. If *Iceman* offers no hope of a revitalized society, like the TV sitcom (e.g. *All in the Family, The Simpsons*) it does affirm the idea that a stable social order depends not on reforming vice and stupidity but on a mutual acceptance of others' weaknesses and false hopes.

This social dynamic is also brought out incisively in the excellent videotaped staging of *Hughie* (1981) with Robards as the washed-up gambler Erie Smith – an empathetic counterpart to his Hickey in *The Iceman Cometh* – especially since a responsive theatre audience at Circle in the Square is very much in evidence throughout the show. In these and two other recorded performances – Lumet's 1962 film of *Long Day's Journey* and the 1975 ABC broadcast of *A Moon for the Misbegotten* – Robards showcases his talents as the pre-eminent O'Neillian actor of the post-World War II era, a standard as imposing as it is definitive. The 1975 *Moon* broadcast is especially important for preserving the collaboration of what may be the most accomplished trio of O'Neillians ever: Robards, Colleen

Dewhurst, and director José Quintero. While Ed Flanders is also superb as the quick-witted Phil Hogan, Dewhurst's Josie Hogan dominates the production with much additional stage business and a vigor that subtly shifts the script's emphasis so that it is Josie's depth of feeling, not her powerful body, that most awes the men in her life. Robards's Jim Tyrone is a valedictory sequel to his Jamie in *Long Day's Journey* that no other actor could match. The television medium itself serves the play well, especially in the final morning scene with its return to domestic normalcy after the emotionally charged exchanges of the previous night.

By the early 1970s Robards had become so fully identified with these roles that John Frankenheimer decided it would be "very unexciting" to cast him in *The Iceman Cometh* film that would be part of the short-lived American Film Theatre project of the early 1970s.[26] After Marlon Brando declined the part, Frankenheimer chose Lee Marvin as Hickey, a move most critics questioned – undoubtedly prejudiced by the image of Robards's Hickey on stage and television. While Marvin has a formidable screen presence, he lacks the swagger and infectiously hammy style that Robards has made integral to Hickey's character. The enduring strength of this production lies more in the rest of its cast, especially two veteran Hollywood actors in their final roles: Robert Ryan as Larry Slade and Fredric March as Harry Hope.

If this is an even more claustrophobic *Iceman* than the 1960 television production, the masterful use of point-of-view shots at tabletop level, the somber lighting by cinematographer Ralph Woolsey more effectively draws the audience into the ironical participatory viewpoint of Larry Slade, the play's center of consciousness. John Orlandello defends the flatness of Marvin's Hickey but acknowledges that Ryan is so commanding as the brooding Larry Slade that "the weight of the production" shifts from Hickey's compulsive activism to Larry's tortured self-awareness.[27] While developing his script for *Iceman* Frankenheimer quickly realized that his tentative plan to open up the action with scenes outside the barroom would be a mistake, since "the whole point is not what [the characters] see but what they *think* they see."[28] The space of the play would thus have to be recreated from within the confines of Harry Hope's saloon, yet the brisk cutting from one shot to the next destabilizes this otherwise oppressive closed space; every point of view is ultimately subjective, opening up the space from within. Marvin's Hickey is a too-solid embodiment of metaphysical certitude which the world of the film cannot ultimately support, but the final shot of Larry staring silently into a world beyond the barroom as Harry Hope leads his revitalized customers in singing "The Sunshine of Paradise Alley" incisively captures the play's simultaneous dimensions of

5   Four haunted Tyrones: Jason Robards (Jamie), Dean Stockwell (Edmund), and Ralph
Richardson (James) watching Katharine Hepburn (Mary) in the 1962 *Long Day's Journey
Into Night*, Embassy Pictures

tragedy and comedy: while Larry has internalized Hickey's crushing revelation, Harry and the others have come back to life by reasserting their
ability to wish this oppressive truth away.

The question of a focal character becomes even more complex in the four
screen adaptations of *Long Day's Journey Into Night*. Who is most to
blame for the Tyrones' troubled family past, and who is most capable of
offering some degree of redemption? How should we as viewers be
positioned within the Tyrones' world? Since the visual economy of the
camera – especially in cinema – is more rigorously controlled and precisely
articulated than that of the naturalist stage, the director must decide not
only how to portray relationships among the characters, but how to relate
this family and its situation to the viewing audience.

In the 1962 film version with Robards, Katharine Hepburn, Ralph
Richardson, and Dean Stockwell, director Sidney Lumet places Hepburn's
Mary at the film's visual and thematic center.[29] From the exterior establishing shot of the Tyrone house with the harbor beyond it to the final
sequence of the three Tyrone men staring at the drug-hazed Mary retreating
to her hopeful youth, Lumet brings us from the outside to the interior of

the Tyrones' family psyche, with Mary providing a mirror of the Tyrone men's guilt and disappointment. Frequent high-angle shots further underscore Mary's isolation from the men, drawing the viewer into a posture of surveillance much like that of which Mary accuses her husband and sons. After the men openly accuse her of relapsing back to morphine use, a 360-degree tracking shot shows Mary at the center of a circle of guilt. Finally, the riveting sequence of closeups as Mary regresses further into girlhood memories affirms her status as the film's emotional lightning rod, and secures the viewer's inescapable link to the family's very specific yet universally resonant predicament.

In a sense Hepburn's Mary establishes her strongest connection not to any of the Tyrone men but to the camera – what Lumet has called the film's "fifth character."[30] According to the elaborate "lens plot" devised by Lumet and cinematographer Boris Kaufman for shooting each Tyrone, the use of increasingly longer lenses brings out Mary's growing isolation within the Tyrone home.[31] Though not especially convincing in evoking a Catholic girlhood and lacking in maternal warmth, Hepburn's performance does realize the crucial irony that Mary Tyrone the housewife, not James Tyrone the famous stage actor, emerges as the most consummate performer in the Tyrone household. Dudley Nichols (Ford's screenwriter for *The Long Voyage Home* and director/writer of the 1947 *Mourning Becomes Electra*) has proposed that the stage is a "medium of action" but cinema is "the medium of reaction," where the audience identifies "with the person *acted upon* on the screen, and not with the person acting";[32] accordingly, Mary's morphine addiction in Lumet's film may be seen as the central action to which the men continually react. Viewed from this perspective, Richardson's superb James Tyrone, Sr. – the romantic stage hero reduced to helplessness in his own house – regulates audience empathy. His pained reactions to Mary's actions and words are so fully articulated by Kaufman's camera that the viewer is drawn into his emotional perspective from which to view the appalling spectacle of Mary's regression.

Of the three television versions of *Long Day's Journey*, the broadcast of Michael Blakemore's National Theatre production in 1973 (directed for television by Peter Wood) is the earliest and most successful. While Laurence Olivier's Tyrone is the featured attraction, Constance Cummings's Mary captures her simultaneously domestic yet spectral quality more subtly than does the aggressive angularity of Hepburn's, and highlights some of the advantages of the television medium over cinema in presenting the rhythms of the Tyrone household. Certainly it is fascinating to watch Olivier playing the part of a failed Shakespearean actor – at one point he even bungles a short recitation from *Julius Caesar* – but even more crucial is Cummings's ability to translate the gothic, madwoman-in-the-attic dimension foregrounded in the Lumet film to the more mundane texture and ambiance familiar to viewers of television genres such as sitcoms and soap operas.

If, as David Grote has argued, the goal of the sitcom is "to reaffirm the stability of the family as an institution,"[33] the 1973 television version of *Long Day's Journey* inverts the sitcom formula by recasting family stability as inescapable destiny. Likewise, seeing the Tyrones' home life on television also evokes the soap opera milieu with its persistent focus on "a sexually bifurcated world" in which "men were obligated to seek an individual destiny that often conflicted with the female world of home and community."[34] Cummings's Mary gives focus to the Tyrones' predicament while very powerfully evoking a nostalgic vision of nineteenth-century American home life that Mary longs for but knows she can never achieve. In Marshall McLuhan's familiar terms, Cummings's open and youthful Mary, like television itself, is a "cool" medium through which a viewer can participate more intimately in the Tyrones' family destiny; like the "hot" medium of cinema, Hepburn's Mary is visually assertive, more completely plotted and delineated, but for that very reason she keeps viewers at a distance. To see the Tyrones in a stage production adapted for television frames the more public aesthetic of theatre within the domestic ambience of the television, underscoring one of the key ideas in the play: home life for the Tyrones is a kind of theatre, a psychodrama, squeezed into a house that is never really a home in the nostalgic sense Mary continually invokes. Through the domesticating lens of the television camera, the strident stage histrionics of Olivier's James Tyrone seem – aptly – awkward and out of place.

The 1982 *Long Day's Journey* with its African–American cast, presented on the Arts and Entertainment network stays even more resolutely within the registers of domestic television naturalism. Like the 1981 New York stage production on which it is based, this television version is directed by the veteran O'Neill performer Geraldine Fitzgerald. Earle Hyman, Jr. (Tyrone), and Peter Francis-James (Edmund) reprise their stage roles; on screen Ruby Dee replaces Gloria Foster, with Thommie Blackwell replacing Al Freeman, Jr., as Jamie Tyrone. As Jack Kroll complained in his otherwise approving stage review, this television version is marred by cuts that are essential to tracing the Tyrones' dense web of guilt and deep attachment.[35] Understandably, all references to the family's Irishness are deleted, but many other cuts serve only to mute the sharp antagonisms essential to the Tyrones' complexity as a family. Virtually all the tense first-act sparring is omitted, and Mary's important speech about never feeling "at home in the theatre" is likewise left out of her conversation with the maid Cathleen, as is Edmund's reference to his own suicide attempt. A characteristic omission is Edmund's searching self-criticism in the final act: "Stammering is the native eloquence of us fog people" (CP III, 812–13). The whole production seems determined not to let itself move too far outside the safe confines of television drama, perhaps to keep attention focused on the unorthodoxy of the casting.

Hyman, Dee, Blackwell, and Francis-James perform well, but a viewer familiar with O'Neill's work may be most struck with the idea that the autobiographical masterpiece of a white playwright who used black characters (Brutus Jones; Jim Harris in *All God's Chillun Got Wings*) to explore his own sense of alienation should be recast in turn as the portrait of a black family. Race is not made an explicit issue, but upon hearing Tyrone's regret-filled recollection of how he has lost the great promise he once showed playing Othello opposite Edwin Booth's Iago, one cannot help realizing that in the nineteenth century there were circumstances more formidable than the lure of a money-making play to keep actors of color from realizing their full potential as artists in the American theatre.

Still, of the four recorded performances of *Long Day's Journey* the boldest departure from O'Neill's text may be the 1987 Showtime version directed by Jonathan Miller and starring Jack Lemmon as Tyrone. Featuring the cast of the successful if controversial 1986 Broadway revival, this performance is most valuable as an object lesson on the dangers of aggressive direction. Of his decision to "liven it up a little" by having actors overlap much of their dialogue, Miller explained that he hoped above all to avoid the "canonical, custodial versions" of *Long Day's Journey*, to render O'Neill's language not reverentially as "dramatic poetry" but as "ordinary, repetitious conversation" so fully naturalized that even the Tyrones themselves have ceased to hear it any more.[36] As Mary, Bethel Leslie speaks her lines with a flatness that decidedly avoids Hepburn's more spectral descent in the final act, and Tony Straiges's compact set design – which retains a unified fourth-wall stage aspect far more than any of the other three *Long Day's Journey* adaptations – stresses horizontal lines, especially in the long, narrow wood paneling that covers the rear walls.

Though Lemmon's Tyrone was described in stage reviews as likeable and graceful,[37] on videotape his quarrelsome, mannered performance comes nowhere close to generating the ambivalent empathy of Ralph Richardson's Tyrone. Just as Miller seems intent to keep Mary from drifting into a morphine haze, Lemmon plays up the cranky, miserly side which his wife and sons despise in Tyrone. For example, when he acknowledges Edmund in the fourth act as "a poor thing but mine own," Lemmon evokes no hint of the "real, if alcoholic, affection" called for in the text (CP III, 804); he even threatens Edmund with a belt and later strikes Jamie, a violence well beyond that of the three previous screen Tyrones or O'Neill's text. In the play's final scene, as Mary recites her life as a young convent girl, Tyrone is shown off to himself praying fervently, a shot that diverts attention from what should be Mary's most luminous and most moving scene, losing all the spare eloquence of O'Neill's scene directions: "Tyrone stirs in his chair" (*CP* III, 828). Peter Gallagher's Edmund and Kevin Spacey's Jamie are the most reliable performances, perhaps because the rebellious tendencies of their characters are closer in sensibility to the generally anti-reverential approach Miller has taken toward O'Neill's magnum opus.

The heavy cost Miller has paid for imposing new rhythms on the Tyrone family is the loss of the play's fascinating emotional oscillation, the wrenching shifts between hatred and love that are the key dramatic element in the play and the most enduring principle of the family's relationships. The brisk linearity of the whole production avoids the relentless repetitions so characteristic of O'Neill's final plays and so necessary to draw an audience, in spite of itself, into a web of complex and difficult emotions.

Miller's resolve to cut against the usual "canonical" fidelity to O'Neill's script points to an issue key to future adaptations: how to convey O'Neill's decidedly modernist angst to viewers accustomed to the different techniques and ideologies of postmodern media. Perhaps future adaptations of O'Neill will need to take similarly anti-traditionalist approaches. Though recorded performances by Robards, Dewhurst, Robeson, and others may serve as the definitive standards, they also challenge directors and actors to formulate new visions for O'Neill's plays. The lack of new O'Neill screen adaptations in the 1990s, despite continued, often strikingly innovative stage revivals, suggests a period of transition. Making available such currently out-of-print videos as *Iceman* and *A Moon for the Misbegotten* may help to spur interest in new adaptations. What seems certain is that in the post-Cold War era, new aesthetic contexts and new electronic media for both presenting and viewing O'Neill will emerge, and will become essential to the persistence of vision by which we see the many "sustained patterns" of O'Neill's art.

NOTES

1 Travis Bogard and Jackson R. Bryer, eds., *Selected Letters of Eugene O'Neill* (New Haven: Yale University Press, 1988), p. 220.

2 "Some Problems in Adapting O'Neill for Film," in Richard F. Moorton, ed., *Eugene O'Neill's Century: Centennial Views on America's Foremost Tragic Dramatist* (New York: Greenwood, 1991), p. 75.

3 A partial list of television adaptations (only those plays that have been adapted for both film and television) may be found in William T. Leonard, *Theatre: Stage to Screen to Television* (Metuchen: Scarecrow Press, 1981), 2 vols.

4 "Film and Theater," in Gerald Mast and Marshall Cohen, eds., *Film Theory and Criticism*, 2nd edn. (New York: Oxford University Press, 1979), p. 364.

5 "Film and Theater," p. 366.

6 See Williams's comparison of television drama and the naturalist stage in *Television: Technology and Cultural Form* (New York: Schocken, 1974), pp. 56–57.

7 *Selected Letters*, p. 546.

8 "Eugene O'Neill Returns After Twelve Years," in Mark W. Estrin, ed., *Conversations with Eugene O'Neill* (Jackson: University Press of Mississippi, 1990), p. 170.

9 Louis Sheaffer, *O'Neill: Son and Artist* (Boston: Little, Brown, 1973), p. 68.

10 *Selected Letters*, p. 122.

11 Richard Watts, Jr., "O'Neill Picks America as His Future Workshop," in *Conversations with Eugene O'Neill*, p. 115.

12 "From Eugene G. O'Neill. [Letter] To the Dramatic Editor." *New York Times* 18 December 1921 sec. 6, p. 1. Reprinted in *Eugene O'Neill: Comments on the Drama and the Theater*, ed. Ulrich Halfmann (Tübingen: Narr, 1987), p. 12.

13 *O'Neill on Film* (Rutherford: Fairleigh Dickinson University Press, 1982), pp. 32, 35.

14 Other discussions of O'Neill on film and television include Linda Ben-Zvi, "Eugene O'Neill and Film," *Eugene O'Neill Newsletter* 7 (Spring 1983): 3–10; Donald P. Costello, "Sidney Lumet's *Long Day's Journey Into Night*." *Literature-Film Quarterly* 22 (1994): 78–92; Edward T. Jones, "The Tyrones as a TV Family: *Long Day's Journey Into Night* Primetime," *Literature-Film Quarterly* 22 (1994): 93–97; Marcelline Krafchick, "Film and Fiction in O'Neill's *Hughie*," *Arizona Quarterly* 39 (1983): 47–61; Edward Murray, "Eugene O'Neill, Expressionism, and Film," *The Cinematic Imagination* (New York: Ungar, 1972), pp. 16–35; William L. Sipple, "From Stage to Screen: *The Long Voyage Home* and *Long Day's Journey into Night*," *Eugene O'Neill Newsletter* 7 (Spring 1983): 10–14.

15 *Selected Letters*, p. 521; Sheaffer, *O'Neill: Son and Artist*, p. 383.

16 "Hollywood's 'Arty Cinema': John Ford's *The Long Voyage Home*," *Wide Angle* 10 (1988): 30–45.

17 Bernstein, "Hollywood's Arty Cinema," p. 32.

18 Bernstein, "Hollywood's Arty Cinema," p. 38.

19 Eugene O'Neill, *Complete Plays: 1920–1931*, Travis Bogard, ed. (New York: Library of America, 1988), p. 128. Subsequent references to this edition will appear parenthetically with these abbreviations: *Complete Plays: 1913–1920* as *CP* I; *Complete Plays: 1920–1931* as *CP* II; and *Complete Plays: 1932–1943* as *CP* III.

20 *Electronic Hearth: Creating an American Television Culture* (New York: Oxford University Press, 1991); see especially pp. 42–83.

21 *Reading Television* (London: Methuen, 1978), p. 111.

22 Quoted in Sandy Flitterman-Lewis, "Psychoanalysis, Film, and Television," *Channels of Discourse: Television and Contemporary Criticism*, ed. Robert C. Allen (Chapel Hill: University of North Carolina Press, 1987), p. 188.

23 "Soap Operas: Search for Yesterday," in *Watching Television*, ed. Todd Gitlin (New York: Pantheon, 1986), p. 49.

24 *Ibid.*
25 Quoted in Jane Feuer, "Genre Study and Television," *Channels of Discourse*, ed. Robert C. Allen, p. 122.
26 Charles Champlin, *John Frankenheimer: A Conversation with Charles Champlin* (Burbank: Riverwood, 1995), p. 133.
27 *O'Neill on Film*, p. 159.
28 Champlin, *John Frankenheimer*, p. 133.
29 Frank Cunningham, *Sidney Lumet: Film and Literary Vision* (Lexington: University of Kentucky Press, 1991), p. 125.
30 Cunningham, *Sidney Lumet*, p. 122.
31 Cunningham, *Sidney Lumet*, p. 125.
32 "The Writer and the Film," in *Film: A Montage of Theories*, ed. Richard Dyer MacCann (New York: Dutton, 1966), p. 78.
33 Quoted in Feuer, "Genre Study," p. 122.
34 Rosen, "Soap Operas," p. 47.
35 "Passionate 'Journey'," *Newsweek* 20 April 1981: 104.
36 Lesley Valdes, "Long Day's Journey Onto Broadway," *Wall Street Journal*, 11 April 1986: 25.
37 See for example Brendan Gill, "Unhappy Tyrones," *New Yorker* 12 May 1986: 93–94; Frank Rich, "A New 'Long Day's Journey'," *New York Times* 29 April 1986: sec. 3: 12.

9

BRENDA MURPHY

O'Neill's America: the strange interlude between the wars

Perhaps because Eugene O'Neill tended to cast his work in universal terms, critics tend to write of him in relation to the world stage and to the recognizably seminal thinkers and playwrights of his time – Nietzsche, Freud, Jung, Ibsen, Shaw. O'Neill is not often thought of as a distinctly American playwright working in an American theatrical tradition and living almost all of his life in the United States, keenly interested in the political, social, and moral developments in his country. Yet, in his last decade of playwriting, O'Neill was at work on a most ambitious treatment of American history, his projected play Cycle about the cultural history of the United States from 1775 to 1932, based on the story of a single American family, a union of the English Harfords and the Irish Melodys, which is dealt with in detail in other essays in this collection. The Cycle's overall title, *A Tale of Possessors, Self-Dispossessed*, indicates O'Neill's point of view, essentially an indictment of America's greed and materialism and its failure to value spirituality or beauty. The number of plays in the projected Cycle varied from five to eleven, and only two are extant, *A Touch of the Poet* (1942/57),[1] the only one O'Neill carried through to completion, and *More Stately Mansions* (1939/62), a draft of which was spared accidentally when O'Neill and his third wife, actress Carlotta Monterey, destroyed the outlines and drafts of the play Cycle in his last year. In 1948, the year before Arthur Miller's seminal treatment of the American success myth in *Death of a Salesman*, O'Neill explained the overarching theme of the play Cycle:

> This country is going to get it – really get it. We had everything to start with – everything – but there's bound to be a retribution. We've followed the same selfish, greedy path as every other country in the world. We talk about the American Dream, and want to tell the world about the American Dream, but what is that dream, in most cases, but the dream of material things? I sometimes think that the United States, for this reason, is the greatest failure the world has ever seen. We've been able to get a very good price for our souls in this country – the greatest price perhaps that has ever been paid – but you'd

think that after all these years, and all that man has been through, we'd have sense enough – *all* of us – to understand that the whole secret of human happiness is summed up in a sentence that even a child can understand. The sentence? "For what shall it profit a man if he shall gain the whole world and lose his own soul?"[2]

The history of the Harford and Melody families embodies a fundamental struggle that O'Neill saw at the heart of American culture – the struggle between pragmatic, materialistic greed, essentialized in the success myth, and the search for spiritual transcendence, whether through God, through beauty, through nature, or through human love. All of his treatments of American culture, whether historical or contemporary, reveal similarly fundamental conflicts within and among Americans. While the oppositions among these values are refracted in various ways and given different emphases in his dramatic representations of the twenties and thirties, the sense of endlessly seeking a higher ground for human experience is never absent from them.

In *Mourning Becomes Electra* (1931), O'Neill's most effective treatment of history, he combined two characteristic strategies of American modernism, mythicizing and historicizing, to endow contemporary human experience with transcendent meaning. *Electra* embodies a struggle between the New England Puritan heritage of the Mannon family and the influence of the "foreigners" who have mixed with them, people who have the capacity to free America from its self-imposed oppression by the Mannons' life-denying Puritan ideology. All but one of the trilogy's fourteen acts take place, as in a classical Greek tragedy, before the exterior of a great building, the ante-bellum Mannon family mansion, a *"white Grecian temple portico with its six tall columns"* (*Plays* II, 893). The house is freighted with significance, as O'Neill makes clear in an early speech by Christine Mannon, one of the "foreigners": "Each time I come back after being away it appears more like a sepulchre! The 'whited' one of the Bible – pagan temple front stuck like a mask on Puritan gray ugliness" (*Plays* II, 903–04). Looming over the action of the play, the house is a constant statement of the failure of the Mannons, and of the United States, to overcome the failures of its native form of Puritanism, which, as a typical American modernist, O'Neill saw as moral hypocrisy and a life-denying repression of emotion, sexuality, and aesthetic response to beauty. Like the false face on the Mannon house, the overlay of a pseudo-classical civilization has served only to emphasize the ugliness of the Mannon values.

O'Neill saw the same struggle between life-denying puritanism and the desire for freedom and sensual experience in the United States of the

Twenties. In his review of *Diff'rent* (1920), Kenneth Macgowan called the play "a vigorous and healthful attack upon the puritanism that eats away so much of the creative happiness of life."[3] The modernist attack on puritanism was at the center of the play, but the opposition was not quite as simple as Macgowan suggested it was. O'Neill represents the struggle of the conflicting forces that define the character of Emma Crosby visually in the setting, even before the play opens. The Crosbys are a fishing family in a small coastal New England village. The set for the first Act, in 1890, is the family parlor, which is *"small and low-ceilinged. Everything has an aspect of scrupulous neatness"* (Plays II, 3). The dismal room is filled with furniture that is dark and old-fashioned for the eighteen-nineties. It is dominated by *"a bulky Bible with a brass clasp"* and *"several enlarged photos of strained, stern-looking people in uncomfortable poses"* (Plays II, 3). In short, it is a pictorial representation of small-town New England puritanism from the point of view of the modernist playwright. Like Emma herself, the room is joyless and life-denying, dominated by the religiosity of its patriarchal puritan past. On the table next to the Bible, however, are *"several books that look suspiciously like cheap novels"* (Plays II, 3), indicating the romantic sentimentality that conflicts with the puritanism in Emma's character. In the first act of the play, the puritanism wins, as Emma breaks her engagement with Caleb Williams when she finds out that he has had a brief sexual relationship with a young woman in the South Seas, proving to her that he was not as "diff'rent' from the others in the seafaring town as she had thought.

The second act takes place in 1920, and O'Neill uses the pictorial image of the set to convey the change that has taken place in the thirty intervening years. *"The room has a grotesque aspect of old age turned flighty and masquerading as the most empty-headed youth. There is an obstreperous newness about everything"* (Plays II, 27). The stage directions go on to describe a room that shrieked "modern" in 1920, with its orange curtains, hardwood floor with *"garnish-colored rugs,"* flowered wallpaper, painted-to-order seascapes in gilded frames, varnished oak and cane-bottomed furniture. Displaying the new conspicuous leisure and the rather frenetic pursuit of entertainment in the postwar years, the room is completed by a brand new piano, a set of unread installment-plan books, a pile of fashion magazines, and a Victrola that is playing a jazz record as the curtain rises. Significantly, however, the family Bible has survived the redecorating, suggesting that the inherited puritanism in this family is not dead, just overwhelmed by the material culture of the Twenties. Like the house, Emma has been transformed. Her heavy make-up, dyed hair, and short skirt make her into *"a pitiable sham, a too-apparent effort to cheat the years by appearances*" (*Plays* II, 27). She is making a fool of herself by flirting with Caleb's nephew Benny, a soldier, who is one of the first portraits of the "lost-generation" veteran in American literature. Caleb expresses the view of a bewildered older generation toward the returned World War I veteran:

> I thought when the war come, and he was drafted into it, that the army and strict discipline'd maybe make a man o' him. But it ain't! It's made him worse! It's killed whatever mite of decency was left in him. And I reckon now that if you put a coward in one of them there uniforms, he thinks it gives him the privilege to be a bully! Put a sneak in one and it gives him the courage to be a thief!
>
> (*Plays* II, 46–47)

After serving his tour in France, Benny has re-enlisted in the army because he was "sick o' this small place and wanted to be out where there was more fun" (*Plays* II, 30). He is callous and unscrupulous, consciously exploiting Emma's rather grotesque attraction to him in order to get some money out of her. He even plans to extort money from his uncle, who is still devoted to Emma, by threatening to marry her and take her money unless Caleb agrees to pay him. As the generation before him had exploited the women of the south seas sexually, Benny has exploited the women in Paris: "Oh, boy! They're some pippins! It ain't so much that they're better lookin' as that they've got a way with 'em – lots of ways. (*He laughs with a lascivious smirk*) ... I don't know about wicked, but they're darned good sports. They'd do anything a guy'd ask 'em" (*Plays* II, 33–34). Emma shows an obsessive interest in Benny's sexual exploits, compensating for the iron repression of her girlhood. When she discovers that Benny has no feeling for her and was simply planning to exploit her desire for him, she is devastated. Learning that Caleb has hanged himself in his barn, she heads out to join him, the force of puritanism conquering desire in the end.

Diff'rent is not a very good play, but it was an early exploration of the ideas that O'Neill was to employ to much better effect in the plays of the Twenties and early Thirties. In a somewhat crude mythologizing of the cultural situation in the United States of the early Twenties, Emma Crosby represents a country that is deeply divided between its inherited puritan culture, which is joyless, repressive, and focused on death, and the postwar world view, which is hedonistic, amoral, and unable to think beyond the present moment. On the positive side, while the puritan heritage offers a purpose in life based on faith in God and a clear set of moral principles, the postwar revolution offers a new creative freedom and a healthy acceptance of the body and its natural desires. This play indicates that the country's situation is tragic, for while Americans of Emma's generation can desire the new modern freedom of body and spirit, their puritan training converts it to something perverse and grotesque, and the "lost generation" simply has no values except the infantile gratification of its immediate desires.

Representing the opposition of cultural forces from a slightly different viewpoint, the conflict between materialistic greed and the desire for spiritual transcendence is at the center of O'Neill's historicized satire of the American businessman, *Marco Millions* (1924/28). O'Neill's version of Marco Polo, who was widely compared to Sinclair Lewis's Babbitt when the play was produced, "has not even a mortal soul, he has only an acquisitive instinct" (*Plays* II, 420). The division O'Neill presents in *Marco Millions* is a division between the materialistic West, personified in Marco, who cannot recognize beauty when it is placed in front of him, and the contemplative East, which values wisdom and beauty above the material.

The least successful of O'Neill's treatments of the opposing forces in contemporary American culture, *Dynamo* (1929), was a complicated representation of the conflict between puritanism and science. Basing his play loosely on Henry Adams's opposition of the Dynamo and the Virgin in *The Education of Henry Adams*, O'Neill combined the forces that are working upon Reuben Light – puritanism, a desire for religious faith, sexual desire for both his mother and his girlfriend, guilt, maternal jealousy, fear, electricity, and hatred for his father – into one unified force that comes into being when Reuben fetishizes the dynamo that produces electricity into a female idol representing the power of science in opposition to the patriarchal Puritanism of his father, a fundamentalist minister. Projecting the sexual prudery of his mother onto his self-created god, Reuben is overcome with guilt for his own sexuality and immolates himself on the dynamo. The last of O'Neill's plays searching for what he called "god-replacements," *Dynamo* demonstrates the futility of trying to replace America's outworn Puritan religion with a worship of power through science.

By far the most ambitious of O'Neill's treatments of contemporary American culture was *Strange Interlude* (1928), a nine-act play that addresses all of the concerns in the other plays in its mythicizing of the cultural condition of the United States in the nineteen-twenties. *Strange Interlude* generates meaning at a number of levels, the most obvious of which is as a Freudian-influenced study of character. For this play O'Neill developed a technique of dialogue that was similar to the "stream-of-consciousness" technique that was being introduced by modernist fiction writers like James Joyce, but had been used in American drama as early as 1913 in Alice Gerstenberg's *Overtones*. The "Interlude technique" involves two levels of dialogue – one that is recognized as regular speech to which the other characters respond and one that is recognized as what in film would be a "voiceover" – the character enunciating his or her thoughts, which are heard by the audience but not by the other characters. This allowed O'Neill to interpolate the characters' analyses of themselves and each other into the dialogue. While the psychology comes across as rather crude Freudianism today, the dialogic method has been successful with theatre audiences as recently as the 1984 revival with Glenda Jackson, directed by Keith Hack, which was well received in both London and New York.

More to the purpose here is O'Neill's use of Nina Leeds as a figuration of the United States in the twentieth century, the central figure in his mythicizing of American culture between the world wars. As the play opens, Nina is trying not very successfully to recover from the devastating effects of World War I on her emotional and psychological health. Like the country, Nina has lost her hope for the future in losing the embodiment of her generation's youthful promise, Gordon Shaw. Gordon, her fiancé, was a college hero who united prowess on the athletic field with the highest marks in his academic courses. Before leaving to be trained as a fighter pilot, Gordon had spent the night with Nina, but, as she says: "Gordon never possessed me! I'm still Gordon's silly virgin! ... I knew it was only the honorable code-bound Gordon, who kept commanding from his brain, no, you mustn't, you must respect her" (*Plays* II, 648). After distinguishing himself in the war, Gordon was "brought down in flames ... two days before the armistice" (*Plays* II, 635). The memories of Gordon expressed by Nina and the family friend Charlie Marsden suggest that he was the epitome of virtue. Marsden remembers that fairness and honor were "Gordon's proud spot" (*Plays* II, 640) and Nina broods over the loss of his spirit, "brave and generous and gay" (*Plays* II, 645). In short Gordon is the village hero, the representative of the bright promise of his generation that is destroyed in the war. His early death is the origin of the "Gordon myth" that develops around him, Nina's idea of male perfection, one that none of the men in her life will be able to match.

For the nation, the loss of Gordon represents a loss of innocence – the loss of those fine-sounding virtues that were an overhang from the nineteenth century. As Ernest Hemingway was to have his disaffected soldier say in *A Farewell to Arms*, published a year after *Interlude* was produced: "I was always embarrassed by the words sacred, glorious, and sacrifice and the expression in vain ... I had seen nothing sacred, and the things that were glorious had no glory and the sacrifices were like the stockyards at Chicago if nothing was done with the meat except to bury it."[4] America entered World War I with Woodrow Wilson's promise to make the world "safe for democracy" and came out of it on the winning side, but instead of a safer world, it was faced with the devastating reality of nine million people killed on both sides, and with the constant reminder of the maimed and the shell-shocked as European Realpolitik destroyed the dreams of world democracy and much of Europe drifted toward fascism. The loss of Gordon is the loss of America's schoolboy ideals.

Like the United States after the war, Nina turns to frivolity and aimless activity to fill the void. O'Neill makes it clear that Nina has become unstable after losing Gordon. After a period of "horrible numbed calm," she spends the summer playing golf and tennis and driving around with her friends, dancing and eating "with a ravenous appetite" (*Plays* II, 638). Having spent a period of mourning, her father notices, "she's gone to the opposite extreme! Sees everyone – bores, fools – as if she'd lost all discrimination or wish to discriminate. And she talks interminably ... intentional nonsense ... refuses to be serious! Jeers at everything!" (*Plays* II, 638). Nina has become a good example of that postwar phenomenon, the flapper, as described by its epitome, Zelda Fitzgerald: "You always know what she thinks, but she does all her feeling alone ... an artist in her particular field, the art of being – being young, being lovely, being an object ... whose sole functions are to amuse and to make growing old a more enjoyable process for some men and staying young an easier one for others."[5] Unable to find forgetfulness in the empty amusements of the flapper, Nina becomes a nurse in a veterans' hospital, trying to assuage her guilt at not having "given herself" to Gordon by having sex with any of the patients who desire her. As Dr. Ned Darrell puts it, "she began to blame herself and to want to sacrifice herself and at the same time give happiness to various fellow war-victims by pretending to love them" (*Plays* II, 663–64). Nina's promiscuity does not help her, and, as Ned suggests, each experience "has only left her more a prey to a guilty conscience than before and more determined to punish herself!" (*Plays* II, 664).

Like the country after the war, Nina has tried to lose the sense of its devastation through empty amusements and ineffectual compensation to the veterans. When her father dies, she finally is forced to face the reality of her disillusionment. Dr. Leeds, a professor in a New England college, represents the overlay of classical Western culture on American Puritanism. As Marsden says, he is "primly classical ... when New Englander meets Greek" (*Plays* II, 634). In the myth of the play, the death of Dr. Leeds represents the passing away of nineteenth-century cultural beliefs – faith in the patriarchal God of the Judaeo-Christian tradition, and faith in the wisdom of the past and in the institutions based on that faith. After her father is gone, Nina tells Charlie: "I was trying to pray. I tried hard to pray to the modern science God. I thought of a million light years to a spiral nebula – one other universe among innumerable others. But how could that God care about our trifling misery of death-born-of-birth? I couldn't believe in Him, and I wouldn't if I could" (*Plays* II, 668–69). Nina is devastated by her loss of faith, which she also recognizes as a loss of human feeling. "I want to believe so I can feel! I want to feel that he is dead – my father! And I can't feel anything" (*Plays* II, 670). She ascribes both losses to the war, realizing that her attempts to make up for her "failure" with Gordon were misguided: "I knew it was a stupid, morbid business, that I was more maimed than they were, really, that the war had blown my heart and insides out!" (*Plays* II, 672).

Like Reuben Light in *Dynamo*, Nina recognizes that the twentieth-century alternative to the dead belief systems represented by her father is the "science God," but unlike Reuben, she realizes its limitations. As she says, the scientist "believes if you pick a lie to pieces, the pieces are the truth ... he's so inhuman" (*Plays* II, 668). Nina imagines another alternative, however, in the God she sees as "God the Mother." The perversion of our view of life, she decides, has been that our "God of Gods – the Boss – has always been a man" (*Plays* II, 670). Instead, she decides:

> We should have imagined life as created in the birth-pain of God the Mother. Then we would understand why we, Her children, have inherited pain, for we would know that our life's rhythm beats from Her great heart, torn with the agony of love and birth. And we would feel that death meant reunion with Her, a passing back into Her substance, blood of Her blood again, peace of Her peace! (*Plays* II, 670)

As represented in the play, Nina's (and America's) search for the peace of God the Mother is thwarted from the beginning by the very patriarchal nature of American culture. Nina's life is always in the hands of the men to whom she attaches herself: her father, Gordon Shaw, the three rivals who want to possess her – Charlie Marsden, Sam Evans, and Ned Darrell – and her son, Gordon, Jr.

Like the other American modernists, many of whom O'Neill knew from his days in Greenwich Village before the war, O'Neill reserved his greatest scorn for the elements of American culture that he saw as deriving from Puritanism – the worship of duty, judgment of and retribution for the human frailties of others, sexual repression and the withdrawal from life experience. In *Strange Interlude*, these characteristics are represented in the figure of Charlie Marsden. Charlie is a writer of novels that even he thinks of as "long-winded fairy tales for grown-ups" (*Plays* II, 795). A character whom Ned Darrell describes as "one of those poor devils who spend their lives trying not to discover which sex they belong to" (*Plays* ii, 662), Charlie has a deep aversion to sex, which O'Neill ascribes to a bad initial experience with a prostitute when he was sixteen. Charlie embodies a puritanical rejection of the new sexual freedom being asserted by the artists of O'Neill's generation in the Twenties. As Charlie thinks to himself: "oh, this digging in gets nowhere ... to the devil with sex! ... our impotent pose of today to beat the loud drum on fornication! ... boasters ... eunuchs parading with the phallus! ... giving themselves away ... whom do they fool? ... not even themselves!" (*Plays* ii, 635). Charlie loves Nina from a distance throughout the play, but is pushed aside, first by Gordon Shaw, then by Sam Evans and Ned Darrell.

Sam embodies the force that O'Neill sees as having taken over the national spirit during the Twenties. In the view of President Calvin Coolidge, the business of America is business. Sam, a character who is more sympathetic than Lewis's Babbitt or O'Neill's Marco Polo, shares essential characteristics with them. While Sam requires Nina's approval and confidence in him to flourish, once he comes into his own, he is as much a personification of "the acquisitive instinct" as Marco is. Like Charlie, Sam is a writer, but a writer of copy for an advertising agency, one of the fastest-growing of postwar American boom-time businesses. As Sam sits in Professor Leeds's study, surrounded by the classics of Western culture, his thoughts as he tries to write indicate the sorry pass to which O'Neill believes the arts have come in the service of business: "No use ... can't think of a darn thing ... well, who could dope out a novel ad on another powdered milk, anyway? ... all the stuff been used already ... Tartars conquering on dried mare's milk ... Metchnikoff, eminent scientist ... been done to death ... But the old man turns over in his grave at my writing ads in his study ... maybe that's why I can't ... bum influence" (*Plays* ii, 693).

Rather presciently in 1928, O'Neill has Sam suffering from a hidden congenital disease that will destroy him eventually, as the booming bull market on Wall Street was about to be destroyed by the crash of 1929. Sam's lack of confidence in his fertility threatens to destroy him as a businessman until he is convinced by Nina and Ned that the child they have produced, Gordon, Jr., is his. As he begins to be successful in the advertising business, he becomes more and more confident, and also more grasping and materialistic. When Charlie's mother dies, Sam immediately considers how he can get Charlie to invest part of his estate in his advertising business. As Charlie, who begins to dislike him, thinks, "he's brash ... a little success ... oh, he'll succeed all right ... his kind are inheriting the earth ... hogging it, cramming it down their tasteless gullets!" (*Plays* ii, 735). Charlie recognizes in Sam the "typical terrible child of the age ...

universal slogan, keep moving ... moving where? ... never mind that ... don't think of ends ... the means are the end" (*Plays* II, 744). As he becomes more wealthy and successful, Sam's love for Nina dies, and he cares only for Gordon, Jr., who embodies the qualities of the "college hero" he was named for. O'Neill implies that, despite its amoral pursuit of the main chance, the greedy, materialistic American business culture desires to claim the myth of innocence represented in Gordon as its own, one of the fundamental contradictions in America's self-conception.

In O'Neill's myth, Ned Darrell, the force of science, temporarily displaces Sam (business success) as the object of Nina's (America's) desire. Ned is first depicted as a man who has placed his human desires and emotions under an iron repression in order to pursue science: "*There is a quality about him, provoking and disturbing to women, of intense passion which he has rigidly trained himself to control and set free only for the objective satisfaction of studying his own and their reactions; and so he has come to consider himself as immune to love through his scientific understanding of its real sexual nature*" (*Plays* II, 661). Nina remarks, "I like him because he's so inhuman" (*Plays* II, 668). Ned analyzes others with the same emotionally repressed "scientific detachment" with which he thinks about his own actions and responses. He convinces himself that cooperating with Nina's plan to have a child together and convince Sam it is his would be his "duty as an experimental searcher after truth ... to observe these three guinea pigs, of which I am one" (*Plays* II, 711). When Nina becomes pregnant and Sam acquires the self-confidence he needs to become wealthy in the advertising business Ned considers the experiment a success, but he had not planned on the emotional effects of his sexual relationship with Nina. As Ned puts it, "the other male, Ned, seems to have suffered deterioration" (*Plays* II, 754) as a result of his love for Nina and his desire to assert his paternity of the child. Recognizing Sam as the provider that she and Gordon need, Nina relegates Ned to an ancillary role, allowing him to be her lover as she allows Charlie to play the role of father. At this point, Nina accepts all three of her men, as she feels "their desires converge in me! ... to form one complete beautiful male desire which I absorb ... and am whole ... they dissolve in me, their life is my life" (*Plays* II, 756). At this point, the end of Act 6, America's fascination with the triangulation of patriarchal Puritanism, business, and science exists in a rather uneasy balance, and all are father to the new generation. As Charlie thinks, "her child is the child of our three loves for her" (*Plays* II, 756).

This tenuously balanced system inevitably breaks down, however, as each of the forces proceeds on its own trajectory. Nina develops the same obsessive love for her son that she has for the idea of the dead Gordon. Taking money from Charlie and Ned to build his business and making them wealthy through his success, Sam also emasculates them by taking away their meaningful work. In the Twenties, America was so enamored of business, and especially the "success myth" of the "self-made man," that the romance of science and the arts had pretty much been displaced in the nation's affections by that of the businessman, F. Scott Fitzgerald's Jay Gatsby being the cultural alter ego of Lewis's boorish Babbitt. O'Neill implies that business money, and therefore business power, now controls the pursuits of art and science in America. Ned, who has given up his medical research and now dabbles in experimental biology, complains, "our backing Sam has made Marsden and me so wealthy that we're forced to take up hobbies. Marsden goes in for his old one of dashing off genteel novels, while I play at biology" (*Plays* II, 761).

The hegemony of business is not permanent, however. By having Ned Darrell find another basis for value than money, O'Neill suggests that the balance of cultural power in the United States is not as stable as it may seem. Ned goes away to work at his research station and returns rejuvenated and empowered. Nina's question about his discovery of the "fountain of youth" brings a clear answer: "Work! I've become as interested in biology as I once was in medicine. And not selfishly interested, that's the difference" (*Plays* II, 785). In pursuing knowledge for its own sake rather than for his personal fame and profit, Ned has found an alternative value-system to that of capitalism as represented by Sam, and for a time he claims a new dignity and a freedom from Sam and all that he represents. This freedom proves illusory, however, for Sam asserts the power of money even from the grave when he leaves Ned half a million dollars for his research, thus proving once again that it is money, and therefore business, that drives science, not the pursuit of knowledge. Wanting to remain pure, and free, Ned at first refuses to accept the money, but then realizes the foolishness of such illusory innocence. Knowing that his protégé Preston will be offered the money if he refuses it, he thinks, "but it's for science! ... he has no right to refuse! ... I have no right to ask him to!" (*Plays* II, 810–11). In Ned's view, Sam has won. Not only did he "own" Ned's "wife" and son during his lifetime, "now in death he reaches out to steal Preston! ... to steal my work!" (*Plays* II, 811).

Sam's money does not have the ultimate power, however. Ned and Sam, science and business, have been fighting for Nina's material body, but it is finally puritanism that claims her immortal soul, in the figure of Charlie Marsden. After Sam's death, and Ned's departure to devote himself single-mindedly to his work, Gordon, Jr. flies off in his plane as Nina calls, "Fly up to heaven, Gordon! Fly with your love to heaven! Fly always! Never crash to earth like my old Gordon" (*Plays* II, 816). The allusion to Icarus, falling from the sky as he tried to reach the sun, is telling in conjunction with the personification of America's myth of innocence in the Gordons. Like all romantic fantasies, this one, O'Neill implies, is headed for ultimate destruction, no matter how much America may still want to believe in it. As Gordon flies off with his fiancée, Nina says to Charlie, "My having a son was a failure, wasn't it? He couldn't give me happiness. Sons are always their fathers. They pass through the mother to become their father again ... they could not give us happiness!" (*Plays* II, 817). Nina's search for the ideal mate and for God the Mother have brought her back once again to the father, the patriarchy that she is finally unable to escape.

Nina ends up with Charlie Marsden, who advises her to "forget the whole affair of your association with the Gordons" (*Plays* II, 817). He suggests that together, the two of them can "forget the whole distressing episode, regard it as an interlude, of trial and preparation, say, in which our souls have been scraped clean of impure flesh and made worthy to bleach in peace" (*Plays* II, 817). And Nina agrees: "Yes, our lives are merely strange dark interludes in the electrical display of God the Father!" (*Plays* II, 817). The implication for O'Neill's America was unmistakable. Rather than waste time on the accumulation of material wealth or the illusion of power through the accumulation of knowledge, in 1928 O'Neill thought that America needed to look to its spiritual health. As Anglo-America began with puritanism, he suggested, it is likely to end with it, although in some debased form like Charlie Marsden, at peace, and "passed beyond desire" (*Plays* II, 818). For American culture, Nina's movement from the influence of her father, the union of classical Western civilization and New England puritanism, to that of Charlie, the repressed writer of fairy tales for adults, implies a decadence that suggests little hope for the future. While O'Neill saw this cultural state as clearly tragic when he implied it in *Diff'rent* in 1920, his implication is more ambiguous at the end of the decade. On the one hand, the search for spiritual transcendence that pervades O'Neill's dramatic representations of American culture is thoroughly defeated in Nina's settling for Charlie. On the other hand, Nina and Charlie may have chosen a form of death-in-life in their acceptance of each other, but they have also found peace, and they have in some degree escaped subjugation to the twentieth century's false gods of money and science. After the cultural upheaval and the moral impoverishment of the Twenties, this state appeared less unthinkable than it had a few years earlier, but its peaceful acceptance was itself only a brief interlude in O'Neill's pursuit of the means of spiritual transcendence.

NOTES

1 The dates given for plays are the dates of the first production, except in cases where there was a long delay between the completion of a script and its production, in which case the date of completion precedes the date of production.

2 Quoted in Hamilton Basso, "Profiles: The Tragic Sense," *New Yorker* (13 March 1948); rpt. *Conversations with Eugene O'Neill*, ed. Mark W. Estrin (Jackson: University Press of Mississippi, 1990), p. 230.

3 "Diff'rent," *Vogue* 57 (15 March 1921): 82.

4 Ernest Hemingway, *A Farewell to Arms* (New York: Scribner's, 1929), p. 196.

5 *Zelda Fitzgerald: The Collected Writings*. ed. Matthew J. Bruccoli (New York: Collier, 1991), p. 398.

WORKS CITED OR CLOSELY RELATED TO THIS ESSAY

Egri, Peter, "High Culture and Popular Culture in Eugene O'Neill: *Strange Interlude*" in *High and Low in American Culture*, ed. Charlotte Kretzoi (Budapest: Lorand Eotvos University, 1986): 55–76.

Estrin, Mark W., *Conversations with Eugene O'Neill* (Jackson: University Press of Mississippi, 1990).

Hinden, Michael, "Paradise Lost: O'Neill and American History," *Eugene O'Neill Newsletter* 12 (1988): 39–48.

Kimbel, Ellen, "Eugene O'Neill as Social Historian: Manners and Morals in *Ah, Wilderness!*" in *Critical Essays on Eugene O'Neill*, ed. James J. Martine (Boston: G.K. Hall, 1984).

Miller, Ronald R., "From Scenario to Script: O'Neill's Use of History in the Creation of *A Touch of the Poet* and *More Stately Mansions*" in *Text and Presentation*, ed. Karelisa Hartigan (Lanham, Maryland: University Press of America, 1990).

Murphy, Brenda, "Fetishizing the Dynamo: Henry Adams and Eugene O'Neill," *Eugene O'Neill Review* 16 (Spring 1992): 85–90.

O'Neill, Eugene, *Complete Plays*, 3 volumes (New York: Library of America, 1988).

Raleigh, John Henry, "Strindberg in Andrew Jackson's America: O'Neill's *More Stately Mansions*," *Clio* 13 (1983): 1–15.

Schmitt, Patrick, "*Marco Millions* and O'Neill's Vision of America," *Canadian Review of American Studies* 20 (1989): 31–39.

10

EDWARD L. SHAUGHNESSY

O'Neill's African and Irish–Americans: stereotypes or "faithful realism"?

Eugene O'Neill came early to recognize the fakery of the commercial theatre. It was in that "hateful" institution, after all, that his own father had gained fortune and celebrity. Yet, no matter how much he ridiculed the cardboard world of popular melodrama, young O'Neill grew in knowledge as he moved about freely in his father's house. "... I was practically brought up in the theatre – in the wings – and I know all the technique of acting. I know everything that everyone is doing from the electrician to the stage hands" (Cargill *et al.*, 112). In the same way he became acquainted with the sensational effects obtained by producer–illusionist David Belasco, who specialized in snapshot realism. But O'Neill, who criticized Belasco, was himself innovator enough to use any device he thought might advance his dramatic intention.

Did O'Neill trade in stereotypes? On the level of surface realism, he probably did. If so, however, he merely followed well-established practice. For, in the end, all characters in drama, even the most complex or eccentric, are chiseled from standing blocks identified as types A, B, C, and so forth. Indeed, it is their surface realism that makes even the greatest characters memorable. Take Lady Macbeth, the very type of ruthless and ambitious wife, who invokes all strategies fair and foul to gain her end. In truth she becomes believable only by virtue of her complexity, that web of drives and motives which gives her madness its riveting power. Great storytellers achieve verisimilitude by rendering the idiosyncratic plausible. O'Neill also came to understand the range of types and the secret of transcending their limitations. Brutus Jones, his *"features ... typically negroid"* (*Complete Plays*, II, 1033) may seem a too obvious neo-primitive, the manchild driven by simple urges and superstitions. Still, as O'Neill explores the logic of the unconscious mind, he moves beyond mere linear realism in *The Emperor Jones*. In *The Iceman Cometh* Larry Slade's *"gaunt Irish face"* gives him the look of a *"weary old priest"* (*Complete Plays*, III, 566), yet Slade is surely one of O'Neill's most complicated characters.

Say what we will, however, an image takes shape as we bring the type to mind: the back-slapping salesman, the red-neck sheriff, the ingenue, the Boston Brahmin. The question is what the artist does with the generalized picture.[1] Shakespeare enlightens; the charlatan distorts. O'Neill's genius was to take from the book of types but to breathe into this clay souls whose terrifying psycho-spiritual histories have become forever fixed in our memories.

In the nineteenth century a particularly virulent form of stereotype was exploited by the American press: the racial and political cartoon. In his depictions of loutish simian Paddies and idiot Sambos, Thomas Nast was no doubt best known of those whose acid portraits sacrificed realism for exaggeration. Nast found nearly all that he hated in the Irish Catholic democrat, whom he mocked again and again as incorrigible brawler and drunkard (in short, the hooligan). O'Neill knew, of course, from background and experience, that both black and Irish–Americans had been hated and alienated, even if he saw differences in the nature of their estrangements.

Black themes and characters

O'Neill did not live to witness the civil rights movement of the 1960s. His reflections on African–American life had been recorded once and for all by 1939. No scene in any of his plays shows blacks in a setting later than the American 1920s. Emancipated *de jure* but never *de facto*, his African–American characters exist in conditions of effective subjugation. They are often forced to behave in ways that confirm the very stereotypes others hold of them. Condemned to live out his prophecy of doom, O'Neill's black exists in a state of resentment and fear, conditions which make him simultaneously suspect and pitiable.

Joel Pfister has examined O'Neill's black portraits very closely. In the end he feels that the playwright did little to enhance the image of African–Americans. In fact, Pfister questions whether O'Neill created sympathy for abused blacks or whether he merely extended the "stereotypes ... that inhabited the cultural swamp of [his] literary imagination" (132). On the other hand, Michael Manheim has taken a view that in O'Neill's Joe Mott, "a descendant of Brutus Jones," we discover

the American black as the American white establishment has forced him to be, though his name suggests that he may also stand for other racial and religious minorities. Desperately isolated, full of indignation, he capitulates not so much because of his personal ghosts, though they exist, as out of a necessity bred by the inescapable vulnerability America has forced upon its racial minorities. (149)

One must concede that a degree of determinism obtains: the effects of applied prejudice are as certain as death. Of course, the victim has little opportunity to view his plight philosophically. But O'Neill saw the immediate damage done, and much more. By representing these effects with fidelity to nuance, the playwright was able to reveal his characters' deeper nature. He thereby accorded his blacks absolute equality in tragic stature.

O'Neill treated human character on three levels: the cultural, which shapes the surface personality; the psychological, which examines the mask behavior that derives from the first; and the spiritual, which depends least on the racial–ethnic. Of course, environmental (i.e., cultural) forces, while they are vastly formative, are essentially accidental. Environment produces the "form," or outward self, that is recognized by others: one's language, codes of dress and deportment, often even one's loyalties, values, and prejudices. On the second level, O'Neill studies the individual's struggle to preserve integrity, his unified self. If he cannot accept the culture's attempt to shape him (to own him), he may seek to preserve his personhood behind an acceptable counterfeit (the mask or *persona*).

But on the third level O'Neill's characters meet on an existential common ground. Here the playwright achieves whatever universality his art may claim. Accepting Nietzsche's "death-of-God" proclamation, the playwright nevertheless sought to invest his characters with a dignity denied by the narrow assumptions of the prevailing literary naturalism. (Indeed, he once proposed to call his work "supernaturalism.") All persons, without regard to the accidents of birth (place, endowment, and race), suffer the ineluctable condition of humanity: the tragedy of time. In this sense O'Neill is more concerned with "fate" than with determinism. Therefore, his major black plays finally deal less with racial matters than with the more fundamental question of what it means to be human.

O'Neill created four important black characters, each of whom searches for his identity by testing the opportunities open to him. The first is an angry and violence-prone teen, now a fugitive, who has found his image in the criminal model. This is Abe, "The Dreamy Kid" (1918). "Dreamy" rejects the advice of those, like Mammy Saunders and Ceely Ann, who caution him to conform. Mortally ill, Mammy asks her grandson to stay by her bedside. Dreamy is torn. Having killed a white man, he is on the run from the police. He whispers to his girlfriend, who insists he leave: "She's croakin', I tells yo' – an' I gotter stay wid her fo' a while – an' I ain't got no time ter be pesterin' wid you" (*Complete Plays*, I, 686). In the brevity of this play, Dreamy's case can be examined in only two stages of human response, the cultural and psychological. His façade of toughness crumbles. (All masks eventually shred in O'Neill.) Fear pierces him, and his behavior becomes perfectly illogical. In panic, he says: "Dey don't git de Dreamy. Not while he's 'live. Lawd Jesus, no suh!" (691).

The Emperor Jones (1920) presents O'Neill's best-known African–American. The surface realism of this *tour de force* is strong, yet by play's end Brutus Jones's blackness has become strangely irrelevant. In a remarkable economy of eight scenes, the play tells of the final day and horrifying death of an erstwhile Pullman porter. Now a prison escapee, Jones has fled to a West Indies island, probably Haiti, where he has exploited the "low-flung bush niggers" and established his "empire." Finally catching on, his "subjects" seek to topple him. In a panicked flight through the Great Forest, as the natives' tom-tom beats ever more rapidly, Jones spirals downward through dream levels and is carried to the place of his personal origin. "... [S]eems like I been heah befo'" (I, 1057). As he moves backward through layers of racial history, Jones at last "beholds" a witch doctor who is making preparations for a sacrifice.

But where had Brutus Jones learned the Darwinian ethic of conquest and gained the skill to deceive the natives? In truth, he had found his models among the successful white salesmen who expound the American business "ethic" in the smoking cars of the Pullmans. The protagonist has merely imitated those who play the power game successfully. Thus, his remark to a crooked Cockney trader is freighted with irony: "For de little stealin' dey gits you in jail soon or late. For de big stealin' dey makes you Emperor and puts you in de Hall o' Fame when you croaks ... If dey's one thing I learns in ten years on de Pullman ca's listening to de white quality talk, it's dat same fact" (1035). Questions of racial superiority have, then, been made to seem superfluous.

The Emperor Jones will probably be disqualified today as "politically incorrect." This is unfortunate, for at bottom O'Neill offers a brilliant study of a soul's unravelling. In this disengagement from reality, we witness the undoing of a man's carefully constructed persona in the moment of surrender to death. In this play of less than an hour's duration the protagonist's destiny suggests something universal. At the end of the action we discover, not the stereotype of the opening scene, but the universal man.[2]

In *All God's Chillun Got Wings* (1923), Jim Harris, a *"studious-looking Negro with an intelligent yet queerly-baffled face"* (II, 292), seeks to make

6 Charles Gilpin as the Emperor Jones in uniform, smiling defiantly, from a 1920 production

himself worthy of his idealized love, Ella Downey. Ella had been his childhood playmate who lived on the Irish side of the street, across from the blacks. This neighborhood might be called Division Street, where groups live in physical proximity but are separated by a gulf of mistrust and cultural differences. Ella comes to feel a profound ambivalence for Jim, who treats her "white" but whom she has been conditioned to look down upon. As a law student Jim has gained a certain verbal dexterity, yet as a black American he has been programmed to fail in self-esteem: "... [W]hen I'm called on – I stand up – all the white faces looking at me – and I can feel their eyes – I hear my own voice sounding funny, trembling – and all of a sudden it's all gone in my head ..." (292).

Ella, first used and then cast off by an Irish prize fighter (Mickey), marries Jim, whom she loves and who wishes to serve her. But so deep has been her training in hatred for her "inferiors" that she belittles him in frenzied attempts to assert her own higher status: "You dirty Nigger" (311). To O'Neill both "the black Jim Harris and the white Ella Downey have internalized racist ideologies and stereotypes that sabotage their 'psychology'" (Pfister, 135). Moreover, says Pfister, "O'Neill's emphasis on psychological determinism in both *The Emperor Jones* and *All God's Chillun* often stands in contradiction to his insights into the internalization of racist language and images" (136). I see the issue in somewhat different terms. Because they breathe and interact in a culture of sickness, both Jim and Ella, even as children, have been infected by America's most lethal virus: racism. To that extent determinism *is* a factor. Their pathology is therefore a kind of synecdoche for the illness that degrades the social organism. Thus O'Neill paints Jim and Ella with fidelity to the logic of an internalized psychology. More important, however, is that they have already been trapped by their human fate of cosmic orphanhood. "The racial factor is incidental," the playwright remarked. "The play is a character study of two human beings" (Sheaffer, *O'Neill: Son and Artist*, 135).

There are three major but no minor male characters in *The Iceman Cometh* (1939). In this sense Joe Mott, a "*one-time proprietor of a Negro gambling house*," is on an equal footing with the other characters. Although he is tolerated by the Irish, Italian, British white African and other "inmates" of Harry Hope's hotel-bar, Joe represents all black Americans who never fully belong. He can sit at the table with the Boer War veterans Piet Wetjoen and Cecil Lewis, but he is taunted by the bartender-pimps, Chuck Morello and Rocky Pioggi. When they call him a "black bastard" and a "doity nigger," he rages like all members of bullied minorities: "You white sons of bitches! I'll rip your guts out" (III, 658). Even Wetjoen calls him Kaffir ("nigger"). *The Iceman* was written near the end of O'Neill's career. By then he had come to believe that all men have reason to create comforting self-deceits. Joe is hardly an exception. He "*grins good naturedly*" but cautions Wetjoen and Lewis:

> ... I don't stand for "nigger" from nobody. Never did. In de old days, people calls me "nigger" wakes up in de hospital. I was de leader of de Dirty Half-Dozen Gang. All six of us colored boys, we was tough and I was de toughest. (589)

Joe Mott's real equality rests in his reinforcing this great theme: "(*Dreamily*) I'll make my stake and get my new gamblin' house open before you boys leave" (594). If it is argued that men and women live by pipe dreams, support for this view may be built on the facts of African–American history, at least as that history resonates in Eugene O'Neill's plays. Perhaps Professor Pfister has some reason to complain about "O'Neill's emphasis on psychological determinism." But, if the playwright's black characters (like all his others) derive support from illusions, that dependency in no way robs them of complexity.

Irish–Americans in O'Neill's plays

The stereotype is a natural, or at least predictable, creation of melodrama and formula fiction: the good guy, the villain, and the like. But the universal character (Everyman, Mother Courage), in addition to type, has been given a kind of protean humanity which, whatever the specifics of his trials or her situation, remains recognizable to men and women of every rank in any period or place. We meet these characters in all of literature, of course, but we encounter them most often in tragedy and the classic novel. No dramatist has been successful in avoiding the stereotype in every instance: not even Shakespeare, and certainly not Eugene O'Neill. The latter, in his early depictions of Irish–Americans, worked too often from a paint-by-the-numbers kit. As he gained confidence, however, he created more convincing characters; eventually, his men and women became fully three-dimensional.

O'Neill, who took pride in his Celtic roots, developed a sophisticated understanding of Irish history. Ironically, however, by practicing fidelity to truth, he sometimes rendered portraits even less flattering than the sketches done by Irish-baiters. For O'Neill refused to sentimentalize Irish America. Indeed, his portrayals often earned him resentment among latter-day Hibernians. As William V. Shannon once observed, "Those who thought him anti-Irish did not comprehend that for an artist telling the truth is the highest act of love" (264). A rejection of stereotype, then, does not imply a denial of ethnic or racial endowment. O'Neill admired the Celtic gifts of wit and lyricism; he knew first-hand the dark and brooding melancholy and the Irishman's debilitating habit of self-medication via alcohol; and he responded to the mysteries of fatalism and mysticism that stalk the Irish soul. Although he never made a journey to the "sod," O'Neill spoke with considerable authority in dealing with all things Irish.[3]

Although the immigrant Irish had long lived in a kind of servitude, they carried fewer handicaps than did blacks, in the struggle for American assimilation. As life was lived in the United States, their most obvious advantage was the protective covering of color. But fluency in English also gave the Irish far greater access to the world of "haves" than was available to blacks. With effort one could defeat the brogue. The case of the playwright's father illustrates the point: James O'Neill became an acclaimed Shakespearean actor. Not only did the Irish come to America speaking English, however; they had long since gained familiarity with English law, customs, and values.

Essentially O'Neill presents two sorts of Irish–Americans. The first group, who accept the logic of the American dream, can be easily lampooned and stereotyped. Like other nineteenth-century immigrants, the Irish wished for success as defined in a brave new world. But O'Neill saw clearly that this surrender to mammon was certain to produce a sense of self-loathing. Long before Arthur Miller, he had isolated the cause of the national sickness: one must sell oneself. Hoping to acquire fortune and high station, the Irish also admired the types who succeed: Marco "Millions" Polo (O'Neill's Babbitt); William A. Brown, architect to the philistines; or the patrician Harfords, who live in stately mansions. In *A Touch of the Poet*, the Irish–American Cornelius and Sara Melody (father and daughter) seek to gain social rank and wealth among well established New Englanders. In the career of his own father, mirrored in James Tyrone's of *Long Day's Journey*, Eugene O'Neill saw evidence of why the Irish immigrants have historically been susceptible to the spiritually enfeebling *virus Americanus*.

The second and smaller group of Irish–Americans are O'Neill's "fog people," a company of existential misfits who can never belong. By nature and inclination, they seem less likely to evoke stereotypes. Perhaps they will be thought of as the "black Irish" or mystics, those who long for some zone of peace and comfort "beyond the horizon." They look to a past, real or imagined, that cannot be recovered. If, politically, they espouse an ideal of social and material justice, they also recognize their dreams as little more than supportive illusions that help keep the void at a distance. As Larry Slade says in *The Iceman Cometh*, "It's a great game, the pursuit of happiness" (III, 572). Such men and women do not await the millennium. In these Irish O'Neill was reminded of what he had experienced himself: a conflict between faith and doubt; the idea of woman as both virgin and whore; the yearning for the Celtic *Tir na n'Og* (the land of eternal youth). Such men, often lost in the modern world, are foredoomed to see life itself as tragic.

O'Neill's first three Irish creations are sailors who surely call to mind stock Irish types. Each speaks with a pronounced brogue, is given to heavy drinking, and conducts his affairs with little regard for the virtue of prudence. Driscoll, *"a powerfully built Irishman,"* ships aboard the S. S. *Glencairn*, the microcosmic stage for O'Neill's one-act sea plays. Nearly all the crew are men of strong prejudices, superstitions, and elements so mixed as to render disaster all but inevitable. Yet the plays' poetic naturalism suggests a deeper, intrinsic menace in the world itself. Driscoll, who carries the scar tissue of the knock-about brawler, somehow responds with pity to the vulnerability of his mates. In "The Moon of the Caribbees" and "Bound East for Cardiff" of the *Glencairn* quartet, the sea's crushing power is always implied, of course. But some other terror haunts the sailors: each man is crippled by a sense of his own isolation and of life's basic injustice. John Synge's heroic Maurya describes the same dilemma with simple eloquence in *Riders to the Sea*: "No man at all can be living for ever, and we must be satisfied" (97). Aboard ship one contends not merely with the cruelty of officers but with something else: the burden of human destiny itself. As Driscoll says, "The divil's own life ut is to be out on the lonely sea wid nothin' betune you and a grave in the ocean but a spindle-shanked, gray-whiskered auld fool the loike av [the captain]" (I, 189).

In *The Hairy Ape* the ancient Paddy, an Irish dreamer who is always a little drunk, recalls a time before sailors were plunged into an inferno of smoke and steel. He pines for the days of clipper ships, when one felt connected to nature and when the very enterprise of sailing exhilarated the spirit: " 'Twas them days a ship was part of the sea and a man was part of a ship, and the sea joined all together and made it one" (II, 127).

Perhaps Mat Burke comes closest to the Irish stereotype. To his bragging and boozing are added equal parts pugilist and virgin-idolator. Like Driscoll, he is powerful and proud. But in a four-act play (*Anna Christie*), a central character ought to be a finished piece of work. Yet we discover in Burke a variation on the stage Irishman: the cork-screw rationalizing to justify his own loutish behavior; a maudlin loyalty to the "faith" and to his mother's memory; and the rascally irresponsibility of the typical boyo. Mat falls in love with Anna, daughter of a coal barge skipper, Chris Christopherson. Under his rough exterior but true to type, Mat believes in all the pieties about marriage to "a rale, dacent woman." So he goes on an epic binge when he learns of Anna's prostitute past. But the flinty Swedish girl is stronger than the two men and creates a far greater impact than either of them. She comforts the father who had abandoned her in her childhood: "There ain't nothing to forgive ... It ain't your fault, and it ain't mine, and it ain't his neither. We're all poor nuts, and things happen, and we yust get mixed in wrong, that's all" (I, 1015). Burke, "that damn Irish fallar" (994), cannot match the wisdom and charity of this woman who delivers an early O'Neillian statement on fate.

Along the way, O'Neill introduced characters whose Irishness contributes little to the plays' significance, e.g., Eileen Carmody in *The Straw* (1919) and Ella Downey in *All God's Chillun Got Wings* (1923). But only in his late plays did he create truly complex studies of Irish–Americans. From his father and from experience, O'Neill learned that the greatest Irish sin was betrayal, especially self-betrayal. In the story of James Tyrone in *Long Day's Journey Into Night* we may be reminded of the parable of a man who buried his talent and thereby suffered its loss (Matt. 25: 14–30). At about twenty Tyrone learned that he was brilliantly gifted. Others quickly saw his promise as Shakespearean actor. But the memory of his immigrant mother's and siblings' abasement by poverty made James into a kind of spiritual pauper. Thus, he took the role of cardboard hero and performed it for decades in a soulless melodrama. That decision exacted a fearful price: the loss of native talent, the loss of self-respect, and finally loss of the memory itself: "What the hell was it I wanted to buy, I wonder, that was worth – Well, no matter. It's a late day for regrets" (III, 810). Perhaps parables carry general meanings, but they surely transcend the limitations of stereotype.

The tragedy of Mary Tyrone, who stands for O'Neill's mother, can also be traced to childhood experience, but an experience of a kind quite the opposite of that which entrapped James. Overly protected by her indulgent Irish father, Mary was much praised in convent school for her unworldliness. Ironically, this very innocence contributes to her undoing. In marriage to the matinée idol, she too loses her life's trajectory. Perhaps the Tyrones' story seems especially convincing because, by the time he wrote it, Eugene O'Neill had mastered the dynamics of character: motivation, reflex, and inner consistency. By then he had given up all dependence on the stereotype and had come to see the Irish (indeed, to see all humans) as driven by powers both within and without themselves. These later portraits were painted in the style of "faithful realism," to use Edmund Tyrone's words.

While eight of the ten characters in *A Touch of the Poet* are Irish, only the leading characters transcend their stereotype. Cornelius Melody, once a major in His Majesty's Seventh Dragoons, now operates (1828) a tavern on the post road near Boston. By imposing scullery and serving chores on his peasant-wife, Nora, and their feisty daughter, Sara, he establishes himself as gentleman of leisure. Both women see the nonsense, of course, but Nora responds with charity, Sara with acerbity. The barkeep Maloy, cousin Cregan, and motley hangers-on (Roche, O'Dowd, and Riley) hardly challenge Melody's pose.

Con Melody seems at first the stereotypical "Mick on the make." A pretender to aristocracy, he is in fact the son of a lowly Galway shebeen keeper who "got rich by moneylendin' and squeezin' tenants and every manner of trick ... and bought an estate with a pack of hounds" (III, 185). War hero or not, Con had offended Anglo-Irish sensibilities by seducing a Spanish noble's wife. He took Nora and Sara to New England where he has been again rebuffed, this time by "the damned Yankee gentry." Tyrone had also sought Yankee approval but retained pride in his heritage. Melody, however, is more than a stereotype. He despises his background and "considers the few Irish around here to be scum beneath his notice" (186). He fails to persuade the ascendant Brahmins to acknowledge his "rightful" place. How galling, then, that his headstrong daughter should trick and then fall in love with Simon Harford, a proper Boston scion.

If Con Melody inveigles and his toadies grovel, Nora is shown to be the very paragon of Irish virtue, faithful and generous in all things familial but more than a stereotype. She is a finely sewn character, not a patch cut from the common cloth. In the opening scene of *More Stately Mansions* (sequel to *A Touch of the Poet*), Nora's spiritual beauty comes fully to light.[4] Melody finally defeated, is being waked. Nora accepts what is and prepares for what remains: first to mourn and then to take up a new life, perhaps as a nun. "... [T]here is a spirit in her that shines through her grief and exhaustion, some will behind the body's wreckage that is not broken, ... an essential humble fineness of character ..." (III, 290–91).

O'Neill had long worried about the traits of greed and possessiveness in the national psyche (e.g., *Desire Under the Elms, Marco Millions, The Great God Brown*). As he grew older, this concern became a near obsession. Indeed, he intended *A Touch of the Poet* and its sequel to be major entries in a projected Cycle on the theme of American materialism, *A Tale of Possessors, Self-Dispossessed. More Stately Mansions* carries the epic forward, its main action tracing the union and fortunes of Sara and Simon Harford, Irish acquisitiveness wedded to Yankee power and wealth.

More important, perhaps, than theme or characterization, where Irishness is concerned, is language. His limitations as wordsmith galled O'Neill. Even so, he occasionally acquitted himself in the manner of Irish wits, orators, and poets. Even the Irish tragedian must offer a convincing show that he can manage the elements of humor, both mordant and merry. O'Neill passes muster in both *A Moon for the Misbegotten* and *Long Day's Journey Into Night*. In the former the lowly tenant Hogan twits the brilliant Jim Tyrone in a spirited exchange worthy of Boucicault: "It's the landlord again, and my shotgun not handy. Is it Mass you're saying, Jim? That was Latin. I know it by ear. What the hell – insult does it mean?" (III, 875). In like manner the "wily Shanty Mick," Shaughnessy of *Long Day's Journey* blisters his millionaire neighbor: "[Shaughnessy] began by shouting that he was no slave Standard Oil could trample on. He was a king of Ireland, if he had his rights, and scum was scum to him, no matter how much money it had stolen from the poor" (III, 726).

Of course, the far greater challenge to the writer than this pepper rhetoric is the evocation of the ineffable. Irish poets are said to be successful at this; at least they seem willing to try. Early and often O'Neill had tried and failed in this test. He both recognized this deficiency and surmounted it in the late plays. Edmund Tyrone's attempt to share with his father the mystical moment at sea ("I belonged, without past or future, within peace and unity and a wild joy, within something greater than my own life, or the life of Man, to Life itself!") seems to vindicate O'Neill. At any rate, he allows himself the comfort of his father's praise in the words of old Tyrone: "Yes, there's the makings of a poet in you all right" (III, 812). Here was the recognition of a fellow artist.

O'Neill understood why a Jim Harris or James Tyrone should have felt the bitterness of unfulfillment. But their histories only accentuated the stabbing fear that everyone feels in his own isolation. It was this understanding, no doubt, that turned O'Neill from topical to universal issues. How fitting it is that three Irish–American characters, each with a deep knowledge of tragedy, deliver his darkest lines.[5] In *The Iceman Cometh* Larry Slade, defeated by life, *whispers*: "Be God, there's no hope" (III, 710). Jamie Tyrone flings his corrosive wit into the teeth of the absurd, as he beholds his deranged mother: "The Mad Scene. Enter Ophelia" (824). Edmund speaks for all impotent and disaffected poets: "Stammering is the native eloquence of us fog people" (812–13).

A note on performers

A word ought to be said about certain performances by black and Irish–Americans in O'Neill's plays. We know, of course, that the playwright generally held little confidence in actors' artistic judgment. (Perhaps he could never forget his father's "hateful theatre" in which the performers were encouraged to play to the gallery.) Most men and women who take to the boards, O'Neill believed, vastly over-estimate their own importance to a given production. Thus, he demanded strict fidelity to the text (including stage directions).

In casting black and Irish roles, O'Neill tried hard to avoid the easy slide into stereotypes. In *A Moon for the Misbegotten*, for example, he created a character (Josie Hogan) with "*the map of Ireland ... on her face*" but searched for an actress who could locate "*the inner state of Josie*." When

Irish-born Mary Welch read for the part in 1946, O'Neill quizzed her: "Are you Irish? What per cent?" Yet such things, he knew, merely enhance the surface realism. Later, when Miss Welch had won his confidence, he acknowledged her maturity by relating to her his sorrow and anger for the injustice done to America's blacks. In her essay, "Softer Tones for Mr. O'Neill's Portrait," Welch says:

> O'Neill brought up his earlier plays, particularly the ones he had written about the Negro people. He had felt deeply about them, and his face grew bitter and forceful as he recalled how some of the New York professional theatre crowd had accepted these works. His words were, "They didn't really understand what I was writing. They merely said to themselves, 'Oh look, the ape can talk!'" (In Cargill, *et al.*, 89)

In the end no actor received a higher accolade from Eugene O'Neill than did Charles Gilpin, the first Brutus Jones. Although Gilpin sometimes created problems by coming to work drunk and by improvising on stage, O'Neill named him one of three actors (with Louis Wolheim in *The Hairy Ape* and Walter Huston in *Desire Under the Elms*) who realized his intentions most fully. In 1946 he went further: "As I look back now on all my work, I can honestly say there was only one actor who carried out every notion of a character I had in mind. That actor was Charles Gilpin" (Woolf, "Eugene O'Neill Returns," 62). Even so, he was more than once infuriated by Gilpin's adlibbing: "If I ever catch you rewriting my lines again, you black bastard, I'm going to beat you up" (Gelbs, *O'Neill*, 449). The brilliant Paul Robeson, who took over the role of Brutus Jones when the play opened in London in 1924, also performed in the 1933 film version of *The Emperor Jones*. As Jim Harris in the controversial New York premiere of *All God's Chillun Got Wings*, Robeson established another theatrical milestone. O'Neill greatly admired the actor's range of talents and his political courage. But the tribute to Gilpin stood and, therefore, remains all the more impressive.

Irish actors who vied for parts in O'Neill have been models for their American cousins. Productions of his late masterpieces at Dublin's Abbey Theatre[6] occurred after O'Neill's death, of course, but he would surely have blessed the acclaimed performances by Ria Mooney (1959 and 1962) and Siobhan McKenna (1985) as Mary Tyrone. Vincent Dowling became a dedicated O'Neillian in Ireland and the United States: as Richard in *Ah, Wilderness!* (1962), as Edmund Tyrone (1959, 1962, 1967), and as Theodore Hickman in *The Iceman Cometh* (1972). Dudley Digges, trained by Frank Fay in the Abbey's early years, came to the United States and performed as Henry Smithers to Robeson's emperor in the film, as Ramsay

Fife in *Dynamo*, Chu-Yin in *Marco Millions*, and Harry Hope in the Broadway premiere of *The Iceman*.

It may be, however, that the most popular actor ever to appear in an O'Neill play was the Irish–American George M. Cohan in *Ah, Wilderness!* (1933). But, after early warm relations (their fathers had worked together to found the Catholic Actors' Guild), O'Neill did not take well to his fellow Celt. Cohan made a hit as Nat Miller, father to young Richard, but he began to puff up the part (more adlibbing!) and to stretch his time on stage. Many years later, and off the record, O'Neill referred to Cohan as "a vaudevillian" (Sheaffer, *Son and Artist*, 422).

Unfortunately, the playwright never saw Dublin-born Geraldine Fitzgerald in a play of his. She has played Essie Miller in *Ah, Wilderness!* (1969 and 1974) and Nora Melody in *A Touch of the Poet* (1978), but her Mary Tyrone opposite Robert Ryan in 1971 fairly stunned critics and audiences alike. Virginia Floyd points out that, in his notes, O'Neill had described a Mary very like the one Miss Fitzgerald created with director Arvin Brown. In researching the effects of morphine, they learned that some addicts experience a "cat reaction" and respond to the drug, not passively, but aggressively. Interpreted in this light, Mary becomes "the victimizer and not the victim" (Fitzgerald, "Another Neurotic Electra," 291).

In affairs of the theatre O'Neill's integrity was unassailable. His black and Irish–Americans must be seen as a "faithful realism." Never a propagandist, he was willing to incur doubts about his racial sympathies in his searing depictions of Brutus Jones and Jim Harris. Nor did he offer an *apologia* for his sometimes unflorid portraits of Irish–Americans. But in the end his Celtic credentials and loyalties were never truly in doubt. Indeed, O'Neill fairly glowed when he was praised by Irish writers. Yeats's esteem pleased him, of course. It was Sean O'Casey's tribute, however, that touched him most profoundly: "You write like an Irishman, not like an American" (Gelbs, 788).

All this given, it seems likely that O'Neill would have approved a 1983 television adaptation of *Long Day's Journey Into Night*. In that production the brilliant Ruby Dee headed an all African–American cast in a brave and moving version of the tragedy. So much for stereotypes.

NOTES

1 In his classic essay on "Stereotypes," Walter Lippmann acknowledges the over-simplifications and dangers that stereotypes can produce, but he also suggests their values: efficiency in categorizing experience.

2 The distinguished black historian, Nathan Irvin Huggins, makes an exceptionally useful observation in this connection in *Harlem Renaissance* (1971): "... here was no stereotype of Negro character. Emperor Jones's ultimate fall, although superstition is involved, occurs because the artifices that have propped him up have been removed. So, exposed and defenseless Jones – like any other man – falls victim to his fear and his essential, primitive nature." (296–97)

3 O'Neill once advised James T. Farrell to read Sean O'Faolain's biography, *The Great O'Neill.* "I learned from it a lot of the Irish past I had mislearned before. You know what most Irish histories are like – benign Catholic benediction-and-blather tracts, or blind jingo glorifications of peerless fighting heroes, in the old bardic fashion. Hugh O'Neill, as O'Faolain portrays him in the light of historical fact, is no pure and pious archangel of Erin but a fascinatingly complicated character ... In short, Shakespeare [his contemporary] might have written a play about him" (*Selected Letters*, 545).

4 It is interesting that in his journal (18 December 1941) O'Neill mentions his "notes on main themes of Cycle": there he observes, "5th Play – Nora as exemplar on simple religious plane – nunnery ideal ..." (*Work Diary*, 425).

5 There are many other O'Neill characters without Irish surnames who might well express the same sentiments: Dion Anthony in *The Great God Brown*, Nina Leeds in *Strange Interlude*, Lavinia Mannon in *Mourning Become Electra*, John Loving of *Days Without End*, the entire cast of *The Iceman Cometh*, Erie Smith in "Hughie," *et al.* As noted earlier, Eugene O'Neill should never be looked upon as parochial.

6 For a history of O'Neill productions (in both the Republic and the North) from 1922 to 1987, see Edward L. Shaughnessy's *Eugene O'Neill in Ireland: The Critical Reception.* (New York: Greenwood Press, 1988).

WORKS CITED

Fitzgerald, Geraldine, "Another Neurotic Electra: A New Look at Mary Tyrone," in *Eugene O'Neill: A World View,* ed. Virginia Floyd (New York: Frederick Ungar, 1979).

Gelb, Arthur and Barbara, *O'Neill.* Rev. edn. (New York: Harper, 1973).

Huggins, Nathan Irvin, *Harlem Renaissance* (New York: Oxford University Press, 1971).

Manheim, Michael, *Eugene O'Neill's New Language of Kinship* (Syracuse, New York: Syracuse University Press, 1982).

O'Neill, Eugene, *Complete Plays* (Vols. i, ii, and iii), ed. Travis Bogard (New York: Library of America, 1988).

  Selected Letters of Eugene O'Neill, ed. Travis Bogard and Jackson R. Bryer (New Haven: Yale University Press, 1988).

  "O'Neill Talks about His Plays" in *O'Neill and His Plays: Four Decades of Criticism,* ed. Oscar Cargill, N. Bryllion Fagin, and William J. Fisher (New York: New York University Press, 1961), pp. 110–12.

Pfister, Joel, *Staging Depth: Eugene O'Neill and the Politics of Psychological Discourse* (Chapel Hill and London: University of North Carolina Press, 1995).

Shannon, William V., *The American Irish: A Political and Social Portrait* (New York: Macmillan, 1963).

Sheaffer, Louis, *O'Neill: Son and Playwright* (Boston: Little, Brown, 1968).

O'Neill: Son and Artist (Boston: Little, Brown, 1973).

Synge, John M., *The Complete Works of John M. Synge* (New York: Random House, 1937).

Welch, Mary, "Softer Tones for Mr. O'Neill's Portrait" in Cargill, *et al.*, pp. 85–91.

Woolf, S.J., "Eugene O'Neill Returns After Twelve Years" (*New York Times*, 15 September 1946).

JUDITH E. BARLOW

O'Neill's female characters

Like many other male writers, Eugene O'Neill created a world populated primarily by men. From the sea plays at the beginning of his career to such late works as *The Iceman Cometh* and *Hughie*, men dominate his theatrical space. A simple number count confirms that only about one-third of the on-stage characters in O'Neill's dramas are female. It is also true that the playwright's conception of women is rooted in a traditional equation of "feminine" with "maternal" that limits his ability to cast women in subject positions rather than as objects of masculine desire. Still, O'Neill's female characters cannot all be easily pigeonholed into neat categories, and even his myriad Madonnas and whores frequently transcend the cultural and theatrical clichés he inherited.

The female characters in what might be called O'Neill's apprentice plays, those written in the years leading up to his Broadway debut in 1920 with *Beyond the Horizon*, are a curious mix, suggesting the influence of two and perhaps even three of the major modern dramatists who preceded him. Among the early works are a handful of problem plays like those favored by Henrik Ibsen. *Servitude* (1914), for example, is an extraordinarily talky drama about David Roylston, a writer whose preachings on "self-fulfill-ment" make him a guru to legions of female readers, including the beautiful Ethel Frazer. But Mrs. Frazer is disgusted to learn of Roylston's disdain for his wife, Alice, who supported his career by working as a stenographer, typing his manuscripts, and keeping house. In what Joel Pfister aptly calls a "weird blend of feminist and antifeminist sentiments,"[1] Roylston comes to appreciate Alice's declaration that "Love means servitude,"[2] although it's unclear how he will act on that knowledge. *The Personal Equation*, written while O'Neill was studying playwriting at Harvard in 1915, includes what might be his most promising feminist. Olga Tarnoff is a radical who scorns marriage as an institution that sanctions male ownership of women and asks her live-in lover: "Aren't we equals when we fight for liberty – regardless of sex?" (*CP* I, 313) Pregnancy and impending motherhood temper Olga's radicalism, but she retains a measure of her revolutionary fervor at the play's ironic conclusion.

Female crusaders are rare in the O'Neill canon, however, and O'Neill's greater debt is to August Strindberg and what critics often call the Strindbergian female "destroyer." Maud Steele in *Bread and Butter* (1914) nags John Brown into marriage, ruins his dreams of a painting career, and finally provokes him into a murderous rage and suicide. The "breakfast" Mrs. Rowland prepares for her spouse in *Before Breakfast* (1916) – equal helpings of mockery, recrimination, and self-pity – proves lethal. Only marginally more sympathetic is Ruth Atkins in *Beyond the Horizon*. In aborting Robert Mayo's dreams of sailing to faraway lands, she destroys Robert and helps turn his brother Andrew into a greedy speculator. The formula for these plays seems to be the venerable myth that domesticity, even when freely chosen, kills the male of the species;[3] woman is a trope for the bourgeois life, the insensitivity and materialism that annihilate the artistic soul. These early denizens of O'Neill's world look forward to more fully developed female destroyers like Ella Harris in *All God's Chillun Got Wings* (1923), who celebrates her husband Jim's failure to pass the bar examination; Margaret Anthony in *The Great God Brown* (1925), who is so terrified of Dion's artistic temperament that she cannot even look at him unless he's masked; and the unseen Evelyn Hickman in *The Iceman Cometh* (1940), whose insistence on conventional morality drives her husband to murder her.

Between 1915 and 1922, several of O'Neill's colleagues at the Provincetown Players were creating dramas centering around women's ambitions. But while Susan Glaspell's Claire Archer conducts botanical experiments in *The Verge* and Neith Boyce's widowed Rachel Westcott plans a career as a dressmaker in *Winter's Night*, O'Neill's female characters are rarely artists, adventurers or dreamers – unless the "dream" is of love. Throughout O'Neill's canon, as Doris Nelson notes, his heroines define themselves primarily or wholly in terms of "their relationships to the men in their lives"[4] or less commonly their offspring; jobs are at best secondary compensations. Lily Miller in *Ah, Wilderness!* (1933) sees teaching primarily as a way to nurture the children she herself hasn't borne. Even Eleanor Cape in *Welded* (1923) only performs roles written by her husband, who scoffs: "Good God, how dare you criticize creative work, you actress!" (*CP* II, 249). (Given O'Neill's often harsh comments about the acting profession, it's hard not to detect his own feelings in Michael Cape's distinction between the writer's creativity and the thespian's rote mimicry.) Hattie Harris, a proud career woman, is both a minor character in *All God's Chillun Got Wings* and an anomaly in O'Neill's universe. To signal her lack of gender conformity, the stage direction indicates that she is dressed *"mannishly"* (*CP* II, 297).

If O'Neill's female characters earn their own living, they are likely to do so on their backs. While O'Neill was no George Bernard Shaw, exposing how capitalism made prostitution one of the few job opportunities for women, he was aware that women are a commodity exchanged among men. For the sailors in *The Moon of the Caribbees* (1918), the price of a pint of rum is three shillings while sex with the island women costs four shillings. Freda in *The Long Voyage Home* (1917) participates in the shanghai-ing of Olson, a sailor who yearns to return to his Swedish homeland. Freda gains little more for her efforts, however, than a vicious slap from the proprietor of the dive where she works. In the melodramatic one-acter *The Web* (1913), Rose Thomas is the consumptive mother of an infant. She tries several times to leave prostitution, only to be scorned by the self-righteous "good people" and ultimately framed for murder by her pimp. The "web" in which Rose is caught is clearly patriarchal: she earns her living pleasing men, gives her money to a man, and ultimately is replaced by a policeman, who informs the crying baby, "I'm your Mama now" (*CP* I, 28). At its worst, prostitution prevents women from fulfilling their primary role: motherhood.

O'Neill's most fully realized prostitute is the protagonist of *"Anna Christie"* (1920). In the play's first version, entitled *Chris Christophersen*, the plot focuses on Anna's father. The Anna of *Chris* is a wholly incongruous figure in O'Neill's universe, a prim British-bred typist who inexplicably falls in love with the sea and a young sailor. As the work evolved into *"Anna Christie,"* Anna developed into a cynical prostitute. Raped by her cousin at sixteen, Anna left the farm where she was raised and escaped to the city. After two years of unsatisfying hard work and unrelenting sexual harassment, she entered a brothel. Anna claims to detest all men and becomes furious when her father and lover fight over her as if she were their property. She insists "I can make it myself – one way or other. I'm my own boss" (*CP* I, 1007), a strong statement even though it fails to acknowledge that Anna has been "making it" by selling herself to the lowest bidders.

From one perspective *"Anna Christie"* is a variation on the oldest stage cliché: the prostitute redeemed by love of a good man, stoker Mat Burke. Yet O'Neill probes deeper, for the feisty Anna challenges the "goodness" of men like Mat who patronize (in all senses) women like her. Margaret Ranald reveals that in an intermediary script between *Chris Christophersen* and *"Anna Christie,"* the version of the drama entitled *The Ole Davil*, Anna is "more aggressive, more damaged by her past experiences, and more turned against men than her later counterpart."[5] Apparently the Anna of *The Ole Davil* was just a little too independent for O'Neill, but the Anna of the final version remains sharper and more articulate than most of her stage predecessors.

On the other hand, O'Neill was equally capable of sentimentalizing prostitution, often in disturbing ways. The amiable "tarts" in *The Iceman Cometh* humor their pimp as if he were a cherished brother. The prostitute in *Welded*, simply named Woman, grins when she acknowledges that her pimp may beat her up "just for the fun of it" (*CP* II, 266). *Welded's* protagonist, Michael Cape, is so impressed with her willingness to accept her brutal life that he announces he's joined her "church" (*CP* II, 267). The *Great God Brown's* Cybel wears the mask of a prostitute, but she is virtually a caricature of O'Neill's favorite version of the whore-with-a-heart-of-gold, the "Earth Mother."[6] The full-breasted Cybel chews gum "*like a sacred cow*," offers a refuge for the tormented Dion Anthony, and eases the suffering Billy Brown into death.

As his playwriting talents developed, O'Neill began to envision more complex female characters. Neither cynical prostitute nor Earth Mother, Nina Leeds stands at the center of *Strange Interlude* (1927), which traces her life from age twenty to a very early dotage at forty-five. O'Neill referred to this nine-act epic as "my woman play," yet three of the drama's four main characters are male, and *Strange Interlude* is the story of a woman who defines herself wholly in terms of the men in her life. Nina goes into nursing not because of some dedication to healing but because she believes she won't have "found" herself until she gives herself to men. When Dr. Ned Darrell prescribes motherhood for Nina because she needs to "find normal outlets for her craving for sacrifice" (*CP* II, 665), he recapitulates a popular Freudian view of female masochism.

In some ways Nina proves Ned's prescription wrong: motherhood is not quite enough for her and she demands a lover as well as a son. But there is little suggestion of the constructedness of Nina's dilemma, the extent to which a patriarchal society has excluded any other definitions of selfhood for women. Bette Mandl observes that Nina is largely the "currency" the men use to relate to one another,[7] yet this does not seem to bother the character. *Strange Interlude's* extended "thought-asides" would seem to give the audience access to Nina's deepest reflections, and these thoughts rarely go beyond the males in her life. In her famous "My three men" soliloquy about her husband, lover, and old friend, Nina muses that "I feel their desires converge in me! ... to form one complete beautiful male desire which I absorb ... and am whole ... they dissolve in me, their life is my life" (*CP* II, 756). It is *their* desire, not hers, that she experiences. Doris

Nelson also makes the astute observation that "The stages in [Nina's] life correspond to physical rather than intellectual changes."[8] Although she has grown from a young virgin to a middle-aged widow, Nina finds herself at the end of the play virtually where she was at the beginning; the only difference is that the devoted Charlie Marsden has replaced her late father. Nina lives in a wholly male world, but neither the character nor the playwright sees this as a major cause of her unhappiness: she does not lament her lack of female friends or – like Darrell and Marsden – a fulfilling career she might have had. Instead, the blame lies with fate, God, and the biological accident of inherited mental illness.

Four years after *Strange Interlude*, O'Neill completed *Mourning Becomes Electra* (1931), which could more accurately be called his "woman play." Although appearing relatively late in O'Neill's career, *Electra* is his first work – and indeed one of very few in his canon – to explore relationships between women in any depth. A discussion of important mother–daughter bonds in the O'Neill canon would begin and end with *Mourning Becomes Electra* and *A Touch of the Poet* (1942).[9] If we are looking for relationships between sisters we are out of luck entirely, and even significant female friendships are few and far between, emerging mainly in the unfinished plays of the "Tale of Possessors Self-Dispossessed" Cycle.[10]

In his depiction of Christine Mannon and her daughter, Lavinia, O'Neill again seems to have taken his cue from Freud. Freud postulated that a girl's "turning away from the mother is accompanied by hostility; the attachment to the mother ends in hate. A hate of that kind may become very striking and last all through life."[11] Lavinia eventually comes to empathize and identify with her mother, but only after her mother's death – a suicide for which Lavinia herself is largely responsible. While Christine is alive there is no sense of love or mutual understanding between the two, and the cause of their conflict, not surprisingly, is jealousy over the men in their lives. Lavinia Mannon is obsessed with her father Ezra, and Christine admits she wouldn't have taken a lover if her son Orin hadn't gone off to war. The spiral of incestuous desire finally concludes with Lavinia, the most courageous of the family, who locks herself in with her memories instead of choosing the suicide into which her mother and brother escaped.

Susan Harris Smith makes the important observation that "Lavinia attains classically tragic stature only when she sacrifices the 'natural' and 'female' aspects of herself to the Mannon furies, the bastions of the political and patriarchal norm."[12] Smith here points to what might be called a female force or principle that figures in several of O'Neill's major works. Eben Cabot's dead mother, who haunts much of *Desire Under the Elms*

(1924), is part of a feminine spirit symbolized by the trees that embrace the farmhouse. These elms, resembling "exhausted women," (*CP* II, 318), stand in diametric opposition to the stone walls built by the farm's rigid patriarch, Ephraim. Nina Leeds thinks yearningly of a beneficent "mother God": "The mistake began when God was created in a male image ... That makes life so perverted, and death so unnatural. We should have imagined life as created in the birth-pain of God the Mother" (*CP* II, 670). Smith sees the same pattern in *Mourning*, where "The dominant if decadent force is male; the 'Other,' doomed to estranged and displaced subservience, is female."[13] Following traditional tropes, O'Neill associates this fertile feminine principle with nature – the nature of childbirth, trees, water, and the "Blessed Islands" sought by so many of the Mannons.

Still, O'Neill's feminine principle is not as benevolent as this suggests. The elms that shade the Cabot house in *Desire* are ominous growths that "appear to protect and at the same time subdue. There is a sinister maternity in their aspect, a crushing jealous absorption" (*CP* II, 318). This female force can destroy, devour, as well as comfort. Further, the "Blessed Islands" of which Orin Mannon dreams have a revealing sexual component. He tells his mother: "The breaking of the waves was your voice. The sky was the same color as your eyes. The warm sand was like your skin. The whole island was you" (*CP*, II, 972). Orin's literalized "Mother Nature" is an Oedipal vision grounded in male desire. The female god, the Blessed Islands, the recuperative powers of the feminized natural world, are all based on O'Neill's equation of womanhood and motherhood.

Virtually every O'Neill scholar has acknowledged the deeply personal nature of his work, and the primary grist for the autobiography mill is his relationship to his mother, Ella Quinlan O'Neill. Biographers like Louis Sheaffer and critics including Michael Manheim, Doris Alexander, and Laurin Porter[14] identify aspects of Ella in many if not most of the playwright's female characters. Less commonly, scholars like Gloria Cahill invoke the influence of Sarah Sandy, the nursemaid who helped raise the young O'Neill.[15] Without denying his deep ambivalence toward the mother who became a drug-addict at his birth, and her temporary surrogate, it is important to see that O'Neill's fascination with the maternal female was as much a part of the cultural and religious air he breathed as it was of the troubled family into which he was born. The Virgin Mary, the image of sexless motherhood, remained a part of O'Neill's iconography long after he ceased being a practicing Catholic. According to Freud, the secular priest of early twentieth-century America, "a marriage is not made secure until the wife has succeeded in making her husband her child as well and in acting as a mother to him."[16] Cahill quotes an equally telling observation from Carl Jung, whom O'Neill admired: "Man leaves his mother . . . and is driven by the eternal thirst to find her again, and to drink renewal from her; thus he completes his cycle, and returns again into the mother's womb."[17] Whether the playwright was influenced by the ideas of these thinkers, or whether his preoccupation with maternal figures confirms their reading of the male psyche (surely the connections go both ways), O'Neill's vision of the feminine has deep roots.

O'Neill's apotheosizing of the maternal female character is a dominant motif throughout his canon,[18] although motherliness has little to do with biology or sexuality. His maternal women are as likely to be prostitutes, virgins, or childless wives as they are to be biological parents, while those they mother are usually adult men.[19] A "maternal" character may be defined, for O'Neill, in traditional terms: one who nurtures, cares for, and protects others; one who is willing to subordinate her own dreams and concerns to her loved one's desires; and one who forgives all transgressions. O'Neill readily exposes the limitations of the male heroes he creates; to assume that he simply speaks through them is to underestimate the complexity of his artistic vision. Still, the extent to which O'Neill's women display these cherished maternal virtues determines not only male characters' attitudes toward them but the playwright's perspective as well.

The large number of O'Neill's female characters who regard their husbands or lovers with maternal solicitude includes such diverse figures as Cybel in *The Great God Brown* and Madeline Arnold in *Strange Interlude*, the latter a woman who, at the advanced age of nineteen, has "*a distinct maternal older feeling in her attitude toward*" her fiancé Gordon (CP II, 803). "My son," "my boy," "my poor little boy," "poor little child," or "my child" are terms uttered, at various times, by Olga Tarnoff in *The Personal Equation*, Hazel Niles in *Mourning Becomes Electra*, Abbie Putnam in *Desire Under the Elms*, Miriam in *Lazarus Laughed*, Nina Leeds in *Strange Interlude*, and Eleanor Cape in *Welded*. In none of these cases are they referring to children. Margaret in *Brown* considers her husband the eldest of her sons, an attitude she shares with Sara Harford in *More Stately Mansions*. One of the most astonishing love scenes in American drama shows Abbie wooing her step-son Eben with "*a horribly frank mixture of lust and mother love*" (CP II, 354). Freudian psychology and Christian miracle join forces in *Lazarus Laughed*, where Lazarus grows younger as his wife Miriam ages. After Miriam's death her husband looks "*like a young son who keeps watch by the body of his mother*" (CP II, 609).

The "good mother's" maternal ministrations extend to husband and progeny alike. The idealized Essie Miller in *Ah, Wilderness!* feeds and nurses her husband and children, and appears to have no ambitions beyond her family's physical and emotional health.[20] Pathetic rather than comic, Nora Melody in *A Touch of the Poet* (1942) declares that she has "no pride at all" (*CP*, III, 280) except in her self-sacrificing love for her husband, Con. She subordinates her own desires to Con's wishes and, while her primary allegiance is to the husband she treats *"as if he were a sick child"* (*CP* III, 271), she still finds time to counsel her daughter, Sara.

Conversely, the numerous "bad mothers" in O'Neill's universe fail their offspring and their spouses. The still-born infant in *Before Breakfast*, one of a large group of dead children in O'Neill's plays, symbolizes Mrs. Rowland's refusal to nurture either husband or child. While Ruth Mayo in *Beyond the Horizon* is victim as well as victimizer, her inability to appreciate her husband's aspirations is mirrored in her impatience with their daughter, who is far more attached to her "daddy." In short order, Robert follows the little girl to the grave. The unseen Rosa Parritt in *The Iceman Cometh*, faithful to neither lover nor son, attempts to impose her ideals of revolutionary conduct on them. The lover escapes into alcoholic skepticism and the son retaliates with betrayal, creating a burden of guilt that he can assuage only by suicide.

If O'Neill seems daring in his often sympathetic portraits of prostitutes, this is largely because to him the distinction between virgin and whore is less important than the division between those women who "mother" men and those women who do not. His male characters rarely seek out prostitutes for the sexual delights they offer; Dion Anthony, Michael Cape, Richard Miller, and Jamie Tyrone would rather talk with prostitutes than sleep with them. The compassionate whore Cybel, pursued by both Dion Anthony and Billy Brown in *Brown*, is a far more appealing figure than the virginal Emma Crosby of *Diff'rent* (1920). Emma's unwillingness to marry Caleb because of his alleged dalliance with a "native" woman, her selfish desire to hold him to her Puritanical sexual ideal, destroys them both. Lily Miller in *Ah, Wilderness!* also lacks the important quality of forgiveness, but O'Neill grants her the virtues of protectiveness and nurturance. Although she too refuses to wed her errant suitor, she soothes the remorseful Sid *"as if he were a little boy"* (*CP* III, 71) and fusses "over him like a hen that's hatched a duck" (*CP* III, 101). Lily is not romanticized as Cybel is but, unlike Emma, she is not "punished" with madness and death.

It is within this matrix of maternity that we can examine O'Neill's late great plays, *The Iceman Cometh*, *Long Day's Journey Into Night*, and *A Moon for the Misbegotten* (1944). The most remarkable fact about the major female characters in *Iceman* (and the one-act *Hughie*, written shortly afterward) is their absence.[21] Unseen women – alive or dead – are important throughout the O'Neill canon, beginning with *A Wife for a Life* (1913), in which two miners discuss a young woman whom both covet. The spirit of Eben's late mother hovers over *Desire Under the Elms*, as the memory of Jim Tyrone's mother dominates O'Neill's last completed play, *Moon*. Ann C. Hall argues that by having the women stereotypically present while absent in *Iceman*, O'Neill illustrates the Lacanian thesis that women are both absent and present in a patriarchal economy.[22] While such an argument has merit, it obscures the more important point: the vast number of O'Neill women who remain both faceless and voiceless. The missing wife in *A Wife for a Life*, like Smitty's former girlfriend in *In the Zone* (1917), "speaks" only through a letter read aloud by the men, while the dead young woman in *Abortion* (1914) is represented on-stage by her brother. We do not see the perspectives of that "damned bitch" Evelyn Hickman, "that nagging bitch" Bessie Hope, or that "damned old bitch" Rosa Parritt, except through the eyes of their spouses, lovers and sons in *Iceman*. It is for the *men* in Harry Hope's bar – however sodden they may be – that O'Neill seeks our understanding and empathy.

Even Mary Tyrone is kept off-stage during most of the last act of *Long Day's Journey Into Night* (1941), while the men exchange stories of past disappointments and future plans. Mary is O'Neill's most fully realized female character, a figure whose suffering exposes the limitations and paradoxes imposed on women in a world shaped around male desires. Yet the playwright himself is not exempt from those desires, and in this most autobiographical of his dramas he simultaneously understands Mary's maternal failures and blames her for them. The Tyrone men, rather than Mary, dominate the stage as the full narrative of the family unfolds.

In part, Mary Tyrone's dilemma is that she has found herself in an O'Neill play. Like most of O'Neill's male characters, her husband and sons demand of her that triumvirate of virtues which Essie Miller and Nora Melody possess: nurturance, forgiveness, and renunciation of her dreams for theirs. But nurturing this family is too much for Mary, who cannot live with the anguish and guilt of a dead baby, a seriously ill son and his alcoholic older brother. It may well be that Mary's refusal to eat, although partly a result of the drugs and perhaps a touch of vanity, symbolizes her refusal to be the mother her men seek. O'Neill's most maternal characters – Mrs. Fife in *Dynamo* (1928), Cybel, Essie Miller, Nora Melody, Sara Harford, Josie Hogan – have the ample female figure, including the large comforting breasts, that Mary is anxious to avoid. Despite her protests to the contrary, Mary is also unable to pardon the men for their transgressions against her and themselves. Her repeated recitations of Tyrone's domestic crimes, dating back to a drunken honeymoon night some thirty-five years earlier, are evidence that to forgive yet never forget is not to forgive at all.

Nor can Mary entirely erase the aspirations she once had that conflicted with her desire to be a wife and mother. Tyrone attributes her reveries about a musical career to the "flattering" of naive nuns, and the playwright himself gives us no evidence of Mary's talent: when she plays the piano, all we hear is the "*stiff-fingered groping*" (*CP* III, 823) of an aging arthritic. But O'Neill gives some credence to Mary's "more beautiful" dream of becoming a nun, for the opening stage directions tell us that "*her most appealing quality is the simple, unaffected charm of a shy convent-girl youthfulness she has never lost – an innate unworldly innocence*" (*CP* III, 718). Had Mary remained virginal, she would have faced few of the troubles she laments throughout *Long Day's Journey*. On the other hand, of course, there would also have been no family – a family that despite everything loves her just as she, despite everything, loves them. Mary Tyrone is finally neither mother nor virgin, and in this lies much of the tragedy of the Tyrone family. The men demand that she be a mother in all senses of the word, but she cannot and will not fulfill that role. Yet even in her drugged stupor she cannot regain the virginal innocence for which she so desperately yearns.

Just as Mary Tyrone is neither mother nor virgin, so Josie Hogan is both, and O'Neill portrays her as the most positive female character in his stage universe. Unlike Mary, Josie is willing to be silent so that others (male) might speak. Disturbed by his drugged mother's recriminations, Edmund begs her to "Stop talking" (*CP* III, 753), and Jim Tyrone repeatedly asks Josie not to talk that "raw stuff." One wonders whether they are troubled only by *what* the women are saying, or by the fact that they are speaking at all. The Tyrone men want a confessor who will sympathize with their fantasies and commiserate with them for their failures. Josie relinquishes her own story, abstains from the liquor that might (like Mary's morphine) free her tongue, and accepts the role of listener to Jim's tale of woe – a double role because she stands for his deceased mother as well. The identification between the two is an ominous metaphor for Josie's renunciation of self: she symbolically merges not only with another woman, but with a woman who is dead. Indeed, in some ways Josie's self-silencing parallels O'Neill's silencing of numerous female "characters" by the simple expediency of leaving them off-stage.

Mary is so desperate for the female companionship she knew at the convent that she bribes the servant Cathleen to spend a few minutes with her. Josie Hogan's world is even more relentlessly masculine than Mary's but, like Margaret Anthony, Abbie Putnam, and Nina Leeds before her, she is content to define herself in terms of men or to let them define her. Even Josie's fantasies of being promiscuous, unacceptable as they are to Jim Tyrone's conventional double-standard, are ultimately forgivable because they revolve around her desire to "give" herself to men, much as Nina Leeds "gave" herself to the wounded soldiers in *Strange Interlude*. Throughout his plays O'Neill created patriarchal worlds into which women could fit only by assuming the narrow roles in which the male characters sought to cast them. All too rarely, however, did O'Neill critique such worlds through a female character like Mary.

Josie Hogan sacrifices her own hope of marriage (itself a "safe" female dream) to Jim's desire that she be his chaste confessor. Josie suffers for her renunciation, yet her consolation, like Nora Melody's, is that she has comforted the man she loves: "I want you to remember my love for you gave you peace for awhile" (*CP* III, 944) she tells him. For O'Neill's perfect mother, the act of giving solace is its own reward. Michael Manheim may be right that the theme of *Moon* is that "kinship between man and woman is finally the most powerful of any,"[23] but the terms of that bond are dictated by the man. The long Pietà pose that opens Act 4 clearly links Josie with the Virgin Mary and echoes a series of tableaux in his earlier plays: Abbie holding Eben in the last scene of *Desire Under the Elms*, Cybel comforting a dying Billy in *The Great God Brown*, Sara cradling Simon Harford in the Epilogue to *More Stately Mansions*. Ann C. Hall argues that "Josie is not a passive reflector of male desire ... but an active participant in the masquerade of gender"[24] because she "consciously chooses the Madonna role."[25] Yet the fact remains that O'Neill asks us to believe both that Josie gets great satisfaction from that "masquerade" and that the only roles she can even *imagine* – wife, prostitute, mother – are those that most reflect male desire.

Martha Gilman Bower identifies what she calls a "gender role reversal" in O'Neill's Cycle plays, on which he was working during his last creative years. She argues that the tenacious, often ruthless female characters in this series may be partly based on O'Neill's third wife, Carlotta Monterey.[26] Although O'Neill's notes for unwritten Cycle dramas do suggest that the playwright envisioned new female representations, the women in *A Touch of The Poet* and *More Stately Mansions* – the submissive Nora, the earthy Sara, and Simon's disturbed mother, Deborah, who alternately smothers and rejects her son – are familiar figures. Elements of Carlotta, whom O'Neill dubbed his "mother, and wife and mistress and friend,"[27] are apparent in nearly every play he wrote after their relationship began in 1926. Finally, the strength of characters like Nora and Sara is nothing new in O'Neill's canon; as Manheim observes, the O'Neillian Earth Mother is "a total provider, a bringer of comfort, a figure in all respects, physical and emotional, more powerful than himself."[28] O'Neill often depicts his women as strong, but their presence – epitomized in the *"oversize"* Josie Hogan – signifies the comforting omnipotence a child sees in its parent.

Suzanne Burr believes that O'Neill has "remarkable empathy with women,"[29] while Hall contends that O'Neill's late plays "expose the process by which patriarchy attempts to oppress women."[30] To a certain extent, this praise is justified. In his portrait of Mary Tyrone, a woman who chafes at the overwhelming demands placed upon her, who imagines a world in which she would have a story separate from that written for her by her male kin, O'Neill creates his most complex and theatrically powerful stage woman. Even as early as the 1917 drama *Ile*, Mrs. Keeney (a forerunner of Mary) embodies a critique of a masculine world driven by greed and ego, in that case the world of whaling. But as Anne Flèche observes, the critic of O'Neill's plays, particularly the feminist critic, "finds herself staring at an Everest of possibilities."[31] For all the "incipient feminism"[32] of a work like *"Anna Christie"* or the unfinished Cycle play *The Calms of Capricorn*, O'Neill's women characters are most commonly perceived from outside, from a masculine perspective that wistfully endows mothers, virgins, and whores with powerful maternal desires or condemns them for lacking such feelings. Even in her private reveries Nina Leeds calculates her value in terms of the men in her life, and the idealized heroine of O'Neill's last completed play is the motherly virgin Josie Hogan, selfless supplier of comfort and peace. While O'Neill exposed many of the flaws in the patriarchal universe both within and outside his plays he was, not surprisingly, also deeply invested in that universe. His female characters, including some of the modern stage's most memorable women, grow out of that ambivalence.

NOTES

1 Joel Pfister, *Staging Depth: Eugene O'Neill and the Politics of Psychological Discourse* (Chapel Hill: University of North Carolina Press, 1995), p. 194.

2 Eugene O'Neill, Complete Plays 1913–1920 (New York: The Library of America, 1988), p. 268. All future references to O'Neill's plays will be to this three-volume Library of America edition (*CP*) and will be given in the body of the text. Although the books are not numbered, I will designate the first (*Complete Plays 1913–1920*) volume "I", the second (*Complete Plays 1920–1931*) volume "II," and the third (*Complete Plays 1932–1943*) volume "III."

3 Comparing the works of O'Neill with those of his Provincetown Players colleague Susan Glaspell, Linda Ben-Zvi discovers that O'Neill's "heroes – male – yearn for the very things Glaspell's women spurn: love, closeness, home, family, and belonging." This "yearning," however, often proves fatal. See

Ben-Zvi, "Susan Glaspell and Eugene O'Neill: The Imagery of Gender," *The Eugene O'Neill Newsletter* 10, 1 (Spring 1986): 24; Ben-Zvi, "Freedom and Fixity in the Plays of Eugene O'Neill," *Modern Drama* 31, 1 (March 1988): 16–27; and Judith E. Barlow, "No He-Men Need Apply: A Look at O'Neill's Heroes," *The Eugene O'Neill Review*, 19, 1 and 2 (spring/fall 1995): 111–21.

4 Doris Nelson, "O'Neill's Women," *The Eugene O'Neill Newsletter* 6, 2 (summer–fall 1982): 3.

5 Margaret Loftus Ranald, *The Eugene O'Neill Companion* (Westport, Connecticut: Greenwood Press, 1984), p. 527.

6 For discussions of O'Neill's "Earth Mother", see Travis Bogard, *Contour in Time: The Plays of Eugene O'Neill*, rev. edn. (New York: Oxford University Press, 1988), and Michael Manheim, *Eugene O'Neill's New Language of Kinship* (Syracuse, New York: Syracuse University Press, 1982).

7 Bette Mandl, "Gender as Design in Eugene O'Neill's *Strange Interlude*," *The Eugene O'Neill Review*, 19, 1 and 2 (spring/fall 1995): 126. Mandl borrows Claude Lévi-Strauss's use of the term "currency."

8 Nelson, "O'Neill's Women," 7.

9 The hostile relationship between Ruth Mayo and her mother in *Beyond the Horizon* is a relatively minor thread in that work. There are other mother–daughter pairings in plays like *Gold*, *The Rope*, and *All God's Chillun Got Wings*, but none that is significantly developed or explored.

10 For a discussion of women in the Cycle plays, see Martha Gilman Bower, *Eugene O'Neill's Unfinished Threnody and Process of Invention in Four Cycle Plays* (Lewiston, NY: Edwin Mellen Press, 1992).

11 Sigmund Freud, "Femininity," *New Introductory Lectures on Psycho-Analysis and Other Works* in James Strachey, trans. and ed., *The Standard Edition of the Complete Psychological Works of Sigmund Freud* (London: Hogarth Press, 1964), p. 121. Although this lecture was composed in 1933, fairly late in Freud's career, it recapitulates ideas he propounded much earlier.

12 Susan Harris Smith, "Inscribing the Body: Lavinia Mannon as the Site of Struggle," *The Eugene O'Neill Review*, 19, 1 and 2 (spring/fall 1995): 45.

13 Smith, "Inscribing the Body," 45.

14 See Louis Sheaffer, *O'Neill: Son and Playwright* (Boston: Little, Brown, 1968) and *O'Neill: Son and Artist* (Boston: Little, Brown, 1973); Manheim, *Eugene O'Neill's New Language of Kinship*; Doris Alexander, *Eugene O'Neill's Creative Struggle: The Decisive Decade, 1924–1933* (University Park: Pennsylvania State University Press, 1992); and Laurin Porter, *The Banished Prince: Time, Memory, and Ritual in the Late Plays of Eugene O'Neill* (Ann Arbor: UMI Research Press, 1988).

15 Gloria Cahill, "Mothers and Whores: The Process of Integration in the Plays of Eugene O'Neill," *The Eugene O'Neill Review*, 16, 1 (spring 1992): 5–23.

16 Freud, "Femininity," 133–34.

17 Jung, quoted in Cahill, "Mothers and Whores," 3.

18 Travis Bogard discusses "the dual wife–mother character" in the introduction to *The Later Plays of Eugene O'Neill* (New York: Random House, 1967), pp. xv–xvi, and "The search for the surrogate mother" in *Contour in Time*, pp. 441–45. See also Doris V. Falk, *Eugene O'Neill and the Tragic Tension* (New Brunswick, NJ: Rutgers University Press, 1958), p. 76.

19 The discussion that follows is partly based on my essay "O'Neill's Many Mothers: Mary Tyrone, Josie Hogan, and their Antecedents," in Shyamal Bagchee, ed., *Perspectives on O'Neill: New Essays* (ELS Monograph, University of Victoria 1988), pp. 7–16. Reprinted in John Houchin, ed. *The Critical Response to Eugene O'Neill* (New York: Greenwood, 1993), pp. 283–90.

20 Trudy Decker dubs Essie Miller "a *Ladies'-Home-Journal* wife-and-mother." See "Sexuality as Destiny: The Shadow Lives of O'Neill's Women," *The Eugene O'Neill Newsletter* 6, 2 (summer–fall 1982): 9.

21 See Bette Mandl, "Absence as Presence: The Second Sex in *The Iceman Cometh*," *The Eugene O'Neill Newsletter* 6, 2 (summer–fall 1982): 10–15.

22 Ann C. Hall, *"A Kind of Alaska": Women in the Plays of O'Neill, Pinter, and Shepard* (Carbondale: Southern Illinois University Press, 1993), pp. 26–35.

23 Manheim, *New Language of Kinship*, p. 159.

24 Hall, *"A Kind of Alaska,"* p. 50.

25 Hall, *"A Kind of Alaska,"* p. 53.

26 Bower, *Eugene O'Neill's Unfinished Threnody*, pp. 1–8, *passim*.

27 Part of O'Neill's 23 April 1931 dedication of *Mourning Becomes Electra* to Carlotta. Reprinted in *Inscriptions: Eugene O'Neill to Carlotta Monterey O'Neill*, ed. Donald Gallup (New Haven: privately printed, 1960).

28 Manheim, *New Language of Kinship*, p. 122.

29 Suzanne Burr, "O'Neill's Ghostly Women," in *Feminist Rereadings of Modern American Drama*, ed. June Schlueter (Rutherford: Fairleigh Dickinson University Press, 1989), p. 38.

30 Hall, *"A Kind of Alaska,"* p. 2.

31 Anne Flèche, "'A Monster of Perfection': O'Neill's 'Stella,'" in Schlueter, p. 25.

32 Flèche, *"A Monster of Perfection,"* 44.

12

DONALD GALLUP

"A tale of possessors self-dispossessed"

> That Eugene O'Neill could not complete the historical cycle as it was designed is one of the greatest losses the drama in any time has sustained. Goethe's comment on Marlowe's *Dr. Faustus*, "How greatly it was planned," has more relevance to *A Tale of Possessors, Self-dispossessed*. It was a work of astonishing scope and scale. Theresa Helburn rightly called it a *comédie humaine*. Nothing in the drama, except Shakespeare's two cycles on British history, could have been set beside it. The two plays that have survived reveal something of the power of life that beat in it, but they show only vestiges of what its full plan realized would have provided: a prophetic epitome for the course of American destiny. (Travis Bogard, *Contour in Time*, p. 369)

O'Neill's own detailed record of his living and writing from 1924 to 1943, the *Work Diary*, now part of the O'Neill collection at Yale, makes possible the following account of the vast Cycle project: how it was conceived and developed, and how it eventually ended. Although much manuscript material relating to the plays was destroyed, their plots can be reconstructed from scenarios and other notes also preserved at Yale. Outlines of all the plays in the nine-play Cycle are given here in the sequence of their conception as part of the series. They are followed by a summary of the four plays outlined by O'Neill in October and November 1940 to replace plays one and two, actually written between 1935 and 1937, but later destroyed. The four gave the plan its final form – a Cycle of eleven plays.

Although the initial idea for a "vast symbolic play of the effect upon man's soul of industrialism" had come to O'Neill in 1927, and he had worked upon it in 1928, 1929, and the early 1930s (he was then calling it the "Bessie Bowen" play), it was not until 1935 that he began to plan a series of plays that would tell the story of an American family, the Harfords, showing the effect upon them of the corrupting power of material things. Its theme would be the Bible's question, "What will it profit a man if he gain the whole world but lose his own soul?" O'Neill had been working intensively on what he called "the Cycle" for only a few months when, on 3 July 1935, he wrote to his friend Robert Sisk of the Theatre Guild about his plans:

> Each play will be, as far as it is possible, complete in itself while at the same time an indispensable link in the whole (a difficult technical problem, this, but

I think I can solve it successfully). There will, of course, be much less hang-over of immediate suspense from one play to another than in "[Mourning Becomes] Electra." Each play will be concentrated around the final fate of one member of the family but will also carry on the story of the family as a whole ... It will be less realistic than "Electra" in method, probably – more poetical in general, I hope – more of "Great God Brown" over- and under-tones, more symbolical and complicated (in that it will have to deal with more intermingling relationships) – and deeper probing.   (*Selected Letters*, p. 447)

Although he had at first thought of four plays dealing with Ethan, Wolfe, Owen ("Honey"), and Jonathan, the sons of Sara and Simon Harford, O'Neill soon discovered that he could not write about the young men without knowing more about their parents. And so, at the very outset, he encountered the problem that became primarily responsible for his failure to complete the project. He explained it much later, in 1946, to his friend Elizabeth Shepley Sergeant, telling her in an interview that "the difficulty after he began to go backwards was to find the starting point ... – [he] could never be sure of [the] place where he ought to begin. Everything derived from everything else" (Unpublished typescript, Yale). The new play O'Neill had planned to devote to Simon and Sara Harford soon became two, thus expanding the series to six plays before he reached the stage of beginning to write detailed scenarios.

The first scenario he wrote was for *A Touch of the Poet* (then called "The Hair of the Dog"). Completed on 24 February 1935, it tells of the courtship of Sara Melody and Simon Harford. Eventually the only part of the Cycle completed to O'Neill's satisfaction, the play was published posthumously in 1957 and is discussed by Normand Berlin in the essay entitled "The Late Plays" earlier in this collection.

As first conceived in the scenario, the plot differs in several ways from the published version. Simon, nursed back to health by Sara and her mother, does not recuperate at Melody's inn, but returns to his Thoreau-like existence in his cabin on the shore. There his mother (here Abigail, later Deborah), visits him in a scene roughly similar to the opening of *More Stately Mansions*. At the tavern, Mickey Maloy, the barman, encouraged by her father, Cornelius ("Con") Melody, courts Sara, who, having fallen in love with Simon, rejects Maloy's suit. She is driven to visit Simon at night by her fears that his family and her own father may succeed in taking him away from her, and it is in his cabin that their love is consummated. In this play, there is no commemoration of the anniversary of Talavera, and the first meeting of Abigail and Sara comes only in an epilogue.

O'Neill completed a scenario for the second play, *More Stately Mansions*, in April 1935 and eventually finished what he described as a third draft, especially, in January 1939. Feeling that the fourth act needed further drastic cutting, he marked the typescript "Unfinished Work," and directed that it be destroyed in the event of his death. Although the handwritten first draft of the play was indeed burned, the typed third draft was accidentally preserved. A version shortened by Karl Ragnar Gierow of the Royal Swedish Theater, edited by me, appeared in 1964. The complete typescript, edited by Martha Bower, was published in 1988. Normand Berlin also discusses this play in his essay.

The original plan does not differ, basically, from the play as published in 1964, but it is less complicated in its depiction of the inter-relationships among the three principal characters. Here, as in O'Neill's typescript, the play opens at Melody's tavern in 1835. Melody has died, leaving some two thousand dollars in debts, and his wake is actually in progress upstairs. Sara and Simon, with the two youngest of their four children, return from their home in Connecticut for the first time since their marriage six years previously. Simon succeeds in persuading Sara that they are honor-bound to pay off her father's debts with the money they have been saving to enable Simon to buy out his partner, and thus free Nora, her mother, to realize her dream of entering a convent. Simon's brother, Joel, rather than the servant Cato, brings the message that Abigail wants Simon to meet her at his old cabin the following day. (This first scene was omitted from the play as first published, but was restored in the version directed on Broadway by José Quintero in 1967.)

From this point the scenario continues with little variation from the play published in 1964, save that it includes a scene between Abigail and two of the children. In the end Sara leaves with her sons, Simon sets fire to the business, and follows them. Abigail deliberately enters the garden house, the symbol of "the Land of Living Death," and becomes insane, with Joel assuming the role of her protector. An epilogue, just after Abigail's funeral, takes place on Simon and Sara's farm, with Simon recuperating and Sara communing with nature.

O'Neill wrote a scenario for the third play, *The Calms of Capricorn*, in May and June 1935. It is summarized as follows. Telling the story of Ethan, the oldest Harford son, it takes place mostly on a clipper ship bound from New York to San Francisco in 1857. Simon Harford having died in the first act, Sara and their other three sons sail with Ethan to begin new lives in California. His ship is commanded by Captain Payne, now in his sixties, accompanied on this voyage by his thirty-eight-year-old wife, Nancy. Among the passengers are the ship-owner, Warren; his daughter, Elizabeth; the Revd. Mr. Dickey; and a company of gold-seekers. Last to arrive are the failed banker, Graber, and his mistress, the adventuress Leda Cade, who acts as a corrupting influence on all her companions.

Ethan, now twenty-eight, has been promoted from second to first mate, in the place of Hull, an old friend and contemporary of the captain, whose doctor has ordered him to stay at home to recuperate from a heart attack. Just before the ship is to leave the dock, Hull appears, insisting that he is well enough to make the trip. He taunts Ethan, who strikes him. Hull falls, hitting his head on the stairs, and dies. Leda Cade gets Ethan to admit that this is what he really wanted, and suggests that he and Nancy Payne would welcome the death of another old man, the captain.

Ethan as first mate hopes for a record run to San Francisco, but in the South Atlantic the ship encounters twenty days of calm. During that period Leda's evil influence continues to corrupt, taking its toll even of the Revd. Mr. Dickey. Captain Payne, depressed by his wife's very evident attraction to Ethan, and with a death-wish, falls on the stairs, and is eventually murdered by Nancy, abetted by Ethan.

With the captain's murder, a favorable wind returns. Ethan and Nancy are married by Dickey. Ethan assumes command of the ship and drives her unmercifully, encouraged now by the owner. They are about to make a record when, just as they near the Golden Gate, the wind again dies down. Acknowledging that the sea has won, Ethan condemns himself to death. Nancy joins him in committing suicide by jumping overboard.

Wolfe Harford has played solitaire through most of the trip, but he is eventually persuaded to gamble with Graber for the favors of Leda Cade. He wins, and Leda confesses that she loves him; but he is cold to her. Elizabeth Warren and Jonathan agree that marriage will be for them a good business proposition. Honey Harford has demonstrated his skill as a politician by becoming the popular leader of the gold-seekers. The play ends as the various Harford family members look forward to their new life in California.

(This scenario as O'Neill wrote it, along with my "development" of it into play-form, was published in 1982.)

O'Neill next took up the fourth play, "The Earth Is the Limit," the story of the second Harford son, Wolfe, the gambler, and by the end of June 1935 had completed a rough outline. In summary, the play opens in 1858, and chiefly concerns the resolution of the love affair between Wolfe and the adventuress Leda. Elizabeth Warren, the shipowner's daughter, has bet Jonathan Harford that Leda will eventually win Wolfe over, and has agreed to marry Jonathan if Leda fails. Wolfe eventually bets Leda in a card-game with his brother Honey, and loses. Then, realizing that he has fallen in love with her, now that it is too late, he commits suicide. Honey embarks on a promising career in politics, while Jonathan enjoys initial business success.

Because so many details were still unresolved in his mind, O'Neill decided not to write the scenario for this fourth play, but to take up similar rough outlines of the others. (It was at this point that the idea came to him of using "Bessie Bowen," the play he had worked on in the late 1920s and very early 1930s, as the conclusion of a final, seventh Cycle play.) He worked steadily on the outline for the fifth play, "Nothing Is Lost but Honor," the story of Honey Harford, the politician, and finished it in July 1935. A summary of its action follows.

The play opens in 1860, the night before Wolfe's funeral. Elizabeth marries Jonathan, and Leda marries Honey, who continues to meet with success in his political career, eventually becoming a United States senator. Jonathan, a railroad magnate, advances ruthlessly, using his brother to help him in Washington by buying influence. He, Jonathan, appeals to Leda as the only one in the family who can understand that his end justifies any means; she shares his enthusiasm, attracted to him by some of the same quality that she had loved in his brother Wolfe.

The climax comes when Jonathan has sold the railroad stock short. To cause a financial panic and achieve his goal of controlling rail lines from coast to coast, he forces Honey to read before the Senate the list of all the bribes he has paid. Honey convinces himself that his brother is doing this to get even for the shipboard affair he had had with Elizabeth – both influenced by Leda Cade – and forgives him. He has become disillusioned with politics anyway, and has lost nothing but a bit of honor. Jonathan persuades him to take Leda and Elizabeth and go to Europe until the scandal blows over and he, Jonathan, can consolidate his gains. In a later revision of the scenario for *The Calms of Capricorn*, Jonathan does not make the voyage with his mother and brothers, but joins them in California as "The Earth Is the Limit" opens. They tell him the story of the trip and thus provide the necessary linkage between the two plays.

O'Neill next began the outline for the sixth play, of Jonathan, the railroad magnate, "The Man on Iron Horseback." He completed a tentative summary of the scenes in August 1935. The play opens in New York in 1874 or 1875. Jonathan has beaten his chief competitor, Goddard, to the control of another railroad, and cables Honey, Leda, and Elizabeth to come home. In Paris, Elizabeth, dominated by Leda, has led a scandalous life, although Leda has remained faithful – to Honey, she thinks, but actually to Jonathan. They return, and Sara, who has been acting as Jonathan's hostess, goes with Honey and Leda to live in San Francisco. Elizabeth finds

Jonathan cold to her, and enters into an affair with Goddard, although she still loves her husband.

Jonathan's doctor warns him that he is jeopardizing his health by overwork. He replies that he hasn't time to die, and continues his fight to gain a railroad monopoly. Using Elizabeth's relationship with Goddard in his campaign, he accuses her of betraying him; but she has actually betrayed Goddard. Jonathan offers to let her divorce him; when she refuses, declaring that she loves him, he is indifferent. In despair, she commits suicide. Overcome by loneliness and a premonition of death, Jonathan travels to San Francisco by train to see his mother, who rallies him to his dream. He asks her to live in order to look after his children, gives her financial advice, and dies.

At the end of August 1935, O'Neill made notes for the seventh and final play, now called "Twilight of Possessors Self-Dispossessed," incorporating in its second part much of the old "Bessie Bowen" that he had tried to write in the late 1920s and very early 1930s. It opens in San Francisco in 1893. Sara has insisted on paying Jonathan's enormous bequests to charity and there is nothing left except her New England estate and the trust fund which covers its expenses but doesn't allow her to sell. To Honey, Jonathan has bequeathed the livery stable that now stands on the site of their Grandfather Melody's inn. The family all return East and live together on the estate, entirely isolated socially. Sara becomes a miser, practicing every economy. Honey, a lecherous, drunken old man, lives in the past. Leda grows enormously fat, exists only to eat, and dies in a fall down the stairs after a midnight raid on the icebox. Sara becomes senile and dies, and the children, free of the past, leave the estate. Further notes for this final play occupied O'Neill in the first days of September, and he commented in his *Work Diary*: "As this 7th Play follows in main plot-outline the old 'Bessie Bowen' theme, nothing further [is] needed ... now beyond the revision notes I've done in [the] past week" (p. 229).

Once again it was his characters' earlier lives that stimulated his imagination and, on 7 September 1935, we find him "Playing around with [the] idea [for a] new first play to precede '[The] Hair of The Dog', to go back to 1806 and show ... [Simon's mother] as [a] girl – [her] marriage to Henry H[arford]. – and their house & parents – Henry's father [the] big character – title, '*Greed Of The Meek*'" (*Work Diary*, p. 230). He couldn't put this new play, the first of an eight-play Cycle, out of his mind. In early November he wrote a detailed scenario for the first act but didn't like it. He decided instead to take up "The Hair of the Dog" and wrote a first draft, but then returned to "Greed of the Meek." He began to write that play in March 1936, and by 9 May, had reached the last act; but at the end of the month he had to admit that he was "getting nowhere – baffled." On 7 June, he came to the decision that he needed a ninth play, telling the story of Henry Harford's father, mother, and three aunts. He got the title "Give Me Death" and wrote an outline. Returning briefly to "Greed of the Meek," and finding that he was still stuck, he decided to put both plays aside. Between July and August (1936) he completed a second draft of "The Hair of the Dog." Uncertain about the epilogue, he decided to let the play rest without one.

O'Neill now went back again to "Greed of the Meek," and by mid-September had completed it; but he didn't like the ending, and the play was much too long. In spite of his dissatisfaction with it, he decided to call the play finished, pending revision and condensation. He spent 19 September reading over and making notes for revising the scenario of *More Stately Mansions*. He began work on actual dialogue on the 24th, and finished the first scene on 1 October. But then an enforced rest, the move to the West Coast, the Nobel Prize, and, finally, an appendectomy put an end to all work for several months. It wasn't until June 1937 that O'Neill was able to do any extensive writing. He then took up the new first two Cycle plays and, by 22 July, had finished his notes for rewriting "Greed of the Meek." These notes, summarized in the following, are the chief source for information about the play, destroyed in 1944.

Jonathan Harford (not to be confused with his great-grandson of the same name, dealt with in "The Man on Iron Horseback"), feeling that his wife Kate and his three half-sisters have stolen from him the love of his son Henry, has left them to go on a series of voyages in search of freedom. He returns, a convert to Buddhism, planning to rid himself of all worldly possessions. His family attempt to get him involved again in their lives. He does finally respond to the beauty of Henry's wife Abigail (later Deborah), and, at his son's urging, becomes interested in and then obsessed with Aaron Burr – the issue of freedom or greed. He becomes confused over his motives, and fights to recover his philosophic detachment.

His family, now convinced that he is sincere, hate him for rejecting – in effect, murdering – them. The idea of killing *him* grows in their minds. Even Abigail is torn between feeling for and against him. She and he exchange vows of love, followed by mutual repulsion. In a fit of anger, he dashes off a will leaving everything to her. He makes plans to join Burr: with him, by treachery and greed, he can rise to the top. He rushes from his room, but meets Abigail returning to warn him against the others. There is real love between them for a moment, then again recoil. At last they bid each other goodbye, and he leaves. She whispers to herself that she will never forget that she was his in her mind; now she will become pregnant.

The Sisters, Kate, and Henry, having decided to murder Jonathan, come to his room, find that he has left, and discover the will. Abigail decides to put Henry in control of the business, but will require that he consult with his mother and his aunts. As for herself, she will keep up the Harford garden. In the final scene, she, now pregnant, is walking there.

The epilogue takes place about a year later, in Kate's bedroom. Jonathan and the Sisters have died, and Kate is on her deathbed. Abigail is nursing her baby, Jonathan's in spirit, Henry's only in body. Henry exults that now the business can go ahead, be reborn into textiles. Abigail asks Kate's consent in giving the business to Henry. She answers, "Yes, let him have his toy," and dies.

On 26 July 1937, O'Neill took up what had now become the ninth play, the old "Bessie Bowen," and made some notes for it. The play now opens in 1900 at Honey Harford's livery stable and bicycle shop. Sara II, daughter of Leda, has married Bowen and had an only daughter Lou, who is eighteen when the play opens. Lou marries the mechanic–inventor Ernie Cade, and they have four children. She markets the automobile that her husband has invented, and builds up a thriving enterprise. In 1932 she announces her retirement, sells the business, and gives a radio interview. She has sacrificed everything to the business and now wants to become a real wife and mother. But her good resolutions are too late: her younger son has become a dope addict and Anarchist, his wife a Communist escapist; one of the daughters, a Lesbian, goes to Paris's Left Bank to live. Honey continues to the end and, in one outline, has the final speech. But O'Neill's plans for this last play, and especially for its ending, never became definite.

On 9 August 1937, he decided on some title changes that had heretofore been only tentative: the new first play would be called "Greed of the Meek" and the new second play "Give Me Death." The third play would be *A Touch of the Poet*, and the ninth and last would become "Hair of the Dog." The entire Cycle would be called "Lament for Possessors Self-Dispossessed" (*Work Diary*, p. 296).

O'Neill began to write actual dialogue for the new "Greed of the Meek" on 11 August, but the play just would not come to life. He worked at it all through the autumn, with many false starts, finally deciding to call the play finished but only a first draft in need of a lot of rewriting. On 23 December, looking it over again, he commented that it is "longer than 'Strange I[nterlude]' – don't want this – but don't see now how it can be drastically cut without ruining it – trouble is [I] want to get too much in these plays for single length" (*Work Diary*, p. 309). Although O'Neill tore up most of his notes for the rewriting of this first play of the nine-play Cycle when he destroyed the holograph manuscript in 1944, he did preserve its title page and the listing of scenes and characters.

The new "Greed of the Meek" opens in 1775 at Evan Harford's farm in Massachusetts, and the action takes place in the farmhouse, at his son Jonathan's house in a seaport town, and on the latter's barque, ending in 1783. Evan is murdered in the course of the first act by a tramp. All four of his children, motivated chiefly by greed, had reasons for wishing him dead, and his three daughters by his first wife imply that they did kill him in their minds. They became convinced that he intended to disinherit them because they had sided with their step-mother in her desertion of him.

Jonathan, their younger half-brother, educated at Harvard, becomes an advocate of freedom and the American Revolution. After the war, he takes up the slave trade and makes a good deal of money. He becomes an apostle of France and Jacobinism, renounces all property and, leaving his wife Kate in charge, sails off to the Far East in search of freedom.

In March 1938, now at Tao House, O'Neill reread this first play, the new "Greed of the Meek." His verdict, recorded in the *Work Diary* on the 25th, was that it "needs a lot done to it – is as long as 'Strange Interlude'! – and too psychologically involved in spots" (p. 316), but he felt it would be best, because of themes repeated in the first and last plays, to postpone rewriting this and the second play until he had finished all the others. He went on to read the scenario for *More Stately Mansions*, found that he liked it, and decided to write that play next. He began on 29 April, and by early September had finished a first draft. His comment on 8 April has a familiar ring: "needs [a] lot of revision & rewriting – is as long as Strange Interlude! – but don't think [I] will be able to cut [the] length much" (*Work Diary*, p. 328). He spent the rest of the year "going over" the play, and finished revising the first three acts in the script typed by Carlotta – the third draft of the whole play – in January 1939.

On the 23rd he reread *A Touch of the Poet*, and by mid-May had finished a third draft of that play. Although he took up *The Calms of Capricorn*, and wrote a prologue, he tore it up on 5 June as "n[o]. g[ood].," and recorded in his *Work Diary* that he felt "fed up and stale on [the] Cycle after $4\frac{1}{2}$ years of not thinking of any other work – will do me good [to] lay [it] on [the] shelf and forget it for a while – do a play which has nothing to do with it" (p. 351). And so, between June and December 1939, he wrote *The Iceman Cometh*, finishing some final "trimming" of that play on 3 January 1940.

On the 6th and 7th, he reread the longhand draft of the new "Greed of the Meek," the first play of the nine-play Cycle, found he liked it better than he'd thought he would, and made notes for its revision. He did further reading in connection with this and the second play, and worked on notes for rewriting the latter, now called "And Give Me Death."

In that year, 1940, O'Neill took more time off from the Cycle to write *Long Day's Journey Into Night*. He again surveyed the first two Cycle plays in October and in his *Work Diary* on the 20th acknowledged that he had made them "too complicated – [he had] tried to get too much into them, too many interwoven themes & motives, psychological & spiritual" (p. 391). It was his determination to simplify and condense that led him to destroy the drafts of those two plays and to plan the four plays that would replace them in an eleven-play Cycle as far less complicated, with fewer "intermingling relationships." Between 24 October and 13 November, he made for the new plays notes and outlines upon which the following plot summaries are based.

Play one, "Give Me Liberty and – ," tentatively titled both "The Poor in Spirit" and "The Pride of the Meek," opens in 1755, at a New England farmhouse, with the Three Sisters spinning. The first Harford, Jonathan (great-great-grandfather of the railroad magnate of the same name) had come to America, from Wales, with Braddock's army. He had been at first taken prisoner, then released, by Indians. He comes to the farm, seeking a temporary job. The girls' mother, Naomi (last name not given), hires and eventually marries him, bearing him a son Ethan (great-great-grandfather of Captain Ethan Harford). The birth is a hard one for her and it ruins her health. She hates the baby, and makes his three half-sisters nurse him, and keep him out of her sight. She becomes jealous of her husband, fears he will leave her, and eventually worries herself into an early grave. Jonathan, free, returns to the wilderness, leaving the upbringing of his son to his step-daughters. The first play ends with his departure in 1757.

The second play, "The Rebellion of the Humble," opens eighteen years later, in April 1775, at the farmhouse. Ethan has graduated from Harvard with a law degree. He persuades his half-sisters that the farm should be sold to help the cause of the Revolution. Jonathan returns, and his step-daughters try to get him to stay on the farm with them, but he has decided to join the fight until he's free. He is impatient with their meekness, and suggests that they take up privateering as an occupation, with motives of both patriotism and profit. He will tell his friend Mardo, a ship captain, to help them. Ethan reluctantly agrees to this plan, and Jonathan again leaves.

The Sisters begin to rebel against their half-brother, and set his pet caged bird free. When he returns from town, where he has sold and been paid for the farm, he becomes furious with them because of their release of his bird. He informs them, quite casually, that he has learned in town that his father was killed in the battle of Bunker Hill. The Sisters grieve, but Ethan reminds them angrily that his father deserted him and left them, his step-daughters, enslaved to the land. Ethan would in conscience have had to disown him, to wish him hung, because some of the things he said amounted to treason.

In an epilogue, all four watch from a nearby hilltop as the farm burns, the Sisters having left lighted candles and shavings soaked in whale oil. They are determined now to grab all they can, to stop being meek; Ethan will be their little pet bird.

The third play, "Greed of the Meek," opens in Newport or Providence, in 1783. The Sisters have become rich, while their half-brother spends his time making speeches and writing pamphlets advocating revolution in other countries. They persuade Captain Mardo to shanghai him – take him on his next voyage – see that he becomes interested in women. This Mardo does, while they groom a young widow, Kate Blaine, to be Ethan's wife. He returns from the voyage in April 1784, forgives his half-sisters, and later proposes to Kate. They all go on a honeymoon trip to France. The ship is blown off course by a hurricane, in the midst of which Ethan is roused to unrestrained passion for Kate. They do not reach France until early 1786, and Kate's baby, Henry, is born at sea. Ethan takes all the ship's money and goes to join the French Revolution. The Sisters think he will come back; and indeed he does, but, pausing in the shadows, he hears them telling Kate that the French will soon tire of his speeches and will "rotten-egg" him. His face hardens, and he turns away.

In an epilogue, in 1794, the Revd. Henry Deane and his daughter Abigail (later Deborah) are with Kate and her son Henry Harford in the garden. The Sisters went back to France when they received the news that Ethan was arrested and thrown into prison as an adherent of Robespierre. They return home, bringing Ethan, whom they managed to free by bribing his captors. He was so unimportant that they simply forgot to guillotine him, but he has made himself believe that his rescue came just as he was about to be executed. He denounces them all, and plans to make the Harford summerhouse into a temple to liberty.

The fourth play, "And Give Me Death," opens in 1804, on the eve of Henry Harford's marriage to Abigail Deane. The Sisters make a will, providing that the bulk of their property is to go to Henry, who will assume responsibility for his parents. Ethan admires Aaron Burr for killing Alexander Hamilton, but is chiefly interested in the espaliered pear trees he has trained against the north wall. The Sisters cannot bear to see him degenerate into a futile crank. They decide that Henry and Abigail will be married at once and they will all go to France to witness the coronation of Napoleon. In Paris on 2 December 1804, they view the parade from a suite of rooms in a hotel. When they return home, a conflict begins. The Sisters change their will to leave everything to Abigail, and finally sign an agreement turning their property over to her. She proceeds to give it all away, with their reluctant consent – to her father, to Ethan, to Kate, and to Henry. She is pregnant now: in her mind the baby's father is Napoleon. Ethan, dressed in his French National Guard uniform, prepares to sail to join Burr. But he goes to have a farewell look over his garden and comes back in a rage: the espaliers are growing all over the place – free! He can't leave after all, there's too much to do at home.

By making the original Harford a much younger person and changing drastically the character of his son (Simon's grandfather), O'Neill had been able to solve some problems. But at the same time the Three Sisters, now Harford *step*daughters, had become even more vitally important characters. Indeed, they had captured the dramatist's imagination to such an extent that he for a time planned to rewrite both *A Touch of the Poet* and *More Stately Mansions* to carry them into those plays (*Work Diary*, pp. 393–94). But he came eventually to realize that in changing the three from half-sisters to stepdaughters and thus making them no longer blood-members of the Harford family, he had destroyed the unity of the Cycle. George Jean Nathan reported, in the *American Mercury* for October 1946, that "O'Neill's dissatisfaction with the work [*i.e.*, the eleven-play Cycle] as far as it had gone proceeded from his conviction that it should deal with the one family and not two, as it presently did" (p. 464). It seems probable that the major reconstruction of his plans for the first four plays that would have been required in order to correct this fault became an additional, final reason why O'Neill, his energies at a low point because of ill health and depression at the state of the world, failed to do any further major new work on the Cycle during the last years of his life.

In March 1941, he completed the third and final draft of *Long Day's Journey*, and in April finished a first draft of the one-act *Hughie*. In October, he read over the outlines of the first four plays of the eleven-play Cycle, and expressed himself as "pleased – can be great stuff – and I mean, great – but too long, tough job to tackle now" (*Work Diary*, p. 419). And so he worked on other new ideas and, between the end of October and January 1942, wrote a first draft of *A Moon for the Misbegotten*.

In mid-February, O'Neill returned to *A Touch of the Poet*, determined to get at least one Cycle play definitely finished. Working on it over a period of nine months, he completed the new version in November, and commented in the *Work Diary* on the 13th that he had "made it [a] much better play, both as itself & as part of [the] Cycle – a triumph, I feel, considering sickness & war strain – still has minor faults – needs some cutting and condensing, but that can wait a while" (p. 451).

Between January and May of 1943, O'Neill worked on a second draft of

A Moon for the Misbegotten. Although he managed to complete that play, and sent a copy of the script off to Random House, he seems to have done very little other creative work that year. In January 1944, Carlotta reported: "When I suggest [to Gene] it might be wise to *not* destroy so many of his 'notes' on plays & scenarios – he replies, 'I want to destroy all these things – I'm through, I'll never work again' –" (Carlotta Monterey O'Neill, "Diary" [Yale]). On the 21st, after Tao House was sold, O'Neill tore up more manuscript material, including the completed drafts of the first two plays of the nine-play Cycle, later explaining that he did not want to be too much governed by them in rewriting those two plays into the four that he now planned to take their place in an eleven-play Cycle. In June, Carlotta reports retyping for her husband some scenes from the Cycle and his "going over" *A Touch of the Poet*. But O'Neill himself wrote on 24 March 1945 to Frederic I. Carpenter that "For the past two years I've done nothing at all." In that same letter he referred to the Cycle by its final title, "A Tale of Possessors Self-Dispossessed," and stated that the last play, "the old 'The Career of Bessie Bowen' will never be written." The Great Depression caught up with its prophecies, for one thing" (Autograph draft letter, Yale).

In August 1946 there was some discussion with the Theatre Guild about a production of *A Touch of the Poet*, but it came to nothing. From time to time, as his tremor seemed to get a little better, O'Neill ventured to hope that he could start writing plays again, but the affliction invariably grew worse, and on 4 February 1949, he admitted in a letter to his lawyer, Winfield E. Aronberg: "I will never write another play and there is no use kidding myself that I will" (*Selected Letters*, p. 585).

In May 1951 the O'Neills sold their Marblehead cottage and moved into the Hotel Shelton in Boston. They burned much manuscript material relating to the Cycle early in 1953, but in the confusion of those troubled days some items, like the revised typescript of *More Stately Mansions*, that O'Neill had marked to be destroyed, were sent to Yale, along with many miscellaneous notes and plans for the Cycle that for one reason or another had not been torn up.

On 27 November 1953, Eugene O'Neill died, and with him all hope that the Cycle to which he had devoted so large a part of his creative life would ever come into the realization that he had so ardently desired for it.

NOTE

(This essay is adapted from Donald Gallup's *Eugene O'Neill and His Eleven-Play Cycle, "A Tale of Possessors Self-Dispossessed,"* © Yale University Press, 1998. Printed by permission of Yale University Press.)

WORKS CITED

Printed

Bogard, Travis, *Contour in Time: The Plays of Eugene O'Neill. Revised Edition* (New York: Oxford University Press, 1988).

Nathan, George Jean, "Eugene O'Neill after Twelve Years." *American Mercury* (October 1946): pp. 462–66. (Based, apparently, on letters from O'Neill during the period and, presumably, on conversations in New York after the O'Neills' return East.)

O'Neill, Eugene Gladstone, *The Calms of Capricorn. Developed from O'Neill's Scenario by Donald Gallup. With a Transcription of the Scenario* (New Haven and New York: Ticknor and Fields, 1982).

More Stately Mansions. Shortened from the Author's Partly Revised Script by Karl Ragnar Gierow and Edited by Donald Gallup (New Haven and London: Yale University Press, 1964).

More Stately Mansions. The Unexpurgated Edition. Edited by Martha Gilman Bower (New York, Oxford: Oxford University Press, 1988).

Selected Letters ... Edited by Travis Bogard and Jackson R. Bryer (New Haven and London: Yale University Press, 1988).

A Touch of the Poet (New Haven: Yale University Press, 1957).

Work Diary, 1924–1943. Transcribed by Donald Gallup. Preliminary Edition. 2 *volumes* (New Haven: Yale University Library, 1981).

Manuscript

O'Neill, Carlotta Monterey, "Diary" (Yale Collection of American Literature. *Acronym*: YCAL).

O'Neill, Eugene Gladstone, Autograph draft letter, dated by Mrs. O'Neill 24 March 1945 (probably when she typed and sent it) to Frederic I. Carpenter (YCAL: O'Neill MS. 118, vol. 3, 4 February to 16 September 1945).

Miscellaneous notes, outlines, scenarios, and drafts of the Cycle plays (YCAL).

Sergeant, Elizabeth Shepley, typewritten notes of interviews with Eugene O'Neill, 3 [*i.e.*, 4], 10 [*i.e.*, 11], and 25 August 1946 (YCAL MS. 3. Sergeant papers, series III, box 16, folder 358).

13

JEAN CHOTHIA

Trying to write the family play: autobiography and the dramatic imagination

"The truth," Eugene O'Neill wrote in 1926, in response to the first draft of Barrett Clark's biography of him:

> the truth would make such a much more interesting – and incredible – legend. That is what makes me melancholy. But I see no hope for this except some day to shame the devil myself, if I ever can muster the requisite interest – and nerve – simultaneously.[1]

And Clark later quoted Carlotta O'Neill's observation, made in 1933, that "he will never tell the truth about himself, because in so doing he would have to tell the truth about others close to him."[2] O'Neill did cooperate with Clark, though, and the biography, first published in 1926, includes an account of O'Neill's wanderings and his collapse with tuberculosis in 1912. It touches on his father's success on the popular stage and regret for the career he might have had as a Shakespearean actor, his mother's dislike of the theatre and his brother's life as a Broadway *flâneur*. But it is silent about more intimate details of the family's life: about the dead infant, Edmund; about betrayals and dependencies; and, most notably, it is silent about O'Neill's mother's drug addiction which had begun with his birth, the family secret of which he was not himself told until he was nearly fifteen.[3] Nor do references to these appear in O'Neill's published letters, even in those to such close intimates as Kenneth Macgowan at the time of the traumatic sequence of deaths of father, mother and brother between 1920 and 1923.[4]

When O'Neill wrote in the dedication to *Long Day's Journey Into Night*, that he had faced his dead at last in this play written with "deep pity and understanding and forgiveness for *all* the four haunted Tyrones," making clear the close identification of the characters and events of the play with his own family history, he indicated that he had, indeed, finally, in this very late work, "mustered the nerve." Given this, it is remarkable that, apart from the dedication itself, there is no sense for the reader or the theatre audience, of voyeurism, of encountering experience too personal or too raw. It takes unusual personal courage to kick away the ladders and supports of fictional disguise and lie down, as W. B. Yeats has it, "where all the ladders start, / In the foul rag and bone shop of the heart." But it also takes art of a very high order to so recreate the private and the personal in the public medium which drama is that it seems both truthful and compelling to its audience, that it achieves intensity without embarrassment and leaves no impression of special pleading. Ben Jonson's short poem, "On My First Son," cannot fail to touch the reader as an utterance of intense and uncontrived grief, and yet it is a most complexly wrought piece of writing. For all the extremity of some aspects of the experience, it is the literary and dramatic skill when casting it in convincing dramatic form that allows O'Neill's late plays to speak to the responding imaginations of their audiences. And it is with this that I am concerned here.

The direct engagement with autobiography came late but, from the outset, O'Neill's plays were concerned with secrets and concealment: with dysfunctional families, isolated from the rest of the community, or with single men, emotionally damaged, in retreat from the dysfunctional family or haunted by the memory of relationship that has foundered, and so doomed to wander and to find temporary consolation in alcohol. Some plays – *Desire Under the Elms, All God's Chillun Got Wings, Mourning Becomes Electra, Long Day's Journey Into Night* – center the one; some – "The SS Glencairn Plays," *The Hairy Ape, The Iceman Cometh* – center the other, but virtually all include at least elements of both. The fictive locales O'Neill creates within the theatrical space derive directly from these basic situations. Two kinds of setting, seemingly opposed but, in fact, only opposite sides of the same coin, recur: they are notably private spaces – the center, usually the living room, of a family home – or they are notably public spaces – the hold of a tramp steamer, a bar, a flop-house, where disparate people are gathered randomly. The one type culminates in the set of *Long Day's Journey Into Night* which, it is now known, recreates the living room of the O'Neill's New London summer home. The other culminates in the set of *The Iceman Cometh* – an amalgam of the flophouse in which as a young man O'Neill sought escape from self and past.

The more one encounters O'Neill's work the more astonishing the range of setting, plot, character seems, and the more remarkable the extent of the dramatic and theatrical experimentation. But, just as O'Neill engaged in a lifelong and often agonized experimentation with language which came to remarkable fruition in the variousness and seemingly complete naturalness of the densely packed, artful and expressive dialogue of the late plays, so, simultaneously, his own emotional experience, sometimes thinly, sometimes deeply disguised, and disguised perhaps even from himself, is the recurrent subject of plays throughout his writing life. With hindsight, the whole career can be read as a clearing of the ground, a sifting of events, a honing of language and structure in preparation for the extraordinary dramatic control and self-exploration of the final three plays. As certain tropes and motifs are worked and reworked in the changing circumstances of successive plays, the more fully evident it is that, as Michael Manheim has put it, "O'Neill had been writing versions of *Long Day's Journey Into Night* throughout his entire career."[5]

From the outset, O'Neill often included in his plays a poet–rebel figure. Evidently quasi-autobiographical, the presence of such figures, usually indulgently treated, often pitted against rather crudely drawn businessmen in the middle years, is of less interest than that patterns of relationship recur, as do perceptions of things hidden, of pressures building and of characters bound together who are, nevertheless, continually withdrawing from each other. In particular, the woman withdrawn into herself figures recurrently in O'Neill's drama before she is given evidently autobiographical form in *Long Day's Journey Into Night*. Until then, the circumstances are never quite those of Mary Tyrone, or of Ella Quinlan O'Neill, although there are shared characteristics of speech or gesture. In the early play, *Ile*, Mrs. Keeney is cut off from her husband by incipient breakdown, as is Ella in *All God's Chillun Got Wings*. Mrs. Keeney's increasing withdrawal into herself is explained by the context – it is horror of the ice in which her husband's ship has been trapped "for nigh on a year" – but she is an early rehearsal of the later character. She speaks "monotonously," "dully," is restless, "clasping and unclasping her hands" and has a certain clinging obstinacy, her need and determination summed up in the simplicity of her utterance, "I wanted to be with you, David, don't you see?" Ella in *All God's Chillun* shifts in a moment, as Mary Tyrone will in her play, from fierce vindictiveness to a pleading dependency on Jim that leeches his energy. O'Neill explores ways of giving dramatic presence to the torment of those closest to such women. In the early play, Captain Keeney stands listening to his wife sobbing in an inner room from which he is excluded. At the end of the piece, her wild playing of the organ signals her total collapse and her husband discovers the incapacity of any words of his to penetrate her consciousness. Sometimes the mother figure is removed entirely but it is a felt absence. Abbie in *Desire Under the Elms* must assuage Eben's pain at the loss of his mother, dead before the action begins, by becoming his surrogate mother as well as his lover. Elsewhere the emphasis is more clearly on the alienation of the man who has in some way betrayed or failed to live up to the expectations of his woman. In "The

Moon of the Caribbees," Smitty, alone, can find no peace. However far he runs he is haunted by the memory of the woman he disappointed. Curt in the abortive early play, *The First Man*, cries out that it is terrible when his wife torments herself and him with her accusatory, "Yes, you love me. But who am I? You don't know." When Mary Tyrone finally comes downstairs at the end of *Long Day's Journey*, wholly under the influence of the drug, she too plays music, a tribute to her fantasy that she might have been a concert pianist. Although her men-folk are as helpless as Captain Keeney, as Curt or as Ella's Jim, the knife is turned much more cruelly for the Tyrones, and for the audience in the theatre who listen with them, because Mary does speak and, speaking, demonstrates how thoroughly they are eliminated from her consciousness.

In play after play, characters seize an opportunity to tell each other their stories. Such story-telling – like that of Yank and Driscoll in the S.S. Glencairn plays, or Anna in *Anna Christie* – might project a better life – in fantasy or daydream. They can be light, bar-room anecdotes, drawing in the theatre audience as well as the on-stage listeners, like those the men-folk tell in *Ah, Wilderness!* or like the farcical tale of Shaughnessy and the pigs in *Long Day's Journey* which O'Neill reworks as the basis of the comic plot of *A Moon for the Misbegotten*. More often, retelling the past, they enable an ordering, albeit only temporary, of the character's sense of self, and thereby an escape from the present. Seemingly hardened characters reveal their vulnerability in confessional sequences often spoken in the presence of another character, but the response to the self-revelation is usually blank. Our inability to hear each other and the inopportuneness of the moment chosen to speak, are recurring motifs. While Ephraim expatiates on his life and loneliness in part II of *Desire Under the Elms*, his wife, Abbie, is preoccupied by her own private longings. Too late, Ezra Mannon struggles to account for himself to an unreceptive Christine in *Mourning Becomes Electra*. Among the multiple narratives of *Long Day's Journey Into Night* are confessions that *are* eventually heard as, in Act 4, father and son, brother and brother explain themselves each to the other and acknowledge a degree of mutual appreciation. If there is some kind of comfort in this, Mary's extended narrative, which concludes the act and the play, is the most painful of all O'Neill's many sequences of self-revelation precisely because, this time, it is the speaker who is unaware of the significance of her words, unaware indeed of the presence of the on-stage listeners, and it is the listeners, both on-stage and in the audience, who feel the knife of her words turning in the wound.

This representation of our propensity to cast experience into narrative form – to tell ourselves stories – is of signal importance to O'Neill's method and to his capacity to bind the audience to the developing action, as is his tendency to rework in finer form the material of his own earlier plays in writing the later ones. But there is frequently, too, a more evidently literary presence, or presences, shaping the material: other people's stories enable him to tell his own. This is particularly the case when O'Neill addresses the most deeply personal themes, as though what he read not only helped him to constitute himself as a writer but as a person. The echoes are more not less evident, the quotation more willingly acknowledged, in the most fully achieved late plays where commentators have picked up echoes of and quotation from Gorki and Ibsen, Strindberg and Nietzsche, Kipling and Richard Dana, as well as Shakespeare, Baudelaire, Swinburne and Dowson.[6] This too, I think, is a crucial part of the autobiography. O'Neill's personal experience of maternal alienation and of fraught family relationships was only too real, but so, deeply engraved, was the reading. Indeed, the reading might be seen as the young O'Neill's place of retreat, the subsequent writing, his response to, or attempt to understand and even come to terms with the alienation and fraught relationships. For escape can also involve discovery and self-discovery. If the extent and density of the echoes of other writers in O'Neill's drama is surprising, even more so is the individuality of the voice that emerges through them. This is not plagiarism, nor is it "anxiety of influence." What we read helps shape our perception of experience. Perhaps, too, when we read, our emotional experience or confusion shapes our response to that reading so that we respond most acutely to writing that in some important way figures our own condition.

The opening description of the set of *Long Day's Journey Into Night* includes a detailed listing of the authors of the two very different sets of books in the room. What might on first encounter with the play-text seem an absurdity of realistic detail, is in fact a telling indicator of the tone and texture of O'Neill's dramatic imagination. Such naming within a staging that recreates the intimate living space of his own adolescence demonstrates O'Neill's recognition that these were essential features of an authentic recreation of the past and records the importance to him of the books named. As the stage direction has it of the family books, *"the astonishing thing about these sets is that all the volumes have the look of having been read and reread."* Moreover, while the audience in the theatre may not be able to distinguish many of the individual titles, the spines and bindings themselves will be indicative. Further, as the play proceeds, gesture, reference, and quotation will interact with the presence of the two sets of books on stage, underscoring *both* the embattled nature of the relationship between father, owner of one, more traditional, set, and son, owner of the other, avant-garde collection of volumes, *and* the greater closeness to each other than either will acknowledge, evident in the propensity of each to quote and refer constantly to their authors, albeit in very different ways, and marked, not least, by the inclusion of Shakespeare's picture above the case of books which belongs not to the father but to the rebellious son.

The child, O'Neill, read and reread the nineteenth-century romances and tales of adventure in his father's library, moving on to the darker and more disturbing stories of men adrift at sea or in cities of Melville and Dana, Conrad, Poe and Wilde. The rebellious adolescent revelled in the avant-garde writing that exposed bourgeois society's grim underbelly, acknowledged personal needs and guilts and was not afraid to reveal psychological disturbance behind supposedly composed surfaces. Zola and Dostoevski, Nietzsche and Gorki, Dowson and Swinburne were only the most prominent of these.[7] And if O'Neill's first encounters with drama included both his father's admiration of Shakespeare and access to *all three* of his sets of the *Complete Works* as well as the Victorian melodramas for which the career as a Shakespearean actor had been abandoned, he soon felt the impact of the new. As a young man he experienced Nazimova's groundbreaking Ibsen season in New York (1906) and the plays of Synge, Yeats and T. C. Murray, as performed by the Irish Players (1911); he caught echoes of the excitement generated by Granville Barker's productions of Shaw and Galsworthy (1904–14) and, perhaps most significantly, discovered for himself the tortured world of Strindberg's plays and autobiographical novels. He returned obsessively to Nazimova's production of *Hedda Gabler*, Ibsen's study of female frustration and self-destruction and revelled in the capacity of Strindberg's representation of a couple bound in a cycle of mutual hostility and need in *The Dance of Death* to "communicate a powerful emotional ecstasy."[8]

Tropes and figures, even plot-lines and patterns of character interaction encountered in literature bring shape and form to the writer's inchoate experiences, sometimes very directly. Examples leap off the pages of O'Neill's preferred authors. A character in Jack London's *The Valley of the Moon* (1913) asks:

> Don't you sometimes feel you'd die if you didn't know what's beyond them hills an' what's beyond them other hills behind them hills? An' the Golden Gate! (p. 266)

The words reverberate in *Desire Under the Elms* and even more evidently in O'Neill's first full-length play, *Beyond the Horizon*, a work whose story of two rival brothers also has in it echoes of the plot and characters of T. C. Murray's *The Birthright* and of Neith Boyce's Provincetown play, *The Two*

Sons. O'Neill's characters are often conscious of their own provenance. The drunken Richard in Act 3 of *Ah, Wilderness!* glamorizes his condition with a direct quotation of Hedda Gabler's fantasy that "at ten o'clock – Eilert Lovborg will come – with vine leaves in his hair." Melville's *Typee* is invoked by Orin in Act 2 of "The Hunted" when he tells of his dreams of warm peaceful islands in *Mourning Becomes Electra*. The obdurate man who rides rough-shod over the needs and fears of others is a strong presence in American writing after *Moby Dick*, and particularly after the rediscovery of Melville's novel by the literary avant garde at the beginning of this century. One such is Captain Keeney in *Ile* who, in his Ahab-like pursuit of whale oil, has broken the spirit of the wife who has insisted on accompanying him. Abraham Bentley in *The Rope* is another and gains subtlety when he and his tendency to sententious biblical quotation are reworked in Ephraim Cabot, in *Desire Under the Elms*. Abraham and Ephraim are as hard and obsessive as Melville's Ahab, but the literary trope, again, is overlaid with the autobiographical when the next generation turn to mocking the autocratic father behind his back and to claiming that their mother was destroyed by his harshness. The Cabot sons even call their father "the Old Man," as, much later, will the Tyrone sons.

The encounter with high naturalism as developed by Ibsen and Strindberg was crucial for O'Neill's own dramatic method. Central to it is the role of environment expressed in the telling interaction of character and the stage space. In Raymond Williams' words:

> In high naturalism the lives of the characters have soaked into their environment. Its detailed presentation, production, is thus an additional dramatic dimension, often a common dimension within which they are to an important extent defined ... The relations between men and things are at a deep level interactive, because what is there physically, as a space or a means for living, is a whole shaped and shaping social history.[9]

In O'Neill's drama it is also a shaped and shaping emotional and psychological history. Rooms have presence, are indicative of the life lived in them. In the early plays O'Neill worked with broad brush strokes to make the set and stage space expressive. The inherent naturalism was overlaid and extended with new ideas in stagecraft and design derived from *Theatre Arts Monthly* and Gordon Craig's magazine, *The Mask*, or gleaned from the explorations of his immediate collaborators, Kenneth Macgowan and Robert Edmond Jones. But these elements in O'Neill are never just decorative; they always have a realist tendency. They are geared to revealing the pressures and tensions, to exposing the faces behind the masks we show to the world. The "two enormous elms" that enclose and overhang the Cabot house in *Desire Under the Elms* are representative of the lost mother. In *All God's Chillun Got Wings*, Ella's possessiveness and anger against Jim are measured in her verbal assaults on the magnificent Congolese mask which, like General Gabler's portrait in Ibsen's play, dominates the stage in Act 2. The very walls of Jim and Ella's living room close in on them, scene by scene.

The painting could be much finer in the later works. Whereas different rooms were opened to the audience's view in *Desire Under the Elms*, in the late plays the same room or, in the case of *A Moon for the Misbegotten*, the same stoop, is seen at different times of the day. Fog is a repeated image in O'Neill's writing from his very crude early play of that name onwards. In *Long Day's Journey* the audience learns through references in the dialogue and through the repeated sounding of the foghorn in the later part of the play that fog has descended on the surrounding world and presses close around the house, isolating its occupants the more thoroughly. As with the impression that the books on the Tyrones' shelves must give of being much read, details that add local colour and an impression of a lived environment also add substance to the assertions and accusations of the dialogue, and contribute to the accumulating sense of the shared past of the characters. The very lights in the Tyrone summer home in *Long Day's Journey* become markers of the texture of family defense and reproach. The opening instructions for the set include the note that, in the center of the room "*is a round table with a green-shaded reading lamp, the cord plugged in one of the four sockets in the chandelier above.*" The contraption is unregarded for the moment, except as a convincing register of the temporary nature of the house, since the first two acts take place during day-light, but it gains prominence in Act 3 as Mary, alone in the sitting room, allows the evening to darken around her. The shaft of light from the hall falling on Mary as her men-folk come in, exposes her drugged state to them, but, before long, she uses the lamp to turn defense to attack when she says:

> Why don't you light the light, James? It's getting dark. I know you hate to, but Edmund has proved to you that one bulb burning doesn't cost much. There's no sense letting your fear of the poorhouse make you too stingy.

That O'Neill directs that this be spoken "*in a matter-of-fact tone*" makes the sting all the sharper. James's reaction further attunes the audience to the sensitivities touched, preparing for the more developed part lighting will play in the final act when the reading lamp and the other three bulbs of the chandelier become bones of contention and display between Tyrone and Edmund and provide the catalyst for self analysis and, thence, the acknowledgement of a degree of mutual respect – a mutuality broken with the return of Jamie who, unconsciously echoing the melodramatic action of his father moments earlier, turns on all the bulbs in the chandelier as he rants mockingly against his father's parsimony. Not only do all the lights remain on for the rest of the play, bathing the front of the stage in light, but their brightness is augmented by the five bulbs of the chandelier in the inner parlor which flare on to announce Mary's final entrance.

And as the reference to the inner parlor suggests, behind these intimate living spaces are even more private spaces, closed rooms like Maw's parlor in *Desire Under the Elms* with a taboo of entrance on them; off-stage places to which alienated characters retreat. O'Neill's registration of off-stage spaces, and his use of off-stage sound, means that it is not just the retreat which is registered but the impact of the retreat on those from whom they have cut off and on the audience who hear with the ears of the on-stage characters. The attic in Ibsen's *Wild Duck*, Hedda Gabler's inner room, lie behind this. As the women in Ibsen's *John Gabriel Borkman* listen to Borkman's endless pacing in the upper room so the Tyrone men hear Mary pacing "above and around us" in the last act of O'Neill's play. The motif figured as early as *Ile* where, according to the stage directions, *"the silence is unbroken except for the measured tread of someone walking up and down the poop deck overhead."* The echo is characteristic. The experience, so evidently real, of hearing the mother pacing in her drug-induced state has shadowed, absorbed into itself comparable experience. It is not that O'Neill is imitating Ibsen, rather that literary and dramatic experience has been a crucial contributory element in giving form to memory.

Ibsen and Strindberg create the impression of a world outside the stage space through the dialogue and gesture of the characters who view and often try to resist it but on whom it impinges. Mrs. Alving in Ibsen's *Ghosts*, looking off-stage as if through her window, sees the uninsured orphanage burn. The neurosis and isolation of the Captain and Alice in Strindberg's *Dance of Death* is marked in their obsessive interest in the activities of the neighbors across the bay. O'Neill's characters are hardly happier in their encounter with the outside world. The Cabots, the Mannons, the Tyrones, live outside or on the edge of the town and have no intimacy with local families – although the men gravitate towards the conviviality of the bar or the club in their off-stage existence. Interaction with or, more often, alienation from the outside world by the characters generally, help establish belief in the isolation and mutual dependence of the family unit. In *Desire Under the Elms* the invasion of the stage space by the outside world binds the audience all the more sharply to the action of the central characters. In part III, the neighbors come to the Cabot house to celebrate the birth of Abbie's son. Their boisterous sniggerings of their suspicions about Ephraim's cuckoldry for a while possess the stage but pale into insignificance before the stamina of the old man, who dances the fiddle itself into silence, and the intensity of the passions of the young people, who come secretly together in the room above the malicious whispering. Inquisitive neighbors similarly perform a choric role as they gossip about the doings of the Mannon household in *Mourning Becomes Electra*. In *Long Day's Journey* other people remain off-stage, although the different responses of the characters, Jamie's dodging behind the hedge rather than be seen less than sharply dressed, Tyrone's confident and careless wave at those passing by, Mary's shrinking from observation, are registered by the audience as is the men's anxiety that others, even their own maid, should not know about the addiction.

Astonishingly, the most moving and most personal sequence of O'Neill's writing, Mary Tyrone's entrance at the end of *Long Day's Journey Into Night*, also seems to have had a forerunner in the last act of Sean O'Casey's Easter Rising play, *The Plough and the Stars*. Perhaps O'Neill knew O'Casey's 1926 play. O'Casey certainly made no secret of his great admiration of O'Neill and there are echoes of *Juno and the Paycock* in O'Neill's *A Touch of the Poet*. Or perhaps the echo by first one then the other writer of Ophelia's mad scene brought them to a similar position. The differences are as telling as the similarities in revealing the shaping and liberating role of other writing within O'Neill's own and the much more thoroughly wrought use O'Neill makes of the sequence. In O'Casey's play, Nora Clitheroe has reacted hysterically to the fighting. Following news of her husband Jack's death, O'Casey directs that:

> *Nora appears at the door, L. She is clad only in her nightdress; her hair uncared for for some days, is hanging in disorder over her shoulders ... her hands are nervously fiddling with her nightdress. She halts at the door for a moment, looks vacantly round the room, and then comes slowly in.*

When she speaks she is back in the past talking to Jack, as if he were present. She exits and other characters take over the stage. Later, while the other characters are dozing, she enters again in a similar state of undress, and wanders about the stage, singing to herself, again back in the past, pausing at one moment to say, "What is it? ... What is it? ... I must think ... I must thry to remember ..." Although affecting, the moment is not climactic as is Mary Tyrone's entrance, since Nora's is one of several responses to the chaos of civil strife.

Nora's appearance is striking, but every element of Mary Tyrone's entrance, which has been anticipated throughout the long fourth act, is registered by each of her now all-too-wakeful men-folk and the theatre audience alike. The lights flashed on, the strains of the Chopin Waltz played, the madonna-blue nightgown and the hair that so often in the course of the play has been nervously neatened and now is gathered into long girlish braids, the wedding dress she carries, have each accumulated meaning in the course of the play which now resonates. Nora will subsequently becomes the unintentional trigger for another violent death as the action of her play moves on; Mary's action, simply this of moving round the stage and speaking, lost in the past, brings her play to its close. The hint from outside has enabled representation of the rawness within.

The bleakness of the truths faced in *Long Day's Journey* – "If my love was with me she must have been a ghost" – gives way in O'Neill's final play, *A Moon for the Misbegotten*, to something kinder to both characters and audience. A different and consciously fictional – even ostensibly farcical – family, the Hogans, is centered. While Josie and Phil Hogan do spar and tease each other, the audience soon realizes the essential mutuality and good humor between them. Almost without precedent in O'Neill, their dead wife and mother, is remembered with whole-hearted affection by both, and remembered as robust, free of reproach, ready to give as good as she got in household argument. The story that presses and succeeds in being told, is Jamie O'Neill's and, in what is a much extended reworking of the parlor scene from *Desire Under the Elms*, both mother and brother are acknowledged and forgiven. Here, as throughout O'Neill's drama, the past is explored within the continuing present of the stage action. Selective, shifting memories and the self-deception and torment to which these give rise, play a part. As Jamie says in the long and gripping narrative, in which he tells his story of the guilty secret of his mother's death, the whore and the train with which he has tortured himself:

> It was as if I wanted revenge – because I'd been left alone – because I knew I was lost, without any hope left – that all I could do would be drink myself to death, because no-one was left who could help me. (Act 3)

But when he says, "It was long ago but it seems like tonight. There is no present or future – only the past happening over and over again – now," although he might seem to be repeating sentiments familiar from other plays, O'Neill does allow him to say this "tonight" and "now" and to be heard and, despite his devastating self-loathing, to find in Josie someone to help him. The altruism of Josie's final words as she not only forgives and speaks a benediction over him but lets him go – makes no demands on him for herself – is, unusually for O'Neill, allowed to stand. The final words of the play, "May you rest forever in forgiveness and peace," figure, too, as O'Neill's final words as a dramatist.

If O'Neill absorbed shaping devices from Ibsen, Tolstoi, Synge, so his dramatic tropes and motifs have been absorbed into subsequent American drama where secrets and concealments abound. The two kinds of setting that recur with remarkable frequency in recent American drama are O'Neill's: the family living room, setting for works by Miller and Williams, Albee and Shepard, and the public place where disparate people are thrown together, be it bar or cheap hotel as in William Saroyan's *The Time of Your Life*, Robert Patrick's *Kennedy's Children* or Jack Gelber's *The Fix* or, more minimally, a bench in Central Park, as in Edward Albee's *Zoo Story* or David Mamet's *Duck Variations*. His theme of bitterness and dependency, reproach and need within the most intimate relationships also recurs, in Edward Albee's *Who's Afraid of Virginia Woolf* and Tennessee Williams' *The Glass Menagerie*, as does disappointment between the generations in, for example, Robert Anderson's *I Never Sang for My Father* and August Wilson's *Fences* and, perhaps most notably and increasingly with passing time, in the work of Sam Shepard in whose writing the sense of the past and the recurrence of such words as "ghost," "moon," and "curse" are as common as in O'Neill's. As Tolstoi's *Power of Darkness* provides the shaping events of *Desire Under the Elms*, there is more than a little of *Desire Under the Elms* in Shepard's *Buried Child*. For Mary Tyrone's house on the Eastern seaboard, that can never be a home, one might read May's seedy motel room in the far West Mojave Desert in Shepard's *Fool For Love*; for the characterizing actors' or salesman's language, Eddie's cowboy lingo.

Importantly, the influence is felt in dramatic method as well as theme. It is evident in the writing of Albee who more than once has acknowledged the impact of O'Neill on him.[10] The interweaving of two or more monologues where the onus is on the audience to understand the connections, hear the echoes and feel the ironies has become a familiar device in the post-Second-War period. And the telling of stories continues – the secrets of Tyrone's lost career, Mary's addiction, Jamie's alcoholism and fraternal jealousy and pride, and Edmund's nihilism, revealed in the successive monologues of O'Neill's play, find a counterpart in sequences as diverse as "THE STORY OF JERRY AND THE DOG" in *Zoo Story* and the account of desperate past recognitions and incestuous love told in the monologues of Shepard's most O'Neillian play, *Fool for Love*.

As part of his attempt in the early 1920s to persuade his associates in the Experimental Theatre to include in their repertoire some of the dramatists whose work meant most to him, O'Neill said of Maxim Gorki's play, *Night's Lodging*, that it "simply shows humanity as it is – truth in terms of human life."[11] And I think that we, like O'Neill, must have recourse to such words as "truth," which offer intuitive response rather than strict definition, in order to express the sense we have of encountering the thing itself, of being disarmed before certain works. As that rigorous critic, T. S. Eliot, put it, "*Long Day's Journey Into Night* seems to me one of the most moving plays I have ever seen."[12]

The intense encounter with writing that in some important way figures the most private and personal experience enables readers and audiences, some of whom are themselves writers, to apprehend such experience. The enigma of autobiography – at least of O'Neill's kind of driven autobiography – is that the writing seems most moving, most truthful, when most subject to the shaping powers of art. These shaping powers, as I have suggested, derive in part from the encounter with other writing while the new work will, in its turn, inform the imaginative life and dramatic method of those who come after. Writing of Strindberg, foremost of his literary mentors, in 1924, O'Neill supplied a testament at least as appropriate to his own achievement. "Strindberg," he wrote,

> knew and suffered with our struggle years before many of us were born. He expressed it by intensifying the method of his time and by foreshadowing both in content and form the methods to come.[13]

NOTES

1 Barrett H. Clark, *Eugene O'Neill, The Man and His Plays* (revised edn., New York: Dover Publications, 1947), p. 7.

2 Clark, *Eugene O'Neill*, p. 8.

3 Louis Sheaffer, *O'Neill: Son and Playwright* (Boston: Little, Brown, 1968), p. 19.

4 For example, among some 560 letters in Travis Bogard and Jackson Bryer, eds., *Selected Letters of Eugene O'Neill* (New Haven: Yale University Press, 1988).

5 Michael Manheim, *O'Neill's New Language of Kinship* (Syracuse, NY: Syracuse University Press, 1982), p. 4. Manheim's book gives a full account of recurrent motifs in O'Neill's drama.

6 References to aspects of O'Neill's reading and observations about specific borrowings or influences are recurrent in the criticism from Sverre Arestad, "*The Wild Duck* and *The Iceman Cometh*," *Scandinavian Studies*, 20 (February 1948): 1–11 onwards. Good sources of information about O'Neill's literary biography are Travis Bogard, *Contour in Time* (Oxford University Press, 1977, rev. 1988); J. H. Raleigh, *The Plays of Eugene O'Neill* (Carbondale: So. Illinois Press, 1965) and the two-part biography by Louis Sheaffer, *O'Neill: Son and Playwright* (Boston, Little, Brown, 1968); and *O'Neill: Son and Artist* (Boston: Little, Brown, 1973).

7 Lists of the contents of O'Neill's library are to be found in the C. W. Post Center, New York, and in the O'Neill Collection in the Beinecke Library, New Haven. A tabulated account of O'Neill's reading is included as Appendix 1

of Jean Chothia, *Forging a Language* (Cambridge University Press, 1979), pp. 198–206.

8 Sheaffer, *O'Neill: Son and Playwright*, p. 122; Arthur and Barbara Gelb, *O'Neill* (New York: Harper and Row, 1973), p. 233.

9 Raymond Williams in Williams and M. Axton, eds., *English Dramatic Forms and Development* (Cambridge University Press, 1977), p. 217.

10 See, for example, "An Interview with Edward Albee" in A. S. Downer, ed., *American Theatre Today* (New York: Basic Books, 1967) and "Edward Albee" in Jackson R. Bryer, ed., *The Playwrights' Art* (New Brunswick, New Jersey: Rutgers University Press, 1995), p. 10.

11 Interview, *New York Herald Tribune* (16 March 1924), quoted in Oscar Cargill *et al.*, *O'Neill and his Plays* (New York: New York University Press, 1961), p. 110.

12 Quoted, Cargill, p. 168.

13 Playbill for *The Spook Sonata*, Experimental Theatre, New York (3 January 1924).

14

MICHAEL MANHEIM

The stature of *Long Day's Journey Into Night*

What Richard Sewall[1] suggests is the most salient characteristic of true tragedy is not its plots, themes, or subjects so much as the range of human feeling it incorporates in a single work, notably the "capacity for suffering" and the "stamina" of its central figures. To this I would add that it is not suffering and stamina alone, important as these qualities are in tragedy, which contribute to the greatness of a work but also the range of often contradictory feelings underlying the characters' statements and actions. In Sophocles' *Antigone*, it is not Antigone's monumental courage and fortitude in insisting on her brother's burial that contributes to our sense of who she is so much as it is that courage and fortitude set next to her equally monumental rigidity. Her heroism does not rule out this rigidity nor does the rigidity discredit the heroism. It is in taking those qualities together that we come to see her as tragic.

Long Day's Journey Into Night requires this kind of full assessment. Those who see the play as overwhelmingly painful, depicting only what one critic calls the "nightmare realities" of family life, tend not to recognize the force of the contradictions within the dialogue. The pain is abundant, of course, but so are the gestures, responses, sometimes even nothing more than pauses in the seemingly endless patterns of recrimination that alleviate the pain.

Such contradictory feelings within the dialogue are first apparent in the opening act during a heated exchange between James Tyrone and his elder son, Jamie – as the two prepare to go out and trim the hedge. Disagreement and recrimination are abundant here – on subjects ranging from Edmund's illness, Mary's possibly revived addiction, James's stinginess, Jamie's apparent failure in life – but each character repeatedly counters the recrimination by appeals for sympathy and reassurances like Jamie's "*almost*" gentle "I've felt the same way, Papa." And if such reassurances are followed by renewed attacks and counter-attacks, nevertheless, the pauses, appeals for sympathy, and assertions of common feeling are periodically so

206

pronounced as to serve as markers of the undercurrent of mutual trust that exists beneath the turbulence of their relationship. Such early encounters establish the constant counterpoint of feelings that will be heard throughout the play.

What one looks for first in any naturalistic play is, of course, the story, the plot – especially in the case of O'Neill, the melodrama, since O'Neill was, from start to finish, subject to the accusation of being a "melodramatist." And melodrama there is aplenty in this play. It is the story of the day in the family's life when the genuine if shaky stability it has somehow always maintained breaks apart from causes that are essentially unavoidable. The melodramatic interest inherent in the plot – what is sometimes called the "suspense" – is rooted in two closely related questions: (1) Has Mary Tyrone reverted to her drug-addiction of long standing, implying that she will be lost to her family, perhaps permanently? And (2) Has Edmund Tyrone contracted the much-feared "consumption," implying that he will be lost to his family, perhaps permanently? These are the basic questions that move the plot from beginning to end, increasingly intensifying the aura of fear, a time-honored attribute of melodrama, surrounding these people.

Concomitantly, James and Mary confront their problems in melodramatic language that leans heavily on James's roles in traditional stage melodrama and on Mary's Victorian upbringing. Mary's lines especially, increasingly influenced by her drug, make the play seem like the kind of old-time melodrama which focuses on such issues as "madness" and the unnatural.

But the play is not melodrama. That Mary has reverted to her addiction and that Edmund will have to go to a sanatorium are really the givens of the play – not what anyone the least familiar with O'Neill's life will first learn from its plot. And the melodramatic poses of James, Sr. which so irritate his sons, are more the stuff of the play's comedy than of any genuine sound and fury. Even Mary's drug-induced arias evoke not so much fear finally as deep compassion. The structure of the last act as it deals with the drugged Mary's threatened appearance illustrates that we are beyond melodrama. Her repeated pacings upstairs and Edmund's glimpses of her about to descend but changing her mind evoke an aura of terror – the madwoman-in-the-attic – that sharply contrasts with her actual appearance at the end, where, totally divorced from reality as she is, she not only arouses pity rather than fear but also seems, for some, to emblemize some of the play's deepest meanings. (See, for example, Normand Berlin's and Jean Chothia's assessments of the play in this collection.)

The melodrama and the melodramatic effects, then, serve as the background of the play – part of the set in a sense – but the foreground consists of the life of these figures as we see them relating to one another under the play's testing circumstances. The foreground evokes not the fear associated with the background melodrama but the compassion and understanding associated with tragedy.

For me, the long final act is the all-important one because it shows the men of the family reaching one another as deeply as people ever do, and that final act will receive the lion's share of this discussion. But the final act (until its very end) leaves out the play's one major woman character, even though her presence upstairs generates the intensity of feeling the men experience. Therefore, since Mary is both the figure the playwright felt most strongly about in writing the play and the one he seems least able to fully to come to grips with, she must receive her due before any comprehensive understanding of the work can be achieved.

Most men have difficulty understanding their mothers. In O'Neill's case that difficulty was exacerbated by his own mother's addiction, the cause he believed of his life-long pain. The character representing her must be looked at carefully in any analysis of this play. But the scene in which Mary's role is most affecting – her monologue constituting the largest part of the third act – is one in which she is under the control of her narcotic. And memorable as this episode is, it may contribute more to our understanding of the effects of morphine than to our understanding of the woman. On the other hand, her appearances earlier in the play show her in her "normal" state, a state in which she plays the role of wife and mother, trying to hide the signs of her habit from the men. The episode I would like to look at in some detail is one in which Mary reveals most about herself in her relatively unnarcotized condition, one in which she struggles to deal openly with herself and with Edmund. It is an exchange late in Act 2, just before her men leave her to go downtown; and while Edmund intends this exchange to be a final appeal to his mother to control her addiction, it develops into something quite different.

Mary, picking up from an earlier discussion of Edmund's deteriorating health, begins by being solicitous of him, saying he should not go up town in "the dirty old trolley" on such a hot day. But the motivation for her concern is of a complex nature that sets the tone for the rest of the exchange. A series of intertwined fears constitutes the mood out of which she speaks and in one way or another color everything she says. They include her natural motherly fear concerning Edmund's health, her fear that he probably has the dreaded consumption, her fear that she is constantly being watched, and her fear of being left alone with her drug. In the midst of these fears is also a clarity, however, about who she is and what she is doing – a clarity that breaks out suddenly, like sunlight that momentarily breaks through the fog but quickly disappears.

Response sets off counter-response. We hear her go into a tirade against Doc Hardy, whom Edmund must visit to be told the truth that he has the illness that killed her father – Hardy, who, she says, can only look "solemn and preach will power" in response to her condition. The mention of Hardy then sets off other responses: that her husband likes Hardy for only charging a dollar, and a few lines later that the upset caused by Edmund's illness is the chief cause of her renewed addiction. But then the intensity of her reactions is suddenly broken as she realizes, with a clarity of thought quite missing up until now that Edmund may feel she is using his illness as an excuse – which Edmund, of course, does feel. Next Edmund's appeals to his mother to give up her drug ("You're only just started – You can still stop") are met with the familiar contradictory denials: from "Please ... don't talk about things you don't understand!" – which at least acknowledges that the problem exists – to "Anyway, I don't know what you're referring to." Mary's denials always represent the nadir of her fear.

Out of this plethora of startling shifts in response come, however, the honesty and clarity of her most memorable statement of the scene. Acknowledging that it is natural for Edmund to suspect she is blaming him, she becomes totally and pitifully open:

> How could you believe me – when I can't believe myself? I've become such a liar. I never lied about anything once upon a time. Now I have to lie, especially to myself. But how can you understand, when I don't myself. I've never understood anything about it, except that one day long ago I found I could no longer call my soul my own.
>
> (*Complete Plays* III, 769–70)

This moment of truth leads to a new theme: that one day, "when the Blessed Virgin Mary forgives me and gives me back the faith in Her love and pity I used to have in my convent days," she will be "sure" of herself, even when she hears herself "scream with agony." The whole idea of Mary's religious faith is moot – often quite contradictory – like much else in the play. On the one hand, O'Neill seems to present it as a genuine means for Mary's recovery (as it may have been for O'Neill's mother in real life). But on the other, especially as she lowers *her voice to a strange tone of whispered confidence*," it sounds like a new version of her drug. This is especially apparent in her reference to her feeling that she will be sure of herself even while she hears herself *scream in agony*. The ambiguity here seems twofold: first in reflecting O'Neill's own ambivalence toward the religion of his youth, and second in reflecting the puzzle he finds at Mary's center. Her statement about her religious faith appears to flow naturally from her most open and honest attempt to understand her addiction. But it reflects a dependence on a religious figure that suggests the workings of the drug itself. So her clearest moment reflects another crucial contradiction.

But she immediately reverts again to cynical denial. Suddenly thinking that Edmund will not believe her confession since he always suspects her of lying, she reverts to the most denying (and rejecting) of all her attitudes: "Now I think of it, you might as well go uptown. I forgot I'm taking a drive. I have to go to the drugstore."

I deal with this passage not primarily to illustrate Mary's cynical denials but to illustrate the manifold nature of Mary's consciousness. A feeling of motherly solicitude leads to one of intense anger, which leads to one of intense anxiety, which leads to one of hysterical accusation, which leads to one of guilt, which leads to one of open acknowledgment, which leads to one of hope rooted in a lost religious faith, which leads to one of cynical rejection. All these are Mary Tyrone – no one more important than the rest. Mary ends this dialogue with her very cynical statement about going to the drugstore. And he concludes the scene on a similarly contradictory note. Alone for the first time, she says that she feels both glad the men are gone and terribly isolated by their departure – altogether contradictory sets of feelings simultaneously experienced.

The Mary we see and hear during her extended monologue opening Act 3 possesses the same characteristics we saw in the short scene just dealt with, but always, and increasingly, under the influence of her drug. She swings from fuzzy remembrances of life at the convent and of her first meeting with the matinee idol who was to be her husband to the harsh self-assessment that seemingly more rational thoughts provide, but both extremes are in large part responses to the narcotic stimulus – working, it is true, upon actual memories and feelings, but coloring them, distorting them, making them seem at times more like ravings than her feelings in the scene with Edmund just described.

With the return of James and Edmund the same distortions continue to characterize the counterpoint of Mary's responses. Her exchange with Edmund while James goes to the cellar to fetch a new bottle of whiskey might be considered a continuation of the exchange discussed earlier. She displays the same hysteria at the prospect of Edmund's illness (now medically confirmed), the same condemnation of Doc Hardy, the same instants of motherly affection – except that it is now clear that what Mary says at both extremes is greatly affected by the drug. Edmund is finally goaded into his famous "It's pretty hard at times, having a dope fiend for a mother!" – a still point in the breakdown of their relationship. It is this attack that sends Edmund off into his most guilt-ridden flight – into the night, with the same, we must suppose, suicidal thoughts that provoked him to the earlier actual suicide attempt he alludes to in his subsequent conversation with James. It is not so much the contradictions, but the dope that Edmund cannot deal with – as it is the dope that none of the men can deal with.

So, in pursuing the family relationships from this point on in the play, the now thoroughly drug-imprisoned Mary must be left out – until the very end. It is the relationship among the men that is the subject of the play's long final act. There is here no segment involving James and Jamie, perhaps because there was one in the first act that potently demonstrated both the savagery of their hostility and the depth of their closeness. There is nothing more the play can tell us about their relationship. So the focus of Act 4 will be first on James and Edmund, then on Edmund and Jamie, the retrograde brother who arrives on the scene fresh from Mamie Burns's brothel much later in the evening.

The oft-suggested idea that tragedy puts before us experience we are familiar with from our own lives, only in more highly charged terms and with more perilous implications, is nowhere better illustrated than in the relationships between James and Edmund, then Edmund and Jamie, that run the gamut of contradictory emotions the playwright creates in this final act. Both relationships rock between genuine hostility and equally genuine fellow-feeling, both extremes intensified by the alcohol they consume, which leads them to speak more openly and emotionally than they might otherwise do.

James and Edmund are very much father and adult-but-*younger* son in a late-night confrontation – the father ever over-confident regarding his wisdom and experience, the son ever insistent upon his individuality and independence. They are intensifications of their progenitors Nat and Richard Miller of *Ah, Wilderness!*, who are nothing if not typical middle-class father and son; but the subject of the Tyrones' discourse is a serious illness and an afflicted mother rather than a late-night fling in a seedy tavern. Those are large exceptions. The difference enlarges *Long Day's Journey* to tragic proportions. The special conditions of their relationship from the start take them beyond that earlier play: James's having once been a promising Shakespearean actor of shanty-Irish background and Edmund's having a disease which at the time of the play was still looked upon the way many look upon AIDS in this day. And, of course, the special circumstance that both are extremely worried about a wife-mother who is a drug addict. All this is heard, of course, in the context of the contra-dictions between them and within each.

At the opening of the scene, a dejected Edmund runs head-on into his father's penny-pinching. Full of clichés all-too-familiar to the family about "making the electric company rich" and the time-honored "learning the value of a dollar," James orders Edmund to turn off the meagre hall light (this is 1912, remember), which Edmund has switched on after bumping his knee in the dark. Much of this interchange is still the stuff of situation comedy – as is Edmund's refusal to obey and the rage with which James responds to the challenge. But the immediate counterpoint comes with James's realization, as he feels moved to strike his son, of Edmund's condition – which prompts an exaggerated outflow of guilt and profuse affection. The pattern is set for what follows.

As he does periodically along the way, James proposes they have a drink while at the same time chastising Edmund for drinking in his condition. In response, Edmund launches into the first of several recitations of then-contemporary poetry – this one from Ernest Dowson's "Cynara" poem, which includes the famous "They are not long, the days of wine and roses." This he shortly follows with Baudelaire's poetic advice to "Be ever drunken ... with wine, with poetry, or with virtue – but be ever drunken." Edmund's immediate purpose in these quotations is to justify his drinking and to challenge his father, but their larger effect is to resonate the deeper ideas of the scene and of the play. Their conflict here is clearly of a different order than those involving Edmund's illness and Mary's addiction. Father and son here are drawn close by their mutual response to the impact of the verse – even if James does compare it unfavorably with Shakespeare and call Edmund's poets "whoremongers and degenerates" – for what the poems all imply is that the vicissitudes of life must be indeed unbearable but for the possibility of being "ever drunken." Edmund is advocating the pursuit of what a later writer was to call the "lightness of being," attitudes which make the experience of living itself inebriating. Although he assaults Edmund's poets, James implicitly shares this outlook in his favorite toast, "Drink hearty," and in his stated admiration for Edmund's poetic efforts.

But the contrapuntal pattern of the scene continues. The discussion of poets and poetry leads to the mention of Dante Gabriel Rossetti, whom James condemns as a "dope fiend" – which directly leads both to thoughts of Mary. Father and son turn on one another with the sound of Mary pacing upstairs. The talk turns again into attack and defense, prompted by Edmund's reference to James's supposed penury concerning doctors. In the midst of this, at James's suggestion, they begin a card game, which has the effect, like the sharings of the bottle, of again breaking the tension – before hostilities are again renewed.

In one of their moments of relative harmony, James, to explain why he is a "miser," commences his extended aria of the scene – the tale of his father's suicide, his long-suffering mother, and his impoverished youth. This leads into the story of his career as a promising young Shakespearean actor working with the great Edwin Booth, and why he took the infamous role which made his fortune but ruined his chances of ever fully realizing his talents. Edmund, as he remarks elsewhere, has heard the story "ten thousand times," but hearing it under the circumstances, and as it is related by the great performer at the height of his powers, it reaches him, perhaps for the first time. For the first time he empathizes with his father, not only with his pain – because shared pain is so much a part of this scene – but also with his father's earlier hopes and enthusiasms.

Edmund then tells his story of his life at sea, which is not involved so much with the pain of his immediate past as with the glimmers of intermittent hope and faith – ever punctuated by renewals of bitterness, of course – the sea has given him. This is significant because, in spite of the pain and regret of his father's narrative, what Edmund tries to equal in talking about his own life is the poetry implicit in the older man's speech. The exchange brings them together as never before as they hear the mood-shattering sounds of the elder brother's return.

This encounter between James and Edmund is best experienced in the theatre (or on screen), of course, where when well performed it seems far less prolonged than it may read off the printed page. What it conveys, beyond anything else, is a sense of closeness and interdependence made more rather than less convincing by the periodic near-violence of their conflicts. The two function as father and son on a deeper level here than in most other such encounters in drama.

If the relationship between James and Edmund is a combination of the universal and the particular, that between Jamie and Edmund is still more so – the universal eminently recognizable in their brotherly camaraderie and competitiveness, and the particular again deriving from the special nature of their mutual pain. Both share the time-honored cynicism of educated youth – even if Jamie's youth is wearing rather thin – and both share the familiar feelings of an older–younger brother relationship, Jamie having long been Edmund's model to emulate – both in his wit and his debauchery. But the particular nature of their brotherly relationship has chiefly to do with Mary. Each knows better than anyone else how the other one feels about her – a mutuality of feeling that closely links them – but each is deeply and irrationally jealous. Jamie, as he says explicitly, cannot help resenting the fact that it was Edmund's being born that started Mary on her morphine. Edmund cannot help resenting Jamie's harboring such feelings and that Jamie's having learned of Mary's addiction so much earlier – "caught her in the act with the hypo" – has set a model of despair that the younger brother cannot escape. Yet, as Jamie also observes, the special nature of their suffering has brought them closer together than most siblings. Much about their mutual affection and resentment is familiar, but have a "dope fiend for a mother" gives their relationship its tragic dimension.

At the heart of this episode lie Jamie's radical swings in behavior and mood, intensified but not really much exaggerated by his drink. He is the "holy sinner" of this play, the epitome of its view of the human condition as innately contradictory. On the negative side, Jamie is its most corrupt figure. Not only is his alcoholism pernicious, but along with it come the other aspects of his corruption: the sardonic tongue, the malicious sexual behavior, the indolence, the gambling and general financial profligacy, and his dependence on the support of his father. So sardonic does he become in this scene that he refers to Mary as a "hop-head," a word which understandably prompts Edmund to strike him in their confrontation's most violent moment.

But on the all-important other hand, Jamie Tyrone is the one truly humane figure in this play – and while this idea might seem incomprehensible to some, it contributes much to the kind of stature the play possesses. This stature has to do with the deepest kind of emotional suffering accompanied by the recognition and understanding of that suffering by the sufferer. When Jamie says early in the play that he knows how his father feels about Mary's condition, he speaks out of an empathy which is his unique gift. Along with the large capacity of his own suffering, he can feel the suffering of others – even Mary's, whose drug dependency he is the only one of the three men can see is parallel to his own alcohol dependency. And her reversion, after a brief period of false hope, has hurt him the most: "It meant so much. I'd begun to hope, if she'd beaten the game, I could, too."

The segment of the episode that tells us most about who Jamie is (how O'Neill sees him) is his rendition of this visit to the bordello, where he chose as his sexual companion "Fat Violet," the whore who is about to be let go because none of the customers want her. Though speaking sarcastically (which is his wont), Jamie's description of his time with her as a "Christian act" is in fact just that. He felt *sorry* for Vi, he says – sorry for *her* when his purpose in going to the brothel was to make him forget his sorrow for himself. The fact of having had sex with her especially fits this definition. He had, he says, "no dishonorable intentions" when he escorted her upstairs. He just wanted, he says, to recite some of the modern poets to her (for example, Dowson's "I have been faithful to thee, Cynara, in my fashion") – which characteristically seems intended both to mock her and to comfort her – but she grew angry and cried. "So I had to say I loved her because she was fat," he says, "and she wanted to believe that, and I stayed with her to prove it, and that cheered her up …" If the "Christianity" of this act may elude some, it may nevertheless be seen as the one act of completely selfless giving in the play.

Yet with all this, the swings to the negative in Jamie's attitudes become ever more savage – the liquor talking, he says, but we know by this time it is always the essential character talking. He persistently returns to his attacks on Edmund – "Mama's baby, Papa's pet, the family white hope" – even to the most savage of all – "it was your being born that started Moma on dope." But he always swings back to the equally heartfelt praise of his brother and pleas for his understanding: 'You're the only pal I've ever had. I love your guts. I'd do anything for you!"

These swings culminate, of course, in his concluding confession, in which he cuts his lifeline with his only friend by warning Edmund of his potentially destructive nature. He will, he says, be waiting to greet Edmund with a genuinely glad hand upon his return from the sanatorium, but he will also be waiting to stab him in the back. This is by no means a confession of hypocrisy but rather an understanding, not shared by the other men about themselves or him, that there are always two parts of an individual speaking, a dead part and a live part: "The dead part of me hopes you won't get well." But while the dead part is to be feared, the live part is equally potent as is revealed in his repeated outbursts of uncondi- tional affection for his brother culminating in his final appeal: "Remember I warned you – for our sake. Give me credit. Greater love hath no man than this, that he saveth his brother from himself." Having Jamie recite this last variant of scripture sarcastically, as some productions do, misses the point. His devotion to Edmund is real, as even James, Sr. observes a few lines later, and it is in his case a devotion the live part of him has for all the people of the play – including Mary. But it is ever juxtaposed with the savagery of the dead part. It is thus that Jamie is O'Neill's spokesman in the play, his exaggeratedly contradictory states focusing tragedy's inescapable light on the human condition.

If the play's tragic force is brought home by the violently alternating emotions of the pairs of men in the last act, its concluding elegiac quality is the mood of Mary's final appearance. Mary is now totally back in her world of the convent. She fumblingly plays the piano in the next room as the men awake from their drunken sleep, more than a little frightened at what they may see when she appears. But what they see is a dazed woman carrying an elegant wedding dress, lost in her romantic past. Still under the spell of her drug, she laments on the one hand her loss of the convent and on the other her marriage – in which she "was so happy for a time."

Unlike her earlier drugged states, this is one of resignation. More deeply under the spell of her drug than she has ever been, she here embodies the play's central, and for O'Neill life's ultimate and most critical, contradictions. Tragedy is by its nature both devastating and uplifting – and so is the appearance of the life-giving/life-destroying mother – the source of their love and their hate – both devastating and uplifting.

The terrible beauty of this scene is captured in the spirit of Jamie's final poetic quote – from Swinburne's "A Leave-taking" – which bespeaks both the pain and the acceptance of their mother's tragedy:

> Let us rise up and part; she will not know.
> Let us go seaward as the great winds go,
> Full of blown sand and foam; what help is here?
> There is no help, for these things are so,
> And all the world is bitter as a tear. (173)

No one can say what a truly great tragedy is. Even the Greeks and Shakespeare are being questioned by the critical pace-setters of the late twentieth century. But for most, Aristotle's measures still hold. It must achieve genuine and widely acknowledged emotional catharsis and it must convincingly portray an image of fallen greatness. *Long Day's Journey Into Night* has certainly succeeded on the first count and for most on the second as well. The rhythmical play of its emotional extremes have affected audiences as have few other dramas of the twentieth century, and the images of fallen greatness in the deterioration of so finely wrought a family has evoked the kind of empathy that has convinced many that the play deserves to be placed beside the Oedipus plays and *King Lear.* It has undeniably been a model for family plays of the later twentieth century and perhaps will be for centuries to follow. The future may test such assumptions, but for the present this play may be held up as the epitome of tragedy in our time.

NOTE

1 Richard Sewall was the person who immediately came to mind when a separate article on *Long Day's Journey* was scheduled for this volume. His essay on the play in *The Vision of Tragedy* (enlarged edition) – Yale University Press, 1980: 161–99 – seems to me to have come closest to articulating in direct, concrete language the nature of the play's greatness. As editor of this collection, I originally asked Professor Sewall, who is at this writing approaching his 88th birthday, to write the piece; but after considering the possibility for some weeks, he declined, feeling he had nothing to add to what he had already published. It is, then, in recognition of what Sewall has done that I have taken the lead from his work in developing further my own thinking about the play.

Most O'Neill critics have dealt with this play. Among those who should certainly be read is Normand Berlin, who discusses it extensively in almost all his publications on O'Neill.

15

MATTHEW H. WIKANDER

O'Neill and the cult of sincerity

"An incredible heroine, a facile application of Freudian thought, a narrative that at times foreshadows today's soap operas, language that rarely rises above the commonplace": here Louis Sheaffer, O'Neill's admiring biographer, describes *Strange Interlude*. "Yet, paradoxically," he concludes, "its defects testify to the author's achievement."[1] Sheaffer's strategy here is commonly applied to O'Neill's work as a whole by critics determined to enlist O'Neill in the pantheon of dramatists of the first rank. First comes an enumeration of O'Neill's artistic flaws – the disparity between his "often egregious intentions"[2] and his achievements; his clumsiness with language; his reliance upon pop-psychology and resynthesized versions of ancient myth – and his personal failings. Then follows the summation: by dint of hard work, a flawless instinct for theatre, wide and deep reading in modern philosophy and literature, courageous exploration of the psyche, O'Neill conquers these flaws. However confused and banal, hysterical and overblown, inadvertently ridiculous and condescending his output may be in its parts, its whole traces a triumphant coming of age and a fruition of talent in the late masterpieces, especially *The Iceman Cometh* and *Long Day's Journey Into Night*. This paradigm, in keeping with O'Neill's own insistence that he be seen large, makes of O'Neill, looking inward, tormented by but ultimately forgiving if not overcoming the ineluctable dynamics of family dysfunction, a model artist for modern times.

In O'Neill's own terms, it offers a kind of transcendence without God. O'Neill's is a story of "a triumph of the will," of "sheer force of character" a recent anthologist proclaims.[3] O'Neill "sees life straight and strong," Kenneth Macgowan wrote after the premiere of *Beyond the Horizon* early in O'Neill's career, "always getting down to the big emotional root of things ... His is a genius that seems incorruptible."[4] O'Neill learns to forgive his intolerable family and enshrine the triad of father, mother, and brother in art: not only in the play which features them undisguised, *Long Day's Journey*, but, as many critics have pointed out, in many plays in various guises leading up to that work. Great suffering does lead to great understanding and great art.

The triumph is also national. "Before O'Neill," *Time* magazine declared in 1953, "the US had theater; after O'Neill, it had drama."[5] O'Neill's struggle to know himself and to know his own family reflects his country's efforts, in the early twentieth century, to know itself and come into its own as a world power. "I'm going on the theory that the United States, instead of being the most successful country in the world, is the greatest failure," he told a press conference on the occasion of the Broadway production of *The Iceman Cometh* in 1946, and he continued, in language that identifies America with his own art: "Its main idea is that everlasting game of trying to possess your own soul by the possession of something outside it, thereby losing your own soul and the thing outside it too." O'Neill's Cycle of plays based upon American history, "A Tale of Possessors Self-Dispossessed," was to trace a single family from the American revolution to the twentieth century; the surviving plays of the Cycle show this family to be recognizably configured like O'Neill's. Greatness and failure are intertwined in O'Neill's sense of America and in O'Neill's sense of his family.

Most studies of O'Neill strike an uneasy balance, suggesting that O'Neill's flaws, like America's, are not only inseparable from his greatness, but in some way complementary to it and confirmatory of it. For Robert Littell, discussing *Strange Interlude*, O'Neill's strengths are inseparable from his faults, and "several of his faults, while they remain faults, serve also as allies of his strength." Littell praises O'Neill for a "groping, smoldering, passionate sincerity many times more intense, relentless and mysterious than that of any other American playwright – and nearly all foreign ones also" (*SA*, pp. 245–46).

Littell's "perceptive analysis" (as Sheaffer calls it) of O'Neill represents an extreme case of what Henri Peyre has called the "cult of sincerity" in literature, a trend which begins with Rousseau in the eighteenth century and continues through the modern period. Like Rousseau, O'Neill demands and receives high praise for sincerity; "faults" of a technical nature serve to confirm the artist's absolute honesty. Peyre, on the contrary, argues that "by itself, sincerity in a writer never sufficed to give merit to a work of art." Peyre deplores the development in twentieth-century literature of a "cult of sincerity": the high value placed upon honesty by critics, he insists, has "led to a large number of works containing no subject matter, referring to nothing (and sincerity should refer to something behind and beyond itself), involving little constraint over a rebellious material or little restraint, banishing even style from many works of literature."[6]

Assessments of O'Neill's achievement tend to glorify sincerity over style.

O'Neill's sincerity, too, has been pitted against an idea of theatre. O'Neill emerged on the scene as a figure waging war against a host of related opponents variously demonized as "theatre," "entertainment," "Broadway." Sheaffer's account of the reception of *Beyond the Horizon* casts O'Neill in the heroic mold: "Here was an author determined to speak his mind and guts without regard for the shibboleths of Broadway," he declares. "James O'Neill's son had already signaled his intent in his one-act plays. In *Beyond the Horizon* he committed the deed: he introduced the American theatre to life, the sad realities of everyday life, and began changing that theatre into one more genuine, more vital, more sensitive to the human condition." The play's unaccustomed length and its other "distinct shortcomings and flaws" are excused in light of its evocation of the "genuine," the "vital," the "sensitive" (*SP*, pp. 418–19).

As Sheaffer makes clear, the movement from a false, Broadway esthetic to a sincere, true one is generational: "James O'Neill's son" is the hero of his narrative. James O'Neill's own oft-quoted response to *Beyond the Horizon* – "'Are you trying to send the audience home to commit suicide?' he asked huskily," according to the Gelbs[7] – is that of a seasoned theatre professional. But literary critics, unlike James O'Neill, have found it hard to resist O'Neill's privileging of sincerity over theatricality, of truth to the human condition over Broadway. O'Neill's attacks upon actors and upon theatre in his plays and interviews beguile his chroniclers, whose praise of O'Neill's literary genius may reflect hostility not just to the theatre of the past, but to the whole idea of theatre itself.

O'Neill's antitheatricalism: melodrama, bad acting, and bad writing

Eugene O'Neill learned from James O'Neill's theatre an intense discomfort with commercial theatre and mistrust of actors, especially star actors, and this mistrust contributes to the playwright's reputation for bad writing. Flora Merrill asked O'Neill about the difference between his and his father's kinds of theatre. "I suppose ... if one accepts the song and dance complete of the psychoanalysts, it is perfectly natural that having been brought up around the old conventional theatre, and having identified it with my father, I should rebel and go in a new direction" (*SA*, p. 181). Despite going out of his way to express his contempt for "romantic stage stuff" and his distaste for "ranting" (*SP*, p. 205), O'Neill often found himself indicted, by friends and critics alike, for drama that seemed frequently to move less in "a new direction" than to run the risk of becoming itself melodramatic, overblown, and artificial.

In 1934, Virgil Geddes inveighed against what he called *The Melodra-*

madness of Eugene O'Neill, and linked it with antitheatricalism. "In the world of theatre, where acting, production, and all the arts of interpretation give body and life to the author's world and complete the theatre as art," Geddes maintains, "O'Neill is not at home." Geddes singles out O'Neill's stage directions for particular comment. "His plays are written with strong dictations to the actor and stage directions which invite antagonism more than they spur the imagination," he continues: "In his plays, he sometimes writes as though nothing but bad acting was possible on the stage and he fills in the actor's part with clumsy explanation. At other times he writes for the reader, as though acting had nothing to do with his plays and had never existed as an art."[8] O'Neill expresses his contempt for Broadway as mistrust of acting.

O'Neill, Geddes continues, describes rather than dramatizes, "constantly relying on the methods of the novelist. His plays are full of writing which never shows on the stage, and even if one eliminates the material which is written between brackets, the dialogue is often undramatically descriptive."[9] The extensive stage directions in O'Neill's published plays speak of frustration with the medium in which he has chosen to work. When *Welded* failed to win the praise he had hoped for, O'Neill blamed the actors: "What was actually spoken should have served to a great extent just to punctuate the meaningful pauses. The actors didn't get that" (*SA*, p. 132). O'Neill complained to Kenneth Macgowan about the "difference there must always be between the author's idea as he sees what he writes and the horrible puppet shows the actors transform it into, willy-nilly, good or bad." The Gelbs, reporting this remark, appear to share O'Neill's inability to imagine any but bad acting: "It never failed to infuriate him that despite his knowledge of actor craft and the pains he always took to forestall an actor's personal interpretation of a role by spelling out every important gesture, look, and vocal nuance, he could still not get the effect he wanted" (p. 591).

What the Gelbs interpret as O'Neill's desire to "forestall an actor's personal interpretation" can lead not just to the novelistic stage directions for which O'Neill is well known; it can also lead to plodding expository dialogue. What actors are trained to think of as subtext frequently finds its way to the surface in O'Neill. The notorious inclusion of spoken "thoughts" in *Strange Interlude* represents O'Neill's insistence that the playwright control subtext. Lynn Fontanne, who played the role of Nina, found herself much confounded by the need to speak her "thoughts" in aside:

> There were a good many lines intended by O'Neill to be taken seriously, that
> I thought would get belly laughs from the audience ... It would have hurt the

play. For instance, I would have to say in an aside something like, "Ned has the bluest eyes I ever saw; I must tell him so." Then I would go to Ned and tell him he had the bluest eyes I ever saw. I felt it was unnecessary to say this twice. I told O'Neill I thought it would be better if I looked at Ned's eyes with admiration the first time, silently, instead of saying the line as an aside. I asked him if I could cut the line. He said, "No, you can't. Play it as I wrote it." But the play was so long that I felt O'Neill wouldn't realize if I cut a line here and there, so, with fear and trembling, I cut a few of those horselaugh lines. O'Neill never knew about this sly business of mine.

After recounting this anecdote, the Gelbs offer a response of sorts from O'Neill: "During rehearsals O'Neill told Langner, 'If the actors weren't so dumb, they wouldn't need asides; they'd be able to express the meaning without them'" (pp. 649–50).

Identifying acting with his father's theatre, and identifying his father's theatre with star actors out of control, strutting and fretting at the expense of literary texts, O'Neill forestalls interpretation, demands fidelity to the lines as written, and elaborates intention in explicit dialogue and stage directions. O'Neill told Barrett Clark: "The play, as written, is the thing, and not the way actors garble it with their almost-always-alien personalities (even when the acting is fine work in itself)" (SA, p. 469). The apparent grudging compliment to "fine work" again insists that what the actor does is alien to and often hostile to the play. O'Neill's frustration with actors may stem from a wholly understandable frustration with the star system and a commercial theatre that undervalued the written word. But O'Neill's aversion to performance and refusal to acknowledge the collaborative nature of theatre affects the "play, as written," as well.

"I don't go to the theatre because I can always do a better production in my mind than the one on the stage," O'Neill once declared (Gelb, O'Neill, p. 559). Yet the production in the mind can be tyrannical: not only do actors find themselves unable to convey in "meaningful pauses" a play's big themes, but readers, too, can find the stage directions a nuisance. George Jean Nathan, ordinarily one of O'Neill's greatest champions, expressed this frustration when he published, as a kind of free-verse poem, the stage directions from Dynamo in the March 1929 American Mercury:

> Arguing tormentedly within himself
> With angry self-contempt
> Furiously clenching his fist
> His eyes lighting up with savage relish
> Suddenly horrified
> Protesting petulantly
> With indignant anger

With evangelical fervor
With lifelong resentful frustration
With bitter self-contempt
With a resentful side-glance
With a gloomy glance   (*SA*, p. 323)

And so on. The experiment can be repeated with many of the plays with similarly comic results.

"EDMUND – (*moved, stares at his father with understanding – slowly*) I'm glad you've told me this, Papa. I know you a lot better now."[10] Here, in a key moment from *Long Day's Journey*, O'Neill attempts to force an interpretation by means of a stage direction. Edmund and Jamie are, in the earlier acts of the play, all too aware of their father's story of youthful promise wasted. The larger context suggests that Edmund's response could be ironic and dismissive; or, that he is moved to "*understanding*" not by any new information his father has given him but by his father's performance of oft-repeated material. (Or, perhaps, Edmund's immaturity and susceptibility to booze may lead him to accept here an account which he would otherwise challenge or criticize.) The playwright attempts to forestall these possibilities, however, by an insistence that real "*understanding*" has happened. Actor and director are discouraged from exploration. But despite the playwright's endorsement of a therapeutic assent on Edmund's part, the options remain open, and different performers have chosen among these possibilities. That actors may take such liberties is not indicative of bad playwriting: but it is a fact of playwriting that declaring one option to be the author's intention will not necessarily make it the actor's.

O'Neill's antitheatricalism accounts in part for his reputation for bad writing. But bad writing in another, special sense dogs O'Neill's career. O'Neill was acutely aware of his failings in poetic language and his difficulty with elevated rhetoric. *Long Day's Journey* represents an attempt on his part to solve this problem through extensive quotation, from Shakespeare and from the Victorian poets. Jamie's recitation of Swinburne's "A Leave-taking" at the end of the play moves in effective counterpoint to Mary's obliviousness. He "*does it well*," runs the stage direction (how the actor is to do "it well" is not specified). The stage direction "*She does not seem to hear,*" for the reader, echoes the recitation: "Let us go hence, my songs; she will not hear ... Yea, though we sang as angels in her ear, / She would not hear" (III, 825–26). George Steiner singles out this kind of citation for special contempt:

> Language seeks vengeance on those who cripple it. A striking example occurs
> in O'Neill, a dramatist committed, in a somber and rather moving way, to the

practice of bad writing. Interspersed in the sodden morass of *A Long Day's Journey into Night*, there are passages from Swinburne. The lines are flamboyant, romantic verbiage. They are meant to show up the adolescent inadequacies of those who recite them. But, in fact, when the play is performed, the contrary occurs. The energy and glitter of Swinburne's language burn a hole in the surrounding fabric. They elevate the action above its paltry level and instead of showing up the characters show up the playwright. Modern authors rarely quote their betters with impunity.[11]

Harold Bloom also struggles with the question of O'Neill's poetic language. *The Iceman Cometh* and *Long Day's Journey* "stage remarkably and hold me in the audience, though they give me neither aesthetic pleasure nor spiritually memorable pain when I reread them in the study." There, on the page, O'Neill's "sheer bad writing" demands attention. But in performance, the case is altered, and Bloom argues that the stage directions themselves point towards successful performance. "Certainly a singular dramatic genius is always at work in O'Neill's stage directions," he ventures, "and can be felt also, most fortunately, in the repressed intensities of inarticulateness in all of the Tyrones." The quotations, according to Bloom, rise to the occasion of the "grim ballet of looks" prescribed in the stage directions.[12]

Steiner and Bloom represents opposite poles of the page-and-stage debate about theatre. Steiner, content in his study with O'Neill's strategy of quotation, finds it ridiculous in the theatre; Bloom, grumpy with the bad writing in his study, confesses to being moved on two occasions by productions of the play. "The old poetic bull, eh? Crap!" snarls Jamie in *Moon for the Misbegotten* (III, 923); the critics' debate about O'Neill's reliance upon snippets and quotations, in the later plays, is enacted in a character's own self-mockery. O'Neill's awareness of his bad writing, then, opens up some broad areas in the discussion and criticism of drama, where text and performance exist in a constant dialectic, with meaning constantly contingent and negotiable.

For Eric Bentley, O'Neill chooses text over performance as a way of "solving the particular problem to which he had addressed himself: rivaling and replacing his father. How better, in any case, can a man outdo an actor than by becoming a playwright? The actor is the playwright's mouthpiece and victim." But O'Neill's particular fear was that the playwright would become the actor's victim, the meaning of the play transformed in performance, and the mouthpiece the transformer and transmitter of meaning. This is not an uncommon anxiety among playwrights, and Bentley's blithe assurance that "the modern theatre is a playwright's theatre" resistant to the interpretive latitude of actors and directors is not convincing.[13]

Instead, O'Neill's reliance on stage directions and his attempts at elevated rhetoric show the influence of nineteenth-century melodrama. To Robert Benchley, the "royal blood of the 'Count of Monte Cristo'" coursed through O'Neill's veins and led him unerringly to strong theatrical effects.[14] John Henry Raleigh has demonstrated the persistence of motifs from *The Count of Monte Cristo* throughout O'Neill's work. Most of O'Neill's theatrical experimentation – "asides, soliloquies, and disguises" – is directly traceable back to romantic melodrama, Raleigh argues. More importantly, Raleigh insists, O'Neill's concept of rhythm as central to dramatic experience comes from this same old source: *Monte Cristo* gave to O'Neill a "temporal heritage" that "was twofold and polar: the long term narrative movement and the brief, explosive, dramatic event."[15]

O'Neill thus writes against melodrama in his attempts to rein in the star actor and curtail the liberties of performance while he at the same time has internalized a rhythm of dramatic action and explosive event that shares much with the discredited, earlier form. In a recent study, Kurt Eisen has pushed the point further, by invoking Peter Brooks's notion of the "melodramatic imagination" in nineteenth-century and modernist novelists. O'Neill's novelistic impulse, in the extensive stage directions and in the taxing of audiences' powers of endurance with long plays, is part of a larger "drive for discovering new ways to use melodrama as a means to express multivalent psychological conflicts." Eisen's argument is that O'Neill's plays succeed by pitting, in the characters' versions of their own lives, individual melodramas against one another: "stagey rhetoric, frequently crude characterization, and predictable plotting," however, remain a problem even in "the best of the early plays."[16] One way in which melodrama achieves its strong effects is through theatrical shorthand, presenting an audience with readily recognizable character types, stereotypical heroes and villains.

O'Neill and stereotypes: race, class, and gender

"I can honestly say there was only one actor who carried out every notion of a character I had in mind," O'Neill once declared. "That actor was Charles Gilpin as the Pullman porter in *The Emperor Jones*."[17] In 1946, when he made this remark, O'Neill had apparently forgotten his disputes with Gilpin in 1920, when the Provincetown Players recruited him to be the first African–American to play a leading role in the American professional theatre. Gilpin, grateful for the role, nonetheless mentioned in an interview the "stone walls" that stood in his way as an actor. "But – what next? If I were white, a dozen opportunities would come to me as a result of a success like this. But I'm black. It is no joke when I ask myself, 'Where do I go from here?'" As the run continued, Gilpin developed (or returned to) a drinking problem. The Gelbs, in language shockingly insensitive to Gilpin's complaint about the career opportunities available for a black actor, tell the story of a blow-up between Gilpin and O'Neill. O'Neill had learned that Gilpin, "suddenly finicky about using the word 'nigger' (called for by the script), was rewriting the role." The Gelbs cast the dispute as one between playwright and actor, and report O'Neill as threatening Gilpin: "If I ever catch you rewriting my lines again, you black bastard, I'm going to beat you up." "Yes, Gilpin is all 'Ham' and a yard wide," O'Neill protested as he gave the role in the London production to Paul Robeson. "Honestly, I've stood for more from him than from all the white actors I've ever known – simply because he was colored! He played the Emperor with author, play, and everyone concerned."[18] O'Neill protested the racist revocation of Gilpin's invitation to the Drama League dinner, his biographers point out in extenuation. His exasperation with Gilpin is in keeping with his determination to keep any actor, black or white, from rewriting or tampering with his role.

But, as Gilpin's remark about the "stone walls" suggests, race is an issue here. Gilpin's objections to the script of The Emperor Jones cannot be shoved aside as "finicky" or ridiculed as the imperial antics of a hard-drinking "ham." Both Raleigh and Sheaffer, to their credit, allow that Gilpin may have been "understandably" disturbed by the role, and Raleigh goes further in noticing that Gilpin "probably resented the play's atavism, whereby the terrors of the jungle night reduce the proud Jones to a cringing, crawling African savage, just before his end."[19] In The Emperor Jones, the stage directions abound in stereotypes ("*Jones's eyes begin to roll wildly. He stutters*" [1, 1048], for example), and the dialect is reminiscent of minstrel shows. While the Players were progressive in offering major roles to actors like Gilpin and Paul Robeson, Langston Hughes reported that the play itself was ridiculed in a revival in Harlem by audiences who found the "ha'nts" preposterous: "Them ain't no ghosts, fool! ... Why don't you come on out o' that jungle – back to Harlem where you belong?"

African–American critics have responded to the play with mixed feelings, balancing its importance as a theatre event, giving a black actor a major role, with concern about its insistence upon atavism and primitivism. Some have seen the play as a direct satire on Marcus Garvey's "back to Africa" movement, a demonstration of the futility of a Pullman porter attempting to survive in the jungle. Others find instead that the play alludes to stereotypical notions of "natural rhythm" on the part of African–Americans. "The Negro is a born actor, where the white man achieves acting," George Jean

Nathan declared of Paul Robeson. "To the African, dancing, singing, and acting are not separate and divorced from life as they are among Western people," Robeson himself concurred.[20] In the case of Gilpin, O'Neill's attitude towards actors mingled in volatile combination with his embroilment in a romantic racist ideology which saw blacks as (admirably as well as deplorably) primitive.

Entrapped in an insidious discourse of racism, O'Neill nonetheless determined to universalize the experience of race. *The Emperor Jones* shows a regression to the primitive that is meant to be universal. Jones stands for mankind. In *All God's Chillun Got Wings*, O'Neill encoded in the names of his interracial couple, many critics have noticed, his parents' names – Jim and Ella. The universalization moves towards the familial, with the O'Neills' unhappy marriage becoming itself a kind of race war. "This is like racial hatred," says the Captain to his wife in Strindberg's play *The Father*.[21] The Swedish playwright uses race as a metaphor to evoke the violence of the struggle between the sexes and to push his play's interest in issues of heredity and environment to a higher pitch. But in the American theatre, where the discourse of race is so much more violently charged than on Strindberg's European stages, O'Neill's atavism and primitivism still raise controversy.

When O'Neill won his Nobel Prize in 1936, the *Daily Worker* pointed to another kind of controversy. "O'Neill," the communist paper stated, "who started out as a dramatist of the working class, has completed his middle period as the dramatist of a sick middle class." No longer "a revolutionary writer, the chronicler of workers, dreamers and rebels, of hairy apes and underdogs," he was taking a safer route (*SA*, p. 460). The inclusion of "hairy apes" in this list raises a question, because in *The Hairy Ape* Yank is not only ridiculed by the high society types outside the Fifth Avenue church, but is also kicked out of the I.W.W. Local; the Wobblies' Secretary calls him "a brainless ape" (II, 159). Yank's yearning to belong is universalized, and it is as a member of the human species that he cannot find acceptance. "I ain't on oith and I ain't in heaven, get me?" Yank asks the gorilla whose embrace will kill him: the sphere of reference is not only evolutionary but cosmic. The *S.S. Glencairn* plays do incorporate a cast of underdogs, misfits, and rebels, but their aspirations, like Yank's, seem religious rather than revolutionary. John Howard Lawson, a leftist playwright who suffered blacklisting for his political sympathies, noticed that Nina's pursuit of "emotion" in *Strange Interlude* "is an insistence on a *fixed social system*."[22] O'Neill analogizes the social system to a kind of ineluctable fate, in which the suffering individual is trapped. Marxist critique, Lawson suggests, would argue instead that the social system is in flux, and that human suffering can be alleviated by improvements in social institutions.

O'Neill's desire to universalize as the human condition what other artists have seen as a particular set of social circumstances has led to charges of misogyny as well as insensitivity to matters of race and class. "Paralleling his mentor Strindberg," Louis Sheaffer puts it, "O'Neill created in the majority of his leading female characters either bitches or other agents of misfortune or impossibly noble souls. He could praise Woman only in exaggerated, unrealistic terms." John Henry Raleigh waxes poetic about the "humiliated heroine" and the "wounded woman" in O'Neill but remembers that "Men – sons, husbands, lovers – and whiskey, these are the sources of feminine sorrow in O'Neill."[23] As Anne Flèche says, "[T]he feminist critic [of O'Neill] finds herself staring at an Everest of possibilities."[24] The stereotypes abound, from the wise whores like Cybel in *The Great God Brown* and The Streetwalker in *Welded* through a whole range of Earth Mothers to Mary Tyrone and Josie Hogan.[25] O'Neill's obsessive reliance upon Madonna/Whore portrayals of women is usually attributed to his ambivalent feelings about his mother. In 1926, Elizabeth Shepley Sergeant offered this image of O'Neill's childhood: "Gazing afar upon a stage where a heroic figure strutted, towards a distant lovely mother to whom he stretched his arms in vain, he conceived the world in which he was at mercy of his affections as disastrous." According to the Gelbs, Sergeant impressed O'Neill with her "sensitive grasp of the forces that shaped his character" (p. 64).

O'Neill reiterates in his plays the Oedipal pattern of mother, father, and rival sons. Robert Benchley offered the "my three men" scene in *Strange Interlude* as one instance in which the asides seemed to work: "In certain scenes, notably the one in Act 6 where the woman sits with her trinity of complementary male units, all thinking out loud, this method justifies itself and gives a hint of its possibilities in the future."[26]

> NINA (*more and more strangely triumphant*)
> My three men! ... I feel their desires converge in me! ... to form one complete beautiful male desire which I absorb ... and am whole ... they dissolve in me, their life is my life ... I am pregnant with the three! ... husband! ... lover! ... father! ... and the fourth man! ... little man! ... little Gordon! ... he is mine too! ... that makes it perfect! ...
> (*with an extravagant suppressed exultance*)
> Why, I should be the proudest woman on earth! ... I should be the happiest woman in the world! ...
> (*then suppressing an outbreak of hysterical triumphant laughter only by tremendous effort*)
> Ha-ha ... only I better knock wood ...
> (*She raps with both knuckles in a fierce tattoo on the table.*)
> before God the father hears my happiness! ...　　　　　　(II, 756)

Despite Nina's evocation here and elsewhere of a religion of God the Mother, the effect is less an affirmation of Nina's power as an individual than of her status as the object of three intersecting lines of male desire. Likewise, in the strikingly similar final scene of *Long Day's Journey*, Mary Tyrone's appearance trailing her wedding gown, oblivious of her three men watching her from the table, places her, too, at the apex of a triangle of male desire. The difference is that Mary Tyrone evades this desire, retreating into a memory of a past without men, where Nina exults in it.

Recent feminist criticism of O'Neill has allowed one woman to escape the "kind of Alaska" into which women are exiled by male playwrights. Josie Hogan, in *Moon for the Misbegotten*, is "the most fully present female character in the O'Neill canon," Ann C. Hall argues. "She is not Madonna, virgin, or prostitute, but instead a woman who offers a glimmer of hope to other women in the male wasteland."[27] Eric Bentley, in the essay "Eugene O'Neill's Pietà," likewise sees Josie as a touchstone, but one that will impress admirers and detractors differently: "I rather think its central image – that of a giant virgin holding in her arms a dipsomaniac lecher with a heart of gold – may stand in all minds as O'Neill's central monument; for admirers will find it characteristic in grandeur and poetry, while others will find in it, clinically speaking, neurotic fantasy indulged rather than exploited and, critically speaking, poetry strained after rather than achieved." Feminist criticism that seeks to find affirmation in this image must address what Bentley calls its "comic–grotesque" potential.[28] Mary McCarthy vividly evokes the incongruity of this particular *pietà*: "The defeat of all human plans and contrivances is suddenly shaped in the picture of the titaness sitting staring at a stage moon with a shriveled male infant drunkenly asleep at her side. The image ... takes on a certain grotesque epic form; the woman, stage center, like a gentle beached whale, appears for an instant as the last survivor of the world."[29] Hall's "glimmer of hope" is McCarthy's "beached whale."

History, autobiography, and psychoanalysis

Racial, class, and gender stereotypes in O'Neill's plays speak to O'Neill's immersion in his own early twentieth-century American context. O'Neill's indulgence of these stereotypes, though, points to a larger failure to think historically about that context. This is not for want of trying. O'Neill's imagination encompassed a vast historical perspective: the Cycle plays were to cover most of American history through the travails of the Melody-Harford family, and *Mourning Becomes Electra* equates the aftermath of the American Civil War with the aftermath of Troy.

"Brecht himself would have admired the little scene in which the capitalist's wife, to demonstrate her new-won belief in the system, blackmails and browbeats into acceptance of the cash-nexus a representative of the pre-capitalist ideal of honor," Eric Bentley jokes about the "social realism" of *More Stately Mansions*, one of the surviving Cycle plays. But the play's whole focus is upon the story of a failed writer.[30] Deborah Harford, dreaming of the court of Louis XVI, thinks not historically but nostalgically: "I admire the customs and manners of that period, that is all. I would have liked to have lived then when life was free and charming and fastidious, not vulgar and ignoble and greedy as it is in this country today. (*She stops abruptly – exasperatedly*) But how stupid! These insane interminable dialogues with the self!" (III, 316). In her exasperation, Deborah retreats even from nostalgia, further into the self.

In *Mourning Becomes Electra*, the timeless quality of the Oresteian myth makes it a key to the psychic dynamics of the family. The mid-nineteenth century America in which the play is set is mostly evoked through the techniques of allusion. Orin asks his mother if she has read Melville's *Typee*; his account of his not-so-heroic charge is derived from Stephen Crane's *Red Badge of Courage*. Adam Brant's clipper ship is symbolic of a way of life displaced by technology: "Aye, but it ain't for long," says the Chantyman, "steam is comin' in, the sea is full o' smoky teakettles, the old days is dyin', an' where'll you an' me be then? (*lugubriously drunken again*) Everything is dyin'! Abe Lincoln is dead. I used to ship on the Mannon packets an' I seed in the paper where Ezra Mannon was dead! (*Brant starts guiltily*)" (II, 987). Such passages do less to cause an audience to think of the large historical issues raised – the end of the age of sail, the assassination of Lincoln, the rise of the popular press – than to stress Brant's anxiety about the domestic crime of Mannon's murder.

In *The Iceman Cometh* and *Long Day's Journey* O'Neill leaves the historical sweep of the Cycle and the trilogy behind and, with the retrospective economy of classical structure, allows one year, 1912, to crystallize both world history and his own. The characters in Harry Hope's saloon have pasts – as anarchists, Socialists, members of opposing armies in the Boer War – which allow the play to reach out to contexts beyond its own confinement. *Iceman* presents a pivotal year in O'Neill's personal history as a pivotal year in European history as well. Despite the diversity of narratives offered by the denizens of the saloon, however, the play resolves its primary conflicts into a "my three men" pattern. In this instance, however, the figure of Woman is offstage. Larry Slade and Parritt meet as lover and son of Rosa Parritt; Hickey is haunted by his murder of his wife. The historical material serves only as backdrop to an enactment of Oedipal crisis. *Long Day's Journey* drops even the pretense of reference to the public world of 1912. The salient history for this play is utterly personal: in the summer of 1912 Eugene O'Neill worked as a cub reporter on a New London paper and was diagnosed as having tuberculosis. Again retrospective in its method, the play reaches back not into public history, as *Iceman* does, but into familial history, for its characters' warring accounts of themselves.

After destroying the Cycle, O'Neill discarded his ambitions for overtly historical drama, and instead set to work on dramas that evoke special turning points in his own life. The two plays set in 1912 are complemented by *Moon for the Misbegotten*, set in 1923, between the deaths of Ella and Jamie O'Neill. The date has only autobiographical significance. Here O'Neill demands comparison with Strindberg, who obsessively returned to dates of intense private significance in his writings. Strindberg insisted that his special study of himself could become part of a "natural history of the human heart." As one of his alter egos states: "It has in fact seemed to me from an early age that my life was staged before me so that I would be able to observe all its facets. This reconciled me to my misfortunes, and taught me to perceive myself as an object."[31] Strindberg simultaneously reads and writes the text of his life in fifty-five volumes of published works and fourteen volumes of letters; O'Neill's output looks skimpy by comparison.

Strindberg, like Freud in the 1880s, found himself intrigued by the mechanisms of repression and denial through which people resist knowing the truth about themselves. While Strindberg anticipated psychoanalytical thought, O'Neill reacted to a popularized, American Freudianism throughout his career. As Pfister puts it: O'Neill's "principal brief against psychoanalysis was that the dramatist – his profession – got there first."[32] Moorton echoes O'Neill's insistence on the timeless nature of his focus on familial dynamics. "Aristotle," Moorton claims, "explains two millennia before the fact why O'Neill was drawn by artistic as well as psychological reasons to a compulsive retelling of the story of his own house ... not merely because his soul compelled him, but because great plays resulted, for reasons that Aristotle grasped with perfect clarity in the fourth century BC."[33]

This analysis jumbles up O'Neill's compulsion to tell his story with its result, "great plays," as though in succumbing to his "soul" O'Neill also bore in mind Aristotle's preference for tragic stories about family members. While O'Neill was certainly free with his discussion of the ancient Greeks, of Nietzsche, and of tragedy and myth in his middle period, it is he who presents *Long Day's Journey* as a therapeutic exercise. The dedication for Carlotta famously inscribes the play as *"written in tears and blood,"* and thanks Carlotta for the gift of *"the faith in love that enabled me to face my dead at last and write this play – write it with deep pity and understanding and forgiveness for all the four haunted Tyrones"* (III, [714]).[34]

The claim of "deep pity and understanding and forgiveness," is grandiose; but biographers and critics who like to see O'Neill's whole career as a kind of "talking cure" for his problems with his family have been reluctant to take issue with it. Nonetheless, they have provided the background that makes this triumph of self-understanding and forgiveness less total than the dedication suggests. While the three Tyrones who are not Edmund correspond rather closely in biographical detail to O'Neill's father, brother, and mother, Edmund Tyrone is markedly different from his model. In 1912, Eugene O'Neill was married, going through a divorce, and the father of a son; these facts are left unmentioned in the play. As a result, the younger son seems much younger in the play, or at least much less mature: Edmund has the "makings of a poet," but whether he will become one or not is left in the air. The play's insistence upon a repetitive pattern of aggression and regression in the family members' assaults upon each other paints a grim picture for the future. But in 1913, Ella O'Neill checked into a convent and kicked her habit; Jamie, dissolute as he was, stopped drinking for the last two years of his mother's life; and James O'Neill unbuttoned his wallet enough to allow Eugene, after two days at the state sanatorium, to go to the private institution where his tuberculosis was cured and he made the determination to become a playwright.

This is not to fault the seamlessness of the play's design or its ruthless portrayal of a guilt-ridden family trapped, in psychoanalytical terms, in a network of *"frozen introjects,"* as Bennett Simon, a psychoanalyst and literary scholar has put it. Rather it is to question the art-and-therapy linkage so prevalent in criticism of O'Neill. "If the play and the act of writing it served to help him work through his conflicts with his parents and his brother (all of whom were dead at the time of the writing), it did not help him with his conflicts with his children and stepchildren," Simon points out. As a therapist, Simon is more concerned with the living than the dead, and the play's presentation of "parents who are murderously destructive toward children," juxtaposed to the sufferings of O'Neill's own children, gives him pause.[35]

Moon for the Misbegotten, too, grants a kind of forgiveness to its haunted Tyrone, Jamie, that elides some of the more unpleasant facts about his younger brother. Eugene O'Neill, on the occasion of his mother's final illness, refused to leave New York, where he was supervising the production of *The Hairy Ape*, claiming bad health (though, Sheaffer tells us, "Eugene was in fairly good health at the time.") The famous train, on which Jamie slept with "that fat blonde pig" (III, 917) with his mother's corpse in the baggage car, arrived the night of the first performance of *The Hairy Ape*, but O'Neill skipped both the premiere and the train (*SA*, pp. 82–85). O'Neill stages Jamie's much more public and humiliating failure, and grants him Josie Hogan's forgiveness.

Documenting the discrepancies with the biographical record and the shifts of perspective that place the autobiographical writer in a better light is an acceptable critical strategy when the writer claims, as Strindberg does, objectivity about himself, or claims, as O'Neill does, to have forgiven and understood his domestic trauma. The claim of sincerity can invite the charge of disingenuousness. Neither Bennett Simon nor Walter Davis can endorse O'Neill's account of his self-transcendence, Simon as a therapist and Davis as a theorist who is concerned with the limitations of psycho-analysis. O'Neill's strength, in Davis's eyes, is to document ferociously the entrapment of the psyche within a family dynamic that can never be transcended, understood, or forgiven. O'Neill's drama amounts to an assault upon the audience. "As the frameworks of explanation we use to prevent facing the reality of interfamilial cruelty collapse, we are forced to regress, along with the characters, toward psychodynamic explorations that we can scarcely comprehend, since the psychological theory that would articulate them has not yet been developed," Davis argues in an extended analysis of *Long Day's Journey*. "Much has been made of O'Neill's supposed dependence on psychoanalytic theory; the secret thereby concealed is the deep challenge his work poses to psychoanalysis by exploring the dimensions of the psyche that it has chosen to repress."[36] Davis's point is that drama as a form can go deeper than psychoanalysis into the "crypt" of the human psyche, finding at its bottom a murderous hatred that only drama can express.

O'Neill's failure to recognize his last works as acts of aggression and revenge rather than of forgiveness and understanding is less disturbing than the endorsement by the majority of his critics of his own self-delusion about these works. The cult of sincerity presents O'Neill as an artist who is wholly sincere and who has worked out his compulsions in great art; this mingles esthetic and ethical concerns. O'Neill's late plays are not better than his middle plays because they are more honest: they are better because they are structurally more economical, because their characters interact more believably, and because they trumpet their great themes less loudly. But they are not humane, not generous, not humble. One reason the vision of the family in *Long Day's Journey* is so compelling is the author's own embroilment in that family's mutual self-destruction.

O'Neill's cruelty is, to put it another way, an Artaudian cruelty; his assaults upon the audience, acts of aggression as well as representations of aggression. His mistrust of actors, his contempt for theatre, his reliance on crude effects and stereotypical characterizations: all these excesses may be said to flow from one source. O'Neill's work is not a testimonial to self-knowledge and forgiveness. It is a testament of rage.

NOTES

1 Louis Sheaffer, *O'Neill: Son and Artist* (Boston: Little, Brown [1973]; rpt. New York: AMS Press, 1988), p. 245. Subsequent citations appear in the text as *SA*.

2 John Gassner, Introduction to *O'Neill: A Collection of Critical Essays*, ed. John Gassner (Englewood Cliffs: Prentice Hall, 1964), p. 4.

3 Richard F. Moorton, Introduction to *Eugene O'Neill's Century: Centennial Views on America's Foremost Tragic Dramatist*, "Contributions in Drama and Theatre Studies, Number 36" (Westport, Conn.: Greenwood Press, 1991), p. xviii.

4 Quoted by Louis Sheaffer, *O'Neill: Son and Playwright* (Boston: Little, Brown, 1968), p. 481. Subsequent citations appear in the text as *SP*.

5 Quoted by Sheaffer, *SP*, p. 481; compare to "Before O'Neill, America had entertainment; after him, it had drama," attributed to John Lahr on the back cover of *File on O'Neill*, compiled by Stephen Black (London: Methuen, 1993).

6 Henri Peyre, *Literature and Sincerity* (1963; rpt. Westport, Conn.: Greenwood Press, 1978), pp. 336, 334. Peyre exempts drama from his polemic, but with a notable exception: the cult of sincerity "does not apply to the drama (except for the expressionist drama of Strindberg and the *Ich*-drama of his German followers)," p. 20. Far more than any German expressionist dramatist, O'Neill portrayed himself as a devoted "follower" of Strindberg.

7 Arthur and Barbara Gelb, *O'Neill* (New York: Harper and Row, 1962; 1973), p. 408. Subsequent references appear in the text.

8 Virgil Geddes, *The Melodramadness of O'Neill* (Brookfield, Conn.: Brookfield Players, Inc., 1934; rpt. Norwood Editions, 1977), pp. 8–9. Founder of the Brookfield Players, a summer tryout theatre, Geddes's main claim to fame was that his first New York production featured the young Bette Davis in her first New York appearance. *The Earth Between*, a tragedy, set on a farm and rich with hints of incest, was performed by the Provincetown Players in 1929; sharing the bill was a revival of O'Neill's 1916 one-act, *Before Breakfast*.

9 Geddes, *Melodramadness*, p. 37.

10 Eugene O'Neill, *Complete Plays*, ed. Travis Bogard (New York: The Library of America, 1988), III:810. All plays of O'Neill are quoted from this edition, with volume and page numbers appearing in the text.

11 Moorton quotes Steiner with disapproval in *Eugene O'Neill's Century*, xviii–xix. Steiner seems fond of using the word "morass" to refer to O'Neill: for example, see his comments on *Mourning Becomes Electra* in *The Death of Tragedy* (London: Faber, 1961): "O'Neill commits inner vandalism by sheer inadequacy of style. In the morass of his language the high griefs of the house of Atreus dwindle to a case of adultery and murder in some provincial rathole" (p. 327).

12 Harold Bloom, ed. Introduction to *Eugene O'Neill: Modern Critical Views* (New York: Chelsea House, 1987), pp. 5, 12.

13 Eric Bentley, "The Life and Hates of Eugene O'Neill," in *Thinking About the Playwright: Comments from Four Decades* (Evanston: Northwestern University Press, 1987), p. 32.

14 Robert Benchley, *Benchley at the Theatre: Dramatic Criticism, 1920–40*, ed. Charles Gethcell (Ipswich, Mass.: The Ipswich Press, 1985), p. 97.

15 John Henry Raleigh, *The Plays of Eugene O'Neill*, with a preface by Harry T. Moore (Carbondale and Edwardsville: Southern Illinois University Press, 1965), p. 184.

16 Kurt Eisen, *The Inner Strength of Opposites: O'Neill's Novelistic Drama and the Melodramatic Imagination* (Athens: University of Georgia Press, 1994), pp. 26, 30.

17 Quoted by the Gelbs, p. 448.

18 Gelb and Gelb, pp. 448, 449. Contrast with Raleigh: "he could not, understandably, continue to utter the word 'nigger' every night and began to substitute euphemisms, such as 'black baby,'" *Plays of Eugene O'Neill*, pp. 108–09. Sheaffer, acknowledging that Gilpin may have been "resentful of all he had had to endure because of his color," reports the threat as "If you change the lines again, I'll beat the hell out of you" (*SA*, p. 35).

19 Raleigh, *The Plays of Eugene O'Neill*, p. 109.

20 Joel Pfister, *Staging Depth: Eugene O'Neill and the Politics of Psychological Discourse* (Chapel Hill: University of North Carolina Press, 1995), offers an extensive discussion of O'Neill and race, pp. 121–37; Hughes quoted from p. 136; Nathan and Robeson, p. 262 n. 73.

21 August Strindberg, *The Father* in *Plays: One*, trans. by Michael Meyer (London: Methuen, 1964, 1994), p. 61.

22 John Howard Lawson, "Eugene O'Neill," in Gassner, *A Collection of Critical Essays*, p. 49.

23 *SA*, p. 500; Raleigh, *The Plays of Eugene O'Neill*, pp. 127–42, *passim*.

24 Anne Flèche, "A Monster of Perfection: O'Neill's 'Stella,'" in *Feminist Readings of Modern American Drama*, ed. June Schlueter (Rutherford: Fairleigh Dickinson University Press, 1989), p. 25.

25 See, for example, Judith Barlow, "O'Neill's Many Mothers: Mary Tyrone, Josie Hogan, and their Antecedents" in *Perspectives on O'Neill: New Essays*, ed. Shyamal Bagchee (Victoria: University of Victoria Press, 1988), pp. 7–17.

26 Robert Benchley, *Benchley at the Theatre*, p. 70.

27 Ann C. Hall, *"A Kind of Alaska": Women in the Plays of O'Neill, Pinter, and Shepard* (Carbondale and Edwardsville: Southern Illinois University Press, 1993), p. 53.

28 Eric Bentley, "Eugene O'Neill's *Pietà*," in *What is Theatre?: Incorporating "The Dramatic Event" and other Reviews* (New York: Limelight Editions, 1984), pp. 18, 19.

29 Mary McCarthy, *Mary McCarthy's Theater Chronicles, 1937–1962* (New York: Farrar Straus and Giroux, 1963), p. 89.

30 Eric Bentley, "A Touch of the Adolescent" in *What is Theatre?*, p. 396. See also Kurt Eisen, *The Inner Strength of Opposites*: "For all its reflections on American history and the individual's struggle to transcend the duality that history has conditioned, *More Stately Mansions* is a play about a failed writer," p. 87.

31 Quoted by Michael Robinson, *Strindberg and Autobiography* (Norwich: Norvik Press, 1986), p. 3.
32 Pfister, *Staging Depth*, p. 99.
33 Moorton, *Eugene O'Neill's Century*, p. xxii.
34 For Sheaffer, the metaphor of writing in blood becomes a key to interpreting O'Neill. and he emphasizes the phrase "emotional hemophiliac" in both volumes (*SP*, p. 351; *SA*, p. ix).
35 Bennett Simon, *Tragic Drama and the Family: Psychoanalytic Studies from Aeschylus to Beckett* (New Haven: Yale University Press, 1988), p. 181.
36 Walter A. Davis, *Get the Guests: Psychoanalysis, Modern American Drama, and the Audience*, "The Wisconsin Project on American Writers," Frank Lentricchia, general editor (Madison: University of Wisconsin Press, 1994), p. 207.

16

MICHAEL MANHEIM

O'Neill criticism

O'Neill criticism falls essentially into two categories: (1) the reception of his plays in critical reviews following their performances, and (2) the interpretation and evaluation of his plays by scholars and historians. The former have obviously appeared in newspapers like the *New York Times* and magazines like *Time, Newsweek, The Nation*, and *The New Yorker*; the latter in scholarly journals and in books devoted to his life and works. From the early 1920s until the late 1930s – the period of O'Neill's heyday as a popular dramatist – journalistic reviews were the chief category, though some quasi-scholarly studies also appeared in that period, most notably Barrett H. Clark's *Eugene O'Neill*, which was originally published in 1926. With the appearance of Sophus Winther's *O'Neill: A Critical Study* in 1934, evaluation of the playwright as *a* (if not *the*) major American dramatist and a significant figure in world drama has come to predominate, though obviously reviews of individual productions in the United States and, increasingly, abroad continue to appear.

The most comprehensive survey of what has been written on O'Neill until the year of its publication is Jordan Y. Miller's *Eugene O'Neill and the American Critic* (1973). Miller's work is unique in giving equal attention to newspaper reviews and scholarly studies. Another important work – Oscar Cargill, N. Bryllion Fagin, and William J. Fisher, eds., *O'Neill and his Plays* (1961) – actually juxtaposes reprints of selected journalists' reviews with both reprinted and original scholarly articles. Other listings and discussions of O'Neill criticism appear, of course, in general bibliographical discussions – e.g., Madeline Smith and Richard Eaton's *Eugene O'Neill: An Annotated Bibliography* (1988) or Margaret Loftus Ranald's *An O'Neill Companion* (1984) – and in general surveys of American drama criticism, notably Floyd E. Eddleman's *American Drama Criticism*, second edition (Hamden, Conn.: The Shoe String Press, 1979, with supplements in 1984, 1989, and 1992). Obviously, since such studies quickly become out-of-date, students of the playwright's work must inevitably consult such general bibliographies as that published annually by *PMLA* and the *Reader's Guide to Periodical Literature* (the latter chiefly for reviews).

Newspaper and magazine reviews are too varied and numerous to allow for much categorization. Suffice it to say, the run-of-the-mill ones tend to follow current fashions – often those established by literary and, increasingly today, theatre scholars. A few notable reviewers – for example, Joseph Wood Krutch, George Jean Nathan, and Brooks Atkinson – led rather than followed, establishing directions for others. Today, such journals as *The New Yorker* and *The New York Review of Books* increasingly blur the distinction between the journalistic and the scholarly in their reviews. But desirable as it may be, a survey and discussion of the reviewing of O'Neill productions is obviously impossible within the limits of such a discussion as this one.

My main concern here is with critical studies – both in the form of books and, to a very small extent, articles. They range from general discussions of his work to discussions that focus on the influence on his plays of his psychological trauma, his philosophical/religious views, his theatrical techniques, his sensitivity to the impact of black and immigrant minorities in American life, and (most recently) the treatment of women in his plays and his desire to win favor with the influential forces of his time. Most of these discussions are admiring of the playwright, some including him among the world's greatest dramatists; while a few are, sometimes virulently, unfriendly to his work. (See, for example, Matthew H. Wikander's essay in this collection. O'Neill rarely provokes an indifferent response among his audience and readers.)

The general study that has undoubtedly had the greatest influence on thinking about O'Neill in the later twentieth century is Travis Bogard's *Contour in Time*, first published by Oxford University Press in 1972 and slightly revised for a second edition in 1988. (The revisions are almost exclusively limited to Bogard's treatment of the Cycle plays.) Bogard's approach is straightforward, looking at O'Neill's development from early adolescence to full maturity, always in the context of his work. Each play is dealt with, as well as the theatrical conditions of its production and the critical and popular response it generated. This one work, supplemented to an extent by research done by Bogard since its initial publication, has made him still the leading voice in O'Neill criticism today.

But there have been other significant books on O'Neill. Barrett H. Clark's *Eugene O'Neill* (1926) anticipated Bogard by looking at the playwright from a broad perspective. A friend of O'Neill's, Clark was a theatre critic of the Twenties whose criticism is both familiar and sensitive. Edwin Engel's *The Haunted Heroes of Eugene O'Neill* (1953) looked at particularly the dark side of the playwright as never before, though like Clark, Engel was in this work puzzled about issues that later were clarified with the appearance of *Long Day's Journey Into Night*. Sophus K. Winther's *Eugene O'Neill: A Critical Study*, originally published in 1934, and Richard Dana Skinner's *Eugene O'Neill: A Poet's Quest*, first published in 1935, are other pioneering critical works written without the understanding that *Long Day's Journey* and the biographies of the 1960s and 70s would bring.

The first important study to use O'Neill's monumental *Long Day's Journey* in its analysis of the playwright is Doris V. Falk's *Eugene O'Neill and the Tragic Tension* (1958), which begins to see O'Neill's work from a psychological perspective. From quite a different perspective, though again with insights drawn from *Long Day's Journey*, is John H. Raleigh's *The Plays of Eugene O'Neill* (1965), which organizes its discussion around such issues as history and form rather than looking at plays individually and chronologically. And to this group should certainly be added the better general introductions to the playwright: John Gassner's *Eugene O'Neill* (1965), Frederick I. Carpenter's *Eugene O'Neill* (originally written in 1957, but revised in 1979), and Normand Berlin's *Eugene O'Neill* (1982), all works analyzing the O'Neill canon in the entire context of the man and his theatre. To this latter group, Virginia Floyd's *Eugene O'Neill: A New Assessment* (1984) might appropriately be added.

Four studies deal with the playwright's emerging dramaturgical techniques: Egil Törnqvist's *A Drama of Souls: O'Neill's Study in Supernaturalistic Techniques* (1969), which deals with his methods of characterization; Jean Chothia's *Forging a Language: A Study of the Plays of Eugene O'Neill* (1979), which is rooted in Chothia's unique perception of growing sophistication in the playwright's dialogue; Michael Manheim's *Eugene O'Neill's New Language of Kinship* (1982), which reaches conclusions for the entire canon based both on the autobiographical context and language of the late plays; Doris Alexander's *Eugene O'Neill's Creative Struggle* (1992), which uses an autobiographical context to concentrate on the years 1924–33; and most recently Kurt Eisen's *The Inner Strength of Opposites* (1995), which sees inner psychological conflict in the plays from the perspective of the twentieth-century novel.

The most recent direction that seems to be taking shape belongs to the currently fashionable historicist critical mode and is represented among full-length studies by Joel Pfister's *Staging Depth: Eugene O'Neill and the Politics of Psychological Discourse* (1995), the title of which fairly well indicates the nature of its contents. Pfister's approach seems in general not friendly to the playwright in seeing him as primarily, though not exclusively, an exploiter of fashions established by the cultural elite of his time.

Other full-length studies are of a more specialized nature, and first among these must come the several extensively researched and, surely in O'Neill's case, indispensable biographies. For some authors, biography might not seem appropriate in a discussion of criticism, but in O'Neill's case it is highly appropriate, and the best-known of the biographies are in themselves important works of criticism. The first of these – Doris Alexander's *The Tempering of Eugene O'Neill* (1962) – led the way in its perception that the events described in *Long Day's Journey* were more than casually autobiographical in dealing with the one, stupendous psychological trauma of the playwright's early life (his mother's drug addiction). But the two massive biographies to follow are certainly works one should look at first – and looking at them takes time. They are Arthur and Barbara Gelb's *O'Neill* (1962), and, especially, Louis Sheaffer's two-volume *Eugene O'Neill: Son and Playwright* (1968) and *Eugene O'Neill: Son and Artist* (1973). Among other things, these works reveal not only the extent to which the life of O'Neill himself was crucial to his work but also the lives of his father, mother, and brother.

Other works of a comparably specialized nature are also important. O'Neill on stage is increasingly the focus of criticism – and pre-eminent among these are Timo Tiusanen's *O'Neill's Scenic Images* (1968), a discussion of how scenic configurations in the plays often constitute their central imagery; and, more recently, Leonard Chabrowe's *Ritual and Pathos: The Theatre of O'Neill* (1976). Most recently, Ronald Wainscott's *Staging O'Neill: The Experimental Years, 1920–1934* (1988) is an important history of O'Neill production during the first of the two major parts of his career. Gary Vena's study of the original staging of *The Iceman Cometh* also fits into this category. And in the parallel area of O'Neill on screen, there is John Orlandello's *O'Neill on Film* (1982), an important work which is being supplemented today by reviews especially of productions of the plays on television.

While the late plays have, of course, been central to almost all O'Neill criticism since the 1960s, two works were among the first to focus on that importance: Rolf Scheibler's *The Late Plays of Eugene O'Neill* (1970) and Judith E. Barlow's *Final Acts: The Creation of Three Late O'Neill Plays* (1985), which was built upon an earlier article by Barlow ("*Long Day's Journey Into Night:* From Early Notes to Finished Play," *Modern Drama* 22 [March 1979]: 19–28). Winifred Frazer's *Love as Death in "The Iceman Cometh"* (1967) has been an influential study of that late play; while Martha Bower's *Eugene O'Neill's Unfinished Threnody and Process of*

Invention in Four Cycle Plays (1988) and Laurin Porter's *The Banished Prince: Time, Memory and Ritual in the Late Plays* (1988) focus attention on O'Neill's massively conceived but uncompleted Cycle – "A Tale of Possessors Self-Dispossessed" – stressing the relationship of *A Touch of the Poet* and *More Stately Mansions* from that Cycle to the last plays. And Michael Hinden's *"Long Day's Journey Into Night": Native Eloquence* (1990) is the most recent full-length study of that play.

O'Neill's relationship to earlier writers – Ibsen, Strindberg, and the Greek tragedians – has been included in several critical studies, but comparisons of his plays with the work of two writers he is not normally compared with is the exclusive focus of two full-length works: Peter Egri's *Chekhov and O'Neill* (1986), which deals more with Chekhov's short stories than his plays; and Normand Berlin's *O'Neill's Shakespeare* (1993), one of the most original approaches to the playwright in recent years. Berlin has also done work in article form on the relationship between O'Neill and Samuel Beckett ("The Beckettian O'Neill," *Modern Drama* 31 [March 1988]: 28–34). And while not a discussion of O'Neill's relationship to one specific dramatist, Edward Shaughnessy's *O'Neill in Ireland* (1988) certainly suggests the influence of John Millington Synge on O'Neill's work. In addition, James R. Robinson's *Eugene O'Neill and Oriental Thought* (1982) has been important in O'Neill scholarship in exploring Eastern ideas in the plays, while Marc Maufort compares the playwright with Herman Melville in *Songs of American Experience* (1989).

The book which led the way in attacking O'Neill's plays is Virgil Geddes' *The Melodramadness of Eugene O'Neill* (first published in 1934, and reprinted in 1973 and 1977). Geddes has had numerous successors, including the critic Eric Bentley.

Articles too numerous and varied to include for discussion here have dealt with and touched on all these subjects, of course, as have sub-sections of books and anthologies of criticism of modern drama. Several articles were among the first to discuss O'Neill's relationship to other modern dramatists: Sverre Arestad's *"The Iceman Cometh* and *The Wild Duck," Scandinavian Studies* 20 (February 1948): 1–11; Sophus Winther's "Strindberg and O'Neill: A Study of Influence," *Scandinavian Studies* 31 (August 1959): 103–20; Egil Törnqvist's "Ibsen and O'Neill: A Study in Influence," *Scandinavian Studies* 37 (August 1965): 211–35; Helen Muchnic's "The Irrelevancy of Belief: *The Iceman Cometh* and [Gorky's] *The Lower Depths*, in Cargill *et al.*, eds., *O'Neill and his Plays* (1961): 431–42; and more recently (as mentioned above) Normand Berlin's "The Beckettian O'Neill." In addition, Travis Bogard compares O'Neill with Shaw in *The Revels History of Drama in English*, vol. 8 (London: Methuen, 1977): pp. 66–76; and

Linda Ben-Zvi deals with O'Neill and Susan Glaspell in *The Eugene O'Neill Newsletter* 10 (Spring 1986): 22–27.

Similarly, Cyrus Day's articles were the first to emphasize the influence of the Last Supper on *The Iceman Cometh* ("The Iceman and the Bridegroom," *Modern Drama* 1 [May 1958]: 1–9) and of Nietzsche's *Beyond Good and Evil* on *Lazarus Laughed* ("*Amor Fati*: Lazarus as Superman and Savior," *Modern Drama* 3 [December 1960]: 297–305). Numerous critics have dealt with the influence of Aeschylus on *Mourning Becomes Electra*, most recently R. F. Moorton in a collection of essays he edited, *Eugene O'Neill's Century*: 105–18.

Articles dealing with autobiographical elements in the plays have been common through the years since *Long Day's Journey Into Night*. The most shaping probably has been Edwin Engel's "Ideas in the Plays of Eugene O'Neill," in John Gassner, ed., *Ideas in the Drama* (New York: Columbia University Press, 1964: pp. 101–24) – shaping because, following his *Haunted Heroes*, which was written before *Long Day's Journey*, it was the first to delineate precisely the importance of that work to the entire O'Neill canon. Among those probing new depths in biographical criticism of the playwright is Stephen Black, whose articles have appeared in *American Literature*, *Modern Drama*, and *The Eugene O'Neill Review*.

Among the most highly regarded pieces on *Long Day's Journey Into Night* is the chapter of that play by Richard E. Sewall in his *The Vision of Tragedy*, revised and enlarged edition (Yale University Press, 1980: pp. 161–74). (This and numerous other engaging essays on O'Neill appear in books and collections which, since they are not devoted exclusively to the playwright, are easily overlooked in listings of significant O'Neill studies.) And one not-so-recent followed by two more recent essays on *The Iceman Cometh* have suggested original approaches to that play: William R. Brashear's "The Wisdom of Silenus in O'Neill's Iceman" (*American Literature* 36 [May 1964]: 180–88); Normand Berlin's discussion of the play in *O'Neill's Shakespeare*: pp. 166–85; and Stephen Black's "Tragic Anagnorisis in *The Iceman Cometh*," in Shyamal Bagchee, ed. *Perspectives on O'Neill: New Essays*: pp. 17–32. The article which has probably had the most influence in attacking O'Neill also focuses on *The Iceman Cometh*: Eric Bentley's "Trying to Like O'Neill" (*The Kenyon Review* 14 [July 1952]: 476–92).

Several articles by Michael Manheim have sought to point the way toward a new approach to O'Neill deriving from post-structuralist criticism: "The Transcendence of Melodrama in *A Touch of the Poet* and *A Moon for the Misbegotten*," in John Stroupe, ed., *Critical Approaches to O'Neill*: 147–59; and parallel articles in the same vein on *The Iceman*

Cometh, in James Martine, ed., *Critical Essays on Eugene O'Neill*: pp. 145–58; and *Long Day's Journey Into Night*, in Shyamal Bagchee, ed. *Perspectives on O'Neill: New Essays*: pp. 33–42. John V. Antush's "Eugene O'Neill: Modern and Postmodern," *The Eugene O'Neill Review* 13 (Spring 1989): 14–26 comes at the issue in rather different terms.

There have been an increasing number of articles using feminist approaches to the playwright and his work. Examples are Suzanne Burr's "O'Neill's Ghostly Women," in *Feminist Readings of Modern American Drama*, edited by June Schlueter (Rutherford, New Jersey: Fairleigh Dickinson University Press, 1989): pp. 24–47; Bette Mandl's "Gender as Design in *Strange Interlude* (*The Eugene O'Neill Review* 19 [Spring/Fall 1995]: 123–28; Gloria Cahill's "Mothers and Whores: The Process of Integration in the Plays of Eugene O'Neill" (*The Eugene O'Neill Review* 16 [Spring 1992]: 5–23; and previously published articles by Judith E. Barlow, referred to in the notes for her essay in this collection. *The Eugene O'Neill Newsletter* 6 (Summer/Fall 1992) devoted a special section to "O'Neill's Women."

Collections of critical articles devoted exclusively to the playwright have been particularly important in O'Neill study. Among the most significant are: Oscar Cargill *et al.*'s *O'Neill and his Plays* (1961); John Gassner's *O'Neill: A Collection of Critical Essays* (1964); Ernest G. Griffen's *Eugene O'Neill: A Collection of Critical Essays* (1976); Virginia Floyd's *Eugene O'Neill: A World View* (1979); James J. Martine's *Critical Essays on Eugene O'Neill* (1984); Harold Bloom's collections of essays on O'Neill generally (1987) and on *Long Day's Journey* (1988) and *The Iceman Cometh* (1987) specifically; Shyamal Bagchee's *Perspectives on O'Neill: New Essays* (1988); John Stroupe's *Critical Approaches to O'Neill* (1988); Marc Maufort's *Eugene O'Neill and the Emergence of American Drama* (1989); Richard F. Moorton, Jr.'s *Eugene O'Neill's Century: Centennial Views on America's Foremost Tragic Dramatist* (1991); and John H. Houchin's *The Critical Response to Eugene O'Neill* (1993). Entire issues of *Modern Drama* were devoted to O'Neill in 1960 (*Modern Drama* 3) and 1988 (*Modern Drama* 31). I have unfortunately been unable to mention more than a few of the significant essays in these collections.

Articles on O'Neill appear regularly, of course, in literary and theatre journals, but the chief source of such articles is the *Eugene O'Neill Review* published semi-annually by Frederick C. Wilkins, and its predecessor the *Eugene O'Neill Newsletter*.

The pre-eminent edition of O'Neill's plays is the three-volume *O'Neill*, edited by Travis Bogard for the Library of America in 1988. His letters appear in *Selected Letters of Eugene O'Neill* edited by Bogard and Jackson Bryer in 1988. Other O'Neill writings have been edited and published by

Bogard in *The Unknown O'Neill* also in 1988. (1988, O'Neill's centennial year, was a banner year for O'Neill scholarship.)

There are also special collections of O'Neill material in the Beinecke Library at Yale University and in the Charles E. Shain Library at Connecticut College (New London, Connecticut).

SELECT BIBLIOGRAPHY OF FULL-LENGTH WORKS

Ahuja, Chapman, *Tragedy, Modern Temper and O'Neill* (Atlantic Highlands, NJ: Humanities Press, 1983).

Alexander, Doris, *Eugene O'Neill's Creative Struggle: The Decisive Decade, 1924–1933* (University Park: Penn State University Press, 1992).

The Tempering of Eugene O'Neill (NY: Harcourt, Brace and World, 1962).

Atkinson, Jennifer McCabe, *Eugene O'Neill: A Descriptive Bibliography* (University of Pittsburgh Press, 1974).

Barlow, Judith E., *Final Acts: The Creation of Three Late O'Neill Plays* (Athens: University of Georgia Press, 1985).

Berlin, Normand, *Eugene O'Neill* (NY: St. Martin's Press, 1988).

O'Neill's Shakespeare (Ann Arbor: University of Michigan Press, 1993).

Bloom, Harold, ed., *Eugene O'Neill* (NY: Chelsea House, 1987).

Eugene O'Neill's "Long Day's Journey Into Night" (NY: Chelsea House, 1988).

Eugene O'Neill's "The Iceman Cometh" (NY: Chelsea House, 1987).

Bogard, Travis, *Contour in Time: The Plays of Eugene O'Neill* (Oxford University Press, 1972, revised edition, 1988).

The Eugene O'Neill Songbook (Ann Arbor, Michigan: UMI Research Press, 1988).

Boulton, Agnes, *Part of a Long Story* (Garden City, NY: Doubleday, 1958).

Bowen, Crosswell and Shane O'Neill, *The Curse of the Misbegotten: A Tale of the House of O'Neill* (NY: McGraw-Hill, 1959).

Carpenter, Frederic I., *Eugene O'Neill* (NY: Twayne Publishers, 1957, revised edition, 1979).

Chabrowe, Leonard, *Ritual and Pathos: The Theatre of Eugene O'Neill* (Lewisburg, Pennsylvania: Bucknell University Press, 1976; London: Associated University Presses, 1976).

Chothia, Jean, *Forging a Language: A Study of the Plays of Eugene O'Neill* (Cambridge University Press, 1979).

Clark, Barrett H., *Eugene O'Neill* (NY: Robert McBride, 1927).

Eugene O'Neill: The Man and his Plays (NY: Dover Publications, 1947).

Clark, B. H. and Ralph Sanborn, *A Bibliography of the Works of Eugene O'Neill Together with the Collected Poems of Eugene O'Neill* (London: Benjamin Blom, 1965).

Cunningham, Frank, *Sidney Lumet: Film and Literary Vision* (Lexington: University of Kentucky Press, 1991).

Dubost, Thierry, *Struggle, Defeat, or Rebirth: Eugene O'Neill's Vision of Humanity* (Jefferson, North Carolina: McFarland and Company, 1996).

Eisen, Kurt, *The Inner Strength of Opposites: O'Neill's Novelistic Drama and the Melodramatic Imagination* (Athens: University of Georgia Press, 1994).

Engel, Edwin, *The Haunted Heroes of Eugene O'Neill* (Harvard University Press, 1953).

Falk, Doris V., *Eugene O'Neill and the Tragic Tension: An Interpretive Study of the Plays* (New Brunswick, NJ: Rutgers University Press, 1958).

Floyd, Virginia, ed., *Eugene O'Neill: A World View* (NY: Frederick Ungar, 1979).

The Plays of Eugene O'Neill: A New Assessment (NY: Frederick Ungar, 1984).

Frazer, Winifred D., *Love as Death in "The Iceman Cometh": A Modern Treatment of an Ancient Theme* (Gainesville: University of Florida Press, 1967).

Frenz, Horst, *Eugene O'Neill* (NY: Frederick Ungar, 1971).

Frenz, H. and Susan Tuck, eds., *Eugene O'Neill's Critics: Voices from Abroad* (Carbondale: Southern Illinois University Press, 1984).

Gassner, John, *Eugene O'Neill* (Minneapolis: University of Minnesota Press, 1965).

Gassner, J., ed., *O'Neill: A Collection of Critical Essays* (Englewood Cliffs, NJ: Prentice Hall, 1964).

Geddes, Virgil, *The Melodramadness of Eugene O'Neill.* (Brookfield, Conn: The Brookfield Players, 1934, reprinted by Folcroft, Pennsylvania: The Folcroft Press, 1973 and Norwood, Pennsylvania: The Norwood Press, 1977).

Gelb, Arthur and Barbara, *O'Neill* (NY: Harper and Row, 1962, second edition, 1987).

Griffen, Ernest G., ed., *Eugene O'Neill: A Collection of Criticism* (NY: McGraw-Hill, 1976).

Hall, Ann C., *"A Kind of Alaska": Women in the Plays of O'Neill, Pinter, and Shepard* (Carbondale: Southern Illinois University Press, 1993).

Hayashi, Tetsumaro, *Eugene O'Neill: Research Opportunities and Dissertation Abstracts* (Jefferson, North Carolina: MacFarland and Company, 1983).

Hinden, Michael, *"Long Day's Journey Into Night": Native Eloquence* (Boston: G. K. Hall, 1990).

Houchin, John H., ed., *The Critical Response to Eugene O'Neill* (Westport, Connecticut: Greenwood Press, 1993).

Josephson, Lennart, *A Role: O'Neill's Cornelius Melody* (Stockholm: Almqvist and Wiksell International, 1977; and Atlantic Highlands, NJ: Humanities Press, 1978).

Kobernik, Mark, *Semiotics of Drama and the Style of Eugene O'Neill* (Amsterdam: Benjamins, 1989).

Leech, Clifford, *Eugene O'Neill* (London: Oliver and Boyd; and NY: Grove Press, 1963).

Liu, Haiping and Lowell Swortzell, eds., *Eugene O'Neill in China: An International Centenary Celebration* (Westport, Connecticut: Greenwood Press, 1992).

Long, Chester Clayton, *The Role of Nemesis in the Structure of Selected Plays by Eugene O'Neill* (The Hague: Mouton, 1968).

McDonough, Edwin J., *Quintero Directs O'Neill* (Chicago: A Capella Books, 1991).

Manheim, Michael, *Eugene O'Neill's New Language of Kinship* (Syracuse, New York: Syracuse University Press, 1982).

Martine, James J., ed., *Critical Essays on Eugene O'Neill* (Boston: G. K. Hall, 1984).

Maufort, Marc, ed., *Eugene O'Neill and the Emergence of American Drama* (collected essays) (Amsterdam: Rodopi, 1989; and Atlantic Highlands, NJ: Humanities Press, 1989).

Songs of American Experience: The Vision of O'Neill and Melville (NY: Peter Lang, 1990).

Miller, Jordan Y., *Eugene O'Neill and the American Critic* (Hamden, Connecticut: Archon Books, 1973).

Moorton, Richard F. Jr., ed., *Eugene O'Neill's Century: Centennial Views on America's Foremost Tragic Dramatist* (Westport, Connecticut: Greenwood Press, 1991).

O'Neill, Eugene, *"As Ever, Gene": The Letters of Eugene O'Neill to George Jean Nathan.* Edited by Nancy L. Roberts and Arthur W. Roberts (Rutherford, New Jersey: Fairleigh Dickinson University Press, 1987).

The Calms of Capricorn. Developed from O'Neill's scenario by Donald Gallup (New Haven and NY: Ticknor and Fields, 1982).

Comments on the Drama and the Theater. Collected and edited by Ulrich Halfmann (Tubingen: Gunter Narr Verlag, 1987).

Complete Plays. 3 volumes. Edited with notes by Travis Bogard (NY: The Library of America, 1988).

"Love and Admiration and Respect": The O'Neill-Commins Correspondence. Edited by Dorothy Commins (Durham, North Carolina: Duke University Press, 1986).

Poems: 1912–1914. Edited by Donald Gallup (New Haven and NY: Ticknor and Fields, 1980).

Selected Letters of Eugene O'Neill. Edited by Travis Bogard and Jackson Bryer (Yale University Press, 1988).

"The Theatre We Worked For": The Letters of Eugene O'Neill to Kenneth Macgowan. Edited by Jackson Bryer, with introductory essays by Travis Bogard (Yale University Press, 1982).

The Unfinished Plays: Notes for "The Visit of Malatesta," "The Last Conquest," and "Blind Alley Guy." Edited and annotated by Virginia Floyd (NY: Frederick Ungar, 1988).

The Unknown O'Neill: Unpublished and Unfamiliar Writings. Edited with commentaries by Travis Bogard (Yale University Press, 1988).

Work Diary, 1924–1943. Transcribed by Donald Gallup. 2 volumes (New York Haven: Yale University library, 1981).

Orlandello, John, *O'Neill on Film* (Rutherford, New Jersey: Fairleigh Dickinson University Press, 1982).

Pfister, Joel, *Staging Depth: Eugene O'Neill and the Politics of Psychological Discourse* (Chapel Hill: University of North Carolina Press, 1995).

Porter, Laurin R., *The Banished Prince: Time, Memory, and Ritual in the Late Plays of Eugene O'Neill* (Ann Arbor, Michigan: UMI Research Press, 1988).

Prasad, Hari M., *The Dramatic Art of Eugene O'Neill* (NY: Advent Press, 1987).

Raleigh, John Henry, *The Plays of Eugene O'Neill* (Carbondale: Southern Illinois University Press, 1965).

Raleigh, J. H., ed., *"The Iceman Cometh": A Collection of Critical Essays* (Englewood Cliffs, NJ: Prentice Hall, 1968).

Ranald, Margaret Loftus, *The Eugene O'Neill Companion* (Westport, Connecticut: Greenwood Press, 1984).

Robinson, James A., *Eugene O'Neill and Oriental Thought: A Divided Vision* (Carbondale: Southern Illinois University Press, 1982).

Scheibler, Rolf, *The Late Plays of Eugene O'Neill* (Bern: Francke Verlag, 1970).

Shaughnessy, Edward L., *Down the Nights and Down the Days: Eugene O'Neill's Catholic Sensibility* (Notre Dame, Indiana: University of Notre Dame Press, 1996).

Eugene O'Neill in Ireland: The Critical Reception (New York: Greenwood Press, 1988).

Sheaffer, Louis, *O'Neill: Son and Playwright* (Boston: Little, Brown, 1968); and *O'Neill: Son and Artist* (Boston: Little, Brown, 1973).

Shipley, Joseph J., *The Art of Eugene O'Neill* (Seattle: University of Washington Chapbooks, University of Washington Bookstore, 1928).

Sinha, C. P., *Eugene O'Neill's Tragic Vision* (Atlantic Highlands, NJ: Humanities Press, 1981).

Skinner, Richard Dana, *Eugene O'Neill: A Poet's Quest* (NY: Longmans Green, 1935; revised edn. NY: Russell and Russell, 1964).

Smith, Madeline and Richard Eaton, *Eugene O'Neill: An Annotated Bibliography* (Hamden, Connecticut: Garland, 1988).

Stroupe, John, ed., *Critical Approaches to Eugene O'Neill* (NY: AMS Press, 1988).

Tiusanen, Timo, *O'Neill's Scenic Images* (Princeton University Press, 1968).

Törnqvist, Egil, *A Drama of Souls: O'Neill's Studies in Supernaturalistic Technique* (Yale University Press, 1969).

Vena, Gary, *O'Neill's "The Iceman Cometh": Reconstructing the Premiere* (Ann Arbor, Michigan: UMI Research Press, 1988).

Wainscott, Ronald, *Staging O'Neill: The Experimental Years, 1920–1934* (Yale University Press, 1988).

Winther, Sophus Keith, *Eugene O'Neill: A Critical Study* (NY: Russell and Russell, 1961, first published in 1934).

INDEX

Separate sub-headings exist under "Characters" and "Plays" in the following list. The plays thus included are O'Neill's only.